*Computers, Cognition and Development*

WILEY SERIES IN
DEVELOPMENTAL PSYCHOLOGY
AND ITS APPLICATIONS

*Series Editor*
**Professor Kevin Connolly**

**The Development of Movement Control and Co-ordination**
*J. A. Scott Kelso and Jane E. Clark*

**Psychobiology of the Human Newborn**
*edited by Peter Stratton*

**Morality in the Making: Thought, Action and the Social Context**
*edited by Helen Weinreich-Haste and Don Locke*

**The Psychology of Written Language: Developmental and Educational Perspectives**
*edited by Margaret Martlew*

**Children's Single-Word Speech**
*edited by Martyn Barrett*

**The Psychology of Gifted Children: Perspectives on Development and Education**
*edited by Joan Freeman*

**Teaching and Talking with Deaf Children**
*David Wood, Heather Wood, Amanda Griffiths and Ian Howarth*

**Culture and the Development of Children's Action: A Cultural-historical Theory of Developmental Psychology**
*Jaan Valsiner*

**Computers, Cognition and Development**
*edited by Julie Rutkowska and Charles Crook*

Futher titles in preparation

# Computers, Cognition and Development

## Issues for Psychology and Education

*Edited by*
**Julie C. Rutkowska**
and
**Charles Crook**

JOHN WILEY & SONS
Chichester · New York · Brisbane · Toronto · Singapore

*Library of Congress Cataloging-in-Publication Data:*

Computers, cognition, and development.

(Wiley series in developmental psychology and
its appications)
   1. Computer-assisted instruction—Psychological
aspects.   2. Cognition.   3. Developmental psychology.
I. Rutkowska, Julie.   II. Crook, Charles.
III. Series.
LB1028.5.C5724   1987      371.3'9445      87–8135
ISBN 0 471 91583 1

*British Library Cataloguing in Publication Data:*

Computers, cognition and development: issues
   for psychology and education—(Wiley
   series in developmental psychology and its
   applications).
   1. Cognition in children—Data processing
   2. Computers and children
   I. Rutkowska, Julie C     II. Crook, Charles
   155.4'13      BF723.C5

   ISBN 0 471 91583 1


Typeset by Input Typesetting Ltd., London
Printed in Great Britain by St Edmundsbury Press,
Bury St Edmunds, Suffolk

# Contributors

BENEDICT DU BOULAY, *School of Cognitive Sciences, University of Sussex, Falmer, Brighton, BN1 9QN.*

ANN BRACKENRIDGE, *School of Education, University of Exeter, St Luke's, Exeter, EX1 2LU.*

JONATHAN BRIGGS, *School of Education, University of Exeter, St Luke's, Exeter, EX1 2LU.*

CHARLES CROOK, *Department of Psychology, The University, Durham, DH1 3LE.*

JACKIE DEAN, *School of Education, University of Exeter, St Luke's, Exeter, EX1 2LU.*

STEPHEN DRAPER, *Department of Psychology, University of Glasgow, Glasgow, G12 8RT.*

MARTIN HUGHES, *School of Education, University of Exeter, St Luke's, Exeter, EX1 2LU.*

HAMISH MACLEOD, *Department of Psychology, University of Edinburgh, 7 George Square, Edinburgh, EH8 9JZ.*

BROCK MEEKS, *8383 Center Drive, Suite C, La Mesa, CA 92041 USA*

JON NICHOL, *School of Education, University of Exeter, St Luke's, Exeter, EX1 2LU.*

DAVID ROTHERAY, *Educational Technology Research Group, Department of Psychology, University of Hull, Hull, HU6 7RX.*

JULIE RUTKOWSKA, *School of Cognitive Sciences, University of Sussex, Falmer, Brighton, BN1 9QN.*

MICHAEL SCAIFE, *School of Cognitive Sciences, University of Sussex, Falmer, Brighton, BN1 9QN.*

DAVID SEWELL, *Educational Technology Research Group, Department of Psychology, University of Hull, Hull, HU6 7RX.*

TONY SIMON, *MRC Applied Psychology Unit, 15 Chaucer Road, Cambridge, CB2 2EF.*

DEREK SLEEMAN, *Department of Computing Science, Kings College, University of Aberdeen, Old Aberdeen, AB9 2UB.*

JOSIE TAYLOR, *School of Cognitive Sciences, University of Sussex, Falmer, Brighton, BN1 9QN.*

STEPHANIE THORNTON, *School of Cognitive Sciences, University of Sussex, Falmer, Brighton, BN1 9QN.*

MASOUD YAZDANI, *Department of Computer Science, University of Exeter, Prince of Wales Road, Exeter, EX4 4PT.*

# Contents

# Foreword

During the twentieth century scientific discovery and technological innovation have raced ahead at a pace greater than ever before, and in so doing they have had profound effects not only on our material culture but also on the very fabric of our society. Inventions such as the motor car and television have had far reaching effects and have changed our way of life quite profoundly. In the developed world they are everywhere and their penetration through the Third World is only a matter of time. Powerful and pervasive though their effects are, it is certain that in time computers will have greater, and probably more ubiquitous, consequences.

When Norbert Wiener, Warren McCulloch and Claude Shannon laid the foundations of cybernetics and information theory they sowed the seeds of a revolution in the study of mind. The basic physical concepts of matter and energy have not proved to be very useful in our efforts to understand mental activity, but *information* as a central construct holds an altogether different promise. And of course computers, like people, are devices that process information.

Over the past twenty years the computer has become an indispensable tool for the psychologist. Initially it was used as a means for controlling experiments and logging large amounts of data, but increasingly it has been used as a tool for thinking. This book is about the computer as an intellectual tool; for children, for educators and for psychologists seeking to understand the development of mental activity. In the rich countries of the world computers are already a significant factor in the lives of children. The *Statistical Bulletin* of the Department of Education and Science revealed at the end of 1986 that over 50 per cent of head teachers in primary schools in the UK considered that microcomputers made a substantial contribution to teaching in their schools. This will surely increase and spread upwards and downwards in the educational system. Children who encounter computers in their primary schools are going to spend the rest of their lives rubbing shoulders with them and almost certainly using them directly or indirectly in domestic, industrial, business and leisure settings.

Growing up with computers will have many effects and consequences for children, as the essays in Part One of this book point out. Computers offer important possibilities for the handicapped, freeing them perhaps as never before from some of the consequences of their disabilities. Also, contrary to what has often been assumed computers offer opportunities for enhancing the social context for development. If we are to make the best use of computers in educational settings we need theories and principles to guide our efforts. Artificial intelligence provides an approach to exploring and understanding cognitive processes, and the framework which it provides for developing computer-based environments for learning is discussed in the essays grouped in Part Two. Part Three focusses on the development of mind and brings together fundamental questions under the heading of the computational metaphor and developmental psychology. Here the computer is being used as an intellectual tool by the psychologist who is trying to understand the nature of mental activities and how they emerge and change during development.

We are at the beginning of a new adventure in understanding cognitive processes and their development. How successful and powerful an approach this will be remains to be seen, but the intellectual challenge is there and the promise of greater understanding is tantalizing. There is every likelihood that this new direction will have significant effects on formal education, on the lives of children generally and also in the work of developmental psychologists. By collecting together these essays Drs Rutkowska and Crook have made an important and timely contribution.

KEVIN CONNOLLY

# Preface

It is surely clear that the recent and dramatic advance of information technology has far-reaching implications for the work of psychologists. This is most easily recognized with respect to the significant role that the computer has come to play in many people's lives: understanding the effective management of exchanges between computers and their human users provides an exciting practical challenge for the psychologist. But the implications of new technology go further than this. Its application often requires a modelling of intelligent human activity and this enterprise has promoted important advances of a conceptual nature. Those advances can not be overlooked by any discipline concerned with understanding the human mind. Thus, for psychology, the challenges of new technology arise from the status of computers as both practical and theoretical tools.

The aim of this book is to pursue these themes in relation to the particular branch of psychology that is concerned with human development. Research in this spirit is still scarce but, typically, it will draw upon a variety of disciplines. Unfortunately, this means that the relevant literature is diverse, seems widely dispersed and contains technical material whose significance for psychological questions is not always clear. If students of development are to face the challenges arising from new technology, they may need a stronger sense of the foundation upon which research and theory could be built. The present volume takes steps towards meeting this need. It brings together representative work from researchers in artificial intelligence, education and developmental psychology. Each of the contributors reflects upon their own problem-fields in ways that help define issues and strategies for future developmental research.

Adopting the above conception of computers as both practical and theoretical tools, we have identified three ways in which computers and notions of computation are important for developmental psychology. Firstly, there are issues posed by the increasing spread of information technology into society. How may the particular ways in which this technology is encountered influence our psychological development? Secondly, insights that arise from the achievements of artificial intelligence may help define new computer environments for human learning. How may these foster intellectual development? Thirdly, there is an enthusiasm within cognitive psychology for computational methaphors of mental activity. How may this contribute to the advance of theory within the study of cognitive development?

The present volume is organized into three sections, each taking up one of the above themes. Associated with each section is an introduction to the issues involved, and an overview of how these issues are to be treated by the various chapters that follow. Given this arrangement, it is sufficient at this point to do no more than offer a very general orientation towards the three themes that comprise the book.

Part I is about computers as practical tools which people, including young children, may now encounter. The recent drive to extend the place of computers in education has created the most significant context in which questions for developmental psychology will arise. It is likely that the presence of this technology is restructuring children's experience of education and leisure in important ways. Central issues would surely include: children's understanding of and attitudes towards computers; the impact of computers on social interaction and communication in school or home; and the technology's potential as a prosthetic tool that can extend learning environments for the mentally and physically handicapped. All of these issues are taken up by the contributors to this section.

Part II addresses issues that arise from the discipline of artificial intelligence (AI). Students of AI address our naturally intelligent abilities – perceiving, reasoning, remembering, and so on – by programming computers to perform them. Certain of the computational systems confronting children in school have been explicitly informed by the concepts and insights of artificial intelligence. Something of their context within that discipline may be a useful background for the developmental psychologist conducting research in this area. For example, the AI community has debated whether representations which underlie human knowledge should be considered imperatively (as procedures or program instructions which control behavioural and intellectual activities) or declaratively (as databases of information together with logical rules for sorting, ordering and correlating related elements in the database). These two approaches gave rise to the procedural language LOGO and the logic-programming language PROLOG respectively, both of which now have their advocates within educational practice. The ensuing debates concern the most 'natural' medium for programming and the way in which it is best mobilized right across the educational curriculum. Contributors to Section II of the book give particularly close attention to claims made for the benefits of learning experiences organized around these theoretical principles.

Finally, Part III attends to the influence that computers have already had on cognitive psychology and considers how this influence may be extended to developmental aspects of cognition. The focus of discussion for cognitive psychology has been the 'computational metaphor' for the mind: a set of concepts which some are confident will remain unsurpassed for phrasing theories of intellectual processes. Now there is a need to determine the contribution that metaphor can make to our understanding of development, and to consider the strengths and weaknesses of current computational models of learning processes. At the same time, we must recognize the other direction of influence: the contribution that developmental studies might make to the cognitive science endeavour of constructing rigorous models of mental processes. Thus, there is an urgent need for an interdisciplinary framework of computational and developmental work that might furnish a 'developmental cognitive science'. From such a basis we could, in particular, more fully cultivate the instructional potential of computer technology.

The preparation of this volume has been helped by a period of leave from Sussex and Durham. For generously offering us research facilities during that time, we are grateful to the Psychology Department of Stanford University and to the Laboratory of Comparative Human Cognition at the University of California at San Diego. Thanks also to Jane Millar and Aaron Sloman for help with the index.

Collecting the work of the various contributors has been motivated by a belief that computers and computation offer a distinctive challenge to students of development. But to meet this challenge it may be necessary to abandon some of the constraints of disciplinary specialization. This situation offers an unprecedented opportunity for innovation, breaking down the barriers between pure and applied research and between disciplinary methodologies. Our hope is that this collection may not only inform developmentalists of the background of issues in this new field, but will also stimulate them to define their own constructive contribution while the field is in its formative stage.

JULIE RUTKOWSKA AND CHARLES CROOK

**PART 1**

# Growing up with Computers

# Editorial Introduction

The recent influence of 'life span' approaches to developmental psychology has stimulated interest in secular trends: it is now argued that theories of development must be more sensitive to circumstances defining the experience of growing up at a particular point in historical time. Where development is studied longitudinally, general principles that emerge may have to be expressed in terms of the cultural ecology of that period in human history that was observed (Baltes, Cornelius and Nesselroade, 1979). So, following the spirit of this new emphasis, how would we describe the circumstances of our own times? We would surely identify information technology as one potent force active in contemporary society: indeed, we might be inclined to speak of growing up into a 'computer age'.

Thinking of research issues in these terms, it is tempting to compare the 'computer age' with an earlier 'TV age'. The parallel is attractive: in each case, an advancing technology is manifest in a tangible product to which children have ready access – the television and the microcomputer. Moreover, both media do cater for children in distinctive ways – ways that recognize them as a particular 'audience'. But these media also display interesting differences. Firstly, casual and routine access to computers is not proceeding at a pace that characterized the spread of access to television. Indeed, chapters in Section I of this volume identify some of the circumstances that can lead children to have a greater or lesser access to computers: gender, class and race (discussed by Meeks and by Hughes, Brackenridge and Macleod).

A second and more profound difference between televisions and microcomputers as technological artefacts lies in the very range of activities that each may support. The computer is more akin to a tool; one that may be adapted to serve the individual owner's particular purposes. A common oversight, then, is to neglect the sheer variety of purposes that such an apparently singular thing as 'a computer' can support. This versatility is apparent from reports of wide-ranging applications for computers within schools (e.g., Reid and Rushton, 1985) – a theme that will be well illustrated by chapters in the present volume. Thus, chapters in Section I refer to computer activities in primary schools (Hughes *et al.* observe early contact with programming, Crook observes problem-solving collaborations), and to activities in special education (Rotheray and Sewell). But Meeks's chapter draws attention to the fact that this technology is a feature of children's domestic life as well – and that there are intriguing applications developing in that setting.

## GROWING UP WITH COMPUTERS: A VARIETY OF CONTACT

As children encounter this new technology in both home and school, what form does their contact take – and with what developmental consequences? The chapters in the first section of this book bear on these central questions. The authors have not set out to give comprehensive reviews of particular research literatures – in every case the relevant literature is still very much in the making. Rather, they each draw upon a distinctive research experience and, in so doing, give a direct indication of the pressing issues for developmental psychology. Taken together, they convey a strong sense of diversity with regard to the settings and purposes that must be studied.

Three of these chapters focus exclusively on children's contact with computers in education. Hughes *et al.* describe the form of children's contact with computers very much through the eyes of the children themselves: how do they understand this technology and their own interaction with it? Then, the chapter by Crook encourages recognition that the form of their experience has a strong social dimension: computers bear on the quality of social participation in classroom life. Finally, from observations of the impact of computers in a broader educational context, Rotheray and Sewell remind us that this contact involves a broad constituency of children, including those developing in the contexts of special education.

Quite reasonably, we expect children to discover the full potential of this technology within such formal schooling. Events and experiences in the classroom must surely become a focal research interest. Yet, there are signs that distinctive and creative applications of computers are evolving within the domestic environment also. Meeks's chapter identifies a suprising context in which children are encountering computers: he provides a close description of communications activity that is developing among young people in North American homes – an application that is now finding a place in the school curriculum. These are developments not easily visible to those not themselves involved; Meeks's data offer us a rare and timely view.

What consequences might this variety of early computer experience have for psychological development? Consider first a social developmental theme. One characteristic of the technology that causes some concern is its capacity to totally absorb: the pace and challenge of many interactions with computers seems capable of sustaining long periods of involvement. The fear is that this will, therefore, become a socially isolating medium. For example, Weizenbaum (1976) paints a gloomy picture of the adolescent drawn to computers: a sullen and lonesome individual hunched over a keyboard for long hours at a stretch.

Two of the chapters that follow question this analysis. Crook argues that an important property of classroom computers is their capacity to function as a forum for collaborative learning. Indeed, the logistics of a resource that is currently so scarce demand that computer work is organized to involve children in small groups. Under the right circumstances there is every indication that this medium can be a powerful catalyst for peer collaboration.

Meeks shows us a different way in which the technology can function to organize social activity – rather than undermine it. In this case, geographically separated individuals are using their home computers to support interpersonal contact and discussion. Meeks observes how this may often lead to the participants coming together for social activity that is quite separate from computer use. Of course, this is not always for healthy purposes and he does remark on the way in which the 'hacker' community has been effectively organized in this manner. A more positive note is struck by the extension of this kind of computer use into the classroom. At the time of writing, there is a busy schools computer network in Britain that serves to support a rich variety of project collaboration among pupils in different parts of the country. Again, computers are mediating socially organized study rather than serving to isolate the learner.

An interesting extension of such communications activity is found in the recent development of multi-user computer games. Given some inexpensive home computer equipment and a telephone, it is possible to dial into an adventure game and develop its narrative partly through interacting with other individuals who are simultaneously logged in and taking part. This is a far cry from the modest intellectual challenge of arcade games. It does seem that, taken together, these examples identify a real potential for computers to mediate social activity rather than suppress it.

Some of the comments made above highlight the difficulty of separating social and cognitive themes. Suppose the computer is conceptualized as a source of 'tools' for augmenting the human intellect (e.g., Bannon, 1986): on this view, the chapters below suggest that one way in which it so functions is by arranging an augmentation based on socially organized joint activity. However, there are, of course, other ways in which computers mediate intellectual activity that are less dependent on such human collaboration. In particular, there may be ways in which computers can create contexts of tasks for thinking and learning that serve to 'release' cognitive potential. The present theoretical mood within developmental psychology is receptive to the idea that competence may be often by 'trapped' in this manner. Rotheray and Sewell make a strong claim of this kind in discussing the needs of special education. A particular appeal of their discussion may be that it discourages a view of special education as a mixed bag of special-purpose needs: in this, there may be a valuable unifying theorectical perspective that serves to drive applied research.

These chapters capture the circumstances of children and adolescents using computers in a variety of settings. What are the implications for research by developmental and child psychologists?

## GROWING UP WITH COMPUTERS: SOME IMPLICATIONS FOR RESEARCH

Firstly, there is a need to highlight the factors that may limit some children's contact with this technology. The chapters by Hughes *et al.* and by Meeks both draw attention to race, class and gender as being relevant social attributes. There may be problems here that are deeply rooted in our culture; others may be more tractable to psychological research. These are certainly important challenges: if the computer is a resource that promotes intellectual development, it is proper to make it available in an equable manner. Even if there is controversy regarding the extent of its potency as such an educational resource, there can be little doubt as to its importance in the world of work. Children who embark on their working lives with a degree of computer fluency will surely be at an advantage. Even the kind of fluency represented in Meeks's communications examples have their analogue in the modern business environment (Hiltz, 1984): as a recreational activity, computer-mediated communication will furnish a more powerful skill than the narrowly idiosyncratic CB radio. For all these reasons, we should be alert to social policies and psychological prejudices that may give children differential opportunities to encounter this technology.

Secondly, there is a need to construct what might be termed a model of the child as 'user'. Hughes and his colleagues touch on this need when they identify the way in which children bring to their encounter with computers particular attitudes and particular modes of thinking. These act as filters through which experience is formed: the character of those filters will be important to understand. More generally, a sensitivity to the character of children's cognition must surely underpin any attempt to ensure that computer-based learning environments truly do serve to release what Rotheray and Sewell refer to as 'trapped' intelligence.

Included in this notion of childish 'user characteristics' must be characteristics of a social nature. The chapters by Crook and Meeks both stress the manner in which computers can socially organize intellectual activity. The character and significance of peer interaction must be explored as it occurs in computer-based settings. This will allow the potential of such social exchange to be fully realized as a resource to promote intellectual development. Even the Genevan tradition of developmental psychology is recognizing the need for a new social dimension to the theory of cognitive development (e.g., Doise and Mugny, 1984). Clearly, the cognitive and social themes that characterize the present discussion of computer activities must be viewed as interacting. One implication of Crook's emphasis is that where cognitive benefits are claimed for particular computer experiences, consideration should be given to whether the classroom logistics for using the resource created new potentials for interpersonal exchange – and that these may be implicated in any benefits.

It is not the purpose of this volume to take up and develop these issues in later sections – that space must be reserved to identify still other research themes important for developmental psychology. However, we do believe it is urgent that the issues identified in this section are recognized. This commentary began with a parallel to the 'television age'. There is a further dimension to that parallel. The advent of television offered a challenge to developmental research which – to developmentalists' present bitter regret – was not responded to at the time. It would be most unfortunate to be sluggish yet again: this early period in which computers are impinging on the lives of young people is already well under way.

## REFERENCES

Baltes, P. B., Cornelius, S. W., and Nesselroade, J. R. (1979). In J. R. Nesselroade and P. B. Baltes (eds), *Longitudinal Research in The Study of Behavior and Development*, Academic Press, New York.

Bannon, L. J. (1986). Extending the boundaries of human computer interaction. In D. Norman and S. Draper (eds), *User Centred System Design: New Perspectives on Human-Computer Interaction*, Lawrence Erlbaum, Hillsdale, N. J.

Doise, W., and Mugny, G. (1978). *The Social Development of the Intellect*, Pergamon, Oxford.

Hiltz, J. (1984). *Online Communities: A Case Study of the Office of the Future*, Ablex, Norwood, N. J.

Reid, I., and Rushton, J. (1985). *Teachers, Computers and the Classroom*, Manchester University Press, Manchester.

Weizenbaum, J. (1976). *Computer Power and Human Reason*, Freeman, San Franciso.

Computers, Cognition and Development
Edited by J. Rutkowska and C. Crook
© 1987 John Wiley & Sons Ltd

CHAPTER 1

# Children's Ideas About Computers

MARTIN HUGHES, ANN BRACKENRIDGE and HAMISH MACLEOD

## SUMMARY

A group of 6- to 12-year-old children originally interviewed about computers in November 1983 were re-interviewed 16 months later. Attitudes were found to be very positive on both occasions although computer experience was strongly affected by sex and social class. Sex-stereotyping had decreased and ascription of human-like qualities to the computer had increased on the second occasion.

This chapter reports some of the main findings of a study in which over a hundred children aged between 6 and 12 years were interviewed about computers. The children were seen on two separate occasions, November 1983 (Occasion 1) and March 1985 (Occasion 2). The interviews covered a number of areas, of which we will focus on the following here:

(1) children's actual experience of computers, at home and school;
(2) children's attitudes towards computers;
(3) sex-stereotyping in children's views on computers; and
(4) children's conceptions of how computers function.

## DESIGN OF THE STUDY

### Background and purposes

Our main initial motive for carrying out these interviews was to obtain some baseline data at a time when children's exposure to computers was still fairly limited. There is little doubt that we are embarked on a period of very rapid technological change, and that by the end of the century information

9

technology in its many different forms will have had a highly significant impact on many aspects of children's lives. At the time we carried out our interviews, concern was being expressed in a number of quarters about the need for some initial observations as a basis for studying future developments. For example, Sage and Smith (1983), in an influential report to the ESRC, noted (p.26) that 'We have no baselines against which future developments may by interpreted, and if no research is carried out in this field very soon, the opportunity for studying comparatively "computer-naive" children may be lost completely,' while Lepper (1985, p.2) argued that 'If we do not act quickly, we may miss the "research window" on microcomputers, as we did with television.' Unfortunately, few researchers appear to have grasped this opportunity: apart from two small-scale studies, one by Fairbrother (1982) in the UK and one by Mawby, Clement, Pea and Hawkins (1984) in the USA, and Turkle's (1984) in-depth interviews with children and adults already immersed in the computer culture, there appears to have been little attempt to capture this important baseline data.

Clearly, any such attempt must necessarily be selective – and to some extent arbitrary – in the choice of measures to be used. For example, we considered but rejected the notion of obtaining some standardized measures of cognitive functioning, despite the claims being made by many (most notably Papert, 1980) that interacting with computers will have a major effect on children's cognitive development. It seemed to us that such claims would have to be investigated by much more specific and tightly controlled experiments. Instead, we set out to obtain as full and detailed a description as possible of children's own ideas and attitudes concerning computers at a time when they were still relatively new. We then followed up this group to see what changes had taken place over a relatively short (16 months) but crucial period of time.

The first area we looked at was the extent to which children had already encountered computers in their daily lives – at home, school or elsewhere – and the kind of activities they were carrying out with computers. At the time of the initial interviews, it was widely believed that children's computer experience was strongly affected by both sex and social class, and so our sample was drawn to investigate the possible effect of these factors.

The second area we looked at was the extent to which children held 'positive' or 'negative' attitudes towards computers. There was (and still is) a widespread belief that virtually all children have a positive attitude towards computers and are free of the fears and anxieties felt by many adults. This claim clearly needs to be investigated in its own right, but it also has a bearing on more general psychological and educational issues. For psychologists, such a powerful source of intrinsic motivation requires theoretical explanation (e.g. Lepper, 1985; Malone, 1981), while for educationalists the questions are more concerned with how this motivation can best be tapped to enhance learning (e.g. O'Shea and Self, 1983). It should be noted, of course, that many observers do not regard this attraction to the computer as necessarily beneficial (e.g. Shallis, 1984), with particular concern being expressed about the computer 'hacker' (usually a young male who compensates for social inadequacy by spending long hours interacting with a computer).

Our third concern, with sex-role stereotyping, was motivated by the desire to explore the extent to which computer technology is seen to be the prerogative of the male sex. There is indeed growing evidence that certain aspects of computers, such as programming, are taken up more frequently by boys. For example, the Equal Opportunities Commission (1983) reports that in the UK boys outnumber girls by more than 2 : 1 in entries for Ordinary-level computer studies (age 15–16 years), while at Advanced level (17–18 years) the ratio is more than 3 : 1. Similar evidence is emerging from other countries such as the USA (Hawkins, 1984) and Australia (Clarke, 1984). Certainly there are strong cultural influences. The computer industry – like the car and motorbike industries – gears its advertising towards males, and this advertising often contains a strong sexist bias: men are likely to be portrayed sitting in full control at the keyboard with women draped provocatively around the VDU. Further, much popular software, such as 'Space Invaders' and wargame simulations, is aggressive and male-oriented, with women either totally absent or, as in 'Killer Gorilla', passive objects to be rescued by skilful males. It seemed therefore worth investigating whether this strong cultural association of males with computers was also to be found in the children of our sample.

The final area we looked at was the child's 'mental model' or 'conceptual model' of how the computer operates. In general, the notion of 'mental models' has become increasingly prominent in psychology in recent years (e.g. Johnson-Laird, 1983), and it has been argued that a user's mental model of any device is likely to have a strong effect on their performance with that particular device (e.g. Young, 1981; Cumming, 1986). This point has been made most cogently by du Boulay, O'Shea and Monk (1980) in their discussion of how to present computing concepts to novices: 'One of the difficulties of teaching a novice how to program is to describe, at the right level of detail, the machine he is learning to control' (p.237). Du Boulay et al. invoke the idea of a 'notional machine' – 'an idealized conceptual computer whose properties are implied by the constructs in the programming language employed' – and propose that the workings of such a notional machine should be both conceptually simple and clearly visible to the user. In a similar fashion Mawby et al. argue that if children's models of computer functioning are badly flawed, then they may acquire low-level skills, but the deeper conceptual understanding that allows skills to develop and generalize may elude them. Mawby et al. point out that knowledge of children's conceptual models is of major importance for educators concerned with developing appropriate curriculum materials.

In view of the above arguments, our interviews included questions aimed at eliciting children's ideas of how a computer operates, or whether they understood the function of a program, and so on. We were also particularly interested in whether the children attributed to computers qualities such as autonomy and intelligence. We asked them whether computers could 'do things by themselves' and whether computers 'wanted to do things'. We also asked them if computers 'think' and, if so, whether their thinking was like 'our' thinking. We tried to avoid giving the impression that there are correct answers to these questions: indeed, they are questions over which philosophers are divided (e.g. Searle, 1984; Hofstadter and Dennett, 1981). Our concern arose from claims (e.g. by Frude, 1983; Weizenbaum, 1984) that one of the most powerful (and dangerous) aspects of computers is the ease with which users can anthropomorphize them. It seemed likely that children would be particularly susceptible to this, given the frequency of claims that children are particularly prone to 'animism' (e.g. Piaget, 1929). But even if they did not go so far, it seemed highly likely that encounters with an object which is both a machine and to some extent 'intelligent' – what Turkle has called an 'evocative object' – must inevitably have an effect on fundamental concepts concerning the physical and the psychological, and we were anxious to see what the children in our sample made of the phenomenon.

**The administration of the interviews**

In November 1983 we interviewed 102 children (48 boys and 54 girls), drawn at random from two mixed primary schools in Edinburgh. Although geographically close to each other, one school was almost entirely middle-class and the other almost entirely working-class. Of the total, 53 children were in Class 3 (age-range 6 years 9 months to 7 years 9 months; mean 7 years 3 months) and 49 were in Class 6 (age-range 9 years 9 months to 10 years 9 months; mean 10 years 2 months). At the time of these initial interviews neither school had yet acquired a computer (although both did so shortly afterwards).

In March 1985 further interviews were carried out on the same sample of children. Seven children of the original sample (one middle-class boy, one middle-class girl, four working-class boys and one working-class girl) were unavailable for these second interviews, because they either were absent or had left the school.

On both occasions the children were interviewed individually using a semi-structured interview schedule. The questions covered such topics as: whether they themselves had used a computer and, if so, whether they had one at home; what they felt about computers; whether they thought they were or would be good with computers; whether they associated computers with boys or girls; how they thought computers worked; and whether computers could think, remember, and carry out operations by themselves.

There were some minor differences in style and content between the two sets of interviews. On Occasion 1 the children were interviewed by one of three male interviewers, while on Occasion 2 all the children were seen by the same female interviewer. On Occasion 1 the children were asked to draw a computer and discuss their drawing with the interviewer, but pressures of time precluded this on Occasion 2. The same constraint meant that on Occasion 1 the interviews were more open-ended than on Occasion 2, allowing for in-depth discussion of certain topics. Some of the questions used on Occasion 1 were omitted on Occasion 2 and replaced by others which examined topics spontaneously raised on Occasion 1. Apart from these differences, the interviews followed a similar pattern on the two occasions.

## FINDINGS

We now consider our findings, occasion by occasion, as they fall under the four main headings: (1) the children's experience of computers, (2) their attitudes to computers, (3) sex-stereotyping in relations to computers, and (4) their ideas about how computers work.

### Children's experience of computers: Occasion 1

At the time of their first interview, the children's direct experience of computers was extremely limited: two-thirds of the children had not used a computer at all, and only seven children had a computer at home. There was no difference between boys and girls in their experience of computers, nor was there a social-class difference for the younger children. However, the older middle-class children were significantly more likely to have used a computer than their working-class counterparts ($\chi^2 = 4.85$, $p < 0.05$).

There was a considerable range in the children's ideas of what computers were, and this was reflected most clearly in their drawings. At one extreme, a few children among the middle-class 10-year-olds drew identifiable models, often connected to peripherals such as tape-recorders (see James's drawing in Figure 1.1). At the other extreme, a few of the 7-year-olds seemed to have little or no idea about computers, and confused them with robots or videos (see Anna's drawing of R2D2). For most of the children, though, a computer consisted of a keyboard (with a large number of buttons) attached by wires to a TV screen: pressing the buttons caused words, numbers or games to appear on the screen (see drawings by Kenneth and Linda).

The most commonly mentioned use for a computer was that you could 'play games' on them (60 unprompted mentions), closely followed by the idea that computers could 'help you' or 'tell you things' (56 mentions). One

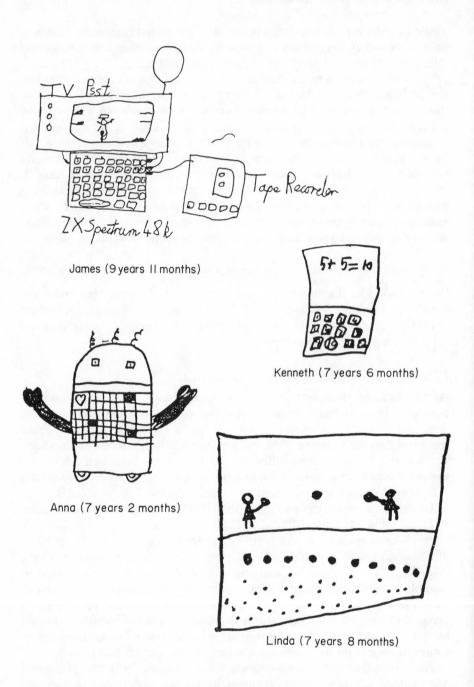

FIGURE 1.1 Children's drawings of a computer on Occasion 1

10-year-old, for example, defined a computer as 'a machine that tells you about things you've not done before', while another defined it as 'a thing to help you with your education and things'. Also frequently mentioned were 'sums' or 'maths' (48 mentions) and 'typing' or 'writing' (43 mentions). After these the next most common mention was 'drawing pictures' (7 mentions). There were no significant sex, social-class or age differences in the frequency with which these features were mentioned.

There was a much greater range of responses to questions concerning who might use computers and where. 'Offices' received the most mentions (30) followed by 'schools' (18), 'factories' (15) and 'hospitals' (13). One 10-year-old boy was particularly vivid about how computers might be used in hospitals: 'If someone has got a fever, or something wrong with someone, if the lines go straight that's them dead.' Universities and banks received 6 mentions each, followed by the police with 5 mentions (one boy suggested that a computer in a police station could 'tell them if there was anybody trying to punch in a car tyre, or something').

### Children's experience of computers: Occasion 2

Between Occasion 1 and Occasion 2 the sale of home computers in the UK experienced a major boom, and this was clearly reflected in our sample: the proportion of children with a computer at home rose from 7% to 40%. As Figure 1.2 shows, this increase was not distributed uniformly across the sample, with the increase in 'home ownership' being statistically significant at the 0.01 level ($\chi^2$ test) for all groups *apart from the working-class girls*. Nearly three-quarters of the home computers were Sinclair Spectrums, with only three BBC 'B' computers (the standard school model) being found at home. Most of the children who did not have a computer at home had used one elsewhere (apart from school), usually at the house of a friend or relative. Nevertheless, just under a fifth of our sample had still not used a computer outside school at the time of the second interview.

The children who used a computer outside school were asked how often they used it and for what purpose: 13% said they used it every day, a further 24% said they used it most days, and another 29% said they used it at least once a week. Over half the children used it just to play games, the most frequently mentioned games being 'Pacman', 'Jet-set Willy', 'Hunchback' and 'Ghostbusters'. Of those children whose use extended beyond playing games, the majority were copying programs from books or magazines. Only a small proportion (13%) of the total sample were actually writing programs themselves: all these children were middle-class and around three-quarters were boys.

As both the sample schools obtained a BBC 'B' computer shortly after Occasion 1, we had expected that by Occasion 2 all the children would have had some experience of using the school computer. However, it had actually

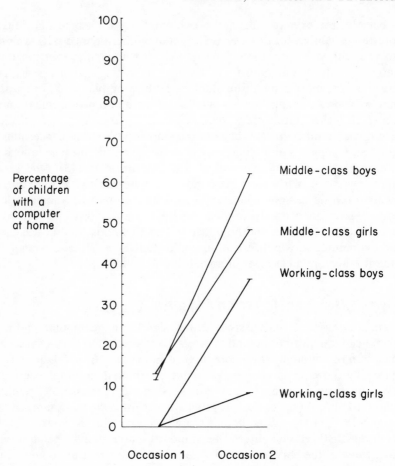

FIGURE 1.2 Home ownership of computers

been used by only one of the four classes, that of the middle-class 10-year-olds. According to these children, the frequency with which they used the computer varied – some weeks they might not use it at all, and other weeks they might use it more than once. As far as we could tell, the children's more recent work involved still and moving graphics. They also referred to mathematics and music programs, and to games of a more or less educational nature, of which 'Travel Agent' (a simulation) seemed to have been particularly memorable.

## Children's attitudes towards computers: Occasion 1

One of the most striking features of the initial interviews was the overwhelmingly positive attitude towards computers shown by the vast majority of the children, irrespective of age, sex, social-class or experience. Given the children's general lack of experience with computers, this enthusiasm usually took the form of an eager anticipation of using computers. For example, those children who did not have a computer at home were asked whether they could like one: 87% of those asked responded positively, usually adding comments such as 'Fantastic!' or 'It would be brill!' The reasons given for wanting one gave some insight into their early conceptions of computers. 'Games' were mentioned 29 times, followed by 'sums' (13) and 'writing' (9). One 7-year-old said she would 'ask it where my granny lives' and 'if my nana's all right', while another said she would 'ask it questions like "what is an apple?" – it would probably think it's a round thing with a stalk on, and you eat it.' Other reasons included 'to find out answers to TV games', 'to learn to read music properly' and 'to tidy my room, if it had special things'. One of the few children who responded negatively gave as her reason: 'It would probably get stolen.' It turned out that this child lived on a rough estate and had previously had a video stolen from her home: her mother now said she didn't want things that cost a lot of money in the house. Other reasons for not wanting a computer at home were 'I can't do it', 'I'm not very keen on computers' and 'I just don't like them'.

There was similar enthusiasm for the idea of using a computer at school, with 84% of the children responding positively. The reasons given for wanting a computer at school were similar to those for wanting one at home, but with an interesting shift in emphasis: 'sums' or 'maths' received 25 mentions, followed by 'to help you in your work' (13), 'writing and stories' (11), 'games' (10) and 'tell you things' (also 10). Once-mentioned reasons ranged from 'to learn more programming' (from a middle-class 10-year-old who was learning programming at home) to 'I could ask my friend a question without talking'. Among the reasons given for *not* wanting a computer at school were that 'It wouldn't help you', 'It would not be very useful' and 'We've got plenty of different things already'. A 10-year-old girl complained that computers would be boring, as 'it takes ages to type it all in', before asking 'Who's going to program it, anyway?'

The most common reason for not wanting a computer at school, however, was that it would 'just do all the work' or 'help too much'. As one 10-year-old put it: 'I think it's helping a bit much, . . . I love computers, I love anything like that, but I don't think in the classroom.' This idea emerged again from the children's answers to another question: 'Do you think your teacher would like a computer in the classroom?' Only 44% of the children said yes, with 16% saying a clear no and the rest showing uncertainty or conflict. Among the positive reasons were that it would generally help her (6 mentions), that she'd use it to get information (also 6), that she would be pleased because it would help children learn (5) and that it would help her with her marking (5). Four children said, in effect, that she could use it as an electronic blackboard, and one girl suggested that 'when the boys were being noisy she could print out "Shut up" on it'. The most common reason why she would *not* want it was that the children would not then do their work (14 mentions): 'We would cheat on it', 'We'd use it instead of our brains', or 'Teachers hate them as they give you the answers'. Five children were concerned about the disruptive effect the computer would have on the classroom: 'She'd get a wee bit cross with the children fighting over it', 'She would be shouting at Mark or Nicholas . . . or David' and 'They'll fight, they'll say "I want a go, I want to do this".' Finally, one 7-year-old boy thought the layout of the classroom was prohibitive: 'You couldn't do it, coz it probably wouldn't stretch into the plug . . . the plug's away over at the other end.'

The conflict between the usefulness of computers and the possibly harmful effects on one's own learning emerged several times in the initial interviews. It was expressed most graphically by Paul (10 years 3 months) in response to a later question:

*Interviewer:*   What sort of things are good about computers?
*Paul:*   Ehm . . . they can tell ye the answer, that'd be good.
*Interviewer:*   Okay, that's a good thing. So it helps you out . . .
*Paul:*   If ye had a wee computer o' yer ain and the teacher didnae see and ye're stuck on a sum, ye could just do it out and the computer might've gave ye the answer.
*Interviewer:*   Yeah . . . is that good or bad?
*Paul:*   Bad. That's cheating – ye willnae learn that way.
*Interviewer:*   So do you think the teachers would like computers in school then, if that was going to happen?
*Paul:*   No.
*Interviewer:*   How would you get round that?
*Paul:*   Well, if they had a computer, I think the teacher wouldnae let people have shots of it.

Paul later explained that the computer could be used to set problems and mark answers, rather than as a device for finding the answers.

One further question in the initial interviews asked children to name 'good things' and 'bad things' about computers. Just under half the children (46%) mentioned both good and bad aspects of computers. For the rest, the over-whelming tendency was to mention only good things about computers with just two children in the entire sample mentioning only bad things. The most commonly mentioned 'good things' about computers were that they 'help you' or 'tell you things' (45 mentions), that they're 'fun' or 'good for games' (34), and that they are good for 'writing' (13) and 'sums' (10). Less frequent responses were that they are quick (7), clever (4) and that 'they talk to you' (4). More idiosyncratic suggestions were that they 'tidy up for Mum', 'wash up', 'work all day without a rest', 'tell the time', 'got different colours', 'help you imagine the past and future', 'are good company' and 'don't argue with you'. Recurring 'bad things' mentioned were that they break down (12 mentions), give you the wrong answers (9), make work too easy (6), are expensive (4), can't be carried around (3) and can't talk to you (3). More unusual suggestions were that 'When the batteries run out and you've no money for any more, you get in a bad mood', 'Some people just use them for games', 'They make people jealous who've not got one', 'You might get a spark in your eye' and 'They're easily confused'. One child even remarked that you have to spend a lot of time with them, and said, as if about a troublesome pet, 'It's not very easy to keep a computer.'

### Children's attitudes towards computers: Occasion 2

Children's responses in the second round of interviews revealed quite clearly that their positive attitude towards computers had been maintained over the intervening 16 months. At the end of each interview the interviewer rated the child's overall attitude towards computers as positive or negative: all but two (one negative and one ambivalent) were judged to be positive.

When asked what they liked best about computers, games were mentioned by about 60 children, and a further seven thought they were 'good fun'. Ten children mentioned programming, while four simply enjoyed playing with the keys – 'They got good buttons', in the words of one of them. 'If you get bored you can switch it off' was what one child liked best. Not so comprehensible was that 'They go from side to side and up and down.' A few children appreciated general qualities such as that computers are quick, easy to use and that with them you can do what you want, or 'so many things'. The most common complaints concerned the keyboard (8 mentions), breaking down (6 mentions), sometimes not doing what you want (6 mentions), taking too long to load or to type in programs (5 mentions) and making too much noise (4 mentions).

Those 38 children who now had a computer at home were asked if it was as good as they had expected and if they ever got bored with it. Only one child was disappointed, and her reason hardly reflects qualities of the computer itself – 'You've always got to get it out and plug it in'. Only eight children – all middle-class and seven of them boys – said they had ever got bored. Their reasons for boredom were mainly to do with playing the same games again and again, but one boy said 'It takes a long time to program it' and another, perhaps referring to the same situation, said 'It seems to drag on sometimes.' As on the first occasion, those children who did not have a computer at home were asked whether they would like one. This time the response was even more positive, with only one child out of the 57 saying no.

The 25 children who had now used the computer at school were also asked whether it was as good as they had expected. All except two said yes, the two girls who said no giving as their reasons: 'Your teacher wants you to do problems and that, and you want to do games and that'; and 'Some of the maths games are boring . . . I don't really like the school computer.' In view of the reservations expressed in the initial interviews about their *teacher's* attitude, these children were also asked if they thought their teacher liked it. This time their answers were virtually unanimous: all but one (who was not sure) replied yes.

As mentioned earlier, the children's responses in the first interview suggested that they envisaged that using computers would be different at home and at school – at home the emphasis would be on games whereas at school it would be on learning. In the second interview we therefore asked the children to compare more directly their use (actual or envisaged) in the two locations.

The first question asked was 'Which do you think is (would be) better – using the computer at home or at school?' Opinion was divided roughly equally: 47% of the children said 'home' and 43% 'school' (the rest said 'the same' or 'I don't know' or described advantages on both sides). There were no clear differences due to sex, age or social class in their answers, nor was there any difference in the responses of the children who had actually used a computer at school. The outstanding reason in favour of home use was that there you have more time (22 mentions); having fun or playing games was mentioned by 10 children, and being able to do what you wanted was mentioned by 6 children. Two children implied that it was quieter at home, but for a further two children the situation in this respect was the opposite: ' . . . you won't have enough peace in your home with your wee brother'. Preferences for school use were most frequently in terms of the helpful and knowledgeable presence of the teacher (14 mentions) who, as one child said, 'puts you onwards'; there were also several references to the school computer itself as being 'better', because it offered a wider variety of things to do (including games), and/or because it was more educational. It was clear from the children's responses to this question that many of them enjoyed learning and being involved, and appreciated any help they could get from whatever quarter, human or electronic.

The second question was 'Do you think you (would) learn more using a computer at home or at school?' Altogether only 15% of the children expected to learn more at home (because of help from parents or from 'looking up the books', for instance, or because they could 'study more' and 'experiment'), while the great majority (73%) thought they learned more at school. There were no significant effects due to age, sex or social class. Of those 21 children who had had experience of the school computer, only one felt that she would learn more at home. Two children who saw two sides to this question explained that it would be better at home once you had learned to do things, because there you had more time, but that at school 'you get shown'.

## Sex-stereotyping: Occasion 1

As reported above, we found no significant sex differences at the time of our first interviews either in the children's use of computers or in their enthusiasm about computers. We nevertheless found strong direct evidence of sex-stereotyping in the initial interviews.

We first asked if 'boys would like computers more than girls, or girls more than boys, or both the same' (the order of the alternatives was randomly varied). As Table 1.1 shows, over half the children said 'boys', and only four children said 'girls'. There were no significant differences in response due to sex, age or social class.

TABLE 1.1 Children's responses to 'Who likes computers more?'

|  | 'Boys' (%) | 'Girls' (%) | 'Same' (%) |
|---|---|---|---|
| Occasion 1 | 55 | 4 | 41 |
| Occasion 2 | 14 | 4 | 82 |

Children not saying 'the same' were asked to justify their answer. The younger children frequently referred to someone they knew: e.g. (from girls) 'My [male] cousin's got one', or 'My brother likes doing it more than me', or even that 'Little boys get more excited when their dad tells them they're bringing the computer home.' Less personal responses were that boys were more interested in computers, used them more, or (from a 7-year-old) 'like pressing buttons more', and several children referred to more general characteristics: boys like electrical toys or mechanical things, or prefer space games, while girls like dolls or 'go to clubs and that'. A working-class girl said that 'Boys have more time: girls have to go to the shops more.' One of the reasons for saying 'girls' was that 'Boys are mostly interested in football.'

The children were also asked in the same way about whether they thought boys or girls would be *better* at computers, and here the association of boys with computers was only slightly less strong (see Table 1.2). Again, there were no significant differences due to age, sex or social class.

TABLE 1.2 Children's responses to 'Who would be better at computers?'

|  | 'Boys' (%) | 'Girls' (%) | 'Same' (%) |
|---|---|---|---|
| Occasion 1 | 42 | 10 | 47 |
| Occasion 2 | 17 | 2 | 81 |

As with the previous question, children were asked to justify their answers. Many of the reasons were similar to those given above: for example, boys 'know about mechanical toys' or 'play more games'. However, some of the explanations were more overtly sexist: 'Coz girls when they grow up just do housework and wouldn't use computers'; 'Men always have bigger brains'; 'Men have got more knowledge'; 'They've got more skill than we don't have'; and 'Boys have got more brains.' Of the few children advancing reasons for girls being better, two noted that more women are typists, while another said 'Boys muck around more in class.' Some of the middle-class 10-year-olds, however, gave more balanced replies: 'Depends on who it is', or 'Depends on how long they've used one'. These children seemed to be aware of factors other than sex which might be more relevant.

The children were also asked if *they themselves* would be good with computers. As Figure 1.3 shows, the boys were clearly more confident than the girls, with significantly more boys than girls answering 'yes' ($\chi^2 = 7.76$, $p < 0.01$).

Further information relevant to sex-stereotyping came when the children were asked who used or would use a computer in their house. By far the most common positively-mentioned person was the father (39 positive, 4 negative mentions). Brothers and sisters received 22 positive, 1 negative and 13 positive, 3 negative mentions respectively. Mothers received 18 positive and 20 negative mentions. Typical comments in answer to this question were: 'Dad would use it, but mum would just wash up dishes'; 'Mum would just do the cooking'; 'My mum hates computers'; 'My wee sister would muck about with it'; and 'My little sister would just press any button.'

### Sex-stereotyping: Occasion 2

On Occasion 2 the children were again asked directly for their views on who liked computers more, who would be better at using computers, whether they themselves were (or would be) good at using a computer, and who else in their house used or might use one. Their responses revealed a major shift away from sex-stereotyping.

The children's responses to the 'who likes computers more' question are shown in Table 1.1. Overall, the number of children saying 'boys' is significantly lower than on the earlier occasion ($\chi^2 = 34.71$, $p < 0.001$). Closer inspection revealed that this change was relatively independent of age or social class, and more closely related to sex: the largest changes were to be found in the number of girls answering 'boys' on the first occasion and 'the same' on the second. Many of the children's justifications were similar to those given on Occasion 1 (e.g. 'Most of the games they have are just like boys' games') but some appeared to show a deeper reflection on the issues

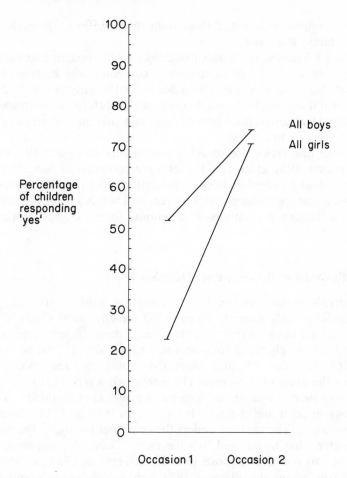

FIGURE 1.3 Children's responses to 'Would you be good?'

(e.g. 'It seems as if boys do but that's because they talk more about it – I think both the same').

A similar reduction in sex-stereotyping was found in the children's responses to the 'who would be better' question (see Table 1.2). Overall, the number of children answering 'boys' is again significantly lower on the second occasion ($\chi^2 = 13.03$, $p < 0.001$), but this time the shift is relatively independent of sex and social class and more closely linked to age: the older children showed a highly significant decrease in the number answering 'boys' ($\chi^2 = 17.98$, $p < 0.001$), while the younger children did not show any significant change in their responses. As before, this question elicited a few justifications such as 'Boys have got bigger brains' (from a younger girl), but it also elicited an increasing number of more balanced replies: 'As long as they're well taught to use it, I think both the same', or 'Depends – some could be brainy, some not.'

As Figure 1.3 shows, the number of children who thought that they themselves were or would be good at using a computer rose between the two interviews. This rise was highly significant for the girls ($\chi^2 = 21.21$, $p < 0.001$), but not for the boys. As a result of this differential increase, there was no significant difference between boys and girls on this measure by the time of the second interviews.

These later interviews also revealed a substantial change in the responses to the question 'Who else (would) use(s) the computer at home?' Mothers and sisters, who had earlier been significantly under-represented so far as positive mentions were concerned, now received nearly as many as the males: in order of frequency – fathers 59 mentions, sisters 45, and mothers and brothers each 43.

### The child's model of the computer: Occasion 1

The children's initial ideas of how a computer works were, with a few exceptions, extremely limited. When asked directly, most children replied that they did not know or that 'you press the buttons'. A substantial number mentioned various electrical components, such as wires (27 mentions), electricity (16), batteries (9) and plugs (6). Some children spontaneously mentioned the ideas of a program (16 mentions), a tape (15) or a memory (10), making such comments as 'You put a program in its mind', 'You just put a program on it and it does what you want it to do', 'You feed things into its memory', 'The tape – it orders the computer around', 'The tape tells the computer what to do' and 'It's the tape'. These children were mostly middle-class 10-year-olds (whose teacher, incidentally, had recently given them a lesson about the silicon chip, which was therefore mentioned by several of them). Two children gave graphic descriptions of the problems involved in loading the contents of tapes into computers, but had only a hazy idea of how the tape might cause the computer to work. A few of the younger children had very misguided notions of what there might be inside the computer that caused it to work: 'a wee engine', 'levers', 'a brain ticket thing', 'prints' and 'a piece of paper with sums on'.

Direct questioning on the nature of a computer program revealed almost total ignorance or confusion: 'Is it a TV programme about computers?' and 'I don't know, I've never watched it.' A few of the most experienced children were familiar with the idea, but even they found it hard to reconcile the electrical nature of the machine with the non-electrical nature of the program. Christopher (9 years 9 months), for example, wrote out a serviceable two-line BASIC program for us, and was then asked how a computer works:

*Christopher:*  By electricity, and the electricity runs through into the computer which is plugged in the television and all the stuff that is programmed into the computer . . . mmm . . . goes through into the television and is printed up on the screen.
*Interviewer:*  So what's inside the computer?
*Christopher:*  Mmm . . . well . . . it is . . . silicon chips, and then people . . . mmm . . . the . . . the program runs through the silicon chips and that is how the thing, the computer works.
*Interviewer:*  So how does a computer know what to do?
*Christopher:*  You tell it what to do and it runs through the wires inside the computer and gets into the computer's memory bank.
*Interviewer:*  And then what happens after it gets into the memory bank?
*Christopher:*  It goes . . . it runs through the computer and is printed. It runs through the wire into the TV and is printed out on the screen.

The remaining quiestions focused more directly on the children's concept of the computer as an intelligent autonomous machine. Table 1.3 shows the percentage of children in the entire sample who responded positively to these questions: there were no major age, sex or social-class differences. As this table suggests, the children considered each question on its own merits, and responded in the way which best fitted both their own interpretation of it and their own particular experience of computers.

TABLE 1.3 Children's responses to 'animacy' questions

|  | \% of children answering 'yes' | | |
| --- | --- | --- | --- |
|  | Occ.1 | Occ.2 | Statistics |
| Can computers do things by themselves? | 17 | 33 | $\chi^2 = 5.2, p < 0.05$ |
| Do computers want to do things? | 45 | 61 | $\chi^2 = 4.2, p < 0.05$ |
| Do computers think? | 48 | 65 | $\chi^2 = 5.1, p < 0.05$ |
| Do they think as we do?* | 13 | 34 | $\chi^2 = 6.1, p < 0.02$ |
| Are they better at thinking than we are?* | 57 | 51 | NS |
| Do computers remember? | 72 | 94 | $\chi^2 = 13.7, p < 0.001$ |

*Percentages of those who answered 'yes' to 'Do computers think?'

The first question asked whether computers did or did not do things by themselves. The majority of children replied in the negative, with every single justification referring to the need for human agency: 'You've got to tell it what you want it to do', 'It's got to be programmed', 'You have to press a button', and 'You've got to turn it on – the computer just can't go and turn itself on'. Several of the children who were not sure referred to the possibility that very big or very clever computers (e.g. 'ones in a university') might be able to do things by themselves. Of the children who said that computers could do things by themselves, only two gave reasons, pointing out that 'you can leave them and they do things while you'r away', and that the computer inside 'Speak n Spell' did itself select the words to be spelt. These affirmative responses, it should be noted, do not necessarily imply an 'animistic' model: they merely reflect accurate observations of situations where computers do indeed function without the need for human agency.

The next question, 'Do computers want to do things?', was also interpreted in more than one way. Although fewer children replied in the negative, their justifications revealed that many of them had in fact interpreted the question along similar lines to the previous one: 'It only does things if you want it to', 'It's not got feelings, it just obeys', 'You want it to do things, not the computer', 'It doesn't really want to do things as it hasn't got a mind, but if you program it, it will do it for you.' However, several of those who replied 'Yes' seemed to interpret it as referring to the computer's *willingness to do things*: 'It wants to help you', 'When you switch it on it wants you to feed things into it, make it do things', and 'It would like to do things, I think, but after a long time it might get fed up, having to do this, do that.' Several children suggested that an essential feature of computers was that they would do things without objecting: 'Coz it wouldn't be much use if it didn't do things', 'It'll have to' and 'It really wants to. *You*'ve got to try, but that computer just goes on and on for ever.' Two children even suggested that computers would find idleness unattractive: 'It maybe likes to be happy because it's got a job', and 'I think it would be bored sitting there all the time doing nothing.' In other words, rather than seeing the computer as having motives and desires of its own, it tended to be regarded as a willing and obedient servant.

The question 'Do computers think?' seemed to come as a surprise to many children. There was usually some hesitation in answering, often accompanied by 'Pardon?' or 'Eh?', as if they thought they might have misheard the question (one child did in fact mishear it and replied that he wouldn't put *his* computer into water to find out!). While the most common answer was 'yes', it was often qualified by an expression of doubt, such as 'I think so'. There were relatively few justifications for a positive response, typical ones being 'It thinks about what it has to do', 'It has to think before it does it, because it will make a mistake', and 'I think so, coz they've got to think about your question.' The most common negative response was that the computer didn't think as it hadn't got a brain. One child made the interesting response that computers didn't think, but just knew everything you typed in: 'We're thinking, but they know the answer.'

Those children who felt that computers *did* think were then asked if computers 'think like we do' and if they 'are better at thinking than us'. The great majority of these children clearly did not believe that computers 'think like we do', with most of their justifications taking the form 'They've not got a brain, only a microchip', and 'We're alive but they're electric.' Our hearts went out to the girl who said 'No, coz I just think daft things!' Over half the children thought that computers think 'better than us', with most of the justifications focusing on the computer's speed, accuracy and calculating power: 'They're quicker than us', 'They don't make mistakes', 'They do bigger sums than I do' and 'They're over the top of teachers'. Some children were more equivocal: 'They know better sums than me, but maybe not better than my mum and dad, coz they've been at school a long time', and 'Probably, but a really good person who had read a lot of history books would be better'. A few of the older children were clear that computers were superior in some areas but not in others: 'It would depend what we were thinking about . . . if it's feelings, they wouldn't be able to, because they don't have feelings, but they would be better than us at different things . . . like sums', and 'Not always, because like . . . we know how many bottles of milk we get. They don't. They haven't a clue about it.'

The final question on this topic was whether computers could remember things. A clear majority of those asked said 'yes' and usually referred to the computers' memories, their memory banks, or the possibility of storing information on a tape. Several children were aware that switching off a computer would cause it to forget much of what it had been doing. As with the previous question, a few children were clear that computers had skills in some areas but not in others: 'It'll remember sums, things like that, but probably wouldn't remember where things go.'

### The child's model of the computer: Occasion 2

By the time of the second interviews, there was no more than a modest advance in the children's conceptions of how computers worked. On this occasion the children were asked directly: 'What is a computer program?' About a third of the children (32%) gave an acceptable definition, such as 'A form of commands put together to make an instruction', and 'You type something into it and it does what you type in – you're sort of telling it what to do actually.' The remaining children either replied that they did not know (43%) or gave an inadequate explanation (25%), such as 'Like a game thing', 'It's a tape', or 'The thing you put in'. The middle-class children were significantly more likely to give an acceptable definition than the working-class children ($\chi^2 = 4.48$, $p < 0.05$), as were the older children compared with the younger children ($\chi^2 = 11.43$, $p < 0.001$), but there were no significant differences between boys and girls. There was, however, a highly significant correlation between the children's *level of use* and the adequacy of their definition of a program – those children whose experience of computers included copying or actually writing programs were much more likely to give an adequate explanation than the others ($\chi^2 = 14.53$, $p < 0.001$). This effect was also present when each age, sex and social-class group was looked at separately.

The children's responses to questions such as 'Do computers do things by themselves?' and 'Do computers think?' are shown in Table 1.3. Somewhat surprisingly, the children now showed a *greater* willingness to attribute 'human-like' qualities to machines, with five of the six questions eliciting a statistically significant increase in the number of affirmative responses. As before, the children's responses to these questions were not significantly related to age, sex or social class, and only one item was significantly related to level of use: children who had written or copied out programs were less likely to say that computers think 'like us' ($\chi^2 = 4.56$, $p < 0.05$).

Closer examination of the children's responses suggested that, as before, they were frequently grappling to relate these puzzling questions to their own actual experiences with computers. For example, as on Occasion 1, many children responded negatively to the question 'Can computers do things by themselves?', by referring to human agency: ' . . . coz somebody's got to work them' and (indignantly) 'Well if we don't press the knobs they can't do anything!' Other children, however, justified positive answers by referring to occasions when computers had selected questions or games, or worked out the answer to a problem, without any apparent human agency: 'If you put a question into it, well it would put the answer back', and 'When your dad wants to find stuff then the computer brings it up for him.'

Similarly, many children again seemed to interpret the question 'Do computers want to do things?' by considering whether computers had ever shown any *unwillingness*. For many children the answer was simple: 'They want to help you', 'Yes, that's what they're made for', 'Yes . . . to help families, to make things easier' and (on the other hand) 'The one that my friend has it seems to take a long time to load so I don't think it wants to.' One child showed some uncertainty: 'Sometimes they can't find your program and I don't know if it's because they don't want to do it or they can't find it.' Other children were more animistic, suggesting that computers wanted 'to be able to talk' or even 'to do important things, like control a railway, or air traffic control'.

As on Occasion 1, the question 'Do computers think?' generated a good deal of uncertainty and puzzlement, for example 'No . . . well, they do . . . sort of', 'Yes . . . no . . . well they've got a brain but it's made up of microchips and wire and they've got to be told what to think', 'They haven't got a mind of their own . . . like chess, you can't just program it to do any old move because it would just get checkmate, so . . . I don't know what it does . . . but it's not thinking' and finally 'Yes, because you press a certain button but it has to go through its memory to get it on the screen so . . . well . . . that wouldn't be thinking . . . No I don't think they do, because you press the button and then they just have to search their memory, they can't think, it's just sort of automatic.' In contrast, there was little doublt that computers could 'remember'.

## DISCUSSION OF THE FINDINGS

The period of time between our two sets of interviews (November 1983 to March 1985) saw a major incursion of computers into the lives of many young children (the proportion of children in our sample with access to a computer at home rose from 7% to 40% during this period). This rapid growth in the availability of a novel and powerful piece of technology raises many questions for both psychologists and educationalists, some of which are illuminated by our findings.

One clear finding from our study is that children's experience of computers is not evenly distributed across the population as a whole. As expected, gender and class emerge as important factors, with the working-class girls being the one group whose access to home computers remained low throughout the study. Such sex differences are hardly surprising, and have indeed been reported elsewhere (e.g. Siann and Macleod, 1985, Fife-Schaw, Breakwell, Lee and Spencer, 1986). The social-class differences are equally unsurprising but less well documented: nevertheless, several observers have already pointed to the danger of information technology increasing rather than decreasing the attainment gap between social classes (e.g. Hannon and Wooler, 1985). In addition, children's access to a computer at school is similarly uneven: only a quarter of our sample had actually used one there. Other studies (e.g. Beard, 1985; Jackson, Fletcher and Messer, 1986) suggest that such limited access to a school computer is not uncommon, and there are many anecdotal reports of the single school computer being either restricted to one classroom (usually that of the oldest children) or even not used at all. This uneven distribution means that by the time of our second interviews some children were using a computer regularly both at home and at school, while others had yet to put their hands on one.

Our interviews also make clear the need to take account of the *context* in which children experience computing. The two main contexts for computing – home and school – do in fact differ on several crucial dimensions – such as hardware, software, type of task, extent of adult involvement, presence of other children and time available. Furthermore, the children themselves perceived the two contexts as quite different: school was seen as primarily concerned with learning, whereas home was more an environment for fun and games. This situation raises some interesting questions concerning the carry-over from one context to another. One characteristic finding of much recent research in developmental psychology is that young children are particularly sensitive to their immediate context, and that skills demonstrated in one context will not necessarily reveal themselves in another (e.g. Donaldson, 1978; Tizard and Hughes, 1984). There is, however, some anecdotal evidence that children using a computer in a classroom will defer to those who have extensive out-of-school computer experience – even if the skills do not transfer, children themselves appear to believe that they do! A further problem is that children may use criteria developed for evaluating games software at home as a means of judging educational software in school, and indeed there is evidence that this is already happening (Smith and Keep, 1986). As software developed for the home market becomes more colourful, ingenious and exciting, it is likely that the educational software used in school will increasingly seem unattractive to computer-sophisticated children.

The second main issue we explored concerned children's attitudes towards computers. Both sets of interviews provided clear confirmation of the popular myth that children almost without exception possess a positive attitude towards computers. Interestingly enough, where doubt was expressed, it was usually by children who were in regular – in some cases daily – contact with a computer at home, and who engaged in some kind of programming activity: these children, while obviously 'heavy users' of computers, were able to see their faults. This finding may provide some reassurance to those concerned that children who use computers a lot will become 'addicted' to them and use them as a substitute for interpersonal relationships. In fact we found no children who fitted the common stereotype of a 'hacker', but it may be that the age-range of our sample (6–12 years) was below that in which the syndrome can be found.

Our interviews provided only a few clues as to the source of this strong feeling towards computers – what others have termed the computer's 'holding power'. Most of the comments from the children suggested that they thought computers were good because they provided a novel source of entertainment through exciting, colourful and noisy games. Psychologists interested in this phenomenon (e.g. Malone, 1981; Lepper, 1985) have noted that the most popular games are challenging on many levels and allow children to set themselves realistic targets which they can then raise as their performance improves. The importance of 'mastery' for children of this age also emerges from Turkle's (1984) in-depth interviews with American children, but we found few spontaneous references to this in our sample. Other factors may be involved – such as the feeling of being in control of the interaction with the computer, or the extent to which expertise gives a sense of identity. Clearly, there are important questions for psychologists to investigate here.

There are also important issues for educationalists arising from the widespread attraction to computers. For some, it may be sufficient that a generation of children will grow up without the fear and anxiety towards computers which characterizes many adults today – provided, of course, that the current quality of computer-use does not lead to alternative negative feelings of boredom and contempt. Others are more concerned with ways in which the motivating power of the computer can be used to help children through difficult or distasteful areas of the traditional curriculum. But there are dangers here, as Lepper (1985) in particular has pointed out. Children may be more motivated to carry out educational tasks when these are presented on a computer, but this does not guarantee that they will necessarily learn any better; furthermore, they may be even less motivated to return subsequently to more traditionally presented tasks.

The third area we explored was the presence of sex-stereotyping in children's attitudes. Our first interviews revealed that nearly half the children – girls as well as boys – believed that boys not only liked computers more than did girls but would perform better with them, and significantly more boys than girls believed that they themselves would be good at computing. These findings will add to the concern of those who believe that girls will be seriously disadvantaged by information technology, although it is unclear whether such attitudes will themselves affect children's actual performance with computers. There is some evidence from an Australian study by Clarke (1984) of such an effect, but the evidence from other subject areas is ambivalent (e.g. Entwisle and Baker, 1983). Nevertheless, some educationalists have already implemented approaches aimed at positive discrimination in favour of girls – for example, using software specially written for girls, setting up girls-only computer classes, or introducing information technology in its less male-oriented aspects (e.g. word-processing).

Such measures may turn out to be unnecessary, in that we found a substantial decrease in sex-stereotyping in children's attitudes on Occasion 2. One possible explanation for this lies in the sex of the interviewer – male on the first occasion, female on the second – but it seems unlikely that this factor could totally explain the differences between the two occasions. It seems much more likely that the children's beliefs were actually modified by the experience of seeing their peers of both sexes interacting with computers. This is an important and encouraging finding, for it suggests that such stereotyped views may not be as deeply rooted and unchallengeable as some may believe.

The final issue we explored was that of the children's mental model of the computer. On both occasions our direct questioning about how computers worked and the nature of a computer program suggested that children's mental models of computers are quite limited. Some confirmation of this comes from a study by Mawby et al.(1984), in which children aged 8–12 years were interviewed about their understanding of how computers function at the beginning and end of a year's programming in LOGO. The authors reported (p.22) that 'In general, the inner workings of computers are largely

unknown to these children . . . ', and argued (p.36) that ' . . . the progress
of even the most advanced students could be hindered by their inadequate
mental models of Logo'. If it is the case that children will not spontaneously
develop an adequate model of how computers function simply through interacting with them, and also that the better the model, the better the children's
potential as users, then it follows that children should be more explicitly
encouraged to acquire an appropriate and adequate model.

We also attempted to find out whether children attributed animistic qualities to computers by asking direct questions such as 'Do computers do things
by themselves?', 'Do computers think?, and so on. Our findings show an
increase in 'animistic' replies on Occasion 2. If one regards these as
representing 'naive' or 'primitive' thinking, then this is indeed a surprising
finding: one would expect that experience with computers would lead to a
decrease in such responses. Our finding, however, confirms a claim made by
Turkle (1984), who noted (p.41) that ' . . . when children get used to the
[computerized] toys, the language they use to talk about them becomes more,
not less, psychological. The more contact children have with computational
objects, the more nuanced and elaborated this psychological language
becomes.' Turkle's explanation for this increase in children's psychological
language ties in with her notion of the computer as an 'evocative object' –
that is, something which exists on the margins of the physical and the psychological, with properties of both. The importance of such evocative objects,
according to Turkle, is that they present a challenge to our conceptual
structures: they force us to reflect on our notions of the physical and the
psychological. The issue for Turkle is not so much whether children do or
do not believe that, for example, computers think: it is rather that the
presence of computers makes us re-examine our notions of what it is to
think, to have intentions and, indeed, to be a human being.

It is certainly true that many children in our study were puzzling over
these notions when we asked them whether computers think or want to do
things. Our impression, however, was that it was our questioning, rather
than the computers by themselves, which had instigated this puzzling –
indeed, many children appeared to be thinking about these issues for the
first time. Nevertheless, in so doing, they gave us some glimpses into their
concepts of what it means to be autonomous, to have agency and to engage
in mental activity. For example, many children interpreted the question of
whether a computer wants to do something more in terms of its willingness
to do what we want it to do than in terms of its having independent desires
and intentions. Similarly, some children appeared to equate 'thinking' with
'having a brain' and so concluded that a computer cannot think; others
considered that if a computer does what for us requires thought (like working
out a sum) then the computer must also be thinking; others again made the
distinction between thinking and knowing – as the computer already knows

the answer (they believe), then it does not need to think. Clearly we have done little more than scratch the surface of an important area for further study.

## CONCLUSIONS

Our initial motive for carrying out these interviews was to establish a baseline against which to measure future developments. The picture which emerged from our first round of interviews was of children looking forward eagerly to the arrival of computers in their lives. They relished the thought of playing games at home (but had some reservations about the ways in which computers would help their learning at school), associated computers with boys rather than girls, and regarded a computer primarily as a willing and obedient servant. Sixteen months later, much had changed. Many of the children now had access to computers, at home or elsewhere. They found them as attractive as ever, but associated them far less with boys and were much more likely to attribute psychological qualities to them. That such unexpected changes could occur in a mere 16 months shows how fluid the situation is. When one tries to take account of concurrent developments in computing technology and software design, it becomes well nigh impossible to imagine what ideas and attitudes children – or adults for that matter – will have in 16 *years* time. We can only hope that the technological revolution will have lived up to the enthusiasm and optimism of the children in our sample.

## ACKNOWLEDGEMENTS

This research was carried out while we were in receipt of grants from the Scottish Education Department and the Nuffield Foundation. We are grateful to John Rodgers, Cathie Potts, Jean Fife and Frances Macnamara for their help in carrying out, transcribing and analysing the interviews.

## REFERENCES

Beard, D. (1985). *The Use of Microcomputers/Information Technology in Devon Schools*, University of Exeter, School of Education, Exeter.
du Boulay, B., O'Shea, T., and Monk, J. (1981). The black box inside the glass box: presenting computing concepts to novices, *International Journal of Man-Machine Studies*, **14**, 237–249.
Clarke, V.A. (1984). Sex differences and attitudes of primary school children using LOGO. Paper presented at the BPS conference 'IT, AI and Child Development', Brighton.
Cumming, G. (1986). Logic programming and education: designing Prolog to fit children's minds, *Pegboard*, **1**, 34–46.

Donaldson, M. (1978). *Children's Minds*, Fontana, London.
Entwisle, D., and Baker, D. (1983). Gender and young children's expectations for performance in arithmetic, *Developmental Psychology*, **19**, 200–209.
Equal Opportunities Commission (1983). *Information Technology in Schools*, Equal Opportunities Commission, Manchester.
Fairbrother, R. (1982). Children's ideas about computers, *Primary Contact*,1, No.2.
Fife-Schaw, C., Breakwell, G., Lee, T., and Spencer, J. (in press, 1986). Patterns of teenage computer usage, *Journal of Computer Assisted Learning*.
Frude, N. (1983). *The Intimate Machine*, Century, London.
Hannon, P., and Wooler, S. (1985). Psychology and Educational Computing. In J.J. Wellington (ed.), *Children, Computers and the Curriculum*, Croom Helm, London.
Hawkins, J. (1984). *Computers and girls: Rethinking the issues*, Technical Report No.24, Bank Street College, New York.
Hofstadter, D.R., and Dennett, D.C. (1981). *The Mind's I*, Harvester Press, Brighton.
Jackson, A., Fletcher, B., and Messer, D.J. (1986). A survey of microcomputer use and provision in primary schools, *Journal of Computer Assisted Learning*, **2**, 45–55.
Johnson-Laird, P.N. (1983). *Mental Models: Towards a Cognitive Science of Language, Inference and Consciousness*, Cambridge University Press, Cambridge.
Lepper, M.R. (1985). Microcomputers in education: motivational and social issues, *American Psychologist*, **40**, 1–18.
Malone, T.W. (1981). Toward a theory of intrinsically motivating instruction, *Cognitive Science*, **4**, 333–369.
Mawby, R., Clement, C.A., Pea, R.D., and Hawkins, J. (1984). *Structured interviews on children's conceptions of computers*, Technical Report No.19, Bank Street College, New York.
O'Shea, T., and Self, J. (1983). *Learning and Teaching with Computers*, Harvester Press, Brighton.
Papert, S. (1980). *Mindstorms: Children, Computers and Powerful Ideas*, Harvester Press, Brighton.
Piaget, J. (1929). *The Child's Conception of the World*, Routledge and Kegan Paul, London.
Sage, M., and Smith, D. (1983). *Microcomputers in Education: A Framework for Research*, Economic and Social Research Council, London.
Searle, J.R. (1984). *Minds, Brains and Science, the 1984 Reith Lectures*, BBC, London.
Shallis, M. (1984). *The Silicon Idol*, Oxford University Press, Oxford.
Siann, G., and Macleod, H. (1985). *Are computers girl-friendly? The origin of gender differences in the response to computer technology*. Paper presented to the BPS Social Section conference, Cambridge.
Smith, D., and Keep, R. (in press, 1986). Children's opinions of educational software, *Educational Research*.
Tizard, B., and Hughes, M. (1984). *Young Children Learning*, Fontana, London.
Turkle, S. (1984). *The Second Self*, Granada, London.
Weizenbaum, J. (1984). *Computer Power and Human Reason*, Penguin, London.
Young, R. (1981). The machine inside the machine: users' models of pocket calculators, *International Journal of Man–Machine Studies*, **15**, 51–85.

Computers, Cognition and Development
Edited by J. Rutkowska and C. Crook

CHAPTER 2

# Computers in the Classroom: Defining a Social Context

CHARLES CROOK

## SUMMARY

The challenge computers make to the interpersonal quality of early education is noted. However, it is argued that the technology does have a potential for catalysing socially organized learning. The case of peer collaboration is illustrated and the theoretical basis for developing computers in this way is outlined.

There are many who will argue that computers have a dehumanizing influence on our lives. What is meant by such a claim? Most likely, it will be inspired by the relentless manner in which this technology encroaches upon areas of human work. But to take some particular activity and complain that it has been 'dehumanized' is not just to express concern for those whose labour gets displaced. This will be a complaint bearing on the interests of all those for whom the activity was conceived. The claim of dehumanization identifies a loss in the quality of our participation in some activity.

Of course, technological encroachments need not have such impact: often they may seem quite benign. The challenge, then, is to be alert to ways in which computer technology might be restructuring our experience of familiar exchanges. Perhaps in many such situations we will not feel perturbed by a loss of human contact. But in other circumstances such loss may seem just too great. Surely, this could well apply to an activity with such rich interpersonal characteristics as schooling.

The social organization of instruction is clearly challenged by present extensions of computers into schools. In a way, this is invigorating: it requires both critics and enthusiasts to identify the social dimension of education that they judge to be important. That is a debate which could well be informed by theory and research from developmental psychology, and one purpose of this chapter is to highlight how such research may contribute to policy in this area.

The plan of the chapter is as follows. First, I shall conceptualize some ways children may interact with computers and consider how such interactions challenge socially organized practices in early education. This analysis invites the suggestion that we stress the computer's potential for supporting collaborative work: two observational studies of such an application will be outlined. I shall then step back and appeal to research in developmental psychology to clarify how interactions among classroom peers could promote cognitive development. The conclusions of this review will highlight the kind of research needed to advance the present conception of peer interaction as a social context for classroom computers.

Two admissions should be made at the outset. Firstly, discussion must be confined to the primary school years. However, this is the period where the anxieties referred to above are greatest. Secondly, it behoves an optimist in these matters to acknowledge that establishing a way in which computer use *could* be developed is no promise regarding how it *will* be developed – but it is a necessary contribution.

## CHARACTERIZING THE PUPIL'S INTERACTION WITH COMPUTERS

One way of expressing that strong interpersonal quality of school learning is to think of it in terms of various 'partnerships' into which pupils will enter. Successful learning depends on success in establishing and developing such partnerships – with tutors or with collaborators. Thus, the growth of children's understanding is socially mediated in this straightforward sense. Insofar as this reflects our general belief, so it follows that we will value the interpersonal dimensions of learning and try to see that the partnerships involved are properly cultivated.

However, such an attitude is not free of complication. It may be argued that one important goal of formal education is to cultivate a capacity to learn independently; in a sense, to find some release from learning-as-partnership. Now, claims of this sort introduce an element of tension: we wish to develop partnerships for purposes of socially mediated learning, but we also wish to cultivate in the learner a certain autonomy. Of course, tension of aims need not imply conflict of aims. Indeed, far from being in conflict, there may be a necessary developmental relation between socially organized cognitive functioning and that which is 'private' or autonomous to the individual (Vygotsky, 1978). Nevertheless, at the practical level of formulating strategies for teaching, there does remain a tension to be handled. Thus, in practice, one thing teachers must surely consider is how they should manage the learning process in terms of a balance of emphasis between pupil autonomy and interpersonal exchange.

### Two varieties of interaction with school computers

A claim central to the theme of this chapter is that classroom computers challenge our thinking about this balance and psychological processes relating to it. This requires us to reflect upon the 'social context' of learning in settings where computers play a significant role – to consider how may disturb the balance of interpersonal processes in the classroom. We should feel some sense of urgency in this challenge, if only to respond to the evident appeal that computer-based activities have for young pupils (cf. Lepper, 1985; Papert, 1980; Turkle, 1984).

Imagine a class of children absorbed in some computer task in much the way that these authors report. How are we to describe their engagement? One account could be in terms of the high degree of apparent autonomy in their learning: perhaps we compare children similarly absorbed in a more familiar task, such as reading or drawing. But a second account could describe their engagement in terms of a kind of partnership: in this case we form a comparison with more socially directed learning and assume the machinery is supporting something that resembles an interpersonal exchange. At first glance, it is not clear which of these two accounts best describes what is actually happening during children's interactions with computers.

In fact, there may be no grounds for unilaterally adopting just one of these possible perspectives. Which is more appropriate will depend on exactly what children are doing in a given situation. So, enthusiasts for the various educational applications of computers may align themselves differently with respect to these two models of computer interaction. For example, Seymour Papert (1980) seems to be expressing the present dichotomy with his much-quoted slogan: 'let the child control the computer not the computer control the child'. Of course, with this plea he is specifically aligning himself with the particular model of computer application that stresses the autonomy it offers the child – it puts the child in charge, it allows learning to occur around the individual's spontaneous activity.

We should not be too rigid about this dichotomy of possibilitilies for interacting with computers. But if we do prefer something resembling a continuum, then Papert's LOGO environment (see Chapters 1 and 6) is surely at one of its extremities. This is self-directed learning; there is no instructional pressure imposed by computers acting as partners-for-dialogue.

So, what kind of activities will lie towards the other extreme of a possible continuum? Papert himself seems to have in mind drill-and-practice routines reminiscent of the teaching machine tradition. Here the computer's role is usually to prompt children with a sequence of problems and provide suitable feedback for responses. In describing such programs, Papert has popularized a model of computers being 'in control' rather than the cosier view of them being 'in partnership'. This attitude is contentious: software that denies children maximum autonomy as 'users' includes more than humdrum drill-and-practice programs. So there is another school of enthusiasts that would develop programs to draw children into powerful learning dialogues – or partnerships (see, for example, Brown (1983) on computer-based coaching or Pea's (1985) discussion of intelligent tutoring systems).

### Recovering an interpersonal dimension

With regard to characterizing the pupil's interaction with computers, the LOGO tradition and the tradition of intelligent tutoring systems seem to proceed from different educational philosophies. Yet they do have a significant common feature: they appear set to dilute an interpersonal quality in the learning experience. A 'microworld' like LOGO is powerful if it supports *self*-directed, discovery learning. Tutoring-style systems are powerful insofar as they promote an instructional dialogue – with the computer. How this shift of emphasis away from interpersonal processes will bear on children's intellectual development is a pressing issue. But suppose we wished to encourage a trend of this kind (say, for reasons of economics), just how convincingly might we thereby dispense with teachers' roles in early education?

Confident answers to that question must definitely wait upon further research, much of it in areas of developmental and educational psychology. In fact, trends of this kind are more easily discussed in terms of how desirable, rather than how imminent, they appear. How do we view models of future classrooms which portray children locked into sustained but solitary interaction with their computers? This is definitely not an appealing image. Perhaps it questions a stubborn intuition that there is something very important about the familiar bustle of primary school classrooms; that the interpersonal dimension of any learning partnership is somehow vital. It may help to reflect upon this intuition.

It is probably not just based on a calculated doubt as to whether technology really can replace particular interpersonal skills of instruction, although research may indeed prove these skills to be precious. Neither is this intuition necessarily based on a respect for the particular discourse practices that teachers can organize in their classrooms, although these too may prove to furnish a precious experience (e.g. Walkerdine, 1982). What may really count is the fact that whether or not we feel committed to regarding intelligence as necessarily *acquired* in socially organized contexts, we do acknowledge that it will most often be *exercised* in socially organized contexts. What may compel us to protect the interpersonal quality of early learning is the belief that cognitive development involves a necessary coordination of our thinking with that of others – in the interests of various kinds of harmony and in the service of various kinds of joint activity.

This belief is central to the remainder of this chapter. Unambiguously, it encourages us to attend to the interpersonal dimension of classroom learning. So, we must consider how computer-based activities could be harmonized into an appropriate social context. My own discussion of this problem will not be comprehensive: in fact, it will completely evade the issue of how the role of teachers might evolve. This may appear eccentric but it represents a view that we may begin to define the social context by attending to interactions among the pupils themselves. In short, I wish to focus on the potential of computer-based activities to support a new priority for peer collaboration.

In the present section, discussion has focused on the child's interaction *with* the computer and how it may be conceptualized; what follows, however, really concerns interaction *around* computers. In contrast to socially isolating conceptions of computer use like those discussed above, the technology could function as a 'medium for joint activity'.

In order to develop this idea, it will be necessary to understand exactly what kind of 'medium' the classroom computer might provide for this purpose. As a forum for joint work, will it reveal distinctive properties? I shall approach this question in the next section where two case studies of such collaborative work will be outlined. They raise a number of issues which will prompt brief consideration of relevant theory and research in developmental psychology. However, at this point, some readers might still welcome further persuasion that collaborative work with computers is a social context that deserves to be studied. There is a more straightforward rationale for discovering what kind of joint activity this medium supports: the very scarcity of computers in the classroom obliges teachers to organize their use on a paired or group basis in order to maximize access. Thus, the typical manner in which computers are used makes them a current focus for collaborative work in primary schools. So, research is also needed to explore the consequences of practices which, at least for the present, are well established.

## COLLABORATIVE WORKING AT COMPUTERS: TWO STUDIES

Hawkins *et al*. (1982) introduced LOGO programing to classrooms of 8–9 and 10–11 year olds. Joint working arrangements were encouraged. Observers recorded measures of collaboration in LOGO and other class activities before, during and after the 6-week period for which it was available. There are three important findings for us to note. Firstly, the computer activity proved especially potent in facilitating collaborative exchanges. Secondly, post-tests revealed no evidence that this richer collaboration carried over to other classroom work. Thirdly, it emerged that the children had formed strong impressions concerning which of their peers were the experts at LOGO: 50% of them identified the same small group of children as LOGO experts – a much higher consensus than was reached for other areas of classroom expertise.

In short, a valuable study. But it's interpretation does require caution. Note that the provision of these computer activities might have been a rather sudden and exciting break from classroom routine. This novelty alone could heighten the children's involvement and even attract their attention towards the achievements of others. Moreover (as the authors note), a lack of carry-over effects might reflect the rather short period of exposure. Such problems of method are difficult to overcome during this early stage of computer use in schools. However, these results do still suggest that computers may prove especially potent in facilitating peer collaboration.

The above remarks imply a special need to look at classrooms where both computer activities and collaborative working are well established. Our second study involves 7–8 year olds from just such a class. (It was carried out by the present author and is to be reported more fully elsewhere.) In this case, more detailed observations were made (but on fewer children) in order to capture some of the quality of the actual exchanges. The activities studied were several self-contained items of software popular in schools at the time. These activities typically mimic familiar curriculum materials but allow the development of a more interactive experience with the problems they pose.

Twelve pairs of children were observed for at least seven sessions each. For all pairs, analysis was carried out on transcriptions of two of their sessions during which three different problem-solving games were attempted and three further sessions which all involved a narrative adventure activity. The three games were:

(i) MAZE, in which a character must be directed along the only possible path through a grid of squares. This route must be composed in advance as a sequence of turns and step instructions.

(ii) SPOT, in which two numbers in an ascending series of six are given and the four blanks must be filled in by 'spotting' the pattern.

(iii) ANAGRAM, in which the jumbled letters of a word must be rearranged; the correct word always being one from a displayed list.

The ADVENTURE activity involved finding a number of hidden children; the discoveries depended on solving problems of reasoning or memory embedded in the narrative.

Space does not permit a detailed account of the collaborations. However, it is possible to identify certain general characteristics of these computer activities that appeared relevant to their success as catalysts for collaborative work.

Each of the three problem-solving tasks prompted a strong *turn-taking* approach for controlling the computer keyboard. At least we may say that the children naturally supposed involvement would be shared. However, these sessions were not universally successful as 'collaborations': how children occupied themselves when not taking a turn is revealing in this respect.

With MAZE, success depended on distributing attention between the maze itself and the developing sequence of steps being written to traverse it. Most children were reluctant to make this effort at times when they were not keystroking the route instructions themselves. Thus, 'collaboration' on MAZE rarely went beyond taking turns at the complete activity. With ANAGRAM, there was greater mutual involvement. However, opportunity for overt, shared discovery remained limited. Often, one child would be slightly swifter in identifying the word and would simply announce it immediately. This could leave one member of a pair merely taking turns at entering (someone else's) solutions.

The number game, SPOT, was the most successful of the three. Here, an overall problem is readily perceived at any given moment and does not demand the close concentration of MAZE. Neither does its answer involve a single response in quite the same sense as ANAGRAM. The solution is, in fact, a rule – the rule defining the sequence. Thus, the approach to solution in this case may be more differentiated, perhaps prompting discussion of competing hypotheses. To some extent, exchanges of this kind did take place. Certainly, the game accommodated a sharing of keyboard turns, while not encouraging simple announcements of the number that one's less speedy partner might be pondering.

The ADVENTURE game provided the richest forum for discussion. Part of its strength lies in the way written language is used to develop a context and, then, to pose challenging problems within it. However, the central place thereby given to fluent reading could be a limiting factor for certain working pairs. All our children could read the text but in some pairs one child would prove more able. This child would invariably end up taking more responsibility for the total activity. He or she would read aloud and so determine the pace of the task, including the pressing of keys to advance the screen text. This keystroke responsibility seemed to generalize so that these children also took greater responsibility for the more important decision making. Thus, relatively small differences in reading ability may serve to cultivate a more general asymmetry of involvement within a pair. Evidently, this problem may only apply at early stages of reading development and it may be partly circumvented by careful pairing. However, it does draw attention to subtle ways in which dominance may arise and spiral within these working arrangements.

In summary, we may say that in each of the two studies described above there is evidence for involvement and cooperation when young children work together at computer-based tasks. However, the finer-grained account of the second study leaves a mixed impression regarding the actual quality of their collaborations. But this claim only draws attention to an obligation neglected in the discussion so far: how are we to define 'quality' in children's experience of collaboration? Any attempt to highlight joint activity as a social context for using computers would be best grounded in a general theory of how children's development is promoted by collaborative exchanges.

To meet this obligation we should examine established theory and research within developmental psychology. Such a course will be taken up in the next section where studies of peer interaction and cognitive development will be discussed. However, it might be useful, at this point, to pose a more specific challenge for existing theory: how far can it clarify the particular issues that could arise in organizing peer interaction around *computer* tasks? Approaching the literature in this way should help us to identify where new research initiatives need to be made.

How might the design of computer-based activities influence possible collaborations? Consider the studies discussed above: the differences in design of those computer tasks do seem significant. LOGO is an open-ended environment that responds to the user's own initiatives. Considered as a vehicle for collaborative work it is probably more distinctive for the levels of involvement it sustains, not for features that might impose particular structure on collaborations among its users. In contrast, the activities of the second study exemplify a more question-and-answer type of format. Here the machine seems to be 'taking part in' a total interaction – as a kind of partner. This role for the computer does seem more likely to define and organize potential interactions among it's users (e.g. Laboratory of Comparative Human Cognition, 1982).

In the simplest of designs, a computer may just issue discrete challenges or problems. Yet even these unsophisticated activities are surely structured quite unlike any other that children might do together in the classroom. One characteristic many activities of this general type display is a typically precise feedback on the adequacy of the user's various solutions. This may exemplify one distinctive feature of the computer partnership that could prove significant. In a collaboration where there is real asymmetry in the abilities of the children involved, this feedback may serve to highlight such differences. In fact, both of the studies that have been discussed in this section do make reference to issues of ability differences between collaborators.

Thus, in reviewing the research literature below we should first seek a general rationale for cultivating peer interaction in classroom settings. But we should also seek insights into the specific influences of *computer*-based activities. So, of particular interest will be studies of peer interaction that focus on variables of task structure and design, but also on considerations of ability composition in groups.

## PEER INTERACTION FOR LEARNING

It is natural to suppose that experience of interacting with peers will serve to promote an individual's social development. This must have implications for life in schools; for schools are forums in which peer relationships can flourish. Certainly, there is ample research indicating how school experience is significant for social development (e.g., Minuchin and Shapiro, 1983). But how far should early education be organized around opportunities for peer interaction? If they are to be cultivated in the classroom, then evidence will be needed to support the (less obvious) claim that peer interactions can also mediate children's *intellectual* development.

Current reviews of research into collaborative learning lead to strong claims for its advantages (Sharon, 1980; Slavin, 1980). Where it is encouraged, it is said to have a favourable impact on children's learning, motivation and attitudes to school. But much of that research merely relates broad classroom strategies to outcome measures; in trying to promote this kind of social context for computer use, we must look for the actual processes that are mediating any effectiveness in peer collaboration.

One possible benefit of peer interaction during classroom activities is that a more expert child may serve as a model for one who is less so. Such learning by observation has been well documented for young children (e.g. Kuhn, 1972; Murray, 1974). However, arrangements of this kind are inherently chancy and possible benefits are, of necessity, unevenly distributed within these collaborations. Activities that promote a properly interactive exchange do seem more appealing: perhaps there are characteristics intrinsic to such interactions that will allow all the participants to exceed what they might achieve as individuals. In other words, there might be something truly distinctive in learning mediated by peer interaction. There is now research that seems to suggest this may be so.

This work is roughly organized around three theoretical frameworks. The first derives from sociolinguistic analyses of communication; an important aim being to expose the structure and functions of classroom discourse. A second body of research is in the Piagetian tradition: there the interest has been in how particular coordinations of peer activity could quite directly facilitate the development of cognitive structures. A third, less fully elaborated framework draws upon the Soviet approach to cognitive development exemplified in the work of Vygotsky. These traditions will be considered in turn.

## A sociolinguistic framework

A study reported by Sinclair and Coulthard (1975) provides a seminal analysis of discourse freely recorded during lessons. Mehan (1979) has since amplified that work, revealing some of the implicit rules of classroom communication and how children come to honour them. Research pursuing these initiatives still further has recently been assembled in one useful volume (Wilkinson, 1982). An effect of all this work has been to focus attention on the role of communicative competence in early education (see Cazden, 1972; or Cook-Gumperz and Gumperz, 1982, for development of this point). In so far as the learner's task is one of accessing information via exchange with a teacher, then mastering the rules of classroom discourse is a prime achievement.

It follows that much research in the sociolinguistic tradition does give priority to the study of teacher–child discourse rather than that associated with interactions among peers. This is an appropriately direct strategy: it looks at the most vital situations where communicative skills are being exercised. But it neglects the possibility that cultivation of these skills may occur, in part, during exchanges with peers.

Nevertheless, some analyses of peer communication have been made within this framework. This is fortunate, because any general argument for collaborative working practices must establish young children's straightforward communicative competence with their peers. This is not to deny that there may be value in exchanges involving only minimal verbal communication – as where an able child functions as effective model for one who is less able. But the available research does suggest that even very young children have the capacity for more useful communication around a shared activity. Hence, we may hope to discover within peer interaction something richer than mere observational learning.

Garvey and Hogan (1973) argue that even pre-school children have linguistic abilities necessary to sustain the dialogues required in collaborative problem solving. An instructive illustration can be found in Gernishi and Di Paolo's (1982) analysis of organization in young children's spontaneous arguments. They demonstrate how such exchanges could be a rich forum for developing strategies of social influence. When such observations are made in the context of children tackling a defined task, it may be possible to identify particular communicative devices associated with success. Such a study has been reported by Cooper (1980). Pairs of pre-school children used a balance to match blocks by weight. Success at this task was associated with the following: greater referential specificity (particularly, use of verbal labels and comparatives), more strategies for focusing a partner's attention, and greater responsiveness to a partner's questions and directives. These represent the kind of communicative skills that may be available to facilitate joint problem solving within the early school years.

A further study by Cooper and colleagues (Cooper *et al*. 1982) considers peer interactions in a school where they are encouraged to take shape spontaneously. The study involved children of 3–7 years; two important findings should be noted. Firstly, this proved a period within which the stability of particular peer groupings became greatly strengthened. Secondly, there were 'striking' individual differences in the extent to which children used peers as classroom resources. Perhaps as a consequence of these differences, there was a tendency for perceived expertise to accrue to individual children. Moreover, Cohen (1984) has shown how children's awareness of these differences can sometimes work to the disadvantage of some members of collaborating groups. Finally, Dickson (1982) has also commented on individual differences of this kind: he shows how, for children in pairs, the stability of such differences is greater within pairs than across the various partners. This implies that communicative competence was located in the dyad rather than the individual.

Our earlier account of collaborative work at computers raised questions both about the process defining effective peer interaction and about the significance of asymmetries in relationships. Sociolinguistic research does offer one theoretical framework. On the question of process, it gives a central place to communicative competence. Revealing the extent of this competence, it encourages us to recognize that peer interation can indeed offer more than learning by mere observation. However, the impact of communication within collaborative work tends to be evaluated in terms of two characteristic distractions of the sociolinguistic tradition – control and status. So, this work does reach beyond processes of passive observation, but it tends to encourage instead an emphasis so something more like 'peer tutoring'.

It would surely be more interesting to discover that peer interaction offered something distinctive in itself, rather than depending on the adult-style tutoring of a more able partner. This may prove a matter of emphasis; it remains implicit that participants of equal ability might also gain from collaborating: they might each employ their communicative skills towards the successful coordination of a joint activity. Unfortunately, this literature provides little indication of how typical or how significant such mutual regulations might be.

On the issue of ability differences among collaborators, this research is certainly sensitive to them and would, perhaps, accord them importance – insofar as tutoring-type processes are judged part of effective collaboration. There is some evidence that differences in expertise are salient to young children and that, in group activities, this knowledge can work to the disadvantage of the less able.

## A Piagetian framework

Piaget (1928) also argued that the value of peer interaction could go beyond passive observation, yet still involve something apart from direct tutoring. The overt disagreements that arise in such interactions may have a special potential for creating cognitive 'disturbances'. He noted how adult–child exchanges must involve asymmetry (in knowledge, authority, etc.), whereas child–child exchanges are more balanced. If other features of early childhood thinking are taken into account (notably an egocentric bias), then problem solving among peers may typically generate some degree of conflict. Piaget claimed a special potency for such conflict. Given the more symmetrical character of peer relationships, the individual is made to recognize the possibility of alternative perspectives. Moreover, this could facilitate more active negotiation of a problem.

Piaget hardly pursued this possibility himself but some recent research has examined the role of conflict in peer interaction. Because of the Piagetian background to this work, the tasks involved tend to call upon the hallmark achievements of operational thinking, particularly conservation and persepctive taking. There are advantages to this choice: these are achievements that may be diagnosed in a fairly clear manner; moreover, this diagnosis involves criteria for determining the real depth of any change in a participant's understanding.

Space dies not allow a detailed review here (see Glachan and Light, 1982). However, the work of Doise and his colleagues (e.g., Doise, 1978; Doise and Mugny, 1984) must be identified as one particularly thorough programme of study. They report broad and stable gains in operational thinking among children allowed to interact around modified Piagetian tasks. Piaget's broad proposal is endorsed: the important experience in peer interaction is disagreement or conflict. This cultivates the child's awareness of responses other than its own and stimulates the elaboration of new cognitive instruments that serve to resolve the disequilibria experienced.

These claims have not been made without controversy. Consider children doing conservation problems together: there is wide agreement that important gains can emerge when a non-conserving child is paired with a conserver. However, Russell (1982) has questioned whether such gains amount to structural change in cognition. He suggests these children's thinking was already, in some sense, 'transitional' and that what their social exchanges influence is the kind of 'propositional attitude' they have towards verbal statements describing dimensional relations. These observations question what it is that is effected by conflict – not the fact that conflict and its resolution are what counts. But Russell urges caution there also. He suggests that real gains through such a mechanism are unlikely when the children involved are both non-conservers. Unlike Doise, he finds that conflict within those dyads would more usually be resolved by social dominance than real coordination of perspectives. Glachan and Light (1982) suggest that differences in research methodology may underly this disagreement, although those authors also describe problem solving characterized by striking social dominance and indicate how it may limit the gains of a less assertive partner.

This Piagetian research identifies conflict as the feature of peer interactions that make them distinctive learning experiences. But, once again, our attention is drawn towards the influence of differences among the individuals comprising a working arrangement. In particular, it remains uncertain whether conflict is only really effective in situations where one participant has a more advanced understanding.

## A framework from Vygotsky

Recently there has been a revival of interest in the work of the Soviet psychologist Vygotsky (cf. Wertsch, 1985). In this view, the very structure of certain social exchanges can function to promote cognitive development. It is claimed that cognitive strategies may first be encountered within an *inter*-individual context – during various joint activities. A process of internatization is proposed as the mechanism whereby these experiences then become *intra*-individual events.

This account tends to emphasize social interactions in which one partner is, in some way, a more advanced thinker. For it is assumed that the richest encounters involve a more experienced collaborator electing to act as a careful support to the efforts of someone less experienced. This perspective has drawn our attention to how an adult will behave in those activities typically shared between children and parents, or children and teachers. It has been less concerned to show how the structure of interactions among peers might contribute to the internalization process.

While such a process may best flourish in collaborations with skilled and sympathetic partners, could there not still be some gain arising from more symmetrical relationships? Perhaps our uncertainty about this reflects a need for greater specification of the particular social events supposed to be so potent. This must imply more observational research that could highlight the particular ways in which cognition can be embedded in the structures of social exchange (cf. Rogoff and Wertsch, 1984; Wertsch, McNamee, McLane and Budwig, 1980). Observations of peer interaction in this spirit would be especially welcome.

For the present, we can only note that ability differences within collaborating peer groups need not constrain any individual from confronting a partner with 'challenges', 'cautions', 'confirmatory comments', and so on. It seems reasonable to suppose that exposure to these exchanges could structure the thinking of the individuals involved. Moreover, it may be that, by being part of a collaborating group, children are encouraged simply to *declare* their thoughts. Even without any strong communicative intent, this may facilitate and organize the thinking of a partner, but it may also be of benefit to the declarer. Indeed, Scardamalia and Bereiter (1983) have argued the value in encouraging children to 'think aloud' for the very purpose of cultivating reflective awareness of their own cognition.

## Implications for promoting computer-based collaborations

Recall that our purpose in examining the peer interaction literature was, first, to help identify whatever processes of a general kind might mediate effective peer collaboration and, second, to help anticipate the special features that computers might have as media for collaborative work. Research within each of several frameworks tends to suggest a potential for learning within peer interactions that does go beyond any benefits from simply watching a more able partner. But we find a strong alternative theme of tutorial influences. This is implicit in the sociolinguist's discussion of communicative competence and control. It is encouraged by the traditional formuation of Vygotsky's perspective. Even some of the Piagetian research suggests that gains may be exclusive to interactions in which one participant is more advanced in operational thinking.

If productive peer interaction does depend on such differences among partners, this seems rather constraining. It may demand too much caution in the organization of pairs or groups. However, this conclusion could be too hasty. There remains other Piagetian research suggesting that conflict within well-matched pairs can indeed have an impact. Moreover, the Soviet perspective of Vygotsky – less concerned with conflict – implies that thinking might be enriched by yet other forms of exchange intrinsic to the public nature of peer interaction. The precocious communicative skills described by sociolinguistic research can only serve to encourage exploration of this possibility.

It is disappointing that the processes within peer interaction have not been more fully articulated. Furthermore, available research gives little guidance regarding the potential of computers as specific media for such collaborative work. It is unfortunate that there has been little interest in exploring the effects of different task structures on patterns of peer interaction. The Piagetian work, in particular, has consciously avoided studying the kind of sustained problem solving that typifies real classroom collaborations. The sheer variety of tasks that children may encounter on computers should prompt more systematic research in this direction.

Finally, it is disappointing that so little consideration has been given to individual differences among collaborators, beyond implications for the tutorial roles that children might adopt. A suggestion arising in our earlier discussion of computer-based collaborations was that, when they worked together on this medium, children's attention could be more easily drawn to their own abilities relative to others. This might be particularly so when computers function more as partners-for-learning and provide very clear feedback about successful choices or decisions. (Although sensitivity to other children's performances was also described above for the very open-ended LOGO activity.) As it happens, there is research indicating that children do become tuned to individual differences of this kind in their early school years (e.g. Nicholls, 1983). Unfortunately, there is little indication of how far such awareness might be cultivated within the context of group work or whether it requires cautious management. This does suggest a distinctive characteristic of computer-based collaboration; one whose significance can not easily be determined by reference to any existing research.

## CONCLUDING OBSERVATIONS

Any regular visitor to primary school classrooms will be aware of the manner in which computer-based activities can engage even very young children. Two perspectives on the computer's role in such interactions were suggested above. Firstly, the computer may function as an instrument facilitating self-directed discoveries – a source of autonomy in the child's learning. Secondly, the computer may function as a responsive 'partner' in more of a learning dialogue. It was not our purpose to debate the merits of these two applications, but we did note that they each lead to an educational experience in which the interpersonal component seems to be undermined.

We may feel uncomfortable about this. In particular, the inherently social character of our lives seems to suggest that we encourage children to exercise intelligence in an interpersonal context. Fortunately, the two models of computer interaction outlined above allow some elaboration: in this chapter I have argued that a social context for computer use can be constructed around a new potential for collaborative work.

To realize an agenda of this kind, research on peer interaction and early learning must be examined to seek the processes mediating advantages that are claimed for collaborative work. We have done this and found such research somewhat disappointing. This literature offers little insight into the consequences of organizing joint work around the specific medium of computers. There are grounds for thinking that this medium would have distinctive properties. One way to express this is to speculate that the characteristic patterns of interacting *with* computers may serve to organize distinctive patterns of interacting *around* computers. For example, I have drawn attention to one possibility: namely, that the rich level of task feedback that characterizes many such interactions may prompt children to reflect more on their own abilities and achievements relative to their partners'. With this kind of consideration in mind, there is a real need here for research that pays more attention to task structures and the way in which they promote different styles of interaction.

At this point it may be argued that the shortcomings in our knowledge are no cause for alarm: the computer has not yet penetrated classrooms to a degree that represents any serious challenge to their interpersonal dynamics. However, it would be wrong to view the present arguments as simply responding to the threats of technological change – when the pace of such change could indeed be debated. If computers can support greater peer collaboration then we should, in any case, seek to understand how they can be mobilized for that purpose. To reinforce the call for further research in this area, I shall conclude on a reminder that the policy of supporting collaborative learning could well use a new impetus.

Ethnographic accounts of classroom life do convey an impression of early learning as a rather solitary affair (e.g. Galton, Simon and Croll, 1980; Kutnick, 1983). Thus, Kutnick (1983) describes the infant school peer group as 'largely an ineffectual gathering of pupils greatly dependent on the parents and the teacher' (p.49). He reports children 'each working for their individual development . . . one might say that the children were co-acting (doing the same thing in the same place as others) but not co-operating' (p.75).

So, although the case for group work is strongly made (e.g. Sharon, 1980; Slavin, 1980), there remains a discrepancy between theory and practice. Indeed, some academics have openly expressed dismay at the modest impact of their research (e.g. Dickson, 1982). Part of the problem here may be the failure of researchers to specify the processes that actually mediate the success of group work. This is a shortcoming already noted above; the same point has been made by Perret-Clermont and Schubaeur-Leoni (1981). They comment that while teachers may strive after joint work, they usually have not been offered formal guidance in how to attend to the structure and function of the groups they create.

A more straightforward reason for the scarcity of effective group work may be the sheer demands of organizing it. Some solutions have involved fairly radical restructuring of classroom routines (e.g., Aronson *et al.*, 1978; Cazden, 1979). More cautious enthusiasts might prefer to start from advice on an itinerary of classroom activities that serve as good catalysts for collaborative work. This may be a real stumbling block: it has been hard to identify activities that do serve to sustain and elaborate the involvement of young children working in concert. I would suggest that much computer-based work has just the dynamic properties that may prove potent in this respect. It is, therefore, important to encourage research that draws attention to this possibility.

Thus, cultivating collaborative work with computers is not simply a strategy for grafting back interpersonal contact that we suspect is threatened by the computer trend. The need for group work in primary education is felt quite independently of any view about the development of computers. Enthusiasts for such working practices might therefore be encouraged to view this technology as an important resource for that purpose.

## ACKNOWLEDGEMENTS

I am grateful for valuable discussions with members of the Laboratory of Comparative Human Cognition during the preparation of this chapter. My research has been supported by an E.S.R.C. grant.

## REFERENCES

Aronson, E., Stephan, C. Sikes, J., Blaney, N., and Snapp, M. (1978). *The Jigsaw Classroom*, Sage, Beverly Hills, Calif.

Brown, J.S. (1983). Learning from doing revisited for electronic learning environments. In M. White (ed.), *The Future of Electronic Learning*, Lawrence Erlbaum, Hillsdale, N.J.

Cazden, C. (1972). *Child Language and Education*, Holt, Rinehart & Winston, New York.

Cazden, C.B. (1979). You all goona hafta listen: peer teaching in a primary classroom. In W.A. Collins (ed.), *Children's language and communication: 12th Annual Minnesota Symposium on Child Psychology*, Laurence Erlbaum, Hillsidale, N.J.

Cohen, E.G. (1984). Talking and working together: status, interactions and learning. In P. Peterson, L. Wilkinson and M. Hallinan (eds), *The Social Context of Instruction*, Academic Press, Orlando, Fla.

Cook-Gumperz, J., and Gumperz, J (1982). Communicative competence in educational perspective. In L.C. Wilkinson (ed.), *Communicating in the Classroom*, Academic Press, New York.

Cooper, C.R. (1980). Development of collaborative problem solving among preschool children, *Developmental Psychology*, **16**, 433–440.

Cooper, C.R., Marquis, A., and Ayers-Lopez, S. (1982). Peer learning in the classroom tracing developmental patterns and consequences of children's spontaneous interactions. In L.C. Wilkinson (ed.), *Communicating in the Classroom*, Academic Press, New York.

Crockenberg, S.B. (1979). The effects of cooperative learning environments and interdependent goals on conformity in school-age children, *Merrill-Palmer Quarterly*, **25**, 121–131.

Crockenberg, S.B., Bryant, B.K., and Wilce, L.S. (1976). The effects of cooperatively and competitively structured learning environments on inter- and intrapersonal behavior, *Child Development*, **47**, 386–396.

Dickson, W.P. (1982). Creating communication-rich classrooms: insights from the sociolinguistic and referential traditions. In L.C. Wilkinson (ed.), *Communicating in the Classroom*, Academic Press, New York.

Doise, W. (1978). *Groups and Individuals*, Cambridge University Press, Cambridge.

Doise, W., and Mugny, G. (1984). *The Social Development of the Intellect*, Pergamon, Oxford.

Galton, M., Simon, B., and Croll, P. (1980). *Inside the Primary Classroom*, Routledge, London.

Garvey, C., and Hogan, R. (1974). Social speech and social interaction: egocentrism revisited, *Child Development*, **44**, 562–568.

Gernishi, C., and Di Paolo, M. (1982). Learning through argument in a preschool. In L.C. Wilkinson (ed.), *Communicating in the Classroom*, Academic Press, New York.

Glachan, M., and Light, P. (1982). Peer interaction and learning: can two wrongs make a right? In G. Butterworth and P. Light (eds.), *Social Cognition*, Harvester Press, Brighton.

Hawkins, J., Sheingold, K., Gearhart, M., and Berger, C. (1982). Microcomputers in schools: impact on the social life of elementary classrooms, *Journal of Applied Developmental Psychology*, **3**, 361–373.

Kuhn, D. (1972). Mechanisms of change in the development of cognitive structures, *Child Development*, **43**, 833–844.

Kutnick, P. (1983). *Relating to Learning*, Unwin, London.

Laboratory of Comparative Human Cognition (1982). A model system for the study of learning difficulties, *Quarterly Newsletter of the Laboratory of Comparative Human Cognition*, **4**, 39-66.

Lepper, M. (1985). Microcomputers in education, *American Psychologist*, **40**, 1–18.

Mehan, H. (1979). *Learning Lessons*, Harvard University Press, Cambridge, Mass.

Minuchin, P.P, and Shapiro, E.K. (1983). The school as a context for social development. In P.H. Mussen (ed.), *Handbook of Child Psychology*, Vol. IV, Wiley, New York.

Murray, F. (1972). Acquisition of conservation through social interaction, *Developmental Psychology*, **13**, 236–243.

Nicholls, J. (1983). Conceptions of ability and achievement motivation: a theory and its implications for education. In S. Paris, G. Olson and H. Stevenson (eds), *Learning and Motivation in the Classroom*, Lawrence Erlbaum, Hillsdale, N.J.

Papert, S. (1980). *Mindstorms: Children, Computers, and Powerfull Ideas*, Basic Books, New York.

Pea, R. (1985). Integrating human and computer intelligence. In E. Klein (ed.), *Children and Computers*, Jossey Bass, San Francisco.

Pellegrini, D.S., and Urbain, E.S. (1985). An evaluation of interpersonal cognitive problem solving techniques with children, *Journal of Child Psychology and Psychiatry*, **26**, 17–41.

Perret-Clermont, A-N, and Schubaeur-Leoni, M. (1981). Conflict and cooperation as opportunities for learning. In W.P. Robinson (ed.), *Communication in Development*, Academic Press, London.

Piaget, J. (1928). *Judgement and Reasoning in the Child*, Harcourt Brace, New York.

Rogoff, B., and Wertsch, J.V. (1984). *Children's Learning in the Zone of Proximal Development*. New Directions for Child Development, No. 23, Jossey Bass, San Francisco.

Russell, J. (1982). Propositional attitudes. In M. Beveridge (ed.), *Children Thinking Through Language*, Arnold, London.

Scardamalia, M., and Bereiter, C. (1984). The development of evaluative, diagnostic and remedial capabilities in children's composing. In M. Martlew (ed.), *The Psychology of Written Language*, Wiley, Chichester.

Sharan, S. (1980). Cooperative learning in small groups: recent methods and effects on achievement, attitudes and ethnic relations, *Review of Educational Research*, **50**, 241–271.

Sinclair, J.M., and Coulthard, R.M. (1975). *Towards an Analysis of Discourse*, Oxford University Press, London.

Slavin, R.E. (1980). Cooperative learning in teams: state of the art, *Educational Psychologist*, **15**, 93–111.

Turkle, S. (1984). *The Second Self*, Simon and Shuster, New York.

Vygotsky, L.S. (1978). *Mind in Society*, Harvard University Press, Cambridge, Mass.

Walkerdine, V. (1982). From context to text: a psychosemiotic approach to abstract thought. In M. Beveridge (ed.), *Children Thinking Through Language*, Arnold, London.

Wertsch, J. (1985). *Vygotsky and the Social Formation of Mind*, Harvard University Press, Cambridge, Mass.

Wertsch, J.V., McNamee, G.D., McLane, J.G., and Budwig, N.A. (1980). The adult–child dyad as a problem solving system, *Child Development*, **51**, 1215–1221.

Wilkinson, L.C. (1982). *Communicating in the Classroom*, Academic Press, New York.

Computers, Cognition and Development
Edited by J. Rutkowska and C. Crook
© 1987 John Wiley & Sons Ltd

CHAPTER 3

# Computers for Communication

BROCK N. MEEKS

## SUMMARY

The use of computers for interpersonal communication among children and adolescents is described. The phenomenon of computer bulletin boards is outlined and data presented from a study of public messages on a large sample of these systems. The development of this phenomenon into schools is noted.

Computers have traditionally been judged to lie within the province of scientists and engineers. But as this technology has grown more powerful, versatile, and inexpensive, so many more people have gained access to it. Although commonly perceived as special-purpose tools for calculations and data storage, actual use of computers may become more elaborate when used on a daily basis. In particular, computers may become general-purpose tools to gather and distribute information and to communicate with others. Such use of the computer as a shared technology incurs some rather striking changes on organizations and social groups.

In fact, this new technology has three distinct orders of effect. The first is the planned technical effects: improved efficiency and productivity that justify the expense of the technology. The second is the transient effects: organisational changes made when a technology is integrated with the daily routine. The third is more subtle: the (often) unintended effects on social exchange. A notable example of the technology shifting to support human communication is found in a decision by the Soviet Union, in October of 1985, to open a channel for daily dialogue between nonpolitical parties in the USSR and the USA. These dialogues are carried on via the electronic conferencing service, EIES (Electronic Information Exchange System). However, the concern of the present chapter is not with such dramatic examples of computers organizing social activity. My concern here is to identify some of the ways in these general developments are starting to impinge on the social lives of ordinary young people.

Although the computer is heralded as 'new' technology, for our present interest it has much in common with two earlier technical advances: the telephone and typewriter. They also had considerable social impact and we may have much to learn from the histories of these other innovations.

The telephone was expected to increase business communication. A hundred years ago, the New York telephone directory contained less than 10 pages and all but a few of the listings were business telephones. Moreover, those residence phones listed were also used by people working from their homes. The telephone did improve business communication: it gave managers a way to contact the office and it provided a ready tool for customers to interact with manufacturers. In the end though, the effects of the telephone on more purely social exchange have been even more significant than technical and transient outcomes (e.g. Short, Williams and Christie, 1976).

Today people use telephones more for social and personal reasons than for business. In the early part of this century, rural areas of the United States were often dismal and isolated places. The telephone made it possible to sustain friendships and obtain help quickly in an emergency. Because it encouraged and sustained interaction outside school, the telephone also made adolescent peer groups socially important. From the use of the telephone, peer group 'networks' could develop.

In considering the history of other modern technologies, there are two general points to note. First, the social effects of new technologies are hard, often impossible, to predict. We tend to exaggerate the technical changes and the significance of transient issues and we underestimate the more interpersonal effects. Second, the long-run social effects of a new technology are not the intended ones, but have more to do with the technology changing interpersonal relations.

In this chapter I shall outline ways in which computers are coming to mediate social exchange among young people. Much of this influence is through the medium of so-called electronic bulletin boards. In what follows, I shall describe the nature of these 'boards' and report my own experience of studying their use. On balance, the impression created is one of the technology enhancing the social experience of children and adolescents; although, as will be indicated, the purposes motivating the social exchange need not always be healthy ones.

## ELECTRONIC BULLETIN BOARDS

An electronic bulletin board system (BBS) is built around a microcomputer linked to a telephone via a device called a modem. The modem allows transfer of text from one computer to another over regular telephone lines. Because such lines are designed to carry human voices as analog signals, the modem serves to translate, or modulate, a computer's outgoing signals (digital) to analog form and then demodulate incoming (analog) signals back to the computer's digital form. In short, to connect with a BBS it is only necessary to have a microcomputer, a modem and a telephone. A BBS is dialled in the same way as making a normal phone call. After the remote computer has been dialled, the caller's own computer and modem take over the process of connection.

Once connected, the remote computer gives instructions on the principal activity: the entering and reading of text messages. Any that are entered are electronically stored for subsequent callers to read and comment on as they wish. Hours later (or days later) a caller may dial in once more to examine any exchange. A BBS will also have provision for communicating person-to-person. This is known as electronic mail and it is a private function: only the addressee can read the contents of the electronic note. In contrast, contributing to a message base allows anyone entering the system to read what has been posted.

The first BBS was started in Chicago by Randy Suess and Ward Christensen as a means of communicating on a collaborative computer project. Since they lived in cities some 50 miles apart, they wanted a way to pass messages to each other without having to remain constantly in reach of a telephone. In this way the computer bulletin board was invented. The BBS allowed two individuals to exchange messages without regard for each other's schedule. Whenever it was convenient for them, they simply called into the BBS and read the comments left there by the other. The resource was such a success that they set about spreading it to a wider public. At the time of writing, there are an estimated 10 000 BBSs operating worldwide.

During the early years of BBS operation, use was mainly by those considered computer hobbyists; those with the technical knowledge to make all the electronics work correctly. As time passed, access to these BBSs became the subject of articles in the popular computer press and so their use became more widespread. Slowly, many of these BBSs started to take on distinctive themes: boards for the discussion of special topics. A significant number have come to be managed by young people and thus cater to the topics and interests of childhood and adolescence.

## Creation of adolescent BBSs

As more children have come to own microcomputers, so many have discovered a particular attraction in computer-mediated communications. The computer that might be used for homework or playing games by day could, by night, become a tool for nationwide communication. In fact, it is no exaggeration to claim these systems are often tools for worldwide exchange.

The majority of existing BBSs are run by adults and, thus, they deal in topics defined by those adults. Inevitably, younger owners of microcomputers have created forums for their own special interests. Quite spontaneously there has emerged in the United States a network of adolescent BBSs.

I have studied these systems in the spirit of participant observer. My research was initiated by making a general 'call for systems' on the US national commercial information utilities, such as CompuServe and The Source. I put out a call for people to forward the names and numbers of any boards they knew, or suspected, were run by someone of adolescent age, or younger. In addition, many BBSs have a file online containing a list of other boards. I devised a database for these numbers. Duplicate entries were automatically deleted and after a period of six months I had compiled some 87 different systems.

During this six months I began my research while still gathering other BBS numbers. I found that 12 had been shut down, and so my work centred on the remaining 75. This figure, therefore, is a good estimate of the number of publicly available boards run by young people at the time of writing (1985). But these systems are volatile and it can be assumed that the number of BBSs functioning at any one time will fluctuate.

My method included dialling into each of these systems and leaving some general information about the study. I dialled into as many as 45 boards in any one week. Any messages left for me were stored and they could only be deleted by myself. A macro capability in the communications software allowed automatic dialling and downloading of messages. Thus, much of my contact was organized to occur during the night hours when telephone rates were at their lowest. In fact, the macro capability did not even require that I be present. If, during the course of this automatic calling, the computer encountered a busy signal, it would continuously redial until a connection was made.

What follows is a partial summary of my experience as gathered over a long period of taking part in communications on a comprehensive sample of young people's boards.

A BBS usually draws its users from the local area. This area typically encompasses approximately a 50 mile radius around the vicinity of the BBS. A likely constraint here is telephone rates: calling a BBS further than this incurs an expense few adolescents can manage. However, it is not unusual to find that a popular BBS will attract callers from out of state, or even from another continent. (A popular BBS is determined by the amount of messages generated in a given period of time. A popular BBS, then, tends to generate between 200 and 400 new messages each month which equates to about 350 individual calls.)

Typically the user base of a BBS is comprised of children of the same ethnocentric background and economic group. This amounts to a white, upper-middle-class community. The primary reason for this is likely to be the current cost of obtaining a computer and modem to operate and communicate with a BBS. Of the 75 BBSs I studied, 95% of the users were white males, 1% were minority males, 3.5% white females and the remaining 0.5% minority females.

It must be remarked that these proportions only serve to reinforce other observations that highlight a more limited female involvement in computer-based activities among young people (e.g. Griffiths, 1985). In this connection it is interesting to note that once a girl became a regular on a BBS she often drew an inordinately high amount of message traffic. Where there might be a large number of males online, a female is something of an anomaly and, therefore, her very presence would attract activity. When I questioned them about this effect, most of these girls (in fact over 80%) said that they appreciated the attention; they knew that if they went online they would most likely be a centre of some attention.

**Analysis of message types**

Most of the messages I gathered were archived on the systems themselves. This simply means that I took a two-week sampling of stored (or online) messages as they already existed within various message bases. Thus, the sampling ensured a real cross-section of message flow and topic discussion – not messages prompted by any announcement that someone would be on a monitoring exercise.

Message traffic averaged 50 messages per week over the two-week period. The total number of messages analysed came to 7500. Of these, 83% were entered by males, 17% (1275) were entered by females. A rough taxonomy of these messages is given in Table 3.1.

TABLE 3.1 A breakdown of message types

| | | |
|---|---|---|
| 1. General topics | 35% | (2625) |
| 2. Computer-related topics | 25% | (1875) |
| 3. Discussion topics | 30% | (2250) |
| 4. 'For sale' messages | 5% | ( 375) |
| 5. Personal messages | 5% | ( 375) |

Topics of *general interest* are a very mixed category of rather business-like messages. Mostly, they took the form of queries to others on the board, such as suggesting that a group gather to attend a concert (an example that is elaborated below). They might generate a flow of traffic for a week or so and then die out as the topic became exhausted. General-interest topics discussed included other BBSs, where to get the best fast food, schools, or the attributes of certain teachers. This general-interest category is more informational in nature. But from within these subjects, full-blown debates often evolved: this moved them into my category of a 'discussion topic'.

*Discussion topics* tend to emerge from controversy within the original message. A body of commentary grows. During subsequent log-ons, users review comments left by others and continue to take the discussion in various directions. If this debate finds some agreement among the various users, solutions to the 'problem' may be bandied about. When such a consensus occurs the discussion may degenerate into a 'name calling' session, where some focal subject in the debate is suitably slandered.

For example, I monitored a lively discussion on government regulation of the Rock and Roll industry. (A Senate subcommittee was proposing that record manufacturers should attach a rating to each record label: parents would thereby be warned of potentially harmful lyrics.) During the course of this discussion (over a period of two weeks) everyone from the President and the Attorney General down was energetically abused. During such exchanges, it is possible to be struck by the potentially subversive quality of this medium.

Naturally, discussion topics often spin-off each other and, in the discussion mentioned above, another topic evolved on the subject of censorship.

*Computer-related discussions* cover everything from the technical aspects of programming, to arguments over the attributes of various machines. In fact, very sophisticated material can be exchanged in this forum. These discussions become a kind of living database for technical information. Because the information is accumulated on disk, it can be called on at the convenience of the users. On some of the BBSs, related information will be compiled into a single file and made available for downloading.

The remaining types of message, for sale and personal, comprise the small groups. *For sale* messages are self-explanatory. They form an online version of the classified section of a local newspaper. The personal messages are more important in their function, and more puzzling because of their small number.

*Personal messages* comprise two groups: 'open' letters to a particular use, and private electronic mail (or 'email'). The former type is often a single response to a request for information. Another use of the open personal message is to draw another user into a private email exchange.

It is hard to escape an impression from all this of something resembling a computer-based subculture. It is in no way a part of the mainstream of daily life, in or out of the school system. Moreover, it is fairly invisible to those who do not regulary 'enter' these systems. There is nothing sinister here: rather, the technology is serving primary interests of the social group, fulfilling various needs that are otherwise unfulfilled by the mainstream of personal contacts.

Sproull, Kiesler and Zubrow (1984) have developed this theme of computers as being part of an alien culture. They comment: 'every culture has values and norms, a status hierarchy, membership signs and boundaries to distinguish members from non-members, a language and its own artifacts.' They go on to discuss some identifiable behaviour of the apparent subculture:

(a) the participants share (or sometimes argue passionately about) concepts concerning good and bad machines, software, programming practices, and systems;
(b) they voluntarily use the computer at all hours of the day and night;
(c) they use an esoteric vocabulary for both technical and non-technical purposes;
(d) they are differentiated from non-members by names and behaviour.

Many of these characteristics are recognizable in the corpus of bulletin board exchanges that I have gathered. However, it would be wrong to imply there is such a strong focus of interest in computing itself. The exchange is broader in scope and – as I shall argue in the following section – it can lead to social activity outside of this electronic context.

**Computers as instruments of social activity**

Because all communication on a BBS takes place asynchronously, one might assume there is no real cohesive bond among its users. This assumption will often prove quite false.

As a BBS begins to establish itself among a number of users, a group identity seems to form. The users begin to refer to a BBS as their 'home base' and may defend it vigorously in discussions on other bulletin boards. It may still be common for an individual regularly to call as many as ten bulletin boards a day: an activity that can take as long as five or six hours and often last far into the night. However, there is usually just one BBS that they would consider 'home' and it is this board that will be defended on other BBSs.

Often a board appears to become a neighbourhood (or township) in microcosm, but one that is dominated by young people. Depending on the general interests of the kids using the BBS, this electronic neighbourhood is shaped into something of a living entity. Each contribution that is posted on the BBS serves to extend a very real culture; one that is evolving, for the moment at least, on a magnetic disk. Distinct topics of discussion soon separate out. For example, a user signing on to a typical system (say, the one called 'Dragon's Lair') will be confronted with the following menu of message bases:

---

### DRAGON'S LAIR

A) Music—Metal Heads only
B) General Interest—Anything goes
C) Politics—How the adults are screwing it up
D) Computers—Technical and non-tech
E) Games
F) Other BBSs
Enter Your Choice >—

As the contributions to a board increase, so a kind of social structure can emerge. That board's users will often begin to align themselves with one another on various matters. These can relate to music, school, or political issues – such as nuclear war. Within a short period of time one observes 'online alliances' building up between kids that have never met each other. All they know of another participant is what they have read online, or what they have learned through exchanges on the board's facility for private electronic mail with others. So, from this message base alone, friendships begin to appear. A typical vehicle for the formation of such friendships might be a banding together for mutual support during a hotly contested online discussion. This might concern a favourite rock group or a preferred computer programming language.

Such groups reinforce contact by then sending messages to each other online. Often what will then happen is that one member of the group eventually suggests they all have a face-to-face meeting. My own observations suggest that the evolution from online autonomy to the creation of electronic alliances, to face-to-face meetings typically covers a period of about five months. So, these face-to-face meetings will be the first personal encounters between individuals who have most likely been conversing and supporting each other electronically for a period of months.

Such initial meetings usually take place in the home of one of the participants amid a party atmosphere. This is an occasion for putting a face to a name. And though usually the group will comprise adolescents from the same socioeconomic background, it is not uncommon for a social 'outsider' to be openly welcomed, with no hint of prejudice or discrimination. The advance contact through participating in the electronic alliance may serve to neutralize possible prejudices.

After these initial meetings there is often a drop in the message traffic. It may be that the novelty of having met in person takes away the appeal of BBS communication. In other words, some of the mystery is removed from the relationship and in return a measure of reality put in its place. It usually takes about a week for the message traffic to pick up again to former levels.

Once the first face-to-face meeting has taken place, other meetings may be regularly held. These typically take the form of going to concerts, travelling to some amusement, or meeting to exchange software and other computer-related material. Always, these social activities are discussed, planned and 'voted' during online conversations. For example, someone might suggest that a particular rock group is coming into town and that they should go to hear them. Others then reply online as to their particular like or dislike of the group's current record and whether or not the idea is a good one. If a consensus is formed, plans are laid to get tickets, provide transport, and so on. In fact, each of these tasks are often delegated online.

There is an interesting parallel between this recreational use of electronic communication by youngsters and the manner in which commercial organizations are now using the medium to organize their business. Much the same categories of activity occur within those corporate planning sessions that are managed within a networked environment: problem identification (is this band worth seeing?); specification of tasks (someone must get tickets, someone else get a car, another determine directions to the venue); suggested courses of action (delegation of activity); reaching a final decision (set the time and place to meet before going to the concert). Perhaps the point is that these youngsters are encountering formative experiences in respect of their later working lives. Certainly, they are becoming fluent with a medium that could be an important tool in any later career. But, more generally, they are evolving skills of organized decision making that transcend the context of this particular medium.

If the sketch above suggests a basically positive role for computers in supporting social activity, then this is probably fair. However, the medium is also capable of hosting exchange with less healthy purposes. This darker side to computer youth has received more publicity than the more positive aspects; it therefore deserves some commentary here.

### The dark side of computer communication

The issue of computer crime – and the role of young people as computer criminals – is well publicized. One popular computer magazine recently expressed the problem in this way: 'There is a dark side to the boom in computer communications. Computers that can talk to each other might also talk to strangers . . . A necessary evil of this new phenomena is the concern for shielding important computer data from unwanted long-distance intruders.' (*Computing for Business*, 1985, **10**(4), 32).

These 'long-distance intruders' are known in the popular press as 'hackers' – electronic vandals, typically teenagers, that wreak havoc on unsus-

64 COMPUTERS, COGNITION AND DEVELOPMENT

pecting mainframe computers. But this is a sensationalized version of their activities.

In tracking down this phenomenon, I have run across more than 200 'pirate' BBSs. These boards do have to be unearthed: they are not open or publicized in the manner of those discussed in the preceding section. The word 'pirate' is used to identify the fact these kids are often stealing something – be it computer time, software or long-distance telephone time. However, a degree of romanticism is involved here: this 'piracy' reflects a belief among the protagonists that they are information-age Robin Hoods, stealing from those that won't miss it, or that don't deserve it.

This pirate community is a community in every respect of the word. These pirates operate their own BBSs, in the manner of those discussed above, and via an elaborate 'electronic underground' network that spans the United States. (There seems to have been no study of pirate BBSs in other countries.)

The community is divided into three distinct groups: 'worms', 'phone phreaks', and 'pirates'. Worms are most noted for worming their way into private computer systems (these are the ones called 'hackers' by the press). Phone phreaks are deft at manipulating the telephone system. This manipulation includes stealing long-distance access codes and the construction of 'boxes' – electronic devices that manipulate the various operating frequencies of the telephone system to furnish free phone calls, and more. Finally, the pirates specialize in breaking the copy protection on commercial software. This lets them distribute 'pirated' copies of such software (sometimes costing thousands of dollars) to anyone that wants it.

Pirate BBSs are the hub that holds this electronic counter-culture together. Their message bases deal almost entirely with illegal subject matter (such as detailing the steps to break into a university computer). Because of their illegal nature, these BBSs are not openly advertised. Their existence is spread by word of mouth – and yet they thrive.

Like any adolescent BBS, these pirate boards comprise a dedicated band of users. Each board usually has several members from each of the three categories mentioned above. From this melting pot separate online 'clubs' will form. Each club draws its membership from the three different groups. A kind of electronic terrorist task force is being built up. Typically these groups range in size from five to twelve. Smaller numbers are preferred because there is less chance for security leaks. On any given pirate board there might exist as many as six different clubs. Competition and rivalry is high among the groups.

Typically the pirate community is made up of white middle-class males. Of the 200 pirate boards I have studied I have found only three female participants. The nature of this activity is extremely technical and this may more readily fit the existing interests and education of young males. Whereas using a regular BBS only requires communication and online skills, participation in the pirate community entails a high level of computing skill. The age range of these pirates is early teens to early 20's, with the biggest concentration being between 14 and 17 years. There is a noticeable drop-off in participation around the 18-year-old period.

Typical of this group is the reluctance to use real names. Each individual picks a 'handle' (i.e. a pseudonym). These handles often draw from historical pirates (such as Bluebeard) to mythical pirates (such as Captain Hook); or from fantasy (Zebulon, Nefertron, etc.). In the pirate community a child's handle is as good as his name. Because the knowledge for making free long-distance phone calls is so readily available, the geographical range of communication within the pirate community is much wider than that of the conventional users. Whereas in regular BBS participation an individual might only call within his immediate locality, pirates communicate regularly with pirate boards up to 3000 miles away. This creates a tight-knit electronic underground network. It also means that news of some fresh computer antic can be made available from coast to coast in less than 24 hours.

The pirates hold face-to-face meetings just like other BBS groups. However, these meetings have a business atmosphere. Pirated programs and passwords are exchanged, while plans are laid out for 'trashing' activities. ('Trashing' is a term that refers to rummaging through corporate trash bins at day's end to try and pick up passwords, or account numbers that have been inadvertently thrown out. Having participated in several trashings for more journalistic purposes, I can confirm that these late-night excursions are surprisingly rewarding – in terms of information gathered.) The motivation for this type of activity is varied. However, my own studies and conversations suggest a few generalizations:

1. They view their activities as 'victimless'. That is, they are playing with electronic data, not holding up a department store or stealing a car. It's just data.
2. They seem aware of adults (perhaps their parents) cheating on taxes and so forth – in effect robbing the government – and they say, 'We are not stealing money or material, just some time. And what is time?'
3. Regarding the breaking of copy-protected software, they use the analogy of adults borrowing a record album and copying it on to a cassette tape. The consensus here is: 'What's the difference?'
4. This activity is more stimulating, and a more powerful learning environment than traditional, secondary educational computer science courses.

It would be inappropriate to conclude this review by dwelling on the less positive communication activities that are facilitated by personal computers. Instead, I shall conclude by drawing attention to the manner in which computer-mediated communication of the kind discussed in this chapter is now finding a place within the curricula of formal schooling.

## COMPUTERS FOR SCHOOL COMMUNICATION

The introduction of computers into the classroom at the beginning of this decade was expected by many to revolutionize the way in which children learn. In fact, progress towards innovation has been rather slow. A great deal of current school computer use is still too firmly at the level of drill and practice routines.

However, there are now emerging projects with rather more flair. One promising line of development can be found in the extension of the kind of computer-based communication that has been discussed in this chapter. As this medium has flourished for recreational purposes, so the possibility for classroom applications has been noticed.

Much of what is happening in this area is guided by a special interest in the cultivation of childrens' skills as writers. An argument has developed that one of the problems in this aspect of the curriculum is motivational: children need to have good reasons for writing. An approach to this challenge is to mobilize a human drive towards communication. By establishing contact with other communities of children (other schools) it is possible to create an *audience* for children's written work. Moreover, this strategy of developing joint activity among school children can generate a new variety of purposes for their writing.

One project, 'Computer Chronicles' at the University of California, San Diego, illustrates this approach very well (see, Levin, Riel, Rowe and Boruta, 1985; Riel, 1985). The work involved secondary students using computers to prepare text with a word processor. At first the result was a series of individual texts that were complied on a single computer floppy disk. These disks were then mailed to other school campuses; some as far away as Alaska. The students at the other participating campuses were also preparing text and thus an exchange of disks took place over a long period. More recently, the project has moved towards using computer networks for more direct contact that allows the stage of transporting disks to be avoided.

Of course, this kind of exchange could, in principle, be supported by other media of communication, although there are few examples of this happening. In fact, there are distinct advantages to using computer-based communication for this purpose. One is that the preparation of text and its transmission can all take place at the same device. But, more important, the pace of communication that can be supported is suitable to sustain the interest and involvement of the participants.

Of course, this kind of project is not an exact parallel of the structure of communication that is characteristic of the bulletin boards discussed earlier.

Communication over that medium has a more public nature. However, computer-based communication activities in schools is already moving towards the versatility that the BBS kind of system offers. In Britain, there is a now a schools' computer network that is accessible from any classroom with a microcomputer and a modem. This functions as both a medium for communication between particular schools (through mailboxes) but also as an arena within which various notices, announcements and data may be active.

There is a significant conclusion that can be made in respect of the computer activities discussed in this chapter. A number of applications in both recreational and educational setting highlight the way in which this technology can support socially organized activity. It is important to recognize that computers need not be isolating in the way that is often feared: they offer considerable potential to enhance human communication – at all stages of human development.

## REFERENCES

Griffiths, D. (1985). The exclusion of women from technology. In N. Faulkner and E. Arnold (ed.), *Smothered by Innovation: Technology in Women's Life*, Pluto, London.

Levin, J., Tiel, M. M., Towe, R. D., and Boruta, M. (1985). Mutak meets jacuzzi: Computer networks and elementary writers. In S. Freedman (ed.) , *The Acquisition of Written Language: Revision and Response*, Ablex, Hillsdale, N. J.

Kerr, E. B., and Hiltz, S. R. (1982). *Computer-mediated Communication Systems: Status and Evaluation*, Academic Press, New York.

Riel, M. (1985). The computer chronicles newswire: a functional learning environment for acquiring litercy skills, *Journal of Educational Computing Research*, **1**, 317–337.

Short, J. A., Williams, E., and Christie, B. (1976). *The Social Psychology of Telecommunications*, Wiley, London.

Sproull, L. S., Kiesler, S., and Zubrow, D. (1984). Encountering an alien culture, *Journal of Social Issues*, **40**, 129–144.

Computers, Cognition and Development
Edited by J. Rutkowska and C. Crook

CHAPTER 4

# The Release of Cognitive Resources: A Unifying Perspective on Mainstream and Special Education

DAVID ROTHERAY AND DAVID SEWELL

## SUMMARY

Application of computer-mediated education indicates certain generally desirable qualities of learning experiences, specifically that the technology and techniques involved in presentation may be more crucial to success than the content itself. This chapter argues that the management of learning needs to examine limitations of the environment rather than of the learner.

There is a sense in which recent research in developmental psychology indicates that intelligence may become 'trapped' at points in normal development. Research in special education encourages a similar conceptualization with respect to the handicapped learner. In one case the 'trap' seems to have been revealed by experiments that give special attention to task structure in the posing of problems. In the other, it arises from the achievements associated with educational technology and accompanying instructional techniques. There is an analogy to be made between these cases, as both involve performance as a misleading guide to capacity. In both, a capacity seems to have been constrained and, as observers, we may have been guilty of underestimating what individuals are capable of achieving. But what is the unifying perspective that our title suggests? This unity may be found only by an examination of psychological theory.

In this chapter we shall attempt to use the perspective of schema theory to describe the effect which the deployment of new educational tools may have on cognitive growth. It is our contention that cognitive 'growth' may in many cases be usefully regarded as the release of potential intelligence which has been denied its expression by the structure of the environment. Various ways in which this environment may be changed are put forward, and it is suggested that there is an unifying quality in all such changes, whether they be changes related to 'hardware' (the use of technology to aid learning) or 'software' (the design of the educational process). Various examples of such processes, taken from research and practice in both mainstream and special education, are given.

A large body of work, both theoretical and experimental, supports a model of the learning process which may be broadly termed 'schematic'. Schema theory, in essence, is an interactive model of learning in which people's cognitive structures (schemata) are seen as internal reflections of their experience of the real world. Experience of the world enforces modification of these structures in line with reality, but, conversely, the interpretation of incoming information does itself depend on the structures already present. Thus we have a circular model of learning, a profoundly dialectical formulation which sees human beings as simultaneously influencing and being influenced by their information environment. While rarely stated in this form, this model in fact underlies thinking in many areas of cognitive and developmental psychology. What is needed is an explication of the common theme which exists in these theories and a review of the practical implications involved, which are considerable. In particular, psychology has failed to assign a clear theoretical role to educational technology.

It was suggested above that schema theory can present a broad coherent picture of intellectual development, a picture which is consonant with current thinking in cognitive and developmental psychology. 'Schema' is the name given to the intellectual structure within which knowledge is represented. In the sense that this structure is tested and modified by experience, schema theory can be seen as a 'hypothesis-testing' model of learning. This does not imply that the learner necessarily forms and tests conscious hypotheses. Rather, since knowledge obviously must be organized (as it serves to plan and control future behaviour) this organization reflects the limitations of experience and hence has all the functional qualities of a hypothesis. For instance, at a certain stage of language development, many children tend to over-generalize language rules (e.g. they put the suffix '-ed' on all verbs in the past tense, including irregulars, producing errors such as 'goed'). The child has, then, a hypothesis about the rules of a language, a hypothesis that will be tested and modified on the basis of future interactions with his language environment. Such a hypothesis is not a consciously formulated theory, but a schema, a cognitive structure which reflects his experience of the world. It must be noted that a schema is not only an organization of knowledge but, implicitly, a plan for action. Thus Evans (1967) offers the following definition of schema: 'a set of rules serving as instructions for producing a population prototype'. Perhaps the most succinct presentation of schema theory is given by Neisser (1976). Discussing perception, Neisser says:

> Although perceiving does not change the world, it does change the perceiver (so does action, of course). The schema undergoes what Piaget calls 'accommodation', and so does the perceiver. He has become what he is by virture of what he has perceived and done in the past; he further creates and changes himself by what he perceives and does in the present.

Learning, then, occurs when a schema attempts to incorporate information which contradicts some aspect of the schema itself; in order to do so, the schema must adapt itself to this information. The same idea is expressed in a rather different form by Robinson (1980):

> Practical activity often has to confront obstacles not conceived of by the thought which initiated the activity. A contradiction arises in which the individual needs to carry out activity yet lacks the ideas necessary to guide this activity. This contradiction, if it is to be resolved, leads to the development of new ideas.

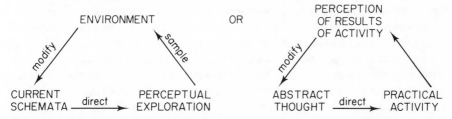

FIGURE 4.1 The schematic model of learning (a) Neisser (1976) (b) Robinson (1980)

These two formulations are represented in Figure 4.1. These are the unifying themes of all those theories herein designated 'schematic'. The most well-known expresssion of schema theory is perhaps that of Piaget. Piaget called the process of incorporating new data into existing models 'assimilation', and the process by which schemata adjust in response to these data 'accommodation'. Many modern psychologists show the influence of this formulation. An example from cognitive psychology is the work of Norman and Rumelhart (1975). Norman and Rumelhart categorize three modes of learning:

(i) 'accretion': the addition of new knowledge to existing schemata;
(ii) 'structuring': the formation of new conceptualizations when existing schemata no longer suffice;
(iii) 'tuning': the fine adjustment of knowledge to a particular task.

Schank (1982), in his theory of dynamic memory, uses the term 'script' rather than 'schema', but his intention is the same. His point is that simply memorizing is not enough; the learner must have a context into which he can slot newly acquired information in order to make intelligent use of this information. It is of course possible for incorrect schemata to develop and persist. This can be explained by saying that the learner can cope with information that conflicts with his schemata by distorting the input to fit the schemata rather than vice versa. This notion is manifested in psychological theories of 'defence' (e.g. Freud, Rogers) or 'cognitive dissonance' (Festinger, 1957).

One of the most important results of this model is the emphasis on interactive communication. The notion of schematic development implies that the nature of learning depends on both the learning environment and on the present cognitive state of the learner, which delimits the operations which can be carried out upon the environment. More accurately, it depends on the matching of the two. Designing learning materials on this basis obviously implies not only a careful analysis of task structures but also a close attention to individual differences. What a learner gains from a situation depends on the matching of the task to his present schemata; information must be within the reach of his current mental model in order for that information to act upon and develop the model. In Piaget's terms, accommodation cannot take place unless assimilation can be attempted. The learner must be capable of carrying out operations upon the learning material, but at the same time the task should serve to display some of the weaknesses or limitations of the strategies the learner uses. Failure to make learning situations thus 'accessible' to the present cognitive state of the learner has fuelled serious psychological misconceptions about the potential abilities of subjects.

Piaget called the process by which schemata adjust in order to incorporate dissonant information 'accommodation'; the integration of experience into an intellectual structure. The essential element in experience is for Piaget the structure which makes an operation possible. Piaget's conclusion was that the learning of new structures is only possible if a complex structure is based on the accommodation of simpler structures. It is possible to argue that the Piagetians themselves failed to take full account of this idea when designing experiments: as Donaldson (1978) shows, it was the failure of the Piagetians to take account of the child's current mental state (i.e. to pose problems in a manner that made them accessible to existing schemata) that caused subjects to fail on Piagetian tasks, resulting in a systematic underestimation of children's abilities.

These findings were accepted, however, because of their congruence with another aspect of Piagetian theory, namely the theory of epigenetic stage limitations upon learning. A body of work has been conducted which contradicts this notion, and its overriding theme has been to present tasks in a manner which makes human sense to the child, which relates to the children's past experience. For example, Piaget claims that children under the age of six are bad at communicating because they are largely incapable of 'decentring', i.e. they are 'egocentric'.

An example of the evidence used in support of this notion is the famous 'three mountains' task. In this task, the subject sits at a table on which a model of three mountains is placed. The experimenter then places a doll at some other position around the table. The task for the child is this: what does the doll see? The child may either select one from a number of alternative pictures of the scene or alternatively rearrange the model to represent the doll's view. There is a reliable tendency for children under six to choose the picture or model which represents the view which they themselves see. This is taken by Piaget as evidence for the children's inability to form a mental picture of a view which they do not actually see. Such as assertion implies serious limitations upon the child's ability to think and reason. And yet there is good reason to believe that such a conclusion is somewhat premature. Hughes (1975) conducted a similar investigation of 'egocentricity', but using a task rather different from that of Piaget. The situation which he used involved comprehensible characters and a social situation familiar to the subjects (the task required the placing of a doll so as to be 'out of sight' of a policeman). The task could be successfully completed only by considering two different points of view; yet Hughes obtained 90% correct responses in a group of children aged between three-and-a-half and five years. This seems difficult to reconcile with Piaget's claim that children under seven are very bad at appreciating points of view other than their own. It seems very likely that children given the 'mountains' task simply do not understand what they are meant to do. Another study by Hughes showed that by using a simplified version of the mountains task and taking great care over the presentation of the problem, it was possible to get a high percentage of correct responses from pre-school children. As Donaldson puts it, it seems that the children in Piaget's experiments did not fail to reason; rather they failed to understand.

Donaldson goes on to quote a number of similar studies, dealing with a range of 'Piagetian' tasks, which suggest similar conclusions. The common theme of these studies is the need to construct tasks which make 'human sense' to the child, i.e. which are not alien to his experience, are related to his knowledge of the world, and are in tune with his expectations and motivations. Another way of putting this is to say that the task must be 'accessible' to the child.

Such considerations have particular significance in the field of special education. For example, children with learning difficulties often demonstrate low motivation and lack of attention on conventional classroom activities, especially when these are placed in an unfamiliar or artificial context. This may be illustrated by a report of learning-disabled children who have problems in carrying out conventional classroom sequencing tasks, yet who can recall, after several months, the sequence of operations necessary to load a program into a computer and then carry out, from memory, the tasks required to play a computer game (personal communication from a teacher of the trainable mentally retarded). This latter task contains the essential operations of a sequencing activity. It differs from traditional 'tests' in that the child needs to carry out these operations in order to achieve a self-imposed, not an externally imposed, goal.

The success of studies such as Hughes's suggests that the limitations in may learning situations lie not within the learner but in the structure of the task. In view of this, one might question the wisdom of premature assertions about cognitive 'capacity'. Papert (1980) re-interprets Piaget in this way:

> Piaget writes about the order in which the child develops different intellectual abilities. I give more weight to the influence of the materials a particular culture provides in determining that order . . . The Piaget of the stage theory is essentially conservative, almost reactionary, in emphasizing what children cannot do.

Papert's own work with the educational computer environment LOGO reflects his philosophy. In particular, Papert draws attention to the notion of 'formal' or 'abstract' thinking as opposed to 'concrete' thinking. What Papert suggests is, in essence, that many learning environments are inaccessible to children because they are too formal; in order to make a concept accessible, you must make it concrete for the learner. Bruner has gone so far as to suggest that almost any problem can be made accessible as long as it is presented in the appropriate manner; for example, the enactive, iconic and symbolic representations of Newton's law of moments (Bruner, 1966). This view can be qualified by the argument presented in this chapter, i.e. that the extent to which a problem can be made accessible depends on the application of the technologies and techniques that are currently available. This is what happens, for instance, in the Hughes experiment discussed above, and it is what Papert claims can happen through the use of LOGO. In the case of LOGO, mathematical and geometrical concepts are made accessible by being linked with the movements of one's own body in space; they are 'syntonic' with knowledge already possessed, in this case 'body knowledge'. In experiments such as that of Hughes, the problem can be seen to be syntonic with the child's social knowledge; the motives and intentions of the 'characters' in the scenario are entirely comprehensible to him. As Papert says of LOGO: ' . . . it can allow us to shift the boundary between the concrete and the formal. Knowledge that was accessible only through formal processes can now be approached concretely.'

Thus, an additional factor affecting accessibility is what may be termed 'world knowledge'; it may often happen that children fail to comprehend tasks because the content of the task concerns unfamiliar or incomprehensible characters or events. We can relate this problem to the Hughes experiment (above), and to Piagetian learning in general, but it is particularly relevant to the handicapped child, whose lack of communication limits his knowledge of the world, which in turn constrains the possibilities for communication and learning. To quote Goldenberg (1979):

> It is so difficult to imagine not having had all the normal experiences – in fact, we are so totally unaware of them that it is difficult even to list them – that we may frequently interpret a handicapped child's failure to comprehend as a lack of intellectual capacity rather than a lack of information.

Making the environment accessible to the individual's existing schemata involves, then, matching the task not just to the cognitive operations they can carry out but to the knowledge which they already possess. These cognitive skills and knowledge base serve as tools for accessing problem domains much as hardware enabling technology does; placing new information in the context of exisiting knowledge will serve to make that information more readily assimilable. Changing the accessibility of new knowledge in this way obviously has significant implications for cognitive development. Olson (1976), discussing the cognitive significance of technological developments, suggests that:

> Intelligence, when considered in terms of underlying abilities, is that set of abilities required to master the tools, artefacts and technologies of the culture; when considered in terms of skilled performance, it is the set of competencies achieved by the mastery of those technologies . . . all tasks or performances that we require from children on intelligence tests reflect competence with our technologies.

This is very much a 'performance' view of intelligence. Olson is talking about hardware technology and the techniques involved in its application. But, as has already been suggested, this category may be too narrow. Romiszowski (1981) defines technology as 'the creative application of science to industrial (or any practical) purposes' and this may include elements which would not be generally recognized as 'technology' in the traditional sense. If, bearing in mind the ideas of Olson, we apply this definition to educational technology, then it can be argued that the bridge between the learner and a cognitive ability which he is required to express may consist of:

1. A piece of technology (the learner may need technology in order to interact with the material).
2. A certain environmental structure (e.g. a testing procedure or an educational objective, is used to shape the interaction: an alternative educational procedure may facilitate the expression of ability).

In addition, one might wish to note a possible third category, which covers situations which one might term as 'genuine' failure to comprehend. Here, the missing element is:

3. Some intermediate cognitive ability (i.e. the learner may lack cognitive prerequisites which are needed in order to deal with the material, however it is presented).

A difficulty at any of these levels may result in a 'trapping' of intelligence, and could be termed a problem of 'technology' in the sense that the application of educational science to the situation may be capable of resolving the difficulty. A trapping at the first level may be resolved by the introduction of new hardware. A trapping at the second level may be resolved by changing the learning/testing environment. A 'trapping' at the third level may be resolved by training based on a consideration of Piaget's dictum that the acquisition of more complex schemata must be based upon the presence of its more simple precursors. A failure at this third level constitutes a situation where the only 'trap' is the learner's own current stage of development (current range of cognitive skills), i.e. the type of 'trap' that Piaget assumed was present in the 'three mountains' experiment. In an ideally designed educational environment these would be the only type of failure to occur; but the contention of the authors is that in many situations the failure is of one of the first two types, and furthermore that these two types of 'trap' are psychologically comparable. Hereafter, the term 'trap' will be used only to refer to the first two categories; the third category is not so much a trap as a statement, à la Piaget, of the individual's level of development.

The significance of 'technologies', for Olson, is that they serve as a medium of interaction between man and his environment. Hence, any inability to use these technologies limits the development or expression of intelligent behaviour. Where these technologies serve merely as the media for expression of other abilities, failure with the technology gives no information about the presence or absence of those abilities, i.e. about cognitive 'capacity'. Improvements in the technology of interaction may show that this ability is in fact present.

What is being suggested here is that this is in fact true of advances in educational techniques in general, and that the notion of 'technology of interaction' may be a very broad category. In many cases redesign of the experiments quoted by Donaldson (1978) enabled young children to express a cognitive ability which Piaget had considered them incapable of possessing. Piaget's subjects failed, not because of a basic incapacity to deal with the problem in question (e.g. conservation, class inclusion) but because the task was not made 'accessible' to their schemata.

The cybernetic model of learning espoused by Landa (1983) embodies this notion, which has been largely ignored by other learning theorists. Landa emphasizes that the learning of rules depends on applying the rule correctly but also on learning to discriminate situations where use of the rule is appropriate from those where it is not. From this notion Landa develops a theory of instruction based on two processes. First of all, analysis of the task situation itself to identify the cognitive abilities necessary to master it. Second, Landa advocates an analysis of the learners, and their existing cognitive abilities, in order to design a teaching situation that will ensure efficient learning. Landa's formulation is highly practical in that he advocates a detailed analysis of the specific operations involved in carrying out a task. In addition, as the present discussion indicates, we must consider the world knowledge assumed by a problem as well as the procedures needed to solve it. The stress Landa places on the operations or algorithms involved in problem-solving reflects his cybernetic orientation:

> The application of rules, particularly the recognition of situations where the rule is applicable, is achieved by means of special operations. Just as it is impossible to solve a manufacturing problem (for example, to make something) without carrying out specific component manipulations (operations), it is also impossible to solve an intellectual problem (a grammatical, mathematical problem or one pertaining to physics, etc.) without carrying out specific intellectual operations. The execution of a specific aggregate of intellectual operations to solve a problem is an objective necessity. (Landa, 1974)

The 'operations' which are required in order to carry out a task must, then, be matched to the cognitive skills which the learner possesses. This includes those operations which are used to decode the task structure and make initial decisions about what is being demanded from the user. Failure on these 'accessing' operations means that the learner cannot interact with the learning environment in question. Redesign of the task presentation may, then, have a dramatic effect on the intelligence that is displayed. Thus, when the opportunity for linguistic creativity can be accessed through a more 'friendly' technology than pen and paper, this learning situation is made available to a greater population of people, and the consequence is that 'trapped' linguistic ability is allowed its expression. Such developments have in fact been demonstrated, both in special and in mainstream contexts. For instance, Geoffrion and Goldenberg (1981) provide examples of communication with handicapped children using interactive communication devices (the 'Talking Typewriter' and CARIS – Computer Animated Reading Instruction System) and conclude that such exploratory learning environments result in the expression of previously trapped cognitive skills. In a similar vein, recent research on the use of word processing has indicated that students using such a tool work longer at improving a piece of written work as well as developing an earlier 'sense of audience' (Womble, 1984). Graves (1984) has argued that the use of word processing can act as a facilitator of thought via the writing process. In these latter cases, technology is being used as a tool to allow for the expression of cognitive ability.

The notion of 'trapped intelligence', as elaborated above, suggests that this can happen not only with the application of technology but with refinements of educational technique. Thus in the case of Piaget's 'three mountains' experiment, the experimenter failed to appreciate the abilities that were required to perform the task and hence misconstrued the performance of his subjects. The experiment of Hughes removed these obstructive complications in the task structure and hence allowed the users to display the ability which was in question (decentring). In other words, the problem is to design situations in which the learner can employ the skills he already possesses. The implication of this is that intelligence is a quality of performance, and that capacity can only be inferred when the limits of performance have been reached. Performance was in these cases an unreliable guide to capacity because adequate opportunity for the expression of ability had not been provided; a refinement in testing technique led to an increase in the intelligent behaviour expressed. What these statements suggest is that in many cases the limiting factor in performance may not be cognitive 'capacity', but rather the quality of the communication between the learner and his learning environment. This 'quality of communication' depends on the design of the learning experience, which forms the interface between cognition and the problem space.

The enhancement of communication via the improvement of educational technique can result in an acceleration of cognitive development, as is witnessed by the studies quoted by Donaldson. The distinction between 'learning' and 'testing' environments is becoming somewhat blurred here; but obviously any testing procedure in which previously unsuspected ability is demonstrated must be a learning environment, by any definition! Although we are talking here in terms of research findings, the relevance of this type of research to normal educational practice is argued convincingly by Donaldson (1978).

Special education provides us with more dramatic examples of the same phenomenon. The notion that performance is often an unreliable guide to capacity is a familiar one to those involved in special education. The idea of 'trapped' intelligence expresses it perfectly; intelligence is 'trapped' by the lack of opportunity for its expression. Consider the case of a physically handicapped child who is provided with an interactive computer environment, together with any necessary input device (e.g. Weir, 1980). Here, the communication problem stems from physical causes but it has a theoretical unity with the learning problems of normal children, as discussed above: the inability to display cognitive ability because of limitations on communication with the learning situations. In the case of 'enabling' technology, the blockage is essentially a 'front end' problem in that the technology merely serves to provide access to an already established learning environment. In the case of the Donaldson experiments, however, the 'blockage' consisted of a processing difficulty, and the release of 'trapped intelligence' was facilitated by the design of a new learning situation. The drawing of an analogy between these situations rests on the notion that both consist of problems of 'access'. The whole learning environment, including the task itself and also the cognitive abilities (e.g. problem-solving strategies) used in tackling it, can be seen as tools which allow the learner to come into contact with some essential central core; some organization of aspects of the environment which constitute a metaphor that embodies what is being learned. To deal with such a model we need a broad understanding of what 'educational technology' may imply. The authors agree with the conception of Lumsdaine (1964) which sees educational technology as being both:

1. Concerned with the use of equipment (as opposed to humans) in the teaching process (the hardware or 'product' aspect of technology).
2. Concerned with the development of learning experiences, through the application of the sciences of learning (the software or 'process' aspect of technology).

The role of educational technology, then, is the extension of the learning environments which are available to the learner. This is the role which is (or should be) played by education in general, of course. 'Educational technology' consists of the appliance of scientific results in the service of education. Both in mainstream and special education this service may be a 'process' contribution; in special education, for example, the use of structured training programmes (Clarke and Hermelin, 1955) has been seen to result in dramatic revisions of our estimates of what the severely subnormal are capable. In terms of our schematic model, a learning environment is brought within range of the individual's schemata. Problems of motor, sensory and mental handicap can be seen to have a certain unity in that they imply a degraded quality of communication with the environment. Changing the learning environment in order to make it more accessible to the learner, making it more syntonic with his cognitive structures or making it available to his physical or sensory ability will enable the learner to interact with that environment.

So what theoretical role can we assign to educational technology? It has been argued above that the role in education of both technology and technique is to increase the accessibility of learning experiences. This occurs when a technology or a technique introduced to the learning experience brings the most essential features of that experience within reach of the learner's current cognitive and physical status. So what, then, is the educational significance of new technology, and, in particular, computer technology? Gagne (1970) wrote that:

. . . the stimuli of instruction of the child in his preschool world are primarily the objects of his restricted world . . . the use of objects to present stimuli continues throughout the school years with the objects themselves growing more refined and more complex.

Although Gagne is a psychologist in the tradition of learning theory, one can see a similarity between his notion of 'objects of instruction' and Papert's 'objects to think with': these objects are essentially features of the environment which in some sense model or exemplify some important concept. Interaction with these objects encourages the development of particular schemata. What educational technology can do is provide a less 'restricted world', a world in which more cognitively significant experiences are available. The computer represents an environment which is extremely accessible physically but which also creates an opportunity for the conscious design of learning environments which are accessible cognitively. As Goldenberg (1979) said, in relation to special education:

. . . the computer's flexibility makes it a perfect extension for a child who is not flexible. We can give the child new opportunities for stimulation using whatever behaviors the child normally exhibits.

For example, we can use a computer to construct a model or analogy of the real world which provides access to powerful ideas more readily than its 'real world' equivalent; consider, for example, the use of the turtle microworld to teach mathematical concepts. This is why Sloman (1978) called the computer 'the most powerful toy devised by man'. Within the active, interactive, schematic model of the learning process outlined above, we can see the significance of the word 'toy'. In a sense it is toys that are needed: objects of learning which are motivating, which allow the user a degree of autonomy, which are personal and informal. The more that educationally significant concepts can be conveyed by such 'toys', the less restricted the environment will be. The notion of a 'restricted world' has obvious relevance to special education. Here, technology provides an otherwise perhaps unavailable opportunity for communication with a meaningful environment. Goldenberg (1979) proposes that:

. . . we can best serve the human being who comes to us for help by trying to remove the barriers to his experiences, thus making room for him to develop his own adaptive and integrative abilities – room for him to develop autonomy.

When this educational philosophy is stated in such a general form it may seem innocuous, uncontroversial and even obvious. However, it is in stark contradiction to several models of learning which have had extensive influence upon educational theory and which still have high currency in many areas of special education. These theories, which take their inspiration from traditional learning theory, are characterized by their position on two particular issues. First, they embody a one-way, receptive model of learning and hence support a purely expository style of teaching. Second, they support a strictly behaviour-centred view of remediation. However, behaviourism has undergone a number of modifications since its original formulation. The hierarchical model of learning and instructional design espoused by Gagne (1982), indicates that behaviourist and cognitive traditions can be combined in a unified approach. However, much current educational software reflects a form of 'crude behaviourism' (Chandler, 1984). Such implicit educational philosophy finds its expression not only in software design but in all areas of educational practice. In many areas certain techniques do implicitly reflect a notion of the learner as a passive receptacle. In special education this position is often seen as an emphasis on the normalization of behaviour rather than the normalization of experience. The 'normalization of experience' entails the provision of an environment which allows the learner to formulate, apply and refine his mental models. From the cognitive point of view, the feature of 'normal' experience which it is most important to capture is the opportunity for interaction. This requires that the environment is meaningful to a learner's existing cognitive structures, that it provides material that can be acted upon by them, and that he is made aware of the effects of his actions by some form of feedback.

Weir (1981) used the phrase 'trapped intelligence' to describe the performance of cerebral palsied children after the provision of computer-based learning environments (specifically, a LOGO project). She writes:

> Introducing computers into the learning environment of severely handicapped students can revolutionize their lives. Students whose intelligence has up till now been trapped because they cannot communicate what they know – either because they cannot write, or because they cannot speak . . . can now look forward to a measure of independence . . .

In these, and similar, cases (e.g. those documented by Goldenberg) the provision of an accessing technology enables the expression of existing schemata. However, technology can also act to provide learning environments which allow communication-impaired children to develop more adequate internal models. Geoffrion and Geoffrion (1983) describe the application of computer technology in the development of more adequate reading schemata in children experiencing difficulties in learning to read. Recent work by our own group has produced restricted interactive language environments for hearing-impaired children (Ward et al., 1985). The software produced allows interactive graphics to be discussed and controlled by means of a simple 'natural' language interface, allowing the user to engage in a conversation with the computer. The nature of the available conversational styles provides access to descriptions, instructions and questions. Use of these computer-mediated environments has resulted in improvements in language performance in these children.

Where communication and interaction are restricted by degraded quality of input, the formation and development of adequate hypotheses about the structure of the input becomes more problematic. Thus, in the case of the hearing-impaired learner the quality of speech input will not allow the formation of precise hypotheses concerning the rule structure and functions of language. Our own work involves the presentation of linguistic information via an alternative mode (visual rather than auditory).

There is a clear analogy with the provision of special technology for the physically handicapped. In both cases, when we bypass, compensate for, or ignore the weak communication modality, dramatic changes are seen in the child's development. Goldenberg notes that:' . . . mental development in general seems to suffer functional retardation when a person can never try out his ideas and get feedback from the trials'.

More significantly, there is an analogy here with education and cognitive development as a whole. The discussion of Piaget, and of the work documentated by Donaldson indicate that educational techniques in general serve the function of making the learning environment accessible to the learner, i.e. matching its structure to the cognitive skills and the world knowledge that the learner possesses. This can occur via technological intervention or by improvements in teaching practice. In either case, Landa's argument is relevant: i.e. that the development and application of an educational device (we use 'device' in its most general sense) must rest on not simply an analysis of the task structure, but on an analysis of the learner. The present discussion is intended to demonstrate that psychology possesses the theoretical tools to enable this analysis.

## ACKNOWLEDGEMENTS

This paper was prepared while D. Rotheray was in receipt of a research studentship from the Joint Committee of the ESRC-SERC. We would also like to thank the Nuffield Foundation who are currently supporting our work.

## REFERENCES

Bruner, J. S. (1966). *Toward a Theory of Instruction*, Harvard University Press, Cambridge, Mass.
Chandler, D. (1984). *Young Learners and the Microcomputer*, Open University Press, Milton Keynes.
Clarke, A. D. B., and Hermelin, H. F. (1955). Adult imbeciles: their abilities and trainability, *Lancet*, ii, 337–339.
Donaldson, M. (1978). *Children's Minds*, Fontana, London.

Evans, S. H. (1967). A brief statement of schema theory, *Psychonomic Science*, **8**, 87–88.

Festinger, L. (1957). *A Theory of Cognitive Dissonance*, Stanford University Press, Stanford, Calif.

Gagne, R. M. (1970). *The Conditions of Learning*, Holt, Rinehart and Winston, London.

Gagne, R. M. (1982). Developments in learning psychology: an interview with R. M. Gagne, *Educational Technology*, June 1982, 11–15.

Geoffrion, L. D., and Geoffrion, O. P. (1983). *Computers and Reading Instruction*, Addison Wesley, Reading, Mass.

Geoffrion, L. D. and Goldenberg, E. P. (1981). Computer-based exploratory learning systems for communication-handicapped children, *Journal of Special Education*, **15**, 325–332.

Goldenberg, E. P. (1979). *Special Technology for Special Children*, University Park Press, Baltimore, Md.

Graves, D. (1984). Computers, kids and writing: an interview with Donald Graves. In J. Green, *Classroom Computer Learning*, March 1984, 20–88.

Hughes, M. (1975). Egocentricism in pre-school children. Edinburgh University, unpublished doctoral dissertation.

Landa, L. N. (1974). *Algorithmisation in Learning and Instruction*, Educational Technology Publications, Englewood Cliffs, N.J.

Landa, L. N. (1983). The algo-heuristic theory of instruction. In C. M. Reigeluth, (ed.), *Instructional-Design Theories and Models: An Overview of their Current Status*, Lawrence Erlbaum Associates, Hillsdale, N.J.

Lumsdaine, A. A. (1964). Educational technology: issues and problems. In P. C. Lange, (ed.), *Programmed Instruction: The Sixty Sixth Yearbook of the National Society for the Study of Education*, NSSE, Chicago.

Neisser, U. (1976). *Cognition and Reality: Principles and Implications of Cognitive Psychology*, Freeman, San Francisco.

Norman, D. A., and Rumelhart, D. E. (1975). *Explorations in Cognition*, Freeman, San Francisco.

Olson, D. R. (1976). Culture, technology and intellect. In L. B. Resnick, (ed.), *The Nature of Intelligence*, Lawrence Erlbaum Associates, Hillsdale, N.J.

Papert, S. (1980). *Mindstorms: Children, Computers and Powerful Ideas*, Harvester, Brighton.

Robinson, J. (1980). Psychiatry and Marxism, *Labour Review*, **4** (1).

Romiszowski, A. J. (1981). *Designing Instructional Systems*, Kogan Page, London.

Schank, R. (1982). *Dynamic Memory*, Cambridge University Press, Cambridge.

Sloman, A. (1978). *The Computer Revolution in Philosophy*, Harvester, Brighton.

Ward, R. D., Lindley, P., Rostron, A. B., Sewell, D. F., and Cubie, R. (1985). An evaluation of the language and thought software, *Journal of Computer Assisted Learning*, **1**(2), 66–72.

Weir, S. (1981) Logo and the exceptional child, *Microcomputing*, Sept. 1981.

Womble, G. (1984). Process and processor: is there room for a machine in the English classroom?, *English Journal*, **73**(1), 34–37.

# PART II

# Artificial Intelligence and Computer-based Environments for Learning and Development

# Editorial Introduction

In their attempt to foresee the future of educational computing, O'Shea and Self (1983) predict a continuation of the advances in hardware technology that have made increasingly powerful machines accessible to home and school to bring us the 'microcomputer revolution'. Trends in software development, however, present a gloomier picture. Much better-quality programs will be needed, but O'Shea and Self find little evidence of systematic, let alone rapid, improvements: 'the awful truth is that over the last ten years the availability of mediocre, computer-assisting learning material has increased in a steady and boring way – the main effect of the microcomputer revolution being to decrease the average quality of computer software' (O'Shea & Self, 1983, pp.260–261; cf. Self, 1985).

A significant positive influence might flow from advances in 'instructional technology' that suggest principles for sound instructional decisions. Unhappily, O'Shea and Self feel unable to predict this; at least, they find no signs of it at the present time. However, they do anticipate a refinement of theory within developmental psychology and a greater concern with implications for education. In particular, they hope that the study and use of computer-based environments will contribute to improved models of how cognitive structures are acquired. Admittedly, developmental psychology has not engaged itself with this context to any great extent. The chapters of this section outline the background to this challenging applied area and suggest mutually profitable forms that greater involvement by developmental psychologists might take.

## ARTIFICIAL INTELLIGENCE AND EDUCATIONAL COMPUTING

Certain computational systems with which the developing individual is faced have been explicitly informed by the concepts and insights of artificial intelligence (AI). We believe that investigating these systems holds most potential for advances in theory and in principled applications; we shall focus on them and the questions they raise. In this, we share O'Shea and Self's view of why so much educational software is unsatisfactory: available programs are too 'unintelligent' to support flexible interaction with the learner. The most important attempts to remedy this draw on the discipline of AI.

What is AI and why should its influence be singled out in this way? AI is often defined as a branch of computer science that aims to make computers do things that would require 'intelligence' if done by people. A popular account of its origins and evolution can be found in McCorduck, (1979), and Boden (1977) provides an introduction that is particularly suitable for psychologists. AI attempts to understand the principles that underlie naturally intelligent abilities – such as perceiving, solving problems, reasoning, or using language – by programming computers to perform them. Hallmarks of AI are its assumption that knowledge is the essential feature of intelligent abilities and its concern with clarifying the cognitive structures and processes that underlie it.

Given this focus, it is unsurprising that AI work has increasingly become associated with various issues pertinent to cognitive development and education. Part III of this volume concentrates on how computational techniques can be used to model cognitive processes and their development. Here we shall be concerned with issues that arise from AI's contribution to computer systems intended to foster the individual's learning and development. Yazdani sets the scene for the chapters of this section by reviewing the relationship between AI, its theories of learning, and the application and testing of these theories in the educational domain. Most of the issues raised by the chapters revolve about the phenomena of LOGO and PROLOG, two significant aspects of AI's contribution in this area. They will be introduced more fully in the chapters. At this point, we shall sketch their origins in AI as a first step towards clarifying their background and significance.

## LOGO AND PROLOG: THEIR AI ORIGINS

The structure of LOGO and PROLOG, as these are used in educational settings, incorporates many dimensions: computational, cognitive and pedagogical. Lying at the computational heart of both systems are AI programming languages. In order to model knowledge structures, AI has devised a number of very powerful computer programming languages; their distinctive characteristics are usefully reviewed in Barr and Feigenbaum (1982). Two of the most influential approaches involve the language LISP (and its descendants) and logic programming: these are associated with LOGO and PROLOG respectively.

LISP was invented by McCarthy in the late 1950s. Particularly in the United States, it is considered to be 'first among equals' (Winston, 1977) and 'the mainstay of AI programming' (Barr and Feigenbaum, 1982). What is so exciting about this type of programming language? Two features relate to the present context and illustrate its importance. First is what programs can be written about. LISP's very general data-structures make it possible for programs to manipulate symbols that can stand for anything the programmer may require, not just for numbers. LISP is short for 'list processing language' because this flexibility is achieved through representing data by linked 'lists'. Second is the structure of programs that can be written. LISP has a special relationship between data and the programs that manipulate it because LISP programs are themselves represented as list structures. This means that LISP expressions can function either as pieces of program, in which case they control the machine's processes, or as pieces of text, in which case they can be manipulated or reorganized by such processes. This enables them to manipulate other programs or even themselves. Longuet-Higgins (1978) remarks that this insight may be among the most important contributions of computer scientists to an understanding of information processing; it captures a distinction that will probably be crucial to any convincing account of human thought. At the practical level of writing programs, it facilitates the construction of interestingly structured and self-modifying programs.

LISP offers AI workers a powerful tool for thinking about thinking. Seymour Papert's seminal contribution was to try to make such ideas accessible to the field of learning and education. He argued that writing computer programs of this kind could offer a concrete context to foster children's understanding of abstract concepts. The focus of his approach is the programming language LOGO, which was designed as a 'junior' version of LISP to make the process of learning to program as simple as possible. Papert blended LOGO with his considerable knowledge of mathematics and with Piaget's theory of cognitive development, especially Piaget's stress on the developmental relationship between sensory-motor activity and abstract reasoning skills (Papert, 1980). The chapters by Yazdani and by Simon outline Papert's highly influential arguments and his LOGO programming environment of 'turtle graphics'. In this 'microworld', program commands control the actions of a mechanical or screen 'turtle'. This illustrates the highly imperative or 'procedural' emphasis of LOGO programming and shows how the powerful LISP-like facilities of the language simplify the design of higher-order programs. For example, programs for drawing simple shapes can be combined to draw more complex ones. This, it is hoped, should offer the learner a deep insight into their structural relationship.

A different approach has its origins in European work on logic programming. Like LISP and other AI programming languages, logic programming is
concerned with the symbol manipulation that is believed essential to produce
'intelligent' computers. However, this perspective endorses the view that
classical logic, which specifies the valid inferences that can be drawn in
deductive reasoning, may offer a superior tool for programming. It regards
computation as a form of 'controlled deduction'. Kowalski (1979), for
example, emphasizes that using logic allows concentration on the structure
of a computational problem or task rather than on the programming itself.
(With many languages, programming is machine-dependent and needs to be
understood primarily in terms of the behaviour it invokes inside the
computer.) The first example of a logic programming language is PROLOG –
short for 'programming in logic' – which was devised by Colmerauer in the
early 1970s. The chapters by Yazdani and by Taylor and du Boulay introduce
important features of the PROLOG style of programming. Most notable is
its emphasis on specifying a database of facts that can be investigated or
questioned through PROLOG's general logical rules for sorting, ordering
and correlating related elements.

Initially, this approach was extended to children's learning with several
objectives: to teach children logic and its application to other subjects; and
to teach the computer-science techniques of database query, program specification and, ultimately, programming itself (Kowalski, 1982; Ennals, 1984).
Proponents of PROLOG stress a 'declarative' use of the language, in contrast
with the 'procedural' style of LOGO. For example, LOGO's turtle graphics
offer a type of procedural geometry; children learn about shapes by writing
programs to draw them. PROLOG's stress is on explicitly stating facts and
relationships; this provides a declarative geometry more compatible with
conventional classroom mathematics teaching.

The design of PROLOG, unlike LOGO, was not motivated by educational
considerations. Early applications in this direction, unlike Papert's work,
were not guided by a particular developmental theory. However, connections
with the Piagetian perspective have again been made. These draw on Piaget's
(1953) assumption that propositional logic accurately captures the structure
of mature human reasoning (see Braine and Rumain, 1983, for a critical
analysis of Piaget's position). In the final developmental stage, he argues,
thought becomes 'formal' in the sense of being abstracted from particular
contexts or contents. The individual can draw valid deductive inferences from
verbal propositions, whatever their content; reason about reasoning itself;
and formulate hypotheses about possible as well as known states of affairs.
The link between Piaget's ideas and PROLOG's logical basis is exploited by
Nichol, Dean and Briggs's work and is discussed in their chapter. Others, as
Taylor and du Boulay show, have found the plausible parallel between
PROLOG and 'natural' human reasoning appealing.

Evidently, the structure of such programming environments and their possible applications are very complex. So, the opportunities and experiences afforded the learner, and the problems faced by any exploration of their effects, are multi-faceted. Too often, this has resulted in claims that are imprecise or unconvincingly substantiated. For instance, this has been particularly the case in respect of LOGO. O'Shea (1985) notes that, despite its exalted status in some quarters, there is hopeless confusion as to whether the 'LOGO experience' connotes an AI programming language, a new way of teaching specific mathematics concepts, a radical educational environment, or a curriculum.

Of course, LOGO could be all or any of these, and it is vital that any claims for its 'benefits' are clear on which dimensions are intended and why. Similarly, questions arise due to the complex background of PROLOG. Are the principles underlying it a good expression of the logic programming ideal? Do microcomputer versions of PROLOG (micro-PROLOG) embody enough of its principles to be considered valid logic-programming languages? Questions of the match between logic programming ideals and particular implementations will not be pursued here. But they should be borne in mind if claims concerning the relationship between reasoning, logic, PROLOG and programming are to be clarified.

Unclear or unsupported claims do not entail rejecting the 'educational computing' enterprise (although caution is being expressed by previous enthusiasts, e.g. DiSessa, 1986). They should alert us to the fact that potential researchers may need to take heed of the more unfamiliar (computational) aspects of this work. In particular, it highlights the need to consider both educational strategy in respect of this enterprise and suitable research techniques for its evaluation. What questions, then, are posed for developmental psychologists by the state-of-the-art in this area?

## GUIDING THE LEARNER'S INTERACTION WITH COMPUTER SYSTEMS

A prominent debate in contemporary work centres on how the learner's interaction with such systems should be structured and guided. We encounter differing philosophies of computer use that, implicitly or explicitly, embody assumptions concerning motivation and development. The first three chapters bear on this issue. They support the view that computers are highly motivating, a feature clearly demonstrated in Part I of this volume. However, they caution against any naive belief that unguided interaction with computer systems can effectively exploit their educational potential.

Yazdani's chapter introduces two traditions from within which AI views of knowledge and learning infiltrated education. Computerized learning environments offer the learner an open-ended opportunity to 'construct' new forms of understanding through exploration and discovery. Not only LOGO but also certain applications of PROLOG can be used in this way. Such environments, it is claimed, embody 'powerful ideas' that, once encountered, will spontaneously transfer and prove valuable outside the computer context. In contrast with this, computer assisted learning (CAL) – including AI developments in intelligent tutoring systems (ITS) – has generally aimed to 'instruct' learners in specific predefined skills or subject matter.

Sleeman's (1985) review of opposing 'ideologies' of ITS and LOGO work, notes that LOGO studies based on this model have not yet convincingly investigated a set of fair questions about its use and impact. How much of the student's evident enthusiasm is due to the computer and how much to LOGO *per se*? Studies often involve very significant teacher and peer support – a circumstance that may be ignored in emphasizing the learner's discoveries. The nature of this social interchange may make an important contribution to any effects that are found in this context, and we need to make their role explicit. Sleeman argues that 'AI researchers are in the business of transforming "ART to SCIENCE", and as such the articulation of pedagogical knowledge, including instructional strategies, must be laid open to systematic and rigorous investigation' (1985, p.27). The problem of teasing out such effects is familiar to developmental psychologists.

One direction for further research involves attempting to isolate the motivational and cognitive consequences of various kinds of learner–computer interaction. Simon's chapter, for instance, discusses the promising approach of Howe and the Edinburgh group, which employed a much more directive approach to LOGO experience than that envisaged by Papert. Nichol, Dean and Briggs's chapter on the use of micro-PROLOG makes a particularly valuable contribution to this issue. They describe three ways in which they integrate micro-PROLOG tools into normal educational practice: to provide information, through pre-prepared programs; as an electronic blackboard for exploring ideas and hypotheses; and as a medium for pupils to write their own programs. Each of these imposes different constraints on the learner.

Evaluation of the developmental consequences of computer-based experience is still out of step with the extreme (positive and negative) claims that are sometimes encountered. Can some things be taught more effectively than others via computer systems? What kind of system has potential at which developmental level(s)? Answers to such questions are sketchy or unavailable. Most studies have been fairly informal, and the following chapters reveal that rigorous assessment is only now getting under way. Is learning with these systems perhaps so novel as to make formal evaluation techniques inapplicable? This seems a needlessly defeatist position. The issue to which we must turn is: what kinds of evaluation are appropriate?

## EVALUATING EFFECTS

In his chapter on LOGO, Simon argues that research in developmental and educational psychology has already addressed pertinent issues elsewhere and has evolved insights that must now be applied within the computer domain. Against a background of developmental research, he assesses claims concerning LOGO to offer a provocative attack on Papert's perspective. In particular, he considers educational research testing the proposal that more meaningful learning follows from spontaneous self-directed discovery and experimental studies of children's problem-solving. Simon's analysis is important in helping us to clarify competing claims and, his key concern, to build a picture of optimal LOGO use that can be tested through further empirical investigations.

Working from the perspective of educationalists, Nichol, Dean and Briggs have studied cognitive processes as they occur during the teaching of a familiar curriculum subject, in contrast with the more restricted settings of mainstream developmental research. They do not favour reliance on psychometric-type measures. Instead, they draw on educational and psychological theory concerned with children's thinking to devise their own tools for analysing the quality of understanding. This approach offers a much richer analysis of children's thinking than is usual; it is explored in detail in their chapter. Methodological issues that arise concern the extent to which such techniques could be extended to areas other than history, and the possibility of combining their rich structured data with suitable quantitative methods of analysis.

These reports indicate that effective evaluation will require a deep theory of the cognitive structures we hope the learner will acquire and of how these relate to specific characteristics of programs that are used or written. This theme is common to the following chapters. Nichol, Dean and Briggs's work, for example, is predicated on their understanding of the structure of historical investigation and how this maps onto various micro-PROLOG tools. Papert's original LOGO concept, whatever its limitations, was based on assumptions about the mathematical 'primitives' it embodied and the way combining these could foster understanding of higher-order concepts. Obviously, it is possible to do research where children are offered '$n$' hours with a computer-based environment and pre- and post-test measures compared. But such research runs the risk of remaining superficial and confusing the 'measurable' with the 'significant' (Sage and Smith, 1983).

This returns us to O'Shea and Self's (1983) suggestion that the computer context may provide developmental psychology with a unique opportunity for refining its theories and enriching its appreciation of cognition. Are there questions that developmental psychologists have posed without, as yet, achieving satisfactory answers? Might their investigation within computer-based environments offer a way forward? Lepper (1985) refers to a range of possibilities in this vein. Here we shall consider just one area of inquiry for which this context seems particularly promising: the development and transfer of reasoning skills.

## REASONING AND TRANSFER IN THE COMPUTER CONTEXT

As we have seen, Piagetian theory is typically implicated in much of the background to this area. Developmental psychologists have, however, now demonstrated that young children appear to have greater cognitive competence than his theory would suggest. For example, Donaldson's (1978) influential *Children's Minds* assembled many studies revealing precocious achievements when the content of Piagetian tasks was made less abstract and more familiar to the child. But unresolved issues remain. In what ways are the child's cognitive structures transferable between tasks and to what extent must they be reconstructed anew in each domain of expertise? How, if at all, do less context-bound reasoning abilities develop?

One difficulty with 'early competence' research is that the tasks on which children succeed may differ considerably from the original ones, making the cognitive processes required to perform them controversial. A worthwhile question is whether assessing children's reasoning abilities in the computer context might offer an advantage. While not beyond dispute, the structure of programs and programming languages is much more precisely understood than that of many task situations in developmental research. It may prove possible to achieve greater agreement concerning the structure and demand characteristics of computer task situations. In this regard, Yazdani's chapter plays a valuable role by emphasizing the importance of distinguishing between potentially important concepts and ideas that can be experienced through programming and the claims made for particular 'brand names'. His chapter details a hierarchy of programming languages, each of which incorporates a larger set of 'powerful ideas'.

As to what the results of further rigorous investigations will be, the following chapters offer varying perspectives. Yazdani confidently invites developmental psychologists to explore untested claims for the transfer of learning from computerized learning enviornments through analogy and metaphor. Simon, on the other hand, doubts that transfer of problem-solving skills will occur in the absence of direct instruction or extremely long periods of intensive learning.

With regard to the nature and development of general-purpose reasoning skills, the final two chapters of this section bear on the pertinent issues within the PROLOG context.

Nichol and colleagues consider that Piaget's account of 'formal' thought reflects the structure of PROLOG's rules. Thus, interacting with PROLOG may furnish experiences necessary for acquiring this type of logical reasoning during adolescence. Their strong emphasis on pupils interacting with pre-prepared micro-PROLOG tools – as opposed to programming as such – means that the pupil is offered a structure for reasoning that is compatible with deductive thought. This may prove a unique medium in which thinking can be structured, externalized and reflected upon. Certainly, it has features that appear quite unlike, for example, traditional literacy. This chapter concentrates on thinking about historical situations, but the approach suggests several routes to testing wider consequences: the impact on logical thinking in other domains and the possibly subtle effects of the children learning to think in the specific manner of historians.

Taylor and du Boulay's research complements this work by focusing on how young adults' ability to handle logic and inference interacts with learning to program in PROLOG. They outline several difficulties with claims that languages like PROLOG should be easy to learn and natural to use. In particular, they have reservations about the supposed compatibility of PROLOG with the structure of spontaneous deductive reasoning. Difficulties with PROLOG provide a context in which the actual organization of reasoning can be studied – as opposed to its ideal organization. A major problem for beginners in any programming language proves to be discovering how to express themselves in a highly constrained formalism; PROLOG's first-order logic appears no easier in this respect. Although PROLOG programs often contain a high proportion of English, Taylor and du Boulay show how this can actually detract from successful learning, when subjects attempt to use their familiar knowledge inappropriately.

## PROGRAMMING AND UNDERSTANDING THE COMPUTER

Understanding 'novice programmers' is the goal of Taylor and du Boulay's work. In the present context, it is natural to consider whether interacting with and programming computers will have particular impacts on aspects of cognition and development. But we must be aware that the computer in its own right poses a challenge for the learner. In conclusion, we turn briefly to consider learning about the computer as an issue in its own right. The overall message conveyed by the chapters is that learning to program, as such, is hard in any language. This should not surprise us; anyone who has used a computer even for word processing will be only too aware of the many forms of understanding involved in appreciating the relation between one's goals, behaviour, information visible on the display screen, and ideas about what goes on 'inside' the machine.

What processes are involved in coming to understand and use computers? Finding a way of conceptualizing and tackling the issues has brought together workers in AI and cognitive psychology in a new field of study called human computer interaction (HCI) or human machine interaction (HMI). The main issues are of clear concern to anyone wishing to investigate the computer context. Taylor and du Boulay's chapter includes an introductory review which sketches six overlapping classes of difficulties that novices must face in learning to use and program computers. This will alert the reader to issues with which they may, as yet, be unfamiliar. It also makes possible a deeper appreciation of certain of the claims made for the 'beneficial' design of particular programming languages and computer environments. Last, but by no means least, it provides another tool for focusing the question: 'How do children come to grips with these complex systems?'

The contributors to this section were originally trained in a range of disciplines: artificial intelligence, computer science, education and developmental psychology. Their chapters demonstrate the truly interdisciplinary nature of the work they are now tackling. The developmental psychologist who moves into this area confronts a good deal of new territory. Some challenges are familiar, others novel, but all are stimulating enough to encourage developmentalists to define their own unique contribution.

## REFERENCES

Barr, A., and Feigenbaum, E. A. (1982). *The Handbook of Artificial Intelligence* Vol. 2, William Kauffman, Los Altos, Calif.
Boden, M. A. (1977). *Artificial Intelligence and Natural Man*, Harvester Press, Brighton.
Braine, M., and Rumain, B. (1983). Logical reasoning. In *Cognitive Development* (Volume eds J. Flavell and E. Markman), Volume 4 of *Handbook of Child Psychology* (Ed. P. H. Mussen), 4th edn, Wiley, New York.
DiSessa, A. (1986). Notes on the future of programming: breaking the utility barrier. In D. A. Norman and S. W. Draper (eds), *User Centred System Design*, Lawrence Erlbaum, Hillsdale, N.J.
Donaldson, M. (1978). *Children's Minds*, Fontana/Collins, Glasgow.
Ennals, J. R. (1984). Teaching logic as a computer language in schools. In M. Yazdani (ed.), *New Horizons in Educational Computing*, Ellis Horwood, Chichester.
Kowalski, R. A. (1979). *Logic for Problem Solving*, North-Holland Elsevier, New York.
Kowalski, R. A. (1982). Logic as a computer language for children, *Proceedings of the European Conference on Artificial Intelligence*, Orsay, France.
Lepper, M. R. (1985). Microcomputers in education: motivational and social issues, *American Psychologist*, **40**, 1–18.
Longuet-Higgins, H. C. (1978). On describing cognitive processes, *Behavioral and Brain Sciences*, **1**, 110.
McCorduck, P. (1979). *Machines Who Think*, Freeman, San Francisco.
O'Shea, T. (1985). AI – future developments in education and training, Paper Presented at the AI for Society Conference, Brighton Polytechnic, Brighton.
O'Shea, T., and Self, J. (1983). *Learning and Teaching With Computers: Artificial Intelligence in Education*, Harvester Press, Brighton.

Papert, S. (1980). *Mindstorms: Children, Computers and Powerful Ideas*, Harvester, Brighton.
Piaget, J. (1953). *Logic and Psychology*, Manchester University Press, Manchester.
Sage, M., and Smith, D. J. (1983). *Microcomputers in Education: A Framework for Research*, Social Science Research Council, London.
Self, J. (1985). *Microcomputers in Education: A Critical Appraisal of Educational Software*, Harvester Press, Brighton.
Sleeman, D. (1985). AI and education: two ideological positions, *AISB Quarterly*, No. 55, 26–31.
Winston, P. H. (1977). *Artificial Intelligence*, Addison Wesley, Reading, Mass.

Computers, Cognition and Development
Edited by J. Rutkowska and C. Crook
© 1987 John Wiley & Sons Ltd

CHAPTER 5

# Artificial Intelligence, Powerful Ideas and Children's Learning

Masoud Yazdani

## SUMMARY

The development of educational computer packages is outlined from 'linear programs' and 'branching programs' to the use of 'expert systems'. An alternative approach is presented based around computational 'learning environments', which incorporate a number of 'powerful ideas'. A hierarchy of programming languages, each of which incorporates a larger set of such powerful ideas, is described.

## INTRODUCTION

As a computer scientist, one of my primary responsibilities has been to design and teach a computer literacy course. As time passed I have become convinced that computer programming has implications for a wider context than the narrowly vocational one which meets the eye. This chapter will, therefore, ultimately provide an invitation to developmental psychologists to explore the claim that the learning of computer programming has outcomes well beyond being a fashion or a means of securing employment.

This paper deals with the relationship between artificial intelligence (AI), its theories of learning and the application and testing of these theories in the field of children's learning. AI attempts to understand the mysteries of intelligence, and computers are sometimes used as a tool in this endeavour (Yazdani and Narayanan, 1984). The concerns of AI include a desire to know 'how people learn' and 'how people teach'. In the pursuit of these aims I have been trying to build systems which are capable of a limited

99

amount of intelligent behaviour in the domain of teaching arithmetic skills (Attisha and Yazdani, 1983, 1984) and language teaching (Barchan, Wood-mansee and Yazdani, 1986). It must be stated that the primary motivation for this lies in the discoveries which might be made regarding the nature of 'learning' and 'teaching', rather than in the actual construction of useful teaching or learning tools. Nevertheless, the results of the research in progress have been offered to practising teachers in a desire to put the evolving theories to an acid test. What better source of feedback can we have than by putting our theories to the test in areas where humans themselves welcome involvement? This approach differs in motivation from the more traditional computer assisted learning, where the needs of the practising teacher, the limitations of the computing devices available, and the dynamics of educational practice have had to be of primary significance.

The main sections of this chapter introduce and contrast two frameworks from within which AI views of knowledge and learning have made their way into education, together with some of the problems and issues which they raise. A general introduction to computer assisted learning (CAL) indicates how AI has enriched the traditional approach. The evolution of CAL is traced, from the early days of 'linear programs' to the use of 'expert systems'. A critique of such approaches is presented, and they are contrasted with an alternative approach based on computerized 'learning environments'. Such environments have been said to embody a number of 'powerful ideas' which can facilitate the process of learning through exploration and discovery. However, the notion of 'powerful idea' has not always been clearly defined. In particular, those new to this area may find it difficult to distinguish between potentially important concepts and ideas which can be experienced via programming and the claims made for particular 'brand names' or program-ming languages. A hierarchy of programming languages is outlined, each of which incorporates a larger set of 'powerful ideas' such as: planning and executing actions; repairing plans as the result of consequences of actions; and simplifying a complex task by dividing it into sub-tasks and dealing with each individually. The chapter concludes by assessing the current status of this framework, together with directions it suggests for future research.

## COMPUTER ASSISTED LEARNING

The advent of computers has had an impact on education, along with all other aspects of human endeavour. From the outset, application of computers in education has been in two separate areas. On the one hand, children follow programming courses (usually in BASIC) in order to learn how to use this new technology. On the other hand, teachers are using this new technology to teach established parts of the curriculum. Developments in computer assisted learning (CAL) have tried to capture – at a greater or lesser level of sophistication – knowledge of a specific domain and evaluate the pupils' performance within that domain.

CAL development has followed an evolutionary path since it was started in the 1950s with simple 'linear programs'. The development of such programs were influenced by the prevailing behaviourist theories (Skinner, 1958) and the programmed learning machines of the previous century. It was believed that if the occurrence of an operant is followed by the presentation of a reinforcing stimulus, the strength of it is increased. To this end a computer program will output a frame of text which will take the student one small step towards the desired behaviour. The student then makes some kind of response based on what he already knows, or by trial and error! Finally the program informs the student whether he is correct. A stream of such steps form what is known as a 'linear program'. The student may work through the material at his own pace and his correct replies are rewarded immediately.

In the 1960s it was felt that one could use the student's response to control the material that the student would be shown next. In this way students learn more thoroughly as they attempt problems of an appropriate difficulty, rather than wading their way through some systematic exploration. 'Branching programs' therefore offered corrective feedback as well as adapting their teaching to students' responses. However, the task of the design of the teaching materials for such systems was impossibly large. This led to the birth of 'author languages', specific languages suitable for the development of CAL material. For more detail interested readers should consult Bitzer (1976) or O'Shea and Self (1983) for a critical view.

In the 1970s a new level of sophistication was discovered (see Woods and Hartley, 1971) in the design of CAL systems where, in some domains such as arithmetic, it was possible to generate the teaching material itself by the computer. A random number generator could produce two numbers to be added together by the student, and then the result of the computer's solution of the addition would be compared with that of the student's, in order to generate a response. Such systems need only therefore to be given general teaching strategies and they will produce a tree of possible interaction with infinitely large numbers of branches. Such 'generative systems' could answer some of the questions from the students, as well as incorporate some sort of measure of difficulty of the task.

By looking at the development of CAL systems over the last 30 years we see that they have improved on the richness of feedback and the degree of individualization they offer the students. However, they are all basically forms of 'learning by being told'. Although CAL seems to have improved beyond expectation in computational sophistication from its humble beginning of replacing the programmed learning machines, it still suffers from a behaviourist and reinforcement theory of learning.

In generative systems there is a mismatch between the program's internal processes (Boolean arithmetic) and those of the student's cognitive processes (rules and tables). None of these systems have human-like knowledge of the domain they are teaching, nor can they answer serious questions of the students as to 'why' and 'how' the task is performed.

Workers in AI have been aware of the importance of teaching along with other human activities. Intelligent tutoring systems (ITS) (Sleeman and Brown, 1982) were the first examples of a radically new approach to educational computing. While CAL has tended to be basically drill and practice, intelligent tutoring systems have aimed to be diagnostic. In Chapter 11 of this volume, Sleeman present an overview of ITS and the types of techniques developed for making such systems adaptive to pupils' individual behaviour in order to diagnose their misconceptions. For the purpose of this chapter, the following subtraction and addition shows the basis of the approach.

$$
\begin{array}{cc}
\begin{array}{r} 170 \\ -\ \ 93 \\ \hline 187 \end{array}
&
\begin{array}{r} 33 \\ +\ 179 \\ \hline 102 \end{array}
\end{array}
$$

An ITS will not print the message 'wrong, you lose a point' on the screen, but will diagnose the pupil's error (forgetting the borrow or the carry-over). These systems succeed by containing clear articulation of knowledge involved in a narrow domain. One such system, DEBUGGY (Burton, 1982), performs as well as, or rather better than, human teachers in diagnosis of misconceptions of pupils when performing subtraction.

There have been two major criticisms levelled against such sophisticated systems. DEBUGGY, for example, 'has not yet been incorporated within a remedial program, with which students can interact to improve their subtraction skill; nor has it yet been presented in such a form as to be usable as a diagnostic aid by any mathematics teacher' (Boden, 1983). The major reason behind these shortcomings has been the complexity of the task involved. Even in such a narrow domain, such as subtraction, there are numerous ways in which a pupil can make mistakes. Therefore a program such as DEBUGGY would be beyond the power of a modest school microcomputer. However, as the cost of hardware is declining, it has become possible to offer some of this level of sophistication to the school teacher.

Attisha and Yazdani (1983) use a taxonomy of possible errors which children make in addition and subtraction in order to provide remedial advice, similar to that of DEBUGGY, using a school microcomputer. This work has been extended (Attisha and Yazdani, 1984) to cover multiplication, which is by nature more complex than subtraction. In multiplication the pupil could make mistakes for various reasons: problems with the multiplication table, with the multiplication algorithm, or with the addition of subtotals. When errors in any two of these areas are combined, the result could appear to be nothing more than carelessness (random) to the best of human teachers. However, the computer system provides exercises in order to isolate different areas of difficulty and diagnose the problem.

A further advance on intelligent tutoring systems is when the knowledge of the domain being taught is made explicit in an independent operational 'expert system'. Expert systems are one of the success stories of AI. They incorporate the knowledge of a narrow domain, such as medicine or law, in a form similar to that believed to be used by trained professionals in the particular domain. Expert systems then manipulate the body of knowledge given to them in order to reach decisions and, if necessary, justify them in a way which is comprehensible to a human being. In this way they can exhibit a degree of competence, within their domain, which matches the performance of human experts and possibly exceeds them.

GUIDON (Clancey, 1979) is one application using an existing expert system MYCIN (Shortcliffe, 1976) for educational purposes. Clancey argues, however, that although MYCIN-like systems are a good means of transferring knowledge from a human expert to a human trainee, the rules representing the knowledge of a domain themselves are not sufficient. He proposes adding two further levels: one a 'support' level to justify rules, and the second an 'abstraction' level to organize rules into patterns in order to transfer such systems into a tutorial medium. Further, he argues that such systems still need 'teaching expertise' of a general kind and 'natural language' competence to carry out a coherent dialogue with the student.

Clancey's work is encouraging in the task of providing computer assisted learning in a domain where the system itself is capable of performing the task that it is expecting the trainee to perform. For example, Barchan, Woodmansee and Yazdani (1986) have chosen a new domain of application (language teaching) which seems well suited to such treatment.

Most language teaching programs rely on a massive store of correct sentences and derivations from them. Despite the large number of legitimate constructs with which they can deal, the programs are really nothing more than a dumb, if effective, pattern matcher, linking unintelligible series of characters to those pre-stored. As a consequence, the programs cannot recognize or comment upon errors encountered, even if the errors are frequent, unless they have been individually and specifically anticipated by the programmer. Therefore, the standard of accuracy required (coupled with the time for preparation of exercises) seems very high indeed. Instead, systems such as FROG (Imlah and du Boulay, 1985) and FGA (Barchan, Woodmansee and Yazdani, 1986), which use a general-purpose language parser, can cope with an indefinite number of possibilities without being programmed in advance to anticipate all the possibilities.

The use of expert systems in education could be considered as the most promising advance in the 1980s on the earlier CAL systems of the previous three decades. However, still more research is necessary before this technology can be considered mature enough.

Most intelligent tutoring systems rely on a good knowledge of the domain where the teaching takes place. For example, Attisha and Yazdani's (1983) system for subtraction relied on a vast amount of existing data in order to build a full taxonomy of children's errors in subtraction. The problem is also encountered by tutoring systems which use other more powerful knowledge representation techniques but which still rely on a reasonable knowledge of the domain while they are being constructed. Such knowledge is not readily available in cases where we have a more complex domain than arithmetic.

Instant feedback and individualization have been the twin gods of computer assisted learning (O'Shea and Self, 1983) for three decades. AI systems seem to provide the possibility of not only instant feedback, but a reasonably rich level of it, in the form of good remedial advice – for example. However, on the individualization side, AI does not yet seem to have offered any advances on traditional CAL. GUIDON, for example, suffers from the fact that it is always comparing a trainee doctor's actions with that of MYCIN while what is needed is a knowledge of what a particular user knows about the topic, his current misconceptions in addition to the terminology with which he is familiar, and the forms of explanation which he finds effective.

These needs are shared by most interactive AI systems and a good deal of research is already in progress in what is called 'user modelling'. A human teacher is constantly learning about the domain and the pupils he is teaching. If intelligent tutoring systems are to succeed they need to be able to modify themselves while in use.


## LEARNING ENVIRONMENTS

CAL and ITS are rather effective for the teaching of narrow domains but are at a loss when dealing with the teaching of general problem-solving skills. An alternative to CAL and ITS is presented in the form of 'learning environments' which provide a student with powerful computing tools. The student engages in an open-ended learning-by-discovery process by programming the computer to carry out interesting tasks. It is therefore argued that the intention is not to learn 'how' to program a computer, but to learn 'through' programming a computer.

The essential strength of such exploratory learning environments is that they can provide individuals with simple, concrete models of important ideas, and their relationships. As compared with arithmetic exercises, which may enhance the knowledge of a specific domain, computer-based learning environments can provide people with new ways of looking at the world.

Central to this thesis is the notion of a 'powerful idea'. A powerful idea is one which, when learned in one domain, can be generalized to guide one's actions in a variety of different domains. Therefore the use of analogy and metaphor is exploited in order that some specific task (such as the use of variables or procedures in computer programming) can be used in one's everyday life.

Papert (1980) has argued that computer programming in an environment rich with powerful ideas has a similar role to that of playing with physical objects in the Piagetian theories of learning. In doing so children build 'objects to think with' in place of sand castles, for example.

The four tables in this section present some concepts found in programming in various computer languages which have been considered candidates as 'powerful ideas'. Languages mentioned in the later tables contain concepts mentioned earlier but introduce new ones not found in their predecessors.

### Programming

Although Papert's arguments are presented in the context of the programming language LOGO, other less complex programming languages share notions with LOGO which are considered 'powerful ideas'. Table 5.1 presents seven such notions which can be found, even in the simplest forms of the BASIC programming language.

Programming in any language involves a good deal of planning which leads to a computer program. However, the program is not executed until an explicit command (such as RUN in BASIC) is given to the computer. This simple separation of the planning (the writing of the program) and the execution of it (the running of it) could be a good way of teaching a similar distance between one's aspirations and achievements.

TABLE 5.1  Some powerful ideas in programming

| | |
|---|---|
| 1.1 | Planning one's actions independently of the execution of the actions |
| 1.2 | Being explicit about one's own thinking |
| 1.3 | Independence of data from procedure |
| 1.4 | To view 'bugs' in a solution as things to correct and learn from |
| 1.5 | The concept of a variable which allows an infinity of instances to be represented and dealt with as one idea |
| 1.6 | Iteration (looping constructs) |
| 1.7 | Making choices (IF THEN ELSE) |

In programming one inevitably faces the issue of having to become more explicit about one's intentions. As a computer language can only accept well-defined concepts, a computer programmer learns to become careful of using vague notions for which he has no explanation.

In most programming languages a sharp distinction is made between information (data) and methods for manipulating it (procedures). This distinction also exists in the real world, where knowing about a task does not equip you to actually perform that task.

Making mistakes and having to cope with the consequences is one of the most common events in real life. Making mistakes and correcting them also happens frequently while programming a computer. Such mistakes are called 'bugs' and the process of rectifying them is known as 'debugging'. The choice of a different terminology is important as it shows the underlying view of mistakes within a computer culture. Bugs, although nasty things, are not important enough for a person to become depressed. One just has to find the right 'insect killer' to debug the program.

The discovery that making mistakes should not lead to a negative estimation of a person's capability is an experience which I believe has widespread character-changing implications for people. In programming one learns to view 'bugs' as the inevitable consequence of attempting to perform a new task which one is not yet fully capable of performing. The search for 'bugs' and the subsequent removal of them is looked on as a positive thing worthy of congratulation and not negatively, as mistakes in real life are often considered by some people. Making bugs is viewed as an activity from which one learns.

On a more technical side we come across a number of specific constructs which also have counterparts in real life not widely recognized. For example, a 'variable' or a symbol which allows an infinity of instances to be represented and dealt with as one idea. Performing a task over and over again (iteration); making choices among alternatives as well as being prepared in advance for choice points (IF THEN ELSE statements) are examples of such useful programming constructs.

**Structured programming**

There is a growing body of opinion that programming languages such as BASIC (which, for the purpose of running on small microcomputers, are kept simple), are too impoverished in the computational constructs they offer to be suitable for general use. This debate is well presented elsewhere by Bramer (1980), Atherton (1982) and Christensen (1982) in the context of a proposal to replace BASIC with COMAL, and by Brown (1982) presenting the case for PASCAL. These two languages are called 'structured' as they offer programming constructs known as 'procedures' and 'functions' which will help the programmer to break a problem down into sub-problems and tackle each sub-problem individually, and then deal with their interaction. Some of the powerful ideas associated with structured programming are listed in Table 5.2.

TABLE 5.2 Some powerful ideas in structured programming

| |
|---|
| 2.1 Attacking the sub-problems of a problem independently, and then with their interaction |
| 2.2 Naming concepts sensibly |
| 2.3 Self-reference/recursion |

A further shortcoming of most dialects of BASIC is the fact that they restrict the user to a small vocabulary for naming the variables. It is argued that being able to name concepts (such as width) sensibly (as WIDTH and not X25) is necessary. Finally, most structured languages offer the possibility of writing self-referencing modules (recursive procedures). In this method an ongoing situation is not viewed as representing one operation a number of times, but the same operation incorporating reference to itself. For example, when two people play chess, each player performs a move, passes the control to the other player, and is then allowed to play again. For a more detailed exposition of this phenomenon interested readers should consult Hofstadter (1979).

Yazdani (1983) presents a full computer literacy course in BBC Structured BASIC which incorporates a number of ideas referred to in Tables 5.1 and 5.2 and some of those in Table 5.3.

## LOGO programming

Papert (1980) has argued that in order to achieve the full educational benefits of LOGO programming, it needs to be carried out in what is known as a 'microworld': a limited portion of the real world whose characteristics can be easily understood. Computer-based microworlds would constitute a very good complement to those normally used by children up to now (such as Meccano sets) and would be as effective, if not more so. The most well known of these computational microworlds has been turtle graphics. This is a computing package (based around a mechanical device with the same name) which will take commands from children in a way similar to their pet 'turtle' if it could understand them. In this way children succeed in drawing wonderful shapes by giving simple commands to the computer.

Figure 5.1, taken from Howe et al. (1984), presents a set of steps used to compose a procedure for drawing a triangle and a square. The programmer then attempts to build a house out of a square and a triangle leading to a shape different to the expected house. He then debugs the procedure for the house and achieves the desired effect in a structured way. Figure 5.2, taken from Burnet (1984), shows how two ideas, those of iteration and the house-drawing procedure, can lead to a totally unexpected new picture. Table 5.3 summarizes the important aspects of LOGO.

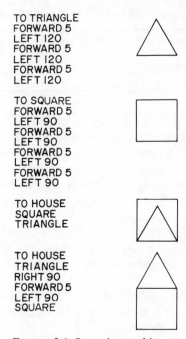

```
TO TRIANGLE
FORWARD 5
LEFT 120
FORWARD 5
LEFT 120
FORWARD 5
LEFT 120
```

```
TO SQUARE
FORWARD 5
LEFT 90
FORWARD 5
LEFT 90
FORWARD 5
LEFT 90
FORWARD 5
LEFT 90
```

```
TO HOUSE
SQUARE
TRIANGLE
```

```
TO HOUSE
TRIANGLE
RIGHT 90
FORWARD 5
LEFT 90
SQUARE
```

FIGURE 5.1 Steps in reaching a
procedure to draw a house

AI is fond of using microworlds in all its area of research, as microworlds can easily be formalized and therefore programmed. The most influential AI work in natural language processing (Winograd, 1972) converses with the users about a small world of a table top with a number of coloured blocks

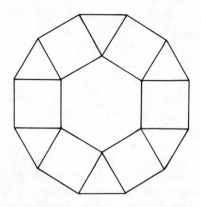

FIGURE    5.2 The    effect    of
combining  iteration  with  the
procedure of Figure 5.1

inhabiting it. The computer program is capable not only of obeying orders in this world, but also of discussing the world in detail. The obvious hope of researchers has been that principles of representing and using knowledge in microworlds would generalize to the real world scale problems, in the same way as a child would, playing with such blocks.

TABLE 5.3 Some powerful ideas in LOGO programming

| | |
|---|---|
| 3.1 | Learning the rules which govern a domain-automated world (a microworld) |
| 3.2 | Learning how people/animals/objects behave on moving from the domain of numbers to objects |
| 3.3 | Learning to instruct others |
| 3.4 | Making lists |
| 3.5 | Interchanging data and procedure – self-modifying programming |
| 3.6 | Recursion in data structures |

On a more technical side, LOGO is a list processing language based on LISP, which means that it incorporates LISP's symbolic manipulation capabilities. Lists, which are the basic data structures in LISP, are more flexible than the 'arrays' of BASIC. People in the real world also have familiarity with shopping lists, etc., where objects of different kinds are all kept in the same list. Furthermore in LOGO, as in LISP, procedures are kept in the same format as data structures and a program, during execution, can modify its own code and therefore its own behaviour.

**PROLOG programming**

The programming languages mentioned so far all belong to a class of language known as 'procedural'. A program is composed of a number of procedures explaining how a task is accomplished. PROLOG presents an alternative approach known as 'declarative' programming where the user specifies objects and the relationships between them and the PROLOG 'inference engine' works out how to get from the given information the user's requested conclusion. PROLOG offers a database and a method for searching this database for special instances of a fact or a relationship. PROLOG's properties are listed in Table 5.4.

TABLE 5.4 Some powerful ideas in PROLOG programming

| | |
|---|---|
| 4.1 | Declarative programming: Say what you want and leave the system to work out how to get it for you |
| 4.2 | Learning to specify facts, objects, actions clearly |
| 4.3 | Dealing with a collection of facts (databases) |
| 4.4 | Learning how to search for a special instance of a fact (pattern-matching) |

In recent years the use of PROLOG in education has been the subject of a number of investigations. Building and querying simple databases of interesting information, when combined with PROLOG's capability to draw higher-level inferences from the facts it has been given (Figure 5.3), seems to offer a very strong educational tool (Ennals, 1984). The pupil learns with enthusiasm, not only the information contained in the database, but also develops logical thinking.

---

*Facts:*
  Elizabeth is_the_mother_of Charles
  Philip is_the_father_of Charles
  Elizabeth is_the_mother_of Anne
  Philip is_the_father_of Anne
  Anne is_the_mother_of Peter
*Rules:*
  X is_a_parent_of Y if X is_the_mother_of Y
  X is_a_parent_of Y if X is_the_father_of Y
*Question:*
  Elizabeth is_the_mother_of Charles?
*Answer:*
  YES
*Question:*
  X is_a_parent_of Anne?
*Answer:*
  X = Elizabeth
  X = Philip
  No (more) answers
*Question:*
  X is_a_parent_of Y and Y is_a_parent_of Peter?
*Answer:*
  X = Elizabeth
  X = Philip
  No (more) answers

---

FIGURE 5.3 Example of PROLOG's ability to draw
inferences

PROLOG, for example, has been used to set up a database of information about particular historical events, and children then query the database in order to discover the cause of events. Nichol and Dean (1984) argue that this would give the children the 'feel' for what it is to be a historian looking for information, sifting the evidence. In addition to acting as a database of information, PROLOG can also be viewed as a general-purpose AI programming language. The difference is, however, in the style of programming: something which Kowalski (1984) has argued is in itself an important turning point. In languages such as BASIC, or even LOGO, the user has to explain to the computer 'how' to perform actions, but when using PROLOG the user only needs to specify 'what' is to be done. The decision how to do the task is left to PROLOG's own powerful search mechanism. It has been argued that this new way of looking at computer programming is, in itself, a very powerful idea.

### AI programming

Some advocates of the use of AI programming environments have gone further than the suggestions made here. They argue that by encouraging as many people as possible to write programs in the same way as AI scientists, we would 'introduce them to ideas about themselves, their minds, and the universe in which they find themselves, which they might otherwise not have encountered' (Coker, 1984).

Pupils can attempt to use AI programming environments in order to produce simple programs which have a certain level of 'intelligence'. They move from the position of being experimented on to doing the experimentation. By trying to write a program which learns to play a game of noughts and crosses, for example, the pupils may begin to realize what learning actually is. This rather more serious claim for the benefits of AI, together with the claims made earlier in this paper, need serious consideration by psychologists.

## CONCLUDING REMARKS

AI programming environments are tailored to human beings, minimizing the cognitive load put on a naive user, as opposed to optimizing the machine's efficiency. Yazdani (1984) presents four such environments based around LOGO, SOLO, PROLOG and POP–11. the practical contribution of such environments is that they make it possible to design computing systems which are educational, fun, and which relate to children's basic feelings.

Using sophisticated AI programming languages, as well as their supplementation with educational microworlds, provides an exciting possibility of learning abstract concepts such as problem solving. What is an open question is whether the pupil who learns powerful new ideas while playing with a microworld could, in fact, reapply them in the real world.

Lighthill (1972) pinpoints the obsession with microworlds in his most effective critique of AI:

> Most robots are designed from the outset to operate in a world as like as possible to the conventional child's world as seen by man; they play games, they do puzzles, they build towers of bricks, they recognise pictures in drawing-books ('bear on rug with ball'); although the rich emotional character of the child's world is totally absent.

AI has not yet been able to translate its successful attempts with microworlds to the real world. There seems to be such a level of increase in complexity of the domain when moving away from the microworlds to the real ones, that most lessons need to be relearned. If AI microworld principles have not yet been generalized for the building of 'real world' scale systems (for an informed view, see Winograd and Flores, 1986, where Winograd complains about this own earlier work), then maybe children will not be able to generalize the lessons they learn either. These are empirical questions to which the answers provided by AI and developmental psychology may amplify each other.

Finding evidence for the role that analogy and metaphor play in cognitive development are issues which need a good deal of research especially from the perspective of developmental psychology. However, the untested claim that computer programming languages are a rich source of powerful ideas, ripe for analogical use, has already shown some positive results after careful preliminary evaluations by Lawler (1985) and Lawler, du Boulay, Hughes and McLeod (1986). My own experience of computer programming and its effects on my students gives me the confidence to invite psychologists to test this claim empirically.

The major weakness of microworlds (Lawler, 1984) and the free-learning environment idea on which they are based may prove to be exactly what makes them so powerful. They can cope with a large variety of possibilities, limited only by the imagination of the user. The user is free to choose his own problems and the route to their solutions. This approach, while increasing the pupil's motivation, simultaneously decreases learning efficiency. The pupil may simply not be very good at selecting his own learning strategy. Developmental psychology research which is relevant to addressing such questions is discussed in detail by Simon in Chapter 6 of this volume.

This shortcoming may be alleviated by designing 'course-ware' within which such activity is fitted. Here a human teacher holds the pupil's hand when necessary and leaves him free to explore when educationally effective. In other words, the shortcoming has so far been in viewing these systems as complete environments. However, they are in fact elements of a larger human environment where the emotional context is provided by the human teacher.

My own personal view is that attempting to build complete tutoring systems or learning environments is fruitless. Teaching and learning are such complex tasks that we should instead attempt to build computational tools for practising teachers who will customize them to their own individual way of teaching. To do this three elements are needed – students, teachers and the computational system.

# REFERENCES

Atherton, R. (1982). *Structured programming in COMAL*, Ellis Horwood, Chichester.

Attisha, M., and Yazdani, M. (1983). A microcomputer-based tutor for teaching arithmetic skills, *Instructional Science*, 12, 333–342.

Attisha, M., and Yazdani, M. (1984). An expert system for diagnosing children's multiplication errors, *Instructional Science*, 13, 79–92.

Barchan, J., Woodmansee, B., and Yazdani, M. (1986). A Prolog-based tool for French grammar analysis, *Instructional Science* (in press).

Bitzer, D. L. (1976). The wide world of computer-based education. In M. Rubmoff and M. Yovits (eds), *Advances in Computers*, Vol. 15, Academic Press, New York.

Boden, M. A. (1983). The educational implications of artificial intelligence. In W. Maxwell (ed.), *Thinking*, Franklin Institute Press, Hillsdale, N.J.

Bramer, M. (1980). *COMAL–80 – Adding structure to BASIC*, Computer assisted learning group, Open University.

Brown, P. (1982). *PASCAL from BASIC*, Addison Wesley, Reading, Mass.

Burnet, D. (1984). LOGO for teacher education. In M. Yazdani, (ed.), *New Horizons in Educational Computing*, Ellis Horwood/John Wiley, Chichester.

Burton, R. R. (1982). DEBUGGY: diagnosis of errors in basic mathematical skills. In D. Sleeman and J. S. Brown, (eds.), *Intelligent Tutoring Systems*, Academic Press, New York.

Christensen, B. (1982). COMAL: an educational alternative, in C. Smith, (ed.), *Microcomputers in Education*, Ellis Horwood, Chichester.

Clancey, W. J. (1979). Tutoring rules for guiding a case method dialogue, *International Journal of Man-Machine Studies*, 11, 25–49.

Coker, M. (1984). Creating a 'good' programming environment for beginners. In M. Yazdani (ed.), *New Horizons in Educational Computing*, Ellis Horwood/John Wiley, Chichester.

Ennals, R. (1984). Teaching logic as a computer language in schools. In M. Yazdani (ed.), *New Horizons in Educational Computing*, Ellis Horwood/John Wiley, Chichester.

Hofstadter, D. R. (1979). *Godel, Escher, Bach: An Eternal Braid*, Basic Books, New York.

Howe, J., Ross, P. M., Johnson, K. J., and Inglis, R. (1984). Model building, in mathematics and LOGO. In M. Yazdani (ed.), *New Horizons in Educational Computing*, Ellis Horwood/John Wiley, Chichester.

Imlah, W., and du Boulay, B. (1985). Robust natural language parsing in computer assisted language instruction, *System*, 13, 137–147.

Kowalski, R. (1984). Logic as a computer language for children. In M. Yazdani (ed.), *New Horizons in Educational Computing*, Ellis Horwood/John Wiley, Chichester.

Lawler, R. (1984). Designing computer-based microworlds. In M. Yazdani (ed.), *New Horizons in Educational Computing*, Ellis Horwood/John Wiley, Chichester.

Lawler, R. (1985). *Computer Experience and Cognitive Development*, Ellis Horwood/ John Wiley, Chichester.

Lawler, R., du Boulay, B., Hughes, M., and McLeod, H. (1986). *Cognition and Computers*, Ellis Horwood/John Wiley, Chichester.

Lighthill, J. (1972). *Artificial Intelligence: Report to the Science Research Council*, Science Research Council, London.

Nichol, J., and Dean, J. (1984). Pupils, computers and history teaching. In M. Yazdani (ed.), *New Horizons in Educational Computing*, Ellis Horwood/John Wiley, Chichester.

O'Shea, T., and Self, J. (1983). *Learning and Teaching with Computers*, Harvester Press, Brighton.

Papert, S. (1980). *Mindstorms: Children, Computers and Powerful Ideas*, Harvester Press, Brighton; Basic Books, New York.

Shortcliffe, E. H. (1976). *Computer-based Medical Consultations: MYCIN*, American Elsevier, New York.

Skinner, B. F. (1958). Teaching machines, *Science*, **128**.

Sleeman, D., and Brown, J. S. (eds) (1982). *Intelligent Tutoring Systems*, Academic Press, New York.

Winograd, T. (1972). *Understanding Natural Language*, Edinburgh University Press.

Winograd, T., and Flores, C. F. (1986). *Understanding Computers and Cognition*, Ablex Publishing Corporation, Norwood, N.J.

Woods, P., and Hartley, J. R. (1971). Some learning models for arithmetic tasks and their use in computer-based learning, *British Journal of Educational Psychology*, **41**, 38–48.

Yazdani, M. (1983). *Start Programming with the Electron*, Addison Wesley, London.

Yazdani, M. (ed.) (1984). *New Horizons in Educational Computing*, Ellis Horwood/ John Wiley, Chichester.

Yazdani, M., and Narayanan, A. (eds) (1984). *Artificial Intelligence: Human Effects*, Ellis Horwood/John Wiley, Chichester.

Computers, Cognition and Development
Edited by J. Rutkowska and C. Crook
© 1987 John Wiley & Sons Ltd

CHAPTER 6

# Claims for LOGO – What Should we Believe and Why?

TONY SIMON

## SUMMARY

This chapter evaluates educational claims regarding LOGO in terms of their theoretical basis, implied model of the learner and supporting evidence. It argues for rejecting Papert's self-discovery approach in favour of structured instructional methods involving analyses of the tasks in question and the processes of learning that they involve.

The LOGO programming language was developed by Seymour Papert and his colleagues for a specific purpose; to revolutionize education. The aim was to create a new generation of children who were 'in love with learning' and whose education was effective and enjoyable. By providing an environment where abstract concepts can be made concrete and then manipulated, Papert predicts that the 'LOGO experience' will change the very nature and benefit of education. He believes more meaningful learning will occur when children deal with the errors in their programming as illustrative exercises in the problem-solving process.

However, it is not clear that these expectations are the necessary consequences of even an intensive experience of working with LOGO. In this chapter I shall argue that the psychological theory which advises the method of LOGO use advocated by Papert is basically insufficient for this purpose. I shall illustrate how previous educational programmes based on the same theory have failed to produce radically superior results than those produced by traditional methods. I shall then consider the conception of learning inherent in current theorizing and advocate the use of process models of thinking and learning as guides to producing the fullest exploitation of the potential of LOGO. Finally I shall address the specific claim that using LOGO will spontaneously result in improved problem-solving skills which will be widely transferable.

## LOGO, EDUCATION AND PIAGETIAN THEORY

The whole philosophy of Papert's approach to educational computing is rooted firmly in Piagetian theory. The relationship, stated both overtly and covertly in *Mindstorms* (Papert, 1980), is based on Piaget's view of the growth of knowledge as 'genetic epistemology'. The essence of this concept is that the knowledge that one acquires is shaped and facilitated by the knowledge that one already has; for Piaget this is the process of accommodation and assimilation of new information by pre-existing schema (see Brainerd, 1978). The consequence of this in both the positions of Piaget and of Papert is that it is the individual who constructs his or her own cognitive processing system; that there is only limited scope for 'acceleration' of this process by external agents. Since others do not share the same knowledge structures as the learner, they cannot 'create' for them new knowledge that is consistent with those structures.

Thus, it is Papert's claim that because children are fed information in educational establishments rather than being active in the process, they are being denied the opportunity to learn in the natural way that Piagetian theory describes development. As a result, Papert advocates the 'learning-by-doing' or self-discovery approach to learning where children are allowed to discover knowledge for themselves, at their own pace and in ways suited to their own individual style of thinking. In this way, he predicts, learning will become a self-generating process where existing knowledge creates new discoveries merely by the process of activity.

'Turtle graphics', the introductory 'baby talk' of LOGO, is intended to be the environment where active learning is expected to occur as children encounter and try to solve fundamental problems in maths and geometry while attempting to achieve such simple goals as drawing a house. The graphics system works by the user giving body-centred commands such as 'forward', 'backward', 'left' or 'right' and some order of magnitude. These commands are then followed by a floor-crawling robot or a 'screen turtle' which leaves a precise trail of the path that it has taken. Thus, by repeating the sequence 'FORWARD 100 (units), RIGHT 90 (degrees)' four times, the end result will be a perfect square. Such instructions can then simply be written as procedures which, when called by name, will execute exactly the same commands. There is also the facility to combine procedures so that individual routines can be used as building blocks, or sub-procedures, in a more complex program.

Thus, having written the procedure 'square' as above, and similarly 'triangle', the larger procedure of 'house' could be defined by simply calling 'square' then 'triangle' (with the necessary de-bugging – see Papert, 1980 p. 61). Using this system, it is envisaged that even very young children will be able to 'teach' the computer to draw simple and complex shapes. Papert believes that, as a result of this process, where the computer literally executes the commands it has been given so that the resulting shape shows any errors that have been made, children can learn in an effective way about concepts in maths and geometry, as well as in other areas.

The question that is to be addressed here is whether such a learning environment can be effective if left almost entirely to the process of self-discovery, as Papert advocates. It has already been pointed out that this assumption is based on his belief in the validity of Piaget's theory of cognitive growth, and herein lies an indication to the answer, for Papert's ideas are not the first, or even the most direct, attempt to translate Piagetian theory into the classroom. At least four major programmes have been developed which created early and pre-school curricula whose content and methods were inspired by Piagetian theory. I will examine just two of them directly but, as can be seen, all of them were of limited success when compared to the radical results that they predicted.

Weikart's (1973) 'Open Framework Program' concentrated on developing classification skills and also used two non-Piagetian curricula as evaluation controls. One of these was an 'interventionist', or direct teaching curriculum, the other was a 'horticulturalist', or self-directed programme (Brainerd, 1983). The 'Open Framework Program' was a fairly intensive course with multiple measures providing assessment of the 3–4 year old students on standardized intelligence tests, teacher ratings and expert assessment. Results showed that all of the assessed programme produced equal and sizeable gains; the Piagetian scheme failing, therefore, to produce significantly better levels of learning.

The most directly translated Piagetian programme was the University of Wisconsin's 'Piagetian Preschool Education Program' (Bingham-Newman, 1974). This long-term programme was carefully evaluated using concrete-operational tests, Peabody Picture Vocabulary and Raven's Progressive Matrices Tests, and was also compared with two traditional pre-schools. Again there were significant improvements in performance from both types of curricula but, leaving aside the fact that what small differences did occur favoured the traditional scheme, this can again be taken as a failure of the Piagetian scheme to deliver the kind of radical benefits that its theorists would predict. Similar results were found for schemes reported by Lavetelli (1970) and Kamii and DeVries (1974). All of this has led Brainerd (1978) to the opinion that 'on the whole, one is forced to conclude that Piaget-oriented educators have failed to establish a case for restructuring traditional curricula along Piagetian lines' (p. 298).

It would seem, therefore, that what evidence does exist leads one to expect that any further implementations of Piagetian education schemes are unlikely to produce spectacular results. Furthermore, there is little reason to expect that merely by introducing an alternative medium, such as the microcomputer, the prospects will significantly change. It is my contention that an answer to the problem of how to exploit the potential of new resources such as LOGO lies in the adoption of an instructional psychology of the type outlined by Glaser (1985) which attempts to solve the problems 'both of understanding and of teaching learning and thinking skills' (p. 616). In other words, using the knowledge generated by new information-processing approaches to learning and cognition to state how learning occurs, under what conditions and how, if at all, these processes can be utilized in instructional settings.

However, before moving on to this alternative approach, I want to return briefly to the issue of using the study of mechanisms of 'natural learning' (or development) to guide the process of instruction. This issue is addressed directly by Gelman (1985) who cautiously urges those interested in undertanding the acquisition of learning skills to look for possible clues in studies of cognitive development. The enormous difference between Gelman's and Papert's positions, however, is their conception of what the mechanisms and processes of development are. Gelman directly states that Piagetian theory does not provide a satisfactory characterization of the ways in which younger children differ cognitively from older children and adults. Instead, she outlines a number of information-processing mechanisms of which all or some may contribute to developing cognition, and possibly learning and knowledge acquisition also. In the next section I shall examine recent investigations into the processes involved in learning and instruction and show how these can be used so that learning with LOGO is more likely to be guaranteed than fortuitous.

## AN INSTRUCTIONAL APPROACH

In this section I shall examine, in some depth, two alternative types of approaches to LOGO. Unlike Papert's, the rationalization for these are based, to a greater or lesser extent, on current information-processing conceptions of learning and development.

The first of these, originating in the work of the Edinburgh group, recognizes the value of one particular method both as a research tool and as an effective learning environment because it has the same benefits in each case. This is the method of learning by model building. Howe (1979) describes in detail how model building enables students to learn about the underlying structure and/or mechanisms of a total entity by building a model of it. Yet, unlike the process where a particular set of components is used to construct a specific object (as a child would construct a model aeroplane), the real learning process begins when the modeller is creative and can define a set of general principles which will serve to model a variety of entities. I shall return to this point shortly.

Using Meccano as an example, Howe outlines six parts of the process of efficient model building which the student will have to master. The modeller must gain total familiarity firstly with the basic building components and secondly with the basic assembly operations. The modeller must fully understand the structure and mechanisms of the object to be modelled and s/he must also be able to apply some knowledge (or theory) about constructing things in general (such as bracing, reinforcing, etc.). The model should be planned and, where possible, split into sub-units to be assembled separately. Finally, the modeller should be able to cope with mismatches between the 'thing to be modelled' and the emerging representation, in terms of the available components.

Howe illustrates how the Meccano system is hierarchically organized into ten levels of difficulty which move from primitive models, built from few components, to elaborate models comprising a multitude of elements. At each level an appropriate 'kit of parts' is provided to enable a range of models to be built and, more importantly, conversion kits are provided to enable the user to move from one level to the next.

It is exactly this type of structured approach which Howe has suggested be used as an optimal environment for learning geometry with LOGO (Howe, Ross, Johnson and Inglis, 1984). Simple shapes can be built from few components (such as houses from squares and triangles) and yet open-ended elaboration is built into the system. It is for the teaching system to help structure the 'kits of parts' for tackling various tasks and also to provide the 'conversion kits' in the form of explanations and examples. Apart from being an effective system this is also desirable because, as Howe states, 'such an approach provides the kind of close guidance which a novice needs on being introduced to new skills, new concepts and new ideas. Yet it does allow him to experiment and to be creative' (1979, p. 217).

As mentioned above, once the modeller passes the novice stage, s/he may be able to begin to define more general components which will allow the modelling of whole classes of concepts or entities. Howe (1979) gives the example of a child defining a 'subprocedure' for a triangle which draws a line and then changes the heading of the turtle. Thus to draw a triangle one need only repeat this three times or, for any other shape, repeat it as many times as the shape has sides. This is just the kind of general rule production that Papert believes will result from children recognizing the similarities between problems when involved in his purely problem-solving approach to

LOGO. Yet Howe argues that this is very unlikely to happen: the weight of evidence from cognitive science would predict that this could only happen 'when a person has extensive domain specific knowledge, suggesting that in the early stages of learning emphasis should be placed on content learning' (Howe, 1979).

LOGO can significantly enhance education by providing children with a tool that enables them to understand geometrical concepts by making explicit all the steps needed to create a model of the desired entity. But what is the best way to expose children to the system? Papert is strongly against content teaching while Howe, on the other hand, believes that not to provide basic knowledge is to disadvantage the child by refusing them the most important information in the process. This surely must provide one of the most important directions for future work. The inference appears to be that the structured approach to LOGO use in present-day schools will be a far more efficient, though less utopian, implementation than Papert's.

Another alternative to Papert has not yet dealt directly with LOGO to any great degree. It is embedded in that fact that, largely in North America in recent years, the field of cognitive development has literally been transformed as information-processing approaches to explaining cognitive growth have replaced traditional Piagetian analyses (see Flavell and Markman, 1983; Siegler, 1983). The most significant transformations that have resulted from this change have been in the level of description and specification of the processes that underly children's cognition, an understanding of the special capacity limitations that apply to the immature processing system and a renewed interest in attempting to specify the precise mechanisms by which development (Sternberg, 1984) and learning (Brown, Bransford, Ferrara and Campione, 1983) take place. It is this new enterprise of rigorously defining the conditions and processes of learning which I will use to guide my recommendations of how LOGO should be used in order to be more certain of obtaining a real increase in the understanding of the learner.

I shall initially mention two recent models which concentrate on the component processes of cognitive activity in order to define the activities of learning and teaching. These are the four-stage approach outlined by Glaser (1985) and the tetrahedral model as explicated by Brown et al. (1983). In his 'letter for a time capsule', Glaser tells the people of the 21st century of the genesis of an instructional psychology that was forming as he wrote in 1985. He tells of a discipline which is beginning to work very hard on the solution of problems relating to four stages of the task of, first, understanding, and then teaching thinking skills to children and adults. These four stages are: (1) the specification of a goal state (or identifying the instructional objectives), (2) specifying the initial state (or assessing the learner's current knowledge and ability), (3) specifying operations to turn the initial state into the goal state (or identifying the teaching techniques and materials), and (4) assessing achievement of subgoals to inform further teaching (or developing achievement and diagnostic tests).

There is a very close relation of these four goals to three of the four points in the more general 'tetrahedral' model of Jenkins (1979) and Bransford (1979), which is discussed in some depth by Brown *et al.* (1983). Their consideration of the 'characteristics of the learner' relates very closely to Glaser's goal of evaluating the initial state of the learner. Likewise, there is a close correspondence between Glaser's instructional techniques goal and Brown *et al.*'s consideration of 'learning activities', although the latter is not solely concerned with instruction. Finally, Brown *et al.*'s consideration of the 'criterial tasks' of learning bears considerable relation (albeit in less instructional terms) both to Glaser's specification of a goal state and to the use of diagnostic and achievement tests. The tetrahedral model also contains a fourth node which urges consideration of 'nature of the materials' when evaluating learning; undoubtedly something anybody interested in instruction must surely do. Let us now take Glaser's four goals and see what current psychological knowledge has to offer which may guide instructional principles.

**Specify goal state**

Specifying the target of any learning or instruction is an obvious first step; how can one know what or how to teach, or whether it has been learned, until a target is set? (The most sceptical reader may at this point suggest that it is possible for unstructured LOGO use to appear effective precisely because no clear end-point is set). Yet the problem remains of specifying the precise goal state that is required. Two available options are to specify a goal ability or some form of goal representation.

If one is going to specify a goal ability, however, one must be very clear about precisely what that ability involves. For example, stating that one wishes to produce memory performance in a 5-year-old that is equivalent to that of a 7-year-old provides very few guidelines for instruction. What is necessary is a detailed task analysis that enables one to restate the intention far more clearly; in this case one might wish to teach the 5-year-old to understand and use the strategy of verbal rehearsal which would likely result in performance similar to that of a 7-year-old (Keeney, Cannizzo and Flavell, 1967). Likewise, it is of little use merely to state a wish to enable a child who fails simple mathematics problems, such as addition and subtraction, to pass them. Unless one is able to clearly state the necessary rules that the child will need to understand in order to successfully and reliably produce the correct answer, no guidance for instruction exists and there can be no certainty about the outcome of any such attempts. Despite expecting that using LOGO will somehow spontaneously produce an understanding of mathematics and geometry principles in the programmer, Papert clearly fails to provide any criteria for evaluating when this process has occurred.

### Specify initial state

Since this second goal is effectively attempting to capture the same information as the first but in the form of a 'baseline measure', the same argument applies; how can one know what to teach if one is unaware of what the student is currently capable of? Similarly, the question of characterization of that knowledge or ability applies. Experimentally, it is reasonably simple to determine whether or not a child is spontaneously rehearsing information or not (Flavell, Beach and Chinsky, 1966), although it is not always so clear in negative instances whether this is because they cannot or, for some reason, do not do so (Brown et al., 1983). Nevertheless, the presence or absence of a target behaviour can, in most instances, be determined.

A somewhat thornier issue arises when attempting to determine what an individual knows about a particular task or problem. Despite an arguably limited scope of application, one very powerful method is the specification of a set of production rules which explicitly state what actions a person will carry out when faced with a given set of conditions. A production rule is the pairing of an antecedent condition (or conditions), such as 'when faced with X', and a subsequent action, such as 'carry out Y'. By building up an individual's rule set, or 'production system', through testing and observation, one can characterize their knowledge of a situation at any given time and, more usefully, predict their performance when faced with a given task. Young (1978) has shown this to be a very powerful technique for characterizing the performance of young children on block seriation tasks.

The two examples given above deal with assessment of the behavioural level and at what one might term the 'procedural knowledge' level, or rules for dealing with certain conditions. What they have not dealt with is assessment of 'declarative' knowledge: knowledge about facts and relations. This is an area which is gaining increasing importance in developmental cognitive theorizing and is one which shows a considerable congruence with Piaget's concept of genetic epistemology. In other words, it is becoming clear that the knowledge that one already possesses will, to a certain extent, guide and facilitate subsequent knowledge acquisition. There are essentially two conceptions of knowledge which bear on instructional issues: those of the 'static' and 'dynamic' views of knowledge (Brown et al., 1983).

A 'static' conception of knowledge concerns facts that are potentially available for the individual to bring to bear on any particular activity. Chi (1978, 1985) has elegantly demonstrated how differences in the knowledge base of novices and experts on subjects as diverse as chess and dinosaurs can completely override age differences on memory and classification tasks. On tasks where the adult subjects are novices, such as a memory for chess pieces, they exhibit typical child-like performances despite producing typical adult performances on a digit-span task. Similarly, child experts perform like adults on tasks where they have considerable knowledge, and like children on tasks where they don't. From such an example it is clear that assessments of existing knowledge are an essential basis for instruction; it is plainly inaccurate to assume that all children know less than do all adults. The more practical issue concerns 'dynamic' conceptions of knowledge for it is beginning to become clear that differences in performance in learning and general academic success are accounted for, in part at least, by differences in the ability to use pre-existing knowledge as a device for further and more efficient knowledge acquisition.

Such a view, that differences in the ability to selectively encode new information and to compare and combine it with existing knowledge lead to differences in general cognition, is explicit in current conceptions of intelligence (Sternberg, 1985) and as a possible mechanism of cognitive growth (Siegler, 1984). In an academic situation such processes have been demonstrated by Bransford, Stein, Shelton and Owings (1981) to account for differences in the learning of text passages. Children were read passages concerning two types of window-cleaning robots; an extendible one for washing the windows of two-storey houses and a non-extendible one for use on high-rise buildings. Further characteristics, such as lightness and the provision of suction cups and a parachute (for the non-extendible robot) and heaviness with spiked feet (for the extendible device) were not explicitly explained. The differences in recall for the passages and comprehension of the relevance of the properties lay in the ability of students to 'activate' knowledge that would help to interpret the significance of these properties. A note far from discordant with Papert's view is struck by Bereiter and Scardamalia (1985) who suggest that traditional educational methods probably encourage this lack of spontaneous activation, creating what they call 'inert knowledge'. Nevertheless, evaluations of the extent of knowledge available and ability to use it in further acquisition must surely play a part in the instructional process.

So it appears that there are at least four ways of determining the initial state of the learner in terms of both knowledge and skills. Almost certainly all of these aspects will bear heavily on the progress of any learning and should all be taken into account when instruction is being designed. Traditional educational methods, about which Papert is so scathing, involve such evaluations, albeit rudimentary ones, and yet the self-discovery approach ignores all such assessments. It is scant justification to argue that since no instruction is involved, no knowledge of the learner is necessary. However, let us now turn to actual methods of instruction and examine whether any effective techniques are available.

**Instructional techniques**

Having established a clear idea of the goal state of learning and also having gained an evaluation of the knowledge and abilities that the learner possesses should considerably aid the process of deciding how to go about transforming the initial state into the goal state. However, since there is never likely to be a single route to this objective, the most fruitful discussion is one which considers the elements that have been found to be necessary to promote effective learning. The use of training, or what is now being called 'intervention research' (Brown *et al.*, 1983), has a long tradition in psychology, both as a method of model testing and of modifying behaviour. A number of studies, both in instructional fields and in mainstream developmental cognitive research, have together begun to build up a picture of what makes for effective, long-lasting, and in some instances, generalizeable learning.

Some of the earliest studies in this field were concerned solely with investigating the nature of memory development in young children. They have since been termed 'blind' training studies (Brown *et al.*, 1983) since they provided only instructions to carry out a given strategy or behaviour without providing any explanation as to its nature or likely benefit. Nevertheless, the immediate results, in terms of recall, of instructing non-rehearsers to whisper the names of stimuli to themselves have shown the technique to be highly effective. The major problem, however, is that very many children who have benefited from using the strategy then fail to maintain its use and their subsequent performance returns to pre-training levels (Keeney *et al.*, 1967).

One solution to this problem is to provide the learner with some extra information which will encourage the maintenance of the target behaviour; termed 'informed' training by Brown *et al.* (1983). Surprisingly, it seems that the nature of this extra information need be no more than the assurance that the target behaviour will produce the desired effect (Kennedy and Miller, 1976), although this may only be true of simple strategies such as rehearsal. The real value of informed-training studies is that they can specify the content and form of valuable instructional experiences. An example of this can be seen from an experiment that some colleagues and I recently carried out to evaluate the role of training on an educational computing task (Simon, McShane and Radley, 1987).

The target activity was a computer game called RAYBOX designed by the Microelectronics in Education Programe to foster problem-solving skills in 10–12 year olds. The screen shows an eight-by-eight grid within which are hidden a specified number of 'atoms'. The player has to fire 'rays' into the box from the perimeter and, by observing the effects that the atoms have on the rays, infer and predict the position of the atoms. Three groups of children were all taught the rudiments of the game. One group was then allowed three 'self-discovery' sessions in which to improve their skill at playing. Also over three sessions, the blind- and informed-training groups were taught three simple atom-finding strategies, but only the informed-training group was provided with explanations as to how and why they worked.

At both an immediate and a delayed post-test, three weeks later, children in the informed-training group were more efficient, planful and uniform in their problem solving than those in either of the other two groups. The experiment, therefore, not only produced effective learning but also specified an instructional environment for the task in question. Informed-training experiments have been shown to be able to satisfy the criteria that educationalists would apply to any measure of learning in that they can produce stable learning and, in many cases, they also produce realistic transfer, both over time and to similar tasks and abilities (see Brown *et al.*, 1983).

A major aim, of course, for any worthwhile educational enterprise, is not merely to teach but also to encourage students to learn for themselves. Intervention research has shown that it is capable of training the development of executive skills such as planning, checking and monitoring so that individuals are effectively providing themselves with informed training. Thus, in 'self-control' training (Brown *et al.*, 1983) explicit guidance (such as self-questioning and checking) is given about the management of cognitive activity and this growing self-provision of information about the effectiveness of performance fosters ideal conditions for the maintenance and transfer of the acquired skill. Meichenbaum (1985) has demonstrated how effective such techniques can be in facilitating stable and self-regulated learning in both normal and non-normal children. With careful guidance, such self-regulated learning can be employed as a means of teaching knowledge acquisition itself. This concept, dubbed 'learning to learn' by Bransford *et al.* (1981), is attracting a considerable amount of research effort in instructional psychology.

Clearly, the specification of instructional techniques is a complex and developing area but strong directions are emerging and some sound principles already exist. The strength of such techniques as do exist is that the learning that they will produce is predictable, stable and uniform. Realistic goals can be set and achieved and little is left to chance. At the beginning of the chapter it was shown how ineffective Piagetian curricula have been in achieving similar results. In contrast, it is hard to deny that there is a growing body of evidence which points to the efficacy of new instructional techniques.

### Diagnostic tests

The last of Glaser's goals is the development of tests for the 'assessment and monitoring of attained performance that provide information for the effective guidance of learning' (1985, p. 618). The aim here is that instruction can become truly dynamic as new goal states are continually developed on the basis of evaluations of attained knowledge and performance. It has already been seen that psychology is currently capable of both kinds of assessments mentioned under the first and second goals: behaviour and, to some extent, representations. However, this topic is particularly interesting from the point of view of future research.

One of the most fruitful approaches to diagnostic testing in recent years has been the method of building models of a student's level of understanding (or misunderstanding) of a problem. A good example of this is the production-system model of simple mathematical ability which Young and O'Shea (1981) developed to characterize the typical mistakes made in such exercises by 10-year-old children. However, such 'static models' are of limited use as direct instructional tools themselves. Far more exciting is the prospect of the large-scale development of interactive modelling systems, such as those developed by Brown and Burton (1978) and Anderson, Farrell and Sauers (1984).

Such systems are usually provided with a formal, or 'black box', model of the task they are trying to teach, such as simple mathematics, and as the student attempts the problems presented, a 'user model' is developed which characterizes the student's level of understanding. By comparison with the formal model, the so-called intelligent tutoring system (Sleeman and Brown, 1982) can identify the student's problems and so present illustrative examples and explanations. These are a few examples of the truly interactive, diagnostic instructional systems of the type envisaged by Glaser which, I believe, illustrate the potential of the contribution that cognitive science has to make to education. At this point I would like to, rather wistfully, suggest that could an 'intelligent LOGO' be produced that could instruct the learning of various problem-solving skills then, and only then, is Papert's vision of children systematically learning 'powerful ideas' (Papert, 1980) merely by interacting with a computer, ever likely to come true.

## REVIEW

This chapter initially illustrated the relationship between Papert's philosophy of the use of LOGO and Piagetian theory and examined the weaknesses of such approaches to learning and education. It then surveyed current approaches to cognitive development, and specifically to instruction. It was demonstrated how process models, both of instructional methods themselves, and of the underlying mechanisms of learning, are beginning to be specified and how these can be used to make reliable predictions about the nature and extent of learning that can be facilitated. It was also proposed that these directions provide the groundwork for the widespread development of intelligent tutoring systems as well as for new classroom teaching schemes.

Given this progress in the understanding of learning and teaching there can be little to recommend rejecting such a position in favour of another unless the alternative has something more convincing to offer in terms of facilitating learning. Papert's belief in the Piagetian system doesn't result in a total rejection of educational intervention. Instead, 'it means supporting children as they build their own intellectual structures with materials drawn from the surrounding culture. In this model, educational intervention means changing the culture, planting new constructive elements in it and eliminating noxious ones' (Papert, 1980. p. 32). I leave the reader to decide which approach they would prefer as a guide to the education of future generations of children.

## WILL THERE BE WIDER BENEFITS FROM USING LOGO?

The final issue that I shall address in this chapter is the claim that grows directly out of Papert's radical vision of the value of LOGO to children's thinking. This is the expectation that, by learning to program in LOGO, children will learn aspects of knowledge-handling and thinking skills which will transfer to far wider areas of cognitive activity and result in more ordered thinking, better problem-solving and a generally higher level of intellectual ability. However, little evidence exists to support Papert's view that this will be the case and this final section will argue that, on the basis of current evidence, no such benefits will accrue without either direct instruction or enormously long periods of intensive learning experience.

In reviewing the issue of the cognitive effects of programming in some detail, Pea and Kurland (1984) outline four levels of programming activity and the sort of transfer likely to accrue from them. While noting the scarcity of evidence on the transfer issue, they make the observation that much of the work that has been done has suffered from a major theoretical weakness which is caused by a 'mismatch between "treatment" and transfer assessments' (p. 158). In other words, most studies have looked for high-level cognitive outcomes from rather low levels of programming activity which, claim Pea and Kurland, would never predict such benefits.

In actual fact, very few rigorous studies have been carried out to evaluate directly the benefits of LOGO for children's thinking, and what has been done has hardly painted a picture of widely generalizable skills emerging. For example, Statz (1973) compared the pre- and post-test performances of sixteen 9- to 11-year-old children who had been taught LOGO for a year, with that of a control group on four problem-solving tests. No significant differences were found on a 'twenty questions' game or the Tower of Hanoi puzzle. These tasks aim to assess the abilities of hierarchical organization, systematic solution and constraint seeking. However, the LOGO group did do better on a game involving the generation of all possible orders of sets of numbers and a word task which assesses classification skills. The most direct inference that one can make from these results is that learning LOGO did not have such a powerful effect as might have been expected from Papert's claims.

Chait (1978) compared individually taught 12-year-olds on comparable concepts but a battery of different tests failed to find any significant changes in scores from pre- to post-test. Gorman and Bourne (1983) compared two groups of children on a variety of rule-learning problems. One group experienced 1 hour of LOGO instruction per week for one school year on top of normal access, while the other group received 0.5 hours per week. The only significant difference was that the 1-hour group made fewer errors than the other group but were no quicker to reach the criterion level. Although one can infer that more LOGO produced less errors, it is not clear that this result is not simply the result of confounding more LOGO with more instruction, thereby invalidating any claim about the inherent benefit of a LOGO experience.

Thus it appears that what little data does exist concerning the qualitative effects on the way children think and solve problems as a result of learning LOGO, tends to support Pea and Kurland's (1984) opinion that Papert's expectations are 'technoromantic' ideas promulgating a 'myth of spontaneous transfer of higher cognitive skills from learning to program' (p. 161). (Perhaps those with a historical sense might be reminded of similar views concerning the claim that learning Latin would improve logical thinking skills.) I shall now turn to an examination of why it is that the hopes of the spontaneous emergence of general problem-solving skills are little more than pipe dreams.

The first confusion that needs to be cleared up is essentially a terminological one. Papert (1980) appears to assume that widely applicable general problem-solving skills are 'powerful ideas', and yet that could not be further from the truth. Newell (1980) uses the analogy of an inverted cone to explain why this should be so. Around the bottom of the cone are very many highly specific problem-solving routines which are very powerful because invoking them in relation to their 'specialist' problem is almost certain to produce a solution. Yet as one travels up the cone, generality is increased at the cost of power. In other words, highly general routines such as knowledge of the utility of planning or checking, can never, in and of themselves, produce a solution to the task. What is essential for general problem-solving skill is a considerable knowledge base of specific routines which are guided by general 'executive' principles.

The problem, therefore, of enabling transfer of general skills is non-existent since by their definition general skills are non-specific and so will apply to many problems. The real problem is the facilitation of the transfer of more powerful specific routines and this, it must be said, is notoriously difficult to do. Having learned to carry out a particular problem-solving task, individuals invariably 'weld' the routines they have acquired to the superficial characteristics of that task and subsequently fail to solve formally identical tasks with even the slightest differences in surface details. Hayes and Simon (1976) demonstrated this phenomenon by translating the Tower of Hanoi task into four 'monster problems' where either monsters or globes are either moved or changed in size to conform to the rules of the problem. What little transfer did occur only did so on functionally equivalent problems; subjects could transfer from one 'moving' problem to the other but not from 'moving' to 'changing' problems.

As Brown et al. (1983) state, the development of problem-solving ability 'consists in part of going from the context-dependent state where resources are welded to the original learning situation to a *relatively* context-independent state where the learner extends the ways in which initially highly constrained knowledge and procedures are used' (p. 142). Furthermore, it appears that not only can this process be aided by instruction, but that unless one is willing to wait an extremely long time for the possibility of this occurring spontaneously, instruction may be the only route. A number of elements to the process of transfer can indeed be isolated and it can be seen that these can be taught very effectively.

Perhaps the major barrier to transfer is the recognition of problem isomorphs, or structurally similar problems. Gick and Holyoak (1980) presented subjects with Duncker's radiation problem where one must kill a tumour in the body by firing low radiation doses from a dispersal of firing sites. These will then cumulatively destroy the tumour but are not individually strong enough to damage the surrounding tissue. Having solved this problem, students were given a structurally identical problem where one needs to attack a castle by sending small groups of soldiers down converging roads, so as not to arouse suspicion but to have a sizeable force at the attack site. Very few students solved the new problem without hints to use the preceding scenario as a guide. Brown et al. (1983, p. 144) review a number of studies which suggest that three principles of instruction can help to overcome this problem.

The first of these is to train problem solving in more than one context; in this way the likelihood of welding a problem-solving routine to any particular set of conditions is lessened. The second technique is to encourage learners to state a general rule since it makes the generality of the routine explicit while it is being learned. Finally, explicit guidance in the range of applicability of problem-solving routines can further facilitate the more flexible use of problem-solving skills that have been acquired. This type of analysis is based on the understanding that transfer and learning are closely related activities and cannot be functionally independent. One aspect of this interdependence is the relation between development of general problem-solving proficiency and the status of one's pre-existing knowledge base.

The issue addressed here is the 'natural' development of general problem-solving abilities. Since Papert would doubtless reject an instructional approach to achieving generality it is important to examine the likelihood of its development without teaching. From all that is currently known about such processes it appears very unlikely that, except in extreme cases of genius, such development is ever likely to occur on a large scale. Hayes (1985) suggests that 'proficiency in some general skills may require vast bodies of knowledge – knowledge that could take years to acquire' (p. 391). This is backed up by Simon's (1980) claim that even a chess grandmaster needs at least 10 years of intensive learning and practice. Hayes (1985) himself shows how almost no 'major' works were produced by the great classical composers until at least the tenth year of their careers. In both of these examples it is likely that both towering genius and intense 'training' contributed to these attainments. Yet, even more closely related findings tend to back up this position. Pea and Kurland (1984) quote an estimate made by Brooks (1980) that a programmer with only three years' experience has usually had some 5000 hours of programming experience. In the face of this necessity for considerable exposure to a problem space, how likely is it that young children using LOGO in an unstructured way for a few hours a week even for a few years will ever attain anything close to general problem-solving skills?

## CONCLUSIONS

It seems that Papert's vision of radical educational advance by a process of self-discovery learning using LOGO is, in truth, little short of 'technoromanticism'. All the available evidence seems to suggest that the method of learning that he advocates will be, at best, unspectacular and, at worst, haphazard and unreliable. Advances in the understanding of the essentials of an instructional psychology based on information-processing analyses of learning appear to hold out hope for sound, stable and, to a realistic extent, general learning. The title of this chapter asks what should we believe, and why. Surely we should believe those who have realistic aims, clear ideas about how to achieve them and evidence that such approaches are effective.

## ACKNOWLEDGEMENTS

I would like to thank John McShane for much fruitful discussion regarding topics covered by this chapter. Thanks also to Rod Nicolson and Chris Smith for their comments on earlier drafts of this chapter.

# REFERENCES

Anderson, J. R., Farrell, R., and Sauers, R. (1984). Learning to program in LISP, *Cognitive Science*, **8**, 87–129.

Bereiter, C., and Scardamalia, M. (1985). Cognitive coping strategies and the problem of 'inert knowledge'. In S. F. Chipman, J. W. Segal, and R. Glaser (eds), *Thinking and Learning Skills*, Vol. 2, Erlbaum, Hillsdale, N. J.

Bingham-Newman, A. M. (1974). Development of logical abilities in early childhood. A longitudinal comparison of the effects of two preschool settings. Unpublished doctoral dissertation. University of Wisconsin, Madison.

Brainerd, C. J. (1978). *Piaget's Theory of Intelligence*, Prentice-Hall, Englewood Cliffs, N. J.

Brainerd, C. J. (1983). Modifiability of cognitive development. In S. Meadows (ed.), *Developing Thinking: Approaches to Children's Cognitive Development*, Methuen, London.

Bransford, J. D. (1979). *Human Cognition: Learning, Understanding and Remembering*, Wadsworth, Belmont, Calif.

Bransford, J. D., Stein, B. S., Shelton, T. S., and Owings, R. A. (1981). Cognition and adaptation: the importance of learning to learn. In J. Harvey (ed.), *Cognition, Social Behaviour, and the Environment*, Erlbaum, Hillsdale, N. J.

Brooks, R. E. (1980). Studying programmer behaviour experimentally. The problems of proper methodology, *Communications of the ACM*, **23**, 207–213.

Brown, A., Bransford, J. D., Ferrara, R. A., and Campione, J. C. (1983). Learning, remembering and understanding. In P. H. Mussen (ed.), *Handbook of Child Psychology* (4th edn), Vol. 3, *Cognitive Development*. J. Flavell and E. Markman (eds), Wiley, New York.

Brown, J. S., and Burton, R. R. (1978). Diagnostic models for procedural bugs in basic mathematical skills, *Cognitive Science*, **2**, 155–192.

Chait, S. (1978). An analysis of children's problem-solving in a graphics oriented computer programming environment. Unpublished Masters thesis, McGill University, Montreal, Canada.

Chi, M. T. H. (1978). Knowledge structures and memory development. In R. S. Siegler (ed.), *Children's Thinking: What Develops?* Erlbaum, Hillsdale, N. J.

Chi, M. T. H. (1985). Interactive roles of knowledge and strategies in the development of organised sorting and recall. In S. F. Chipman, J. W. Segal, and R. Glaser (eds), *Thinking and Learning Skills*, Vol. 2, Erlbaum, Hillsdale, N. J.

Flavell, J. H., Beach, D. H., and Chinsky, J. M. (1966). Spontaneous verbal rehearsal in memory tasks as a function of age, *Child Development*, **37**, 283–299.

Flavell, J. H., and Markman, E. M. (1983). *Cognitive Development*, Vol. 3 of P. H. Mussen (ed.), *Handbook of Child Psychology* (4th edn), Wiley, New York.

Gelman, R. (1985). The developmental perspective on the problem of knowledge acquisition: a discussion. In S. F. Chipman, J. W. Segal, and R. Glaser (eds), *Thinking and Learning Skills*, Vol. 2, Erlbaum, Hillsdale, N. J.

Gick, M. L., and Holyoak, K. J. (1980). Analogical problem solving, *Cognitive Psychology*, **12**, 306–355.

Glaser, R. (1985). Learning and instruction: a letter for a time capsule. In S. F. Chipman, J. W. Segal, and R. Glaser (eds), *Thinking and Learning Skills*, Vol. 2, Erlbaum Hillsdale, N. J.

Gorman, H., and Bourne, L. E. (1983). Learning to think by learning LOGO: rule learning in third grade computer programmers, *Bulletin of the Psychonomic Society*, **21**, 165–167.

Hayes, J. R. (1985). Three problems in teaching general skills. In S. F. Chipman, J. W. Segal, and R. Glaser (eds), *Thinking and Learning Skills*, Vol. 2, Erlbaum, Hillsdale, N. J.

Hayes, J. R., and Simon, H. A. (1976). Psychological differences among problem isomorphs. In N. Castellan Jr., D. Pisoni, and G. Potts (eds), *Cognitive Theory*, Vol 2, Erlbanm, Potomac, Md.

Howe, J. A. M. (1979). Learning through model building. In D. Michie (ed.), *Expert Systems in the Micro-electronic Age*, Edinburgh University Press, Edinburgh.

Howe, J. A. M., Ross, P. M., Johnson, K. R., and Inglis, R. (1984). Model building, mathematics and LOGO. In M. Yazdani (ed.), *New Horizons in Educational Computing*, Ellis Horwood, Chichester.

Jenkins, J. J. (1979). Four points to remember: a tetrahedral model and memory experiments. In L. S. Cermak and F. I. M. Craik (eds), *Levels of Processing in Human Memory*, Erlbaum Hillsdale, N. J.

Kamii, C., and DeVries, R. (1974). Piaget for early education. In R. K. Parker (ed.), *The Preschool in Action* (2nd edn), Allyn & Bacon, Boston.

Keeney, T. J., Cannizzo, S. R., and Flavell, J. H. (1967). Spontaneous and induced verbal rehearsal in a recall task. *Child Development*, **38**, 953–966.

Kennedy, B. A., and Miller, D. J. (1976). Persistent use of verbal rehearsal as a function of information about its value, *Child Development*, **47**, 566–569.

Lavatelli, C. (1970). *Early Childhood Curriculum – A Piaget Program*, American Science & Engineering, Boston.

Meichenbaum, D. (1985). Teaching thinking: a cognitive-behavioural perspective. In S. F. Chipman, J. W. Segal, and R. Glaser (eds). *Thinking and Learning Skills*, Vol. 2, Erlbaum, Hillsdale, N. J.

Newell, A. (1980). One final word. In D. T. Tuma and F. Reif (eds), *Problem-Solving in Education: Issues in Teaching and Research*, Erlbaum, Hillsdale, N. J.

Papert, S. (1980). *Mindstorms*, Harvester, Brighton.

Pea, R. D., and Kurland, D. M. (1984). On the cognitive effects of learning computer programming, *New Ideas In Psychology*, **2**, 137–168.

Siegler, R. S. (1983). Information processing approaches to development. In P. H. Mussen (ed.), *Handbook of Child Psychology* (4th edn), Vol. 1, *History, Theory and Methods*. W. Kessen (ed.), Wiley, New York.

Siegler, R. S. (1984). Mechanisms of cognitive growth: Variation and selection. In R. J. Sternberg (ed.), *Mechanisms of Cognitive Development*, W. H. Freeman, New York.

Simon, H. A. (1980). Problem-solving in education. In D. T. Tuma and F. Reif (eds), *Problem-Solving in Education: Issues in Teaching and Research*, Erlbaum, Hillsdale, N. J.

Simon, T., McShane, J., and Radley, S. (1987). Learning with microcomputers: training primary school children on a problem solving program, *Journal of Applied Cognitive Psychology*, **1**, 35–44.

Sleeman, D., and Brown, J. S. (1982). *Intelligent Tutoring Systems*, Academic Press, London.

Statz, J. (1973). The development of computer programming and problem-solving abilities among ten-year-olds learning LOGO. Unpublished Ph.D. thesis, Syracuse University, New York.

Sternberg, R. J. (1984). *Mechanisms of Cognitive Development*, Freeman, New York.

Sternberg, R. J. (1985). *Beyond IQ*, Cambridge University Press, London.

Weikart, D. P. (1973). Development of effective preschool programs: a report on the High-Scope-Ypsilanti preschool projects. Paper presented at High/Scope Educational Research Foundation Conference, Ann Arbor, Mich.

Young, R. M. (1978). Strategies and the structure of a cognitive skill. In G. Underwood (ed.), *Strategies of Information Processing*, Academic Press, London.

Young, R. M., and O'Shea, T. (1981). Errors in children's subtraction, *Cognitive Science*, **5**, 153–177.

Computers, Cognition and Development
Edited by J. Rutkowska and C. Crook
© 1987 John Wiley & Sons Ltd

CHAPTER 7

# Computers and Cognition in the Classroom

Jon Nichol, Jackie Dean and Jonathan Briggs

## SUMMARY

This chapter is concerned with the computer programming language PROLOG as a tool for developing children's logical understanding. Three uses of micro-PROLOG in normal classroom practice are outlined: to provide information; as an electronic blackboard; and for writing programs. Their impact on children's historical thinking is explored.

## INTRODUCTION: MICRO-PROLOG AND ITS CLASSROOM USE

The computer language PROLOG (PROgramming in LOGic) was developed in the early 1970s for mathematical and linguistics research. PROLOG is based upon predicate logic. A PROLOG program consists of logical rules and statements of fact – together they form the database. PROLOG's goal-based logical rules can sort, order and correlate related elements in the database. The database can describe a 'state of the world'. PROLOG has facilities which enable the computer to ask the program-user questions and add the answers given to the database. A PROLOG program can also explain the logical steps which it has taken in arriving at an answer to a query (Sergot, 1984; Briggs, 1984). Thus PROLOG is potentially a very powerful tool for developing children's understanding of a subject, either through their interrogation of a program written in PROLOG or through their writing of programs which represent their knowledge and understanding of a topic. An introduction to the educational potential of micro-PROLOG (a version of

PROLOG for use on microcomputers) is contained in Briggs (1984) and Conlon (1985).

Since May 1983 we have run a small-scale experimental project at an English comprehensive school to investigate the use of PROLOG in normal teaching. We have concentrated on PROLOG for the teaching of history to 11–14 year olds and its use as an aid for the linguistic development of pupils with specific literacy difficulties (SLD). Below we analyse some of the findings concerning PROLOG's impact upon our pupils' learning from September 1983 to June 1984. During this period we regularly taught history to a first- (11/12 year olds) and a second-year form (12/13 year olds) for one seventy-minute period a week each. From January 1984 to June 1984 we also taught a group of three third-year SLD pupils (13/14 year olds) on the same basis. For the first- and second-year forms we used the computer during 8 and 12 lessons respectively out of 30 (see Table 7.1). Computer-use in the teaching of the two forms was limited as it was only one of a range of resources and techniques employed. With the SLD pupils the computer was the key element in 14 out of 15 lessons.

TABLE 7.1. Number and type of 70-minute sessions for the 1983/84 academic year

| Types of computer-use (see text) | Pupils involved Form 1 11/12 years $n = 32$ lessons | Form 2 12/13 years $n = 31$ lessons | SLD pupils 13/14 years $n = 3$ lessons |
|---|---|---|---|
| Prepared-program use | 7 | 6 | 1 |
| Electronic blackboard | 1 | 6 | |
| Writing programs | | | 13 |
| No. of lessons using computer | 8 | 12 | 14 |
| No. of lessons with no computing | 22 | 18 | 1 |
| Total no. of lessons | 30 | 30 | 15 |

An axiom for our use of micro-PROLOG is that it must be an appropriate element in our normal teaching. In history we use the computer as one of several teaching aids in a course based upon the pupils solving historical problems and re-creating historical situations. Such history lessons employ resource materials ranging from textbooks to artefacts and original documents. The problem-solving approach, based on an understanding of the processes involved in working in the subject domain (i.e. historical methodology), reflects similar development in other areas, such as Nuffield Science (Barker, 1977). The main element in our computer work with the two forms was the use of prepared programs. In contrast, we introduced the SLD pupils to writing programs in PROLOG. They explored prepared programs as a preliminary to writing their own.

In our lessons the use of prepared programs was part of an overall teaching strategy. We tried to see if the computer would enable us to teach more effectively than alternative methods. Our hypothesis was that effectiveness might be attributable to the nature of the interaction between pupils and programs based on predicate logic. PROLOG might force the pupils to see the logical connections between discrete pieces of information, and to apply carefully structured logical thinking in the form of rules. Application of the rules would provide answers to questions, test hypotheses and solve problems. In developing pupil understanding, the computer was used for three distinct purposes: for providing information, as an electronic blackboard and for pupil writing of programs.

(a) The computer as a *provider of information*: pupils' learning developed through their interaction with a program. Here the computer functioned alongside other aids such as slides, pamphlets, books and documentary packs. In our class teaching we had a single computer which we used with three VDUs. Pupils worked in groups of between two and five members. There were two or three groups per VDU. The standard teaching pattern for the use of programs was:
   – Teacher introduction.
   – Pupil formulation of questions, either in groups or as a class.
   – Information from the computer in response to questions.
   – Pupil discussion of computer's answers in groups and as a class.
   – Pupil formulation of new questions.
   – Resolution of problem, in the form of either oral, graphic or written work.
   The hallmark of computer–pupil interaction is that the pupils push on the enquiry at their own pace. They gain confidence and motivation from their mastery over their own learning process. Analysis of taped lessons indicates that computer-use helps the class to achieve the conditions necessary for 'mastery learning' (Bloom, 1971). Here the time constraint on pupil learning is removed, i.e. the pupil moves to the next stage once mastery has been achieved. Concerning pupil interaction with the programs, we have favoured pupils' free exploration of the programs. Examples of free exploration are the pupils' use of the programs BOGBOD, GREENDIE and VIKING TRADER. BOGBOD and GREENDIE ask the pupil to work as a journalist and detective respectively to solve murder mysteries. GREENDIE concerns the murder of John Green, while BOGBOD deals with a body discovered in a Danish peat bog. In VIKING TRADER the pupils question the computer as if

it were a Viking trader who had visited their valley on the Isle of Man. The trader can tell them about the Viking world – its ports and towns, their relative geographical locations, and the goods which they produce and trade.

(b) We used the computer as an *electronic blackboard* in lessons to record, order, classify, analyse logically and then test ideas and hypotheses. Two subjects were treated in this way: the murder of Prince Arthur of Brittany in the reign of King John, and an extremely popular investigation into the burning down of a school. The lessons on these subjects followed the same pattern – the extraction of factual information from written sources, which we typed into the computer as a database; the framing of questions; and the formulation of logical rules to answer these questions. Here we and the pupils were using the computer to express and test our logical understanding of a problem and its solution.

(c) *The writing of programs:* our third approach was to use PROLOG as a vehicle for the SLD pupils to write their own programs, in a group. Individual or group programming with the history classes was impossible, as we had only one computer. Ennals (1982) examined pupil programming in micro-PROLOG. Such successful programming relies on the pupils carefully structuring their data and writing rules which will produce answers to their questions. The problems of teaching pupils in a class sufficient PROLOG to write programs when only seeing them once a week limited our application of this concept.

Before we can ask questions about developing understanding, we need a way of characterizing the thinking of the children concerned. In classroom studies, we cannot capture what is going on through the use of standard tests of reasoning ability. The following section summarizes the development of a classificatory scheme for thinking which is applicable to the types of protocol obtained during classroom interaction. In the final section, this framework is used to provide an analysis of our subjects' thinking, based on tape recordings of lessons and pupil interviews and analysis of their written responses. The analysis relates to the teaching of two programs, PLACE-NAMES and VIKING TRADER, a single electronic blackboard lesson dealing with King John's murder of his nephew and one example of the dyslexic pupils' programming.

In terms of pupil thinking we make no claims that the computer is *developing* their minds. This is because computing work is only one element in a more general teaching strategy, that of involving pupils in the historical process. In a different context, Booth (1978, 1980) and Shemilt (1980) have evaluated pupils' mental development in relation to this strategy. What we hope is that computer-use improves pupil understanding of historical processes and situations and, more generally, makes them aware of the logical steps involved in problem solving. Our analysis is set against recent work on pupils' historical thinking and understanding.

## HOW CAN WE ANALYSE CLASSROOM THINKING?

Most analysis of 11–14 year old children's thinking in both history (Peel, 1967; Hallam, 1972; Dickinson and Lee, 1978; Shemilt, 1980; Booth, 1980) and computing (O'Shea and Self, 1983) is related to Piaget's general theories of cognitive development and his specific account of the maturation of the adolescent mind (Piaget and Inhelder, 1958). Here he dates the development of formal thinking from the age of 11–12. The child's mind has reached a state of equilibrium by the age of 14–15. Of interest for the educational user of a computer language based on logic is Piaget's stress upon the logical structuring of information and ideas which allow for abstract thought:

> Formal thinking is both thinking about thought (propositional logic is a second-order operational system which operates on propositions whose truth, in turn, depend on class, relational and numerical operations) and a reversal of relations between what is real and what is possible (the empirically given comes to be inserted as a particular sector of the total set of possible combinations). (Piaget and Inhelder, 1958, pp.341–42)

Formal thought is based upon reflective thinking which enables the adolescent to move from the concrete to the abstract and the possible. In framing theories and hypotheses the thinking has to be abstract and possibilistic. Piaget's account of possibilistic thinking contains a section which reflects the structure of PROLOG's rules:

> . . . the role of possibility is indispensable to hypothetico-deductive or formal thinking . . . a deduction logically derived from a hypothesis . . . is necessarily true from the formal point of view independently of the value of the assumed hypothesis. The connection indicated by the words 'if . . . then' (inferential implication) links a required logical consequence to an assertion whose truth is merely a possibility. (Piaget and Inhelder, 1958, p.257)

Piaget relates but does not directly link the development of formal operational thinking to physiological change at puberty. He lays greater stress on the social and cultural factors, including education, which cause maturation of the brain. The use of a computer language which mirrors the patterns of thought involved in formal thinking could have major implications (Piaget and Inhelder, 1958, p.337). Already significant advances in pupil maturation have been recorded in schemes using the problem-solving approach to history (Shemilt, 1980; Booth, 1980). Our project uses the same methods. Computer-use is merely one of the teaching strategies.

Edwin Peel extended Piaget's work on adolescent thinking (Peel, 1971).

In the development of formal thought Peel stressed the role of imagination based upon the thinker's experience and insights. 'Formal thought implies a thinker capable of imagining possibilities, conjured up in the form of generalizations, concepts, analogies, cause-and-effect relations and such contingencies' (Peel, 1971, p.68). Peel used three main categories to analyse pupils' thinking. These relate to their responses to test materials. Usually the items were short passages of prose, but could include pictorial evidence, aerial photographs, maps etc. The three categories were:

(a) Restricted – tautological, premise-delaying, irrelevant.
(b) Circumstantial – bound solely by the content of the passage, often taking account at first of only one element.
(c) Imaginative-comprehensive – involving the invocation of independent ideas and the consideration of the problem in their terms.

In analysing historical thinking Peel subdivided and expanded his categories. He recorded that one of his researchers produced six grades for classifying the historical thinking of pupils (Peel, 1971, p.126). These grades remain general, crude instruments of analysis. They reflect the pattern of testing which Piaget developed within a scientific and mathematical environment. Hallam (1972) further developed Peel's ideas and produced four categories for classifying pupil thinking. The transfer of the categories to a different subject domain raises serious questions about their appropriateness, and the validity of conclusions based upon them (Dickinson and Lee, 1978; Booth, 1978).

Dickinson and Lee (1978, pp.97–99) heavily criticized the mechanistic Piagetian approach. They argued that historical understanding involves pupils being able to see historical situations from two different perspectives – that of people in the past, the *historical agents*, and that of the *historian*. To understand historical agents pupils must take into account the factors affecting such agents' actions within their historical context. Such factors are a subtle blend of motives, feelings, contingencies and immediate response to circumstance. Dickinson and Lee identify four main levels of pupil thinking (1978, pp.86–88). The ideas of Piaget, Peel, Hallam, and Dickinson and Lee need to be set against a view of children's thinking which stresses the imaginative element in *associative thought*. Here the associations made between disparate elements complement the rational, logical, scientific and deductive pattern of thought. Watts (Nicholls, 1980) proposes:

. . . that many, if not most, cognitive processes in both children and adults are of the nature of spontaneous associations of images and concepts; that not only can people think associatively, but that much day to day thinking is of such a kind that we use rational and logical thinking much less often than the problem solving model would imply and that 'intelligent' thinking is the result of the fusion of rational and associative elements.

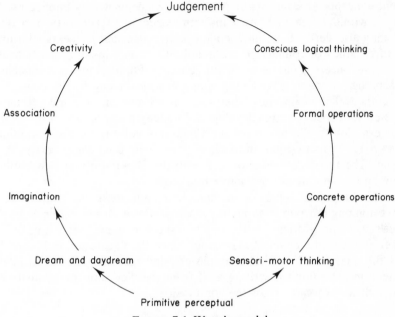

FIGURE 7.1 Watts's model

Watts's model can be represented diagramatically (see Figure 7.1). The more creative, open-ended, imaginative and empathetic pattern of thought is shown in the associative strand. Booth's work on the historical thinking of adolescents (Booth, 1978, 1980) supports analysis similar to that of Watts. Booth argues that pupils can make associations in two distinct ways. At the first level their thinking relates to the immediately observable features of a set of evidence. At a deeper level the thinking is more imaginative and abstract. Here the conclusions go outside the immediately observable and rely on inferred qualities and ideas. Such thinking had developed by the age of 16 in a majority of pupils. Significantly, the quality of their understanding related to the nature of their syllabus and the quality of the teacher.

To analyse pupils' thinking we produced two tools. The first, Table 7.2, was used for holistic analysis of stages in pupil thinking. The other, Figure 7.2, aimed to tease out the precise nature of the thinking which a pupil engaged in, inferred from the external representation of his thoughts. The tools are based on a synthesis of the views outlined above. The four stages in Table 7.2 take as their starting point the stages of Hallam, and incorporate the findings of Dickinson and Lee, Booth, Peel, and Watts.

The use of stages in Table 7.2 is a rough-and-ready procedure for analysing pupil thinking. Peel (1975) provided a framework with a different perspective, based on the division of textual response into two categories: in-concepts and out-concepts. In-concepts he defined as 'concepts wholly implied by the language within T (text) (they are in- with respect to T)' (Peel, 1975, p.109). Ideas may also derive from independent knowledge: out-concepts. Within a text, three kinds of connection are possible: between in-concepts, between in- and out-concepts, and between out-concepts. Pupil responses form chains of reasoning. A chain of reasoning is one in which a single idea/focus/point is developed. The chain ends when there is a break in the pupil's thinking and a new idea/focus/point is developed. The length and nature of the chains can give a clue to the nature of the thinking involved. We have modified Peel's system to analyse the thinking of pupils who used computers in their learning. The modifications allow for both the Dickinson and Lee critique of Peel and the nature of associative thinking.

Figure 7.2 reproduces part of an example of an analysis sheet that we used for investigating our pupils' thought processes. For each separate element in a response, a line is drawn on the analysis sheet to show how it is linked to another element in a chain of reasoning. Thus, the illustration in Figure 7.2 shows the analysis of the first example of pupil reasoning discussed in the next section. The pupil is writing as if from the viewpoint of an historical agent, a Saxon walking across the countryside.

## ANALYSIS OF PUPILS' THINKING USING TABLE 7.2
## AND FIGURE 7.2

Below we analyse pupil responses to two programs, PLACE-NAMES AND VIKING TRADER. We also examine pupil responses to the use of the computer as an electronic blackboard and for pupil programming.

The PLACE-NAMES program enabled the pupils to explore the origins of Saxon place-names in the locality of the school. Each pupil was given a 1-inch Ordnance Survey map of the area and a blank outline map on which to fill in details and ancillary information. The class could ask the computer about any place-name on the map. The computer could tell the class the meanings of a place's name elements, the date when the name was first recorded, its grid location and any relevant additional information. The program cross-correlates data from different place-name entries to yield a rich variety of information. For example, it can tell us which places were mentioned in the Domesday Book, or which places were near water or which places were settled by people with Norman names. It can also produce answers to combinations of questions, for example, those places which were settled near water between 739 and 1066.

Using the program the pupils worked out the meanings of the names of present-day villages and towns on the map. Follow-up work asked them to imagine a walk across the area in Saxon times. For this they used information

TABLE 7.2 Four stages in children's thinking

**Stage 1**

PIAGETIAN   Pre-operational thinking. Not relating the question to the information provided. Isolated centrings on one feature only. An unstable, discontinuous cognitive life. Transducive reasoning – moving from one element to another without considering all the factors involved. Failure coherently to grasp agent's intentions or situation. Direct contradictions of explicit information.

ASSOCIATIVE   Imagination and reconstruction related to the immediate evidence. Linkage between images, evidence and external evidence at the most superficial level. Purely descriptive in nature. No going outside the frame provided by the evidence. No chain of imaginative reconstruction.

**Stage 2**

PIAGETIAN   Intermediate between pre-operational and concrete operational thinking. More than one feature of the situation considered. The attempts to relate differing facts not too successful. Uncertainty of judgements. Action explained by reference to the agent's intentions and situation, where the former includes an important 'conventional' element, and no differentiation is made in the latter between the agent's view of the situation and the historian's view.

ASSOCIATIVE   Able to relate single images and ideas to build up a simple picture. Restricted to the available evidence. No sign of imagination moving to images outside the picture beyond general stereotypes.

**Stage 3**

PIAGETIAN   Concrete operational thinking (COT) linked to the immediate evidence available to solve the problem. Centred on the concrete world of sense experience. Able to give an organized answer but limited to what is immediately apparent in the text. Able to forecast a result from the evidence available. Compensates one statement by another or negates a statement. Not able to coordinate negation and reciprocity. Action explained by reference to the agent's particular intentions and his own view of the situation, but seen relatively locally in the context of the description under which the action requires explanation.

ASSOCIATIVE   Tied strictly to observable evidence. Less adventurous, creative and imaginative than stage 4. Ability to extrapolate from the available evidence and use the imagination to build up a picture of the situation. Thinking does not move outside the world being recreated. Inside that world, able to draw on own imaginative processes to fill in gaps and expand the imaginative web the evidence provides. Highest level where all the evidence is fully exploited for the imagery it is capable of having built on it.

**Stage 4**

PIAGETIAN   Formal operational thinking. Realization of a multiplicity of possible links. Uses logical analysis to find out which is true. Hypotheses are postulated and these can be confirmed or discarded by testing against the data. 'Commits himself to possibilities, there is a reversal of direction between reality and possibility.' Sees a relatively complex relationship between different factors as part of an intelligible total picture.

ASSOCIATIVE   Ability to comprehend and analyse material and group evidence into sets. Not based on immediately observable features. Able to detach self from the situation – relate imaginative reconstruction to external abstract ideas and hypotheses. Brings to the reconstruction a complex set of images and ideas and information from outside the available evidence.

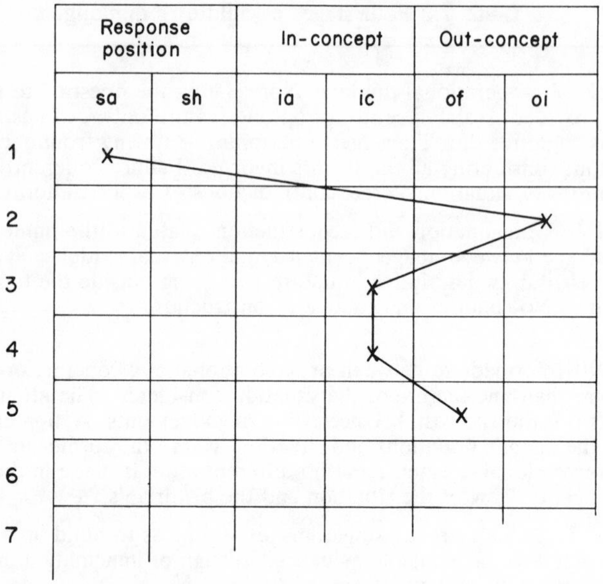

| Response position | | In-concept | | Out-concept | |
|---|---|---|---|---|---|
| sa | sh | ia | ic | of | oi |

Figure grid with rows labelled 1 through 7 and the marks plotting the chain.

Key:
sa = viewpoint of historical agent in the historical context
sh = viewpoint of the historian
ia = in-concept, ancillary material given the pupils (e.g. books, pamphlets, illustrations, computer program, documentation)
ic = in-concept, information derived from the computer program
of = out-concept, factual information
oi = out-concept, imaginative thinking

FIGURE 7.2 Example of analysis sheet used for investigating pupils' thought processes

derived from the computer. Analysis using Table 7.2 and Figure 7.2 indicates a range of thinking from stages 2 to 4 and chains of reasoning related to the stages. One first year (11/12 year old) produced five chains of reasoning. The pupil linked the chains together through taking the role of an historical agent, a Saxon, as he walks across the map through given places. The first four chains reproduced the information from the computer, using its translation of the place-name elements. The fifth shows the pupil introducing an imaginative element:

I [sa] saw a sign saying Copplestone [oi] means Copelan Stan. Copelan means peaked or round [ic] stan means a stone [ic]. As I passed through I saw a stone cross in the middle of the village [of].
[There is such a cross.]

The chain sa–oi–ic–ic–of (see Figure 7.2) shows stage 2 thinking (see Table 7.2).

An example of more purely *associative* thinking came from a second-year pupil's response to the same exercise. On the blank map she drew accurately the meaning of the place-names – for example, Bradly, a wide clearing, was drawn as a large clear area in the forest with a fence around it. In her walk she drew heavily upon her previous knowledge and her imagination. Her first paragraph is associative thinking at stage 3:

> Cheriton Fitzpain which to us [sa/sh] is better known as cyric tun fitzpaine [ic] is a pretty little village [of] with a quaint church [ic] in the centre [of]. People bustle about [oi], women doing their washing [oi] and their husbands going off to work in their horse driven carts [oi]. A man who I know to be the lord-Fitzpaine [ic] sets off on his weekly visit to Crediton [oi] riding with a large white stallion [oi] and dressed all in red with a golden sash [oi]. The village is now riddled with children [oi] as I pick my way through the muddied streets [oi] out on to the common [of] on my way to Yeoford [of].

Here are four linked chains of reasoning, related to seeing the situation originally from both the viewpoint of the historical agent (sa) and the historian (sh). The imaginative element is uppermost. The four chains are relatively short, i.e.

|  |  |
|---|---|
| 1. sa/sh-ic-of-ic-of | 2. oi-oi-oi |
| 3. ic-oi-oi-oi | 4. oi-oi-of-of |

The next step in fostering the pupils' understanding of the nature of the Saxon landscape and its development was for the pupils to use the program to plot key features on their blank maps. The first-year class of 11/12 year olds chose Saxon farms and clearings.

Previously only research historians have carried out such work (Gelling, 1979, pp.116–18). Once the pupils had plotted the place-names, group and class discussion followed. During these talks the class noted down ideas about early settlement. Ideas came from class members. One jotting and response read:

> bog person. few clearings. wash drinking near streams. water supply. war. lost land. apart. farms. lots of them (13). rich land.

The written resolution revealed deductive and associative thinking at stage 3:

> A few reasons for Saxon settlement around Crediton are [sh]: If a bog person [i.e. from Jutland – previous work] [of] lived in Crediton he could easily get water from a stream [ic] or the same other people. They could get water easily by a stream because people liked to settle by streams [ic]. They would need it to wash, drink, etc. [oi] Where the people settled never seemed to be near each other [ic]. There used to be loads of farms and forests around [ic]. They probably came from

the north-east [ic/oi]. The people settled all over the place but still made sure that they were never near each other [ic]. Some people were rich and some were quite poor [oi] so of course the rich probably had a larger settlement than the poor [oi]. There were a lot of settlements altogether there are 13 [ic]. On the map all the clearings [ic] seem to be quite close to a church [ic].

Here the pupil is weaving together the information obtained from the map to gain some general understanding of the nature of the settlement. The pupil is willing to generalize and draw inferences, although judgements are related to concrete evidence. The chains of reasoning run:

| | | | |
|---|---|---|---|
| 1. | sh-of-ic-ic-oi | 4. | oi-oi |
| 2. | ic-ic | 5. | ic |
| 3. | ic/oi-ic | 6. | ic-ic |

Using the computer's information one pupil produced a more abstract synthesis. Taking the historian's perspective he wrote:

Back around 750 AD [sh/of] the scenery would have been very different from today. There were no big villages like Sandford [of] or Bow [of] but little clearings [oi/ic] and farmsteads [ic] which were small [oi]. Crediton at that time was only a farm [ic]. The forests covered most of the land [oi/ic], and the clearings [ic] and farms [ic] were often far apart [ic], near streams [ic] for a good water supply [of]. The Saxons [of] seemed to come from the North-East [of/ic]. They could have moved here because of rich land [oi] or to explore [oi] and claim the land for themselves [oi].

The writer develops several ideas and hypotheses, and tests them against the data. The analysis is moving into stage 4. The chains of reasoning, and the movement between the different possible elements, confirm the sophisticated nature of thought involved. The thinking has a major associative element in the weaving together of facts from the computer, ancillary material and external knowledge. The chains are:

1. sh/of-of-of-oi/ic-ic-oi-ic-oi/ic-ic-ic-ic-of
2. ia-of/ic-oi-oi-oi

Similar patterns of thinking emerge from analysis of pupils' written responses to the VIKING TRADER program. In groups the class asked the VIKING TRADER (the program) about the Viking world – ports, distances apart and directions from one another, goods traded. Ancillary material took the form of a booklet about the Vikings, including details of their trade. On the basis of the information received each pupil drew a map of the Viking world on a blank piece of paper. All were able to produce a mental map (see Figure 7.3) based on the transfer and organization of information from the computer. The less able faced certain problems – one group did not know the difference between north and south. Then the pupils planned out

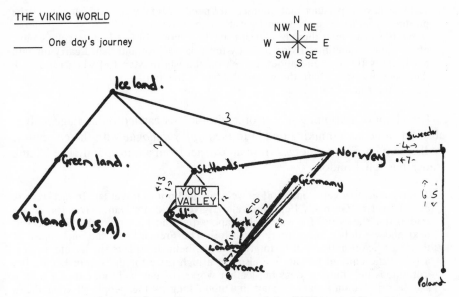

FIGURE 7.3 Pupil's mental map of the 'Viking world'

a trading journey to provide the valley where they lived with goods. Written responses ranged from stage 2 to stage 4. Every pupil in the class produced a coherent narrative chain, linking up ports and their goods. A less able pupil wrote:

> I was going to dublin [ic] It took me two days to get there [ic]. I went two the trader place [ii]. I said have you any slave to trade [ic]. He said yes I will so I got a slave [ic] as I give him a neckless [ic] and two ring [ic]. His name was Jonny [oi]. He was a hard working man [oi]. He was very skinny [oi]. I was finished there. I had two go to London to get some hores [ic]. London was very dirty place [oi]. there are lot of people with dirty cloths [oi]. London have thousands of hores I said can I have 3 hores [ic] He said have you any bronze [ic]. I said yes I have a load of it.

Thinking is at stage 2. Ideas are related to the immediate evidence, and the immediate circumstances of the historical agent are understood. More able pupils produced sophisticated abstract frameworks against which to place the data gained from the computer. One pupil listed the ports and their goods, and wrote:

> The list above shows what I can get and where I can get it from as a viking trader. I also trade at the places mentioned above. When I first started to work as a trader I used to sell most things but people only wanted certain things so now I have cut back my stock to what people mostly seem to want. The places where I sell, all

seem to have a product that another city needs. Usually the city cannot get the produce from anywhere else so I get it for them [ic/oi].
In my life as a trader there is a lot of travelling about. In fact I am travelling most of the time. Sometimes I stop at a city for a day or two and then I carry on with my journey [ic/oi] spend about a week on the isle of Man [oi] when i get back there because it is where the rest of the family live [ic].
This is the route I take . . .

The chain of reasoning – sa-ic/oi-ic/oi-oi-ic – is carried on at stage 4. It is abstract, reflective thinking tied in to *the pupil's dialogue* with the computer. A different emphasis emerges from an extract from a third pupil. The Viking trader has left London:

The sea was now very rough [oi] so we were glad not to travel far. In fact, it took days to get to Germany [ic]. Our valley [given] did not want slaves [oi] so we traded our slaves [ic] for wine [ic] weapons [ic] and millstones [ic]. France was next and we didn't like it there much [oi]. The French knew the importance of their salt [ic/oi] and so got us to give swords, helmets, spears shields etc. [ic] for a very little amount of salt. We also got a high price for the salt in Dublin [ic] iron goods [ic], hunting dogs [ic] leather works [ic] etc. were all ours for a little salt [ic/oi]. I didn't want to stay in Dublin long as the people in Ireland are cutthroats and thieves [oi].

There is an interplay between the historical evidence and the pupil's external knowledge and imagination. Again the thinking is based upon information gained from the computer program, and reveals clear linkages between the extracts in building up a mental picture of the Viking world and trade. The writing is at stage 3.

Our second area of computer application, its use as an electronic blackboard (see above, p.00), arose from our work on King John with a second-year form of 12/13 year olds. The computer's ability to record statements and apply rules to that data can help develop pupil understanding of historical problems. Understanding arises from their extraction of propositions (facts) from the historical evidence which they are working upon, and the application of logical rules to those propositions in order to test hypotheses. In our work on King John we gave the class extracts from a textbook (Nichol and Downton, 1981) which contained accusations against King John with related historical evidence. The first accusation was: *Did King John kill Arthur?* (his nephew).

The computer was used to see if an accusation against King John was true when tested against the facts teased from the evidence. The writing of rules to test the accusations allowed for possibilistic thinking. The pupils worked in groups and then as a whole class to list the facts and then produce the rules. One such rule took the form of:

*King-John guilty if monks told truth*

A pupil who had done a week's PROLOG course the previous year shows how PROLOG can be used to develop understanding. In his week's course he had been introduced to PROLOG's declarative, or descriptive, approach to programming. The pupil saw the problem declaratively, in terms of a network of facts, and the application of general rules to that network:

**Facts**
John was drunk
John was Arthur's Uncle
Arthur ruled Brittany
Arthur claimed throne off John
Arthur hated John and disobeyed him
Lots of witnesses – some stories coincided
Evidence could be true or false
Monks gave evidence against John
Fishermen gave evidence
Baron gave evidence

**Rules**
Monks could tell truth because holy and religious
Monks couldn't tell truth against John because John was against church.
Fisherman has no reason to give evidence at all and had nothing to gain from exciting John.
Baron could tell lies because he might gain something if John was killed although this unlikely because some of his evidence coincided with that of monk and fisherman.

**Conclusion**
John killed Arthur
Because – John felt Arthur was a danger to the throne. John was drunk and therefore could have took stupid action at the spur of the moment.
Arthur hated John – John wouldn't like this and if I was King and someone openly disobeyed and hated me in the time of John I'd kill him. Also there were a lot of witnesses telling the same stories.
Very disisive.

The use of the computer as an electronic blackboard is at an early stage, but it could be of value in developing the kind of approach to problem-solving illustrated above – thinking of a formal operational kind (Piaget and Inhelder, 1958). The pupil is able to extract the facts, frame ideas and hypotheses and reach abstract conclusions. There is evidence of an awareness of the situations of the historical agent (sa) and the historian (sh).

Our third use of micro-PROLOG, for pupil programming, outlined on page 138, relates to Ennals's (1982) work. In producing programs the pupils have to decide what they want their program to do, and then organize their data into a logical order and produce any rules required. Working weekly with three 13-year-old SLD pupils provided the environment within which we could experiment with the introduction of the teaching of logic programming as an element in such children's normal education. Such work was impossible in our whole class teaching. An early problem we faced our SLD pupils with was the writing of a murder mystery around the discovery

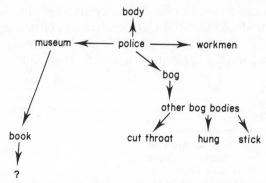

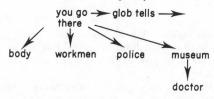

FIGURE 7.4 Tree-diagram of information for murder mystery

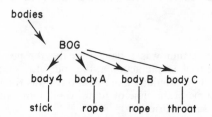

FIGURE 7.5 Tree-diagrams of information for murder mystery

of a body in a Danish bog. They were given information from a textbook (Nichol, 1979) which provided them with the data they required. This they organized in the form of tree-diagrams (see Figures 7.4 and 7.5).

Using their diagrams the pupils wrote a program which was similar to BOGBOD (Nichol and Dean, 1984). An indication of the kind of thinking required for PROLOG programming comes from the considered judgement of one of our pupils on our efforts:

Although I had little expirence with computers I soon caught on to 'prolog' the liverly new language based on logic, with witch a vast selection of rules could be built up, and fited together like a childs building blocks. Soon, I found that computer jargon was part of my everyday language, as it was a part of the Doctors . . . We began work on 'the battle of Jutland'. We hoped to program this into the computer as a game in witch the German fleet fought the British for supremisy, useing completly compat rules and sentences. Unfortunately, there was a scientific dispute between the Doctor and his assistant as to the practicality of this venture and it was droped . . . Despite a little tomfoolery from the groups intellectuel, I thoroughly enjoyed these lessons. I think they improved ore spelling and coordination as well as creative skills. Here's to the good Doctor and a fine terms computing.

Since February 1985 we have developed a whole range of PROLOG authoring programs, or toolkits, which enable pupils to express their knowledge as PROLOG programs. Potentially this places the computer at the centre of the learning process. Analysis of our work from February 1985 to June 1986 will be the topic of a subsequent paper. If micro-PROLOG can provide a powerful tool to help pupils extend their thinking and understanding, and related linguistic skills, it will make a genuine contribution ot education.

## Note

An earlier version of this chapter appears in R. Ennals, R. Gwyn, and L. Zdravchev (eds.) *Information Technology and Education* (1986), Ellis Horwood, Chichester.

## REFERENCES

Barker, B. (1977). History situations, *Teaching History*, No. 17, 19–23.
Bloom, B. S. (1971). Mastery learning. In J. H. Block (ed.), *Mastery Learning: Theory and Practice*, Holt, Rinehart & Winston, New York.
Boddington, T. (1980). Empathy and the teaching of History, *British Journal of Educational Studies*, **28**, 13–19.
Booth, M. (1978). Children's inductive thought, *Teaching History*, No. 21, 3–8.
Booth, M. (1980). A recent research project into children's historical thinking and its implications for history teaching. In J. Nichol (ed.), *Developments in History Teaching – Perspectives 4*, School of Education, University of Exeter.
Briggs, J. H. (1984). *Micro-PROLOG Rules!* Logic Programming Associates, England (also available from PEG-Exeter, School of Education, University of Exeter, EX1 2LU).
Conlon, T. (1985). *Start Problem Solving with Prolog*, Addison-Wesley, Reading, Mass.
Conlon, T. (1985). *Learning micro-PROLOG: A Problem Solving Approach*, Addison-Wesley, Reading, Mass.
Dickinson, A. K. and Lee, P. J. (1978). *History Teaching and Historical Understanding*, Heinemann, London.
Ennals, R. (1982). *Beginning micro-PROLOG*, Ellis Horwood, Chichester.
Gelling, M. (1979). The evidence of place-names I. In P. H. Sawyer (ed.), *English Medieval Settlement*, Edward Arnold, London.
Hallam, R. N. (1972). Piaget and thinking in history. In M. Ballard (ed.), *New Movements in the Study and Teaching of History*, Temple Smith, England.
Little, V. (1983). What is historical imagination, *Teaching History*, No. 36, 27–32.
Nichol, J. (1979). *The Saxons*, Basil Blackwell, Oxford.
Nichol, J. and Downton, D. (1981). *The Middle Ages*, Basil Blackwell, Oxford.

Nichol, J., and Dean, J. (1984). Pupils, computers and history teaching. In M. Yazdani (ed.), *New Horizons in Educational Computing*, Ellis Horwood, Chichester.

Nicholls, W. H. (1980). Children's thinking in history. Watt's model and its appropriateness. In J. Nichol (ed.), *Developments in History Teaching – Perspectives 4*, School of Education, University of Exeter.

O'Shea, T., and Self, J. (1983). *Learning and Teaching with Microcomputers – Artificial Intelligence in Education*, Harvester Press, Brighton.

Peel, E. A., (1971). *The Nature of Adolescent Judgment*, Staples Press, Crosby.

Peel, E. A. (1975). The analysis of comprehension and judgment from textual material, *Educational Review*, **27**(2), 100–13.

Piaget, J., and Inhelder, B. (1958). *The Growth of Logical Thinking*, Routledge & Kegan Paul, Boston, Mass.

Sergot, (1984). A query-the-user facility for logic programming. In M. Yazdani (ed.), *New Horizons in Educational Computing*, Ellis Horwood, Chichester.

Shemilt, D. (1980). *History 13–16, Evaluation Study: Schools Council History 13–16 Project*, Holmes McDougall, Glasgow.

Thompson, F. (1983). Empathy: an aim and a skill to be developed, *Teaching History*, No. 37, 22–26.

Computers, Cognition and Development
Edited by J. Rutkowska and C. Crook
© 1987 John Wiley & Sons Ltd

CHAPTER 8

# Studying Novice Programmers: Why They May Find Learning PROLOG Hard

JOSIE TAYLOR AND BENEDICT DU BOULAY

## SUMMARY

Claims that logic programming languages are natural and easy to learn may
be untrue for novice programmers, who typically lack experience with logic
formalisms. They find themselves writing programs for which they lack
underlying conceptual models. The problems they face are discussed with
reference to observations of novice PROLOG programmers.

## INTRODUCTION

One of the aims of workers in artificial intelligence (AI) is to develop
programming environments and programming languages that can be used to
produce 'intelligent' systems. Such environments (e.g. Interlisp, Poplog) and
languages (e.g. LISP, PROLOG and POP-11) are specially designed for this
kind of task in the same way that other programming languages such as
FORTRAN and COBOL are tuned to the needs of the scientific and commercial programmer. The success of this tool-building activity, whether within
AI or some other field, can be judged on a number of criteria, one of which
is the power of the tool and another of which is the usability of the tool.
Investigating how the human user copes with the complex task of learning
to use and exploit computing facilities is the concern of the field of human/
machine interaction (HMI).

153

There are many aspects to the 'interface' between humans and machines – HMI research addresses such psycho-physical, ergonomic issues as the layout of keyboards and terminal screens, as well as more cognitive issues to do with programming practices and programming languages. It is interested both in the qualities of a system that affect expert performance as well as in the learnability of the systems by both naive and experienced users (for general discussions of the relevant issues see e.g. Smith and Green, 1980; Coombs and Alty, 1981; Monk, 1985; Shneiderman, 1982).

Psychologists – in particular cognitive psychologists (e.g. Anderson, 1982; Norman and Draper, 1986) – have turned to the development of a user psychology, not only because of the necessity of identifying the needs of users in interaction with increasingly complex computer systems, but also because computing offers a microcosm of many of those perceptual and intellectual issues in which psychology has always been interested and, in many cases, a ready means of capturing useful data about human performance.

In this chapter we focus on a particular, new type of 'high-level' programming language, PROLOG. This is used mainly in AI although education is showing a growing interest in it for teaching such diverse subjects as history, logic and mathematics (see e.g. Ramsden, 1984). Our main objective here is to delineate some of the issues that PROLOG beginners have to deal with, but first we explain the notion of a 'high-level' language, and the concept of a 'notional machine'.

The term 'high-level' suggests two ideas. One is that the kinds of entities one can manipulate in the programming language are similar (in some way) to the kinds of entities in the problem situation. The other is that the means provided for such manipulations fit the task, are powerful and easy to use. Broadly speaking, the higher-level a language is, the less it need be constrained by the particular hardware upon which it runs and the more it is designed for a specialized class of problems.

Because the design of high-level languages tends to reflect the structure of problems rather than the structure of the computer on which they run, they allow beginners to write interesting programs when they may know very little about how a computer is physically constructed (i.e. its hardware), or about how its internal workings are organized on a global scale (i.e. the operating system software which allows different kinds of operations to be carried out).

For most programming languages, including PROLOG, the crucial notions for the beginner are first, the 'workspace' area where activities are conducted, second, the 'building blocks' provided by the particular programming language for constructing 'mechanisms', and third, the means of making these mechanisms perform. This idealized view of the system, shorn of irrelevant detail, is described as the 'notional machine' (du Boulay *et al.*, 1981) – where the notional machine is an 'idealized conceptual computer whose properties are implied by the constructs in the programming language employed'. An analogy here is to think of a programming language as being like a Meccano set or a Lego set with standard parts for standard tasks, such as a wheel and bearing. Building a program is not unlike building a model mechanism with one of these sets. As a beginner, one needs to master the accepted means of putting the parts together, ways of translating problem descriptions (e.g. a crane) into the 'language' of the parts provided and the expected uses for what at first may seem rather oddly shaped bits and pieces. Of course, one also has to master pragmatic issues, such as what to do when the model does not work as intended or how to divide up a complex mechanism sensibly into buildable constituent assemblies.

Until recently most programming languages for beginners stressed a procedural/command oriented approach to structured problem solving, and the language constructs supported this approach (e.g. LOGO, BASIC). A facet of this problem-solving approach is that it fits well within the architecture and design of computing machinery, where the computer is directed by the programmer to execute step(a), step(b), . . ., step (*n*). Analysis of beginners' difficulties has typically focused on the development of goals and plans in the programming process with emphasis placed on the way that novices build mal-formed plans or join sub-plans together incorrectly (see e.g. Soloway and Ehrlich, 1984). In their analysis it is the plans which express the procedural knowledge of how to get things done in the particular programming language.

However, the development of PROLOG (Colmerauer *et al.*, 1973) has introduced a new type of language which is based on first-order predicate logic. Here the programmer specifies what is true of the eventual problem solution, leaving the computer to sort out the steps towards finding the solution. Ideally, in the logic programming ethos the programmer can specify a problem solution in logic, and that specification will run as a program. This is the distinction made much of in the PROLOG literature between telling the machine *how* to solve the problem (by issuing commands in a procedure) and telling the machine *what* has to be true of the solution in the end.

It has been claimed, primarily by Kowalski (1979), that 'logic' programming languages like PROLOG are easier to learn and use than other, high-level, AI languages because predicate logic is 'human-oriented', and is therefore more readily understood than other programming formalisms. This argument would not convince a psychologist, and, in fact, given the low level of performance on logical deductive reasoning tasks noted in the psychological literature one might predict a whole host of potential problems. Unsurprisingly, observations of students learning PROLOG confirm that many of them do not find it easy or natural (Taylor, 1984).

Most languages tend to be adopted by a band of people eager to claim that their language is natural, easy to learn and just right for this or that class of problem. Despite the hyperbole, it is clear that learning to program in any language is not necessarily easy. The interesting question that PROLOG poses because of its structure (which we discuss below) is whether problems in learning to program centre around learning to cope with the machine and its idiosyncracies, or whether problems are to do with thinking in a particularly constrained and sometimes counter-intuitive manner (i.e. in a formal logical way). An issue of particular concern to developmental psychologists is the question of how a student's general cognitive competence, especially the ability to handle logic and inference, interacts with the ability to learn PROLOG successfully.

PROLOG does offer some automatic facilities which, in theory, ought to relieve the beginner of certain chores associated with understanding the machinery in learning to program. PROLOG can, for example, make inferences from statements. Given the information that 'Firemen wear red braces' and that 'John is a fireman', PROLOG can automatically infer that John wears red braces. Furthermore, by a process called backtracking, PROLOG can find as many solutions to some query as there are in the database. After finding the first successful answer to a query, the user can ask PROLOG to look for any others, and so obtain, on occasion, multiple solutions to one question.

This process, in turn, is facilitated by the use of 'variables'. The way in which PROLOG uses variables is interesting, and differs from the way that most other programming languages use them. Discussion of these subtleties is not essential for our purposes here, but we occasionally need to refer to the concept of variables so we provide a somewhat simplified example of their use.

The easiest way to think of a variable is as an empty slot which can be filled by anything that 'matches' and is of the correct form. The most straightforward case of filling a variable is when the variable is empty at the outset (i.e. in the query, say) and the database contains information of the correct form which allows the variable to be filled. The following example illustrates the basic process. The database in the computer has an entry regarding the colour of elephants:

DATABASE ENTRY:          grey (elephant).

The user types in a query asking 'what do we know about that is grey?':

USER'S QUERY:            grey(X).

'X' here represents the variable, or empty slot that will be filled. PROLOG will match the query with the database item, and X will represent, or be linked to 'elephant' in the query. PROLOG will answer:

PROLOG'S RESPONSE:          X = elephant

This example illustrates the use of a variable in its most elementary form, and there are many ways in which this basic idea can be elaborated and extended. The relationship of variables to backtracking is that if the user wishes to search further to see if there is anything else in the database which is grey, he or she can say, 'OK, but now look for any other instances of database entries that match my original query.' At this point, X (the variable) goes back to being empty (the link between 'X' and 'elephant' being broken), and PROLOG continues looking down the database for any other legal match. If the database contains the statement that 'skies are grey', e.g.

DATABASE ENTRY:          grey(skies).

then X in the query will stand for 'skies' and PROLOG will respond:

PROLOG'S RESPONSE:          X = skies

and so on.

So at first sight PROLOG looks as though it should be fairly easy to learn. However, the language's apparent simplicity is beguiling, beginners occasionally being lulled into a false sense of security and then finding themselves quite at sea with no idea how to proceed and some uncertainty about whether they have correctly understood those topics they thought were secure. The automatic facilities, while simplifying certain sorts of tasks, introduce their own subtle difficulties for the unwary beginner, and a large part of a PROLOG programmer's skill lies in knowing how to constrain them.

Our objective is to see what, if anything, is special about PROLOG in this respect, and to discuss some of the more misleading claims made on its behalf. One of the issues that will emerge is that we do not yet have a convincing picture of what the ideal PROLOG notional machine should look like, nor do we yet have good strategies for teaching the language (see Bundy and Pain, 1985).

## DIFFICULTIES FOR NOVICE PROGRAMMERS

Difficulties associated with learning most languages, including PROLOG, can be separated into six overlapping classes. These classes should not be thought of as general stages in learning to program or particular stages in the process of producing a working program. Rather they represent views of the programming process at different levels. Each of these views needs to be elaborated and assimilated by the student in order to become expert.

1. There is the general *Problem of Orientation*, finding out what programming can be used for, what general kinds of problem can be tackled and
   what the eventual advantages might be of expending effort in learning
   the skill. For example, at Sussex University we run short introductory
   courses for Arts undergraduates who want to acquaint themselves with
   AI approaches and programming techniques (du Boulay, 1986). Such
   students sometimes find the high-level theoretical discussions of AI interesting and stimulating, but find the programming component of the course
   difficult because it is not clear to them what they could ever use it for – the
   problems computers can solve are not part of these students' conceptual
   framework.
2. There are the difficulties of *Interpreting Problem Descriptions*. This
   includes getting a precise enough understanding of what the problem is
   in order to determine what might count as a solution. This will normally
   involve identifying what elements, relations or objects in the given situation need to be taken into account and what links there are between the
   solution and important factors in the problem. Even if the beginner does
   not know what the solution to the problem will eventually be, he or she
   does have to know the kind of shape a solution would take in order to
   progress to the next stage.
3. There are difficulties associated with the mapping from an understanding
   of the problem to an understanding of the general properties of the
   *notional machine* (i.e. the simplified conceptual computing system with
   which the beginner is working; see above). Furthermore, the beginner is
   often not only dealing with one notional machine, that is the one associated with the language they are using. The beginner will usually also have
   to master an editor, and an operating system, and both of these have
   notional machines associated with them, i.e. at no point are we talking
   about the actual physical machine built of metal and silicon with wires and
   disks, but idealized mental models of part of the computer's functioning. If
   the beginner is lucky, the three notional machines of the programming
   language, the editor and the operating system may be seamlessly inter-
   woven, or at least not conflict with one another. Whether it is one notional
   machine or many, this will entail realizing how the behaviour of parts of
   the tangible machine (the keyboard and screen) relate to these notional
   machines – for example whether the information on the terminal screen
   is a record of prior interactions between the user and the computer, or is
   instead a window on to some part of the machine's innards.

   Second, there are difficulties in transforming an understanding of the
   problem into the terms of reference of the programming language. If the
   concepts embodied in a language are entirely new to the student, this can
   sometimes be a slow and difficult task. One of the subtle changes that
   occurs in the programmer is that he or she comes to view new problems

in terms of the potentialities (and limitations) of the available tool. Those who argue that a particular language is 'natural' are usually right: they have been changed by their own exposure to the language and now see problems in its terms, which may prevent them from perceiving the difficulties that a new learner is having.

The beginner has to recognize and then integrate these two components of the notional machines to gain an understanding of the sometimes complex execution of a program.

4. There are problems associated with the notation of the various *formal languages* that have to be learned, including mastering both the syntax and their underlying semantics. Understanding syntax usually means knowing what kinds of symbols are legal, and how they may be strung together to produce certain kinds of effects. The semantics may be viewed as an elaboration of the properties and behaviour of the programming language's notional machine, crudely sketched above. Relating syntax to semantics involves realizing which strings of symbols will make the computer produce what particular types of 'actions'.

In practice this would entail understanding how the notional machine works in its own terms, mostly independent of any particular problem (which is what distinguishes this level from that described in 3 above).

5. Associated with notation are the difficulties of acquiring *standard structures*, cliches or plans that can be used to achieve small-scale goals, such as working down a list of items performing some operation, or transforming one structure into another. For example, Ehrlich and Soloway (1982) have investigated the 'tacit plans' that experts construct from experience for dealing with standard situations. The plans are tacit because the expert may not be consciously aware of their presence. So, an expert can look at some problem description, decide that a certain type of construct is appropriate, and employ the corresponding plan of action without devoting special thought to the matter, whereas beginners have to generate a plan afresh every time.

The hypothesis is that experts assign a functional role to programming structures and eventually disregard the execution details (i.e. how the computer actually does it) thus enabling them to take a higher-level view of the programming process. Beginners, on the other hand, understand programs by examining how the computer does something, which is a correspondingly lower-level view. So, given a program to read and understand, experts will be concerned with *what* it does, what are the inputs, what are the outputs, and so on, whereas novices interpret *how* it does it, and may not retain information about what the overall goal of the program was.

Since there often are standard ways of accomplishing certain effects in

any computing language, it is useful for these to be taught directly to students, rather than have them laboriously work them out for themselves.
6. Finally there is the issue of mastering the pragmatics of programming, that is learning the skill of how to specify, develop, test and correct ('debug') a program using whatever tools are available.

None of these six issues is entirely separable from the others and much of the shock of the first few encounters between the learner and the system are compounded by the student's attempt to deal with all these different levels of difficulty at once.

This paper concentrates on four of the above issues:

* interpreting problem descriptions;
* moving from problem descriptions to PROLOG programs;
* the semantics of PROLOG;
* pragmatics.

At various points we will mention experimental work that we have undertaken with PROLOG novices (mostly undergraduates and postgraduates) and PROLOG experts (mostly research fellows and faculty).

## INTERPRETING PROBLEM DESCRIPTIONS

**Entities and relations**

One of the skills that the beginning programmer has to master is that of reading a piece of text expressing a problem and deciding what that problem is. This requires an analysis of the major entities involved, of their relationships and how a solution may be obtained in principle. For some programming languages the kinds of entity about which problems can be stated are numerical or at least similarly well delineated. These quantities stand out from the surrounding description and are thus automatically highlighted. As PROLOG allows statements to be made about any relationships and implications, there is no clear boundary between things that can be described in PROLOG and those that cannot. This means that it is much harder for the beginner to use the kind of landmarks that might serve, say, in a numerical problem to see what the major entities are. One way to reduce this difficulty is to stress the notions of relationships and individuals and give the students lots of practice in using a given restricted vocabulary to express limited aspects of English sentences (see Ennals, 1984, for examples of this approach).

Even if the major entities and relationships are clear there is the problem of deciding how these should be represented. A problem that involves 'John liking Mary' might be thought of as problem involving a relationship, 'liking', and two individuals, 'John' and 'Mary', which in PROLOG might look like this:

EXAMPLE 1:          likes(john, mary).

Perhaps it should be thought of as a single event with three parameters, 'John', 'liking' and 'Mary'.

EXAMPLE 2:          event(john, likes, mary).

Another possibility is to think of it involving a single individual, 'Mary', who happens to be in the state of being 'liked-by-John'.

EXAMPLE 3:          liked_by_john(mary).

There are further possibilities as well. Each of these looks rather different when translated into PROLOG and has repercussions on how the rest of the program should be expressed and on what kinds of inferences can be drawn by the program. Questions of how best to solve this kind of issue depend very much on what kind of solution is being sought. In general, changes of representation can have a profound effect on how easily a problem can be tackled (and on how efficient a program may eventually be). For example, although at some levels each of these representations refers to the same state of affairs, the ease with which they can be manipulated and changed in the context of a database differs. Example 1 could probably be thought of as the standard way of representing relationships in PROLOG, and allows for the creation of a database in which we can represent the 'likes' relationship holding between multiple 'partners' or 'objects', i.e. the representation is easily extensible:

```
likes(john, jane).
likes(jane, mike).
likes(sally, susan).
etc.
```

Example 2 has a structure which is more general – 'events' might be of many different types:

```
event(likes, john, reading).
event(likes, susan, sally).
event(likes, judith, pasta).
event(helps, judith, john).
etc.
```

But this very flexibility may be a trap, because the minimal amount of structure is imposed on the database. We could represent other things:

```
event(world, war, two).
```

event(fido, fights, cats).
event(anything, you, like).
etc.

Example 3 could be seen as an over-reaction to Example 2. The datastructure is somewhat overconstrained so that we can only talk either about things which are liked by John:

liked_by_john(apples).
liked_by_john(school).

or about a particular individual (Mary):

liked_by_peter(mary).
liked_by_mother(mary).

Of course for some purposes this constraint may be exactly what is needed, but the point is that PROLOG allows the learner to represent information in a variety of ways, and the learner must acquire a sense of what is a 'good' way for any given problem.


**Generality of solution**

A widespread problem that beginners face when interpreting problem descriptions is deciding how general a solution should be. This problem may occur in PROLOG to a larger degree than in other languages for the reasons given above. This issue was thrown into sharp relief when we asked a selection of PROLOG experts to provide solutions for the following problem.

> Write a program for designing an architectural unit obeying the following specifications: Two rectangular rooms, each room has a window and interior door, rooms are connected by interior door, one room also has an exterior door, a wall can have only one door or window, no window can face north, windows cannot be on opposite sides of a unit. (Coelho, Cotta and Pereira, 1982, p. 63)

Although this is a very loosely expressed specification, we were rather surprised by the very wide range of interpretations that were placed upon it. Some saw it as a problem to design a general-purpose architectural planner which could solve the problem automatically, using the given data as an example of the class of data that such a planner should handle. Others saw it more specifically as a puzzle about the stated unit. Others again couched their solutions as essentially constraint-checkers and as a memory aid to help someone who would do the actual problem-solving for him or herself.

# FROM PROBLEMS TO PROGRAMS

## High-level languages

Certain forms of logic have a long history of being used as problem-solving tools, and in computing such forms are frequently used as specification languages (i.e. 'intermediary' languages which express the logical correctness of some problem solution prior to its being couched in any particular programming formalism). What PROLOG has to offer is that it is both a form of predicate logic and a runnable programming language with machine-independent syntax and semantics. So if a programmar specifies the logic of some solution, he or she can then simply run it (it may run slowly) instead of having to translate it into a more conventional programming language with idiosyncracies due to its dependency on hardware. This streamlines the process of program development by disposing of the need for major translations from one representation to another, and allows for more effective deployment of programmer time and effort, though minor changes within the representation may be needed for the purposes of efficiency.

At both a practical and a theoretical level we can see the advantages that logic programming languages have for the programmer (indeed one of the authors uses it for research). But the programmer here is often a professional who can appreciate the freedom of programming in such a machine-independent language. The situation is less clear-cut for beginners. Note that we are not arguing that beginners should not be taught PROLOG or that it is unteachable. What we are arguing is that teaching it to beginners poses special problems, above and beyond those posed by other more conventional languages, precisely because it is higher level. It presents the beginner with the double-edged blade of freedom to create interesting programs quickly, and the freedom to make serious errors equally as quickly.

## Claims for PROLOG

In common with other languages, PROLOG has suffered from enthusiastic claims for its ease of use. The particular line of reasoning to support this claim for PROLOG is that since PROLOG is based on logic it will be simple to learn (implying that everybody is good at logic) and that it will be easier for novices to express themselves in the language because logic can be understood in terms of its natural-language equivalents (Kowalski, 1979).

We believe this argument is a liberal interpretation of the more formal discussion of PROLOG's high-level status described above and is based on assumptions about people's natural reasoning abilities. Apart from leading novice programmers into false expectations of what the process of programming is about, and what they can expect of their own performance, this kind of interpretation runs counter to what we know of people's logical deductive reasoning abilities.

### Logic, reasoning and natural language

There are three assumptions which will be questioned here: first, that predicate logic captures the logic underlying human reasoning and language; second, that logic is natural; and third, that logic has natural language equivalents. We shall take each in turn.

The crux of the argument is this: although most adults are capable of formal reasoning, the suggestion that such reasoning either conforms to, or is captured in, the precise rules of predicate logic is unwarranted. Formalisms such as classical logics and programming languages attempt to be unequivocal. In the study of deductive reasoning – and of programming – we see people struggling to solve problems within the framework of a formalism which, in the interests of maintaining its formality, embodies certain necessary, but counter-intuitive, constraints. Such tasks are difficult and require practice, so the argument that PROLOG somehow short-circuits this learning pattern simply because it is based on predicate logic is meaningless.

The significant difference to grasp is between the formalisms of classical logic as devised by logicians, and the hypothesized 'logical' thinking processes used by people in their everyday lives, and it is this difference which is frequently blurred in the PROLOG literature.

Psychologists are uncertain about whether a 'natural' logic exists, let alone what kind of classical logic it might resemble, if any (see Johnson-Laird, 1983). It may be true that first-order predicate logic usefully formalizes some aspects of the human reasoning process, but so do many other formalisms (e.g. various branches of mathematics). Predicate logic is not special in this respect, nor should we expect untutored people to have a natural aptitude for using it any more than we would for a more mathematically oriented logic. Evidence produced by psychologists in fact supports the view that, in general, people have no natural aptitude for formal logic (see Evans, 1982, for a review of this literature).

Finally, the claim that logic has natural language equivalents throws our previous remarks into relief because part of the explanation in the psychological literature for poor performance at deductive reasoning is attributed to people failing to understand the difference between expressions couched in natural language and expressions in the formalism. The extraction of 'meaning' from natural language expressions often depends on knowledge of causal or temporal factors known by the listener, who may, in fact end up misinterpreting the expression by importing too much knowledge into the discussion domain. Logic, on the other hand, conforms to quite a different set of rules, often dealing simply with truth functional relations between elements of expressions, regardless of the meaning. In propositional calculus, for example, propositions have one of two truth values – they are either true or false – which is not the case in natural language. Connectives are defined solely as functions of the truth values of the propositions they interrelate (see Johnson-Laird and Wason, 1977). Furthermore, standard logic does not deal with temporal or causal events, and basing interpretations on the semantics of natural language may lead to all kinds of difficulties. For example, the two English sentences: (taken from Johnson-Laird and Wason, p. 79)

*She inherited a fortune and he married her*
and
*He married her and she inherited a fortune*

could be attributed different meanings by someone untutored in logic, but in the predicate calculus with its restricted meaning for 'and', they are identical.

People are quite naturally inclined to misinterpret logical expressions if these differences are not spelled out to them clearly. Furthermore, misinterpretations can arise from the content and form of the material to be analysed. Students may be led astray by 'atmosphere effects' (Begg and Denny, 1969), i.e. assertions couched in natural language create an atmosphere which, in the absence of rigorous logical analysis, may seduce people into deriving conclusions which favour that atmosphere (for example, people are disinclined to draw a 'negative' conclusion from 'positive' assertions). Lastly, untutored people are led into fallacious reasoning by not considering all the relevant information. Some diagrammatic representations of logic (e.g. Venn diagrams) try to overcome this well-known problem. Interestingly, this kind of difficulty also surfaces in the programming environment, where people tend to underspecify algorithms, e.g. telling the computer what to do if some situation arises, but forgetting to tell it what to do if it doesn't.

In theory, therefore, rather than appearing to be an easier programming language to learn than any other, one could argue that PROLOG might be disastrous as a first language, since the combination of logic and programming at the same time, each with their independent constraints and their relationship in programming, would make the novice's task extremely arduous. For example, we have seen that failure to consider the full scope of the problem/solution domain in programming will result in underspecification of algorithms; in logic, it will lead to fallacious reasoning. In PROLOG it may lead to both.

For practical purposes, however, the dilemma is this: if the problem statement refers to abstract notions then the task is often difficult; if concrete material is substituted for abstract (e.g. natural language expressions are substituted for symbolic expressions) then task difficulty diminishes greatly, but the reasoning process becomes error-prone because people feel free to use their natural language comprehension skills where it is inappropriate. Their interpretations of formal expressions are based on what they know of the real world, which, in certain cases, will lead them astray in the logical domain.

From a teaching point of view, we would emphasize the need to encourage learners to view PROLOG programming as a problem-solving exercise, and discourage the notion of 'translation' from English to PROLOG and back again, since the semantics of each is quite different.

We have some evidence of this tendency to confuse the rules governing natural language and the rules governing a formalism. At Sussex University we teach PROLOG to first-year Arts undergraduates who frequently have no strong science or mathematical background. One course lasts 9 weeks and is designed to introduce them to artificial intelligence ideas and techniques. It is not a programming course as such, but they learn how to use a high-level AI programming language, in this case PROLOG.

We asked a group of these students to perform two straightforward tasks: the first was to give us an English rendering of some PROLOG clauses, the second was to create a PROLOG database from information expressed in English. While the first task presented no difficulties at all, the second task was problematic. The English sentences were a mixture of facts and conjunctions, such as

*John works hard and likes music*
which are easily represented in PROLOG:
works-hard(john), likes(john, music).
and some causually dependent sentences such as
*John is a good student because he works hard*

which are not easily represented, because PROLOG, like logic, doesn't deal with causal relationships.

So how do our logically unsophisticated students cope with such a problem? We had a variety of responses, but none of our students explicitly said that this sentence could not be represented because of the limitations of the basic formalism. Some students argued that the solution to this problem is to create a rule which says: if I can prove that John works hard then I can infer that he is a good student. In PROLOG form this can be read: infer that John is a good student if you can prove that he works hard.

good_student(john) :- works_hard(john).

Note that ':-' in PROLOG means 'if' and the inclusion of this rule in a program would enable PROLOG to infer that 'John is a good student' by using another fact in the database, i.e. 'John works hard'. This is an interesting solution because it highlights the sometimes subtle differences between causal reasoning and logical inference in natural language. Our students, in effect, are asking 'Will this happen?' rather than 'Does this logically follow?', more clearly illustrated in the sentence: 'If I tip my cup then my tea will fall out.' This kind of causal reasoning requires an intuitive temporal dimension (one thing must happen before another). PROLOG viewed as logic has no such dimension, but PROLOG viewed as an executable programming language does – the way PROLOG actually works through a program allows for a non-linear (because of the backtracking), but plausible sense of time. Provided that our students do not make the mistake of thinking they are being logically correct, and provided they are consistent in this somewhat unorthodox interpretation of the ':-' operator, they will probably progress quite happily.

Another response was for students to declare that the sentence was impossible to represent. For them, 'if' and 'because' 'don't mean the same and so it can't be done'. In fact, although none of these students were logically trained, this response is closest to the logical stance. However, we suspect that rather than being correct for this reason, these students were actually trying to translate English into PROLOG, and expected PROLOG to have corresponding operators to the English connectives 'because', 'so', 'therefore'. Interestingly, though, while fretting about the causal links, they were quite happy to drop quantifiers such as 'all' and 'every' from statements like 'All Misha's students work hard', and 'Every student of Misha's works hard'. Quantifiers are another feature of English with which PROLOG does not deal directly, but which are usually dealt with by careful use of variables. It may be that the techniques for dealing with quantifiers are less obviously altering the meaning of a sentence than the 'if/because' substitution. But, either way, if students are inclined to construct the meaning of a program from the meaning of English and not from the semantics of the programming language, they may find life difficult.

The situation is problematic both at the level of predicate logic and at the level of computer programming. From the point of view of logic, students who do not realize that logical expressions are subject to the rules of logic, and not the rules of natural language, may find themselves in very deep water later on in trying to interpret the 'meaning' of sentences such as 'Either some dogs are animals or no animals are not dogs' which doesn't have a very sensible English meaning but which is logically sound. From the point of view of computing, there are two issues.

First, data or information in computer programs, whether in PROLOG or not, have to be structured 'sensibly' for the current purpose, whatever that may be, or else programs will produce meaningless or incorrect answers. Learning how to sensibly represent knowledge is arguably the most important issue to be confronted by the beginner in learning to program. So long as students think that they merely have to embark on a surface translation from English into the hieroglyphs of PROLOG, they avoid the crucial issue of knowledge representation which is relevant to all aspects of computing and AI. Such students will confuse themselves by writing disorganized programs which will either take a long time to run, or which will not run at all. Students may then have to waste time debugging badly conceived programs.

Second, from the beginner's point of view, programming involves the notion of problem solving, which usually means devising an algorithm which the computer will use to work out the answer to some problem. The difficulty in adopting the 'translation' view is that simply re-representing the English text in PROLOG is not going to solve the problem – the student must work out how the algorithm will proceed, and what information it needs to succeed. Students who lose sight of this goal are likely to be severely hampered in their learning.

Another facet of the natural language issue is that students may try to understand a program in terms of natural language, and not in terms of the functional relations between different parts of the program. They may think that PROLOG 'understands' the meaning of words, or that some words are significant to PROLOG. This becomes particularly apparent in database manipulation tasks. Ross (1982) points out that beginners are usually presented the declarative viewpoint of PROLOG (see next section) angled towards database creation and search programs which often use a lot of English words. In his opinion this approach promotes complacency because PROLOG looks very easy at this level. Beginners can fool themselves that they are learning to program, when in fact they are understanding the program by understanding the English, i.e. by attributing meaning to the words used. This can allow students to ignore various important aspects of the PROLOG notional machine, and its behaviour, which will cause a great deal of confusion later.

Debugging will be difficult if there is a disparity between what students think their program is saying (described at a linguistic level), and what it is actually doing (at the notional machine level). For example, we have noted that, when asked to describe what their PROLOG programs were supposed to do, some students at Sussex were able to give quite competent English descriptions. But the code they had written either simply did not reflect this English description, or did not work in the desired way because the logical structure of the problem solution had not been extracted from the English. The solution, as expressed in these programs, lay in understanding the meaning of the English words, which of course PROLOG cannot do.

So encouraging beginners to understand logic/PROLOG by the use of natural language may not be the great advantage it at first appears. Kowalski (1979) makes the caveat that natural language will only provide an 'informal guide' to understanding logic. This is fine for someone who understands either logic, or programming, or both. He or she will have a fundamental grasp of the limitations of the 'informal guide' as an aid to understanding. But the warning is not adequate for the optimistic novice.

## SYNTAX AND SEMANTICS

The general problem for beginners with PROLOG is that the underlying notional machine is both powerful and complex, with a surface behaviour that is hard to predict accurately. Most of the preceding section concentrated on what is called the declarative semantics of PROLOG (and the difficulties that novices have with it). The declarative semantics describe PROLOG programs in terms of the high-level logical specification of what it will do (i.e. with no emphasis on 'how' it will be done). There is, however, another view of PROLOG that links back to the remarks about mechanisms in the introduction.

PROLOG is not just a means of recording and then interrogating static observations about a world. It is also a programming language in which things can be made to happen (inferences) and these will occur in a particular order. The user needs to understand this in order to predict accurately what a PROLOG program will do. The procedural semantics is a formal account of what PROLOG programs do and how they do it. A competent PROLOG programmer must reconcile the declarative and procedural view of the language and recognize the circumstances when each is the best way to interpret what is presented. These two views are not in conflict, they are complementary.

Unfortunately, PROLOG syntax does not offer any clear pointers to what is happening 'behind the scenes', i.e. what changes are taking place in the internal state of the machine. Much of the machine's activities have to be interpreted from dense and compact syntax, and because there are few indications of flow of control (i.e. the order of events) through the program, students sometimes find it difficult to interpret how the code will run. PROLOG presents a particular difficulty for beginners in this respect because although it is true that in other languages identifying and sustaining the correct flow of control is important, part of PROLOG's power is in its automatic inferencing and backtracking mechanisms. Backtracking is the mechanism that enables PROLOG to try further rules, if available, when it fails in its attempt to use a particular rule to establish the truth of some inference. This mechanism ensures that PROLOG automatically attempts every possible way of trying to prove an inference before giving up and reporting that it cannot.

The novice must learn how to control these processes by learning how to order sentences in the program, recognizing circularities within a rule, ordering sub-goals within a goal and employing certain special controlling primitives (such as the the the 'cut') to achieve a solution.

PROLOG provides a facility, called a 'trace package' with which the programmer can observe the internal chain of events, such as inferencing and backtracking, while a program runs. These packages are not without their own drawbacks for the novice. Sometimes they present a view of the system which is at odds with the notional machine that the beginner thinks is there, or they provide either too much or too little detail, or indeed are just hard to control in their own right.

Beginners tend to write programs which PROLOG can run away with by drawing an endless chain of useless but true inferences. This happens because they include rules that are in some sense circular e.g. that 'John is a good student if John is a good student'. The system can end up fruitlessly trying to find the end of the chain of identical inferences that such a rule would generate. The actual problems are often more subtle than this, of course, and involve the complex use of variables.

We asked students to write a small program on paper, and then describe what the machine would do with it. Most of them were capable of outlining one possible solution (the one they were expecting) but they gave incomplete descriptions of *all* the work the machine would have to do to get there. When we ran the program and switched on the tracing package they were surprised to see how much variable 'matching' and backtracking was involved during the solution process. This lack of knowledge about how much work PROLOG may have to do behind the scenes even to produce an apparently simple – and to the human user often obvious – answer can make it difficult for students to debug faulty programs. In other words, if the solution is not correct first time, students may have great difficulty identifying where the error lies.

Backtracking confuses beginners in other ways. There have been a number of studies to identify common misconceptions about what PROLOG does when it backtracks, whose results are confirmed by our own work with novices (see e.g. Coombs and Stell, 1984; Van Someren, 1984). One of the issues is that it can only be understood properly in dynamic terms and the static text of the written program is only a partial guide and may even, according to Coombs (1985), be a positive hindrance!

## PRAGMATICS

One of the findings from our work with experts was their much greater reliance on the PROLOG tracing facilities to debug their programs. It did not merely seem a matter that they were more skilled in using these facilities (which of course they were); there seemed to be a difference in what they perceived as a reasonable course of action when developing a program. The experts appeared to be much readier to admit the difficulty of predicting exactly what a PROLOG program would do under various circumstances and used the system itself to help with the prediction and hence the debugging. The novices, on the other hand, seemed to want to undertake this hard predictive task for themselves without help. It was as if they perceived their task as putative programmers to be doing this job unaided.

It has to be admitted that learning to use the tracer and interpret its output can itself be hard. The messages from the tracer and dynamically changing layout of information on the screen require that the student understands the procedural semantics of PROLOG if they are to be fully appreciated. In particular, PROLOG's backtracking behaviour is much in evidence and we have already discussed above some of the problems that students have with this. Students who only partially understand this aspect of PROLOG will probably be helped by trying to interpret the trace output, but they may be reluctant to turn to this as a source of help for debugging.

## CONCLUSIONS

PROLOG provides beginners with the means to write interesting, non-trivial programs at an early stage in the learning process, using powerful computational mechanisms, so capturing the interest of the learner from the outset. The language allows for various types of computing-related activities – aside from writing programs, it can be used as a database creation and search language, as a representation language for problem solving, and because the principles on which PROLOG operates are machine independent, the learner can get a global view of computers and their operations without getting unnecessarily bogged down in highly specific machine-related details.

A problem common to all computing languages is that if a beginner suffers from woolly thinking, then the computer will highlight deficiences with unpitying relentlessness. A specific problem with PROLOG is that up to a point it will allow the user to write some fairly silly, usually contradictory, things without complaining. But clearly, at some point, things will go awry, leaving the beginner in a state of confusion.

There is much that technology can do to ease the load on the user. Improved debugging tools and friendly environments for PROLOG are under development. However, learners have to be made aware of the fact that learning to program, just like acquiring any complex skill, requires effort and practice. It is unlikely that any language will be able to do away with hard work and application. Similarly, it may be tempting for the tutor to think that because PROLOG is a high-level language then less effort needs to be put into the teaching materials – it will be easier to teach as well as to learn. This does not seem to be the case. We have seen that some difficulties are related to PROLOG's internal structure (i.e. the backtracking mechanism) which require the careful development of clear and adequate models of the language to present to students (see Pain and Bundy 1985). Other

problems are to do more generally with students' expectations of themselves –
that they should be able to learn programming effortlessly – and of computers
(i.e. thinking they can understand the meaning of English words). This class
of problem can sometimes combine with a student's limited problem-solving
skills (or abilities) to make the task of learning to program appear an impossible task.

This chapter scratches the surface of many complex problems which we
are continuing to investigate. There are a number of further interesting issues
thrown up by our current experiments which need further analysis. One
example is the apparent unwillingness of novices to use the closed-world
assumption and their wish to represent negative information explicitly rather
than leaving it to be 'discovered' by PROLOG as an absence of positive
information.

## ACKNOWLEDGEMENTS

We thank Maarten van Someren for helpful comments on early drafts of this
chapter, and Jon Cunningham for discussions. This work is supported by a
grant from SERC/Alvey.

## REFERENCES

Anderson, J. R. (1982). Acquisition of cognitive skill, *Psychological Review*, **89**, 369–
406.
Badre, A., and Shneiderman, B. (1982). *Directions in Human Computer Interaction*,
Ablex Publishing Corporation, Norwood, N. J.
Begg, I., and Denny, J. P. (1969). Empirical reconsideration of atmosphere and
conversion interpretations of syllogistic reasoning errors, *Journal of Exp.
Psychology*, **81**, 351–354.
Coelho, H., Cotta J. C., and Pereira, L. M. (1982). *How to Solve it with PROLOG*
(3rd edn), Laboratorio Nacional de Engenharia Civil (Obra 03/53.752), Lisbon,
Portugal.
Coombs, M. J. (1985). Alvey Conference, Edinburgh.
Coombs, M. J., and Alty, J. L. (1981). *Computing Skills and the User Interface*,
Academic Press, London.
Coombs, M. J., and Stell, J. G. (1985). *A Model for Debugging PROLOG by
Symbolic Execution: The Separation of Specification and Procedure*, Dept. of
Computer Science, University of Strathclyde
du Boulay, J. B. H. (1986). Poplog for beginners: a powerful environment for
learning programming. In R. Hawley (ed.), *Artificial Intelligence Programming,
Environments*, forthcoming, Ellis Horwood, Chichester.
du Boulay, J. B. H., O'Shea, T. and Monk, J. (1981). The black box inside the glass
box: presenting computing concepts to novices, *International Journal of Man-
Machine Studies*, *14*, 237–249.
Ehrlich, K., and Soloway, E. (1982). An empirical investigation of the tacit plan
knowledge in programming, Department of Computer Science Research Report
No. 236, Yale University.

Ennals, R. (1984). *Beginning Micro-Prolog*, Ellis Horwood, Chichester.
Evans, J. St. B. T. (1982). *The Psychology of Deductive Reasoning*, Routledge and Kegan Paul, London.
Johnson-Laird, P. N. (1983). *Mental Models*, Cambridge University Press, Cambridge.
Johnson-Laird, P. N., and Wason, P. C. (eds) (1977). *Thinking – Readings in Cognitive Science*, Cambridge University Press, Cambridge.
Kowalski, R. (1973). Predicate logic as programming language, Memo No. 70, Department of Computational Logic, School of AI, University of Edinburgh
Kowalski, R. 1979). *Logic for Problem Solving*, North Holland Inc., New York.
Monk, A. (1985), *Fundamentals of Human-Computer Interaction*, Academic Press, London.
Norman, D. A., and Draper, S. W. (1986). *User Centred System Design – New Perspectives on Human-Computer Interaction*, Lawrence Erlbaum, Hillsdale, N. J.
Pain, H., and Bundy, A. (1985). What stories should we tell novice PROLOG programmers?, work in progress report, University of Edinburgh.
Ramsden, E. (ed.) (1984). *Microcomputers in Education*, Ellis Horwood, Chichester.
Ross, P. (1982). Teaching PROLOG to undergraduates, *AISBQ*. Autumn 1982.
Shneiderman, B. (1980). *Software Psychology*, Winthrop Publishers, Cambridge, Mass.
Smith, H. T., and Green, T. R. G. (1980). *Human Interaction with Computers*, Academic Press, London.
Soloway, E., and Ehrlich, K. (1984). Empirical studies of programming knowledge, *IEEE Transactions on Software Engineering*, Sept. 1984.
Taylor, J. (1984). Why novices will find learning PROLOG hard, *Proceedings ECAI*, 1984.
Van Someren, M. W. (1984). Misconceptions of beginning Prolog programmers, Memorandum 30, Dept. Of Experimental Psychology, University of Amsterdam.

# PART III

# The Computational Metaphor in Cognitive Science and Developmental Psychology

# Editorial Introduction

The chapters of this final section explore direct links between computational concepts and methods of theory construction and those of developmental psychology. From various perspectives, they address the question: 'How can a computational approach contribute to framing more precise and useful theories of cognitive development?'

A feature of contemporary development psychology is its growing awareness of the need for process-models of cognitive abilities. Thornton's chapter highlights the climate of controversy that surrounds current theoretical perspectives on cognitive development. There is no consensus as to what changes in development, or how change should be conceptualized. As she emphasizes, the questions facing developmentalists do not concern children's behaviour so much as our ideas about the underlying processes which generate that behaviour. A promising source of ideas is the 'computational metaphor' for the mind – many are confident that the concepts it provides will remain unsurpassed for phrasing theories of cognitive processes (e.g. Johnson-Laird, 1983).

Similar directions emerge from applied considerations. Constructing models of knowledge organization and learning processes is given first priority in Sage and Smith's (1983) influential framework for research on microcomputers in education. Research workers, they suggest, will need to be open to 'unorthodox' methods, without compromising essential standards of rigour. In particular, they forefront the need for psychological research to proceed within a framework directed toward computational modelling. The probable payoff of this strategy, they argue, will justify the high cost and inherent difficulty involved.

Concern with process-models, computational modelling, and the interplay between developmental and computational approaches, brings us squarely into the province of 'cognitive science'. In these introductory comments, we shall briefly outline those aspects of the cognitive science framework that inform the discussions of the following chapters. These chapters explore possibilities for interchange between developmental psychology and cognitive science. Each suggests ways in which developmentalists can profitably question their own assumptions and methods and give serious consideration to the techniques of computational approaches. Equally, emphasis is placed on the reciprocal benefits that a fusion of computational and developmental methods can offer cognitive science.

## COGNITIVE SCIENCE AND THE COMPUTATIONAL METAPHOR

Cognitive science is still an emerging discipline and lacks clearly defined boundaries. However, several themes are fairly uncontroversial, and they feature in the coming discussions:

(a) Cognitive science is interdisciplinary. It draws on insights and methods from artificial intelligence (AI), computer science, linguistics, philosophy and psychology – although, as yet, little from developmental psychology.

(b) It aims to provide us with a better understanding of the mind, cognition and intelligence than individual disciplines have so far achieved.

(c) Contrasted with mainstream psychology, its approach to theory construction is less concerned with the prediction and experimental study of human behaviour. Rather, its focus is on methods for specifying a set of mechanisms whose interaction can actually be shown to produce the behaviour of interest.

(d) Its practitioners are committed to some version of the computational metaphor. This provides concepts for phrasing theories; and it justifies a novel empirical method for exploring those theories by means of computer programs.

   Behind the computational metaphor for the mind are closely allied notions of *representation* and *computation*, which can briefly be outlined as follows. The core concept is that of a 'physical symbol system': a class of physical systems capable of producing symbols that correspond to or *represent* aspects of their internal and external environments (Newell, 1980; Newell and Simon, 1976). The major force of the 'physical symbol system hypothesis' is found in the claim that computers, as well as humans, belong to such a class of systems. The idea that a subject's abilities depend on, and are constrained by, their knowledge is familiar in cognitive-developmental psychology. What cognitive science's exploitation of the computational metaphor purports to offer is a uniquely precise and fine-grained approach to the nature of that knowledge.

Knowledge is viewed as an active process of *computation*, which is generally defined as rule-governed symbol-structure manipulation (e.g. Solman, 1982). The basis of understanding and behaviour – whether these are embodied in humans or computers – is assumed to lie in computational processes. A key attraction here for developmental psychologists is that they are offered a supremely active metaphor to guide their understanding of cognition. They are invited to move beyond descriptive accounts of what subjects know and do, to explanations of how this is possible in terms of systems of interacting processes. Computational concepts, it is argued, are necessary to express the content, structure, construction, comparison, transformation, function, and development of differing representations (Boden, 1983).

Much of the conceptual and empirical basis of this framework hinges on the relation between computers and symbolic computation. The structure that controls what a computer does – the program – can be thought of as a series of instructions that make explicit its computational rules. When these instructions are activated, they determine which symbol-manipulation processes or computations the computer will perform and when. The computational metaphor assumes that the mind can be viewed in a similar way: the relationship between the brain and cognitive processes is envisaged as analogous to that between a computer and its program.

The distinction between the program and the physical characteristics of the machine on which it runs is vital. A program is, in principle, independent of the machine that it controls. It is possible to run the same program on a range of computers with quite different physical structures. Thus, the program controls the computer, but it can be specified and studied in its own right. The conclusion that is generally drawn for cognitive science is clearly stated by Johnson-Laird:

> Once you know the way in which a computer program works, your understanding of it is in no way improved by learning about the machine on which it runs on this occasion or that. The same program may be translated into completely different codes for controlling different makes of computer that operate in different ways, and yet it is the same program that computes the same function however it is physically realized . . . our understanding of the mind will not be further improved by going beyond the level of mental processes (1983, p.9).

This perspective offers cognitive scientists the possibility of constructing artificial intelligence and a deeper appreciation of natural intelligence. AI researchers, for example, hope to be able to embody 'intelligence' in computers by writing appropriately structured programs. The psychologist's task can be redefined as that of understanding the 'human program', and a new empirical tool becomes available for advancing that understanding: computational modelling. If the computational processes underlying an ability can be specified independently of the particular (brain) wetware or (computer) hardware that happens to support them, then a computer program can serve as a working model of the human program.

A completely specified computational method for performing a particular task is often called an algorithm. By analogy with the more familiar notion of algorithmic methods in problem-solving, which guarantee success, this can conjure up an image of the brute-force computer which cannot fail because it has been 'told' what to do (see e.g. Pylyshyn, 1984, p.88). In the context of computational models of cognition, however, a significantly different meaning comes into play. All of the processes involved must be spelled out by the algorithm – it should be 'deterministic'. But the interaction of these processes should produce a range of behaviour in different contexts – it should be 'generative'. What the algorithm provides is a deterministic method for generating the processes believed to underlie the performance of interest, whether that performance is always successful, only sometimes successful, or is consistently in error. The aim is to generate the successes and errors of human subjects, without succeeding where they fail or making errors of a type that they do not exhibit (Brown and Van Lehn, 1980). In principle, therefore, it should be possible and useful to build computational models of the processes underlying many types and 'stages' of human ability. This is well illustrated in the following chapters, which consider computational attempts to illuminate phenomena ranging from infant object understanding to adolescent competence with algebra.

## COMPUTATIONAL CONCEPTS AND TECHNIQUES AND DEVELOPMENTAL PSYCHOLOGY

There are several levels at which developmental psychology might draw on this framework. The most general involves use of the notion that cognition, like the functioning of a computer, can usefully be seen as a type of information-processing. This idea has become common currency, and it is far from novel (e.g. McVicker Hunt, 1961). However, stated in this broad form, there are no clear implications for interdisciplinary research.

Within more focused enterprises, we might expect to find interest in specific computational concepts and methods – these are the concern of the coming chapters. Developmental psychologists could make use of computational ideas from other disciplines about the organization and use of knowledge, and attempt to evaluate their plausibility as psychological accounts. An extensive and profitable vein of research in language acquisition was established through attention to formal linguistic accounts of syntactic organization. By comparison, the concepts and formalisms of disciplines such as AI remain neglected. Specific and important suggestions have been made as to how they could help to overcome the imprecision of some developmental theories

(Boden, 1982), and there are promising attempts to understand representational development in such terms (see Mandler, 1983, for a useful review). However, several chapters in this section point to the lack of engagement that developmentalists have shown with potentially relevant areas of AI – the field of machine learning being a prime example. Also, they stress the importance of critical evaluation of such areas from a developmental perspective as opposed to one-way borrowing of ideas.

Finally, in regard to empirical research methods, there is the opportunity to employ computational methods for refining and testing theories. Some attempts are being made to further developmental theory by exploiting such techniques, as the coming chapters will show. But Neisser's (1976) early assessment for cognitive psychology continues to apply in the developmental arena: 'Most of the resistance to computer modelling is passive; psychologists simply continue to make theories of other kinds' (p.12).

## WHAT DOES COMPUTATIONAL WORK OFFER?

One reason for restricted take-up of computational possibilities must surely lie in the highly technical nature of the material involved. Potentially relevant work is rarely presented with the developmentalist in mind; it remains inaccessible to those without the requisite background. Accordingly, the chapters of this section aim to introduce pertinent work so as to provide the reader with a basis for further exploration and assessment. Each introduces a major area of concern and asks: what can it offer developmental psychologists, and what have been its achievements so far?

The first three contributions – from Rutkowska, Thornton and Draper – address these questions to computational work whose immediate concern is with theories of cognition, learning and development.

The argument that effective theories should be expressed as computer programs provides the focus for Rutkowska's chapter. The justification for this approach is outlined, and consideration is given to the main steps in developing a computational model, as well as the supposed advantages over reliance on verbally-stated theories. Psychology experiments are reported in familiar, conventional formats making for straightforward evaluation of their strengths and weaknesses. But what should we expect to find in a useful account of a programming experiment? And what issues and criteria need to be borne in mind in assessing computational theories and programmed models? These questions are explored through detailed comparison of two theories that feature working programs and purport to explain data from the same developmental experiments.

Most AI work directly attempting to illuminate theoretical problems in developmental psychology has been based on a way of structuring a computer program known as a 'production system'. Thornton's chapter outlines the major features of a production-system model and shows how they have been implemented successfully to model children's behaviour at various ages on tasks such as length and weight seriation, class inclusion, conservation and arithmetic. In many respects, they promise to provide tools that can sharpen up our attack on developmental issues, and open up possibilities for tackling theoretical problems in a constructive way. However, Thornton's analysis goes on to stress several ways in which present-day production systems are far from fulfilling their potential as psychological theories.

Within AI, the sub-field of research on 'machine learning' is concerned with the nature of, and conditions for, improved preformance and structural change in a range of knowledge domains; it provides the focus for Draper's chapter. Unlike production-system models, machine learning has not explicitly addressed the problem of human development. However, it offers a different perspective on questions long posed by developmentalists and specific models of learning that they could well explore and test. Draper provides a clear overview within a framework organized around the different ways of defining learning that AI workers have adopted. The main types of machine-learning system are introduced with key examples: how they work, their 'motivation' for learning, what they tell us about learning, and their limitations are considered.

The chapters by Sleeman and Scaife locate their discussion of computational approaches and developmental psychology within the context of learner–computer interaction.

Cognitive modelling and intelligent tutoring systems (ITS) are the concerns of Sleeman's contribution. Examples from work with adolescent algebra students provide the basis for conveying the interplay between collecting data, inferring a cognitive mechanism/theory to explain details of subjects' performance, and using this as the basis of the student-user model component of an ITS. Besides giving the reader a feel for what goes into designing an ITS, there are several ways in which this research tradition bears on theory-construction issues in developmental psychology.

The detailed analysis of students' problem-solving protocols is particularly relevant in highlighting great individual variations in performance strategies and learning paths. The problem, for cognitive scientists or for developmentalists exploiting this type of data, is to build and test a theory that is rich and precise enough to explain both the commonalities and the differences in subjects' performance on particular tasks. Here, Sleeman outlines his own theory of part of the algebra data and shows how it can be expressed computationally to provide a student-user model for an algebra ITS. The model is expressed as a production system, and it illustrates two things: first, how the generativity of this type of process-model is achieved by combining basic rules to capture a range of patterns of task performance; and second, the fact that the model is used predictively as its diagnostic powers must constantly be pitted against the performance of new subjects. Unlike many computational models based on production systems and other AI formalisms, ITS's avoid the criticism of being limited to a *post hoc* summary of the data.

In the final chapter, Scaife stresses the lack of a comprehensive developmental theory in which to locate the interactions between children and computers. In the previous section, we discussed how AI had become involved in learning and education. But could ideas from cognitive science – such as those sketched above – provide us with a psychological account of the learning processes of the user of information technology? In this introduction, we noted the (prevailing) cognitive science view that mental processes can be studied independently of their physical basis. Scaife's analysis challenges this assumption. From this perspective, he suggests, most theoretical cognitive modelling is 'disembodied', lacking an explicit relationship between knowledge structures and the physical-social world. This has implications for understanding child–computer interaction: the general assumption, common to workers in AI and developmental psychology, that learning to program is a purely cognitive activity requires revision. Both cognitive science and developmental psychology need to clarify how sensory-motor restructuring is implicated in preparing, mediating, and assisting cognitive changes. Scaife proposes that theory and research from the French-language and Soviet literatures can provide valuable insights.

## FUTURE LINKS BETWEEN DEVELOPMENTAL PSYCHOLOGY AND COGNITIVE SCIENCE

Scaife's challenge to cognitive science and developmental psychology reflects a further theme common to these chapters: developmental psychology and computational approaches have something to learn from one another, but significant gains will be made only if both perspectives are willing to question their assumptions and participate in new, genuinely interdisciplinary research. There are, however, no pre-packaged answers as to how this rapprochement should be achieved, although the following chapters each outline their own suggestions.

Possibilities for more profitable links between empirical techniques are explored in several chapters. Theories expressed as computational models can certainly offer detail and flexibility without sacrificing rigour; and programming experiments allow a number of unique evaluative questions to be posed. Nevertheless, their potential is not always realized. For instance, examples discussed by Rutkowska and Thornton illustrate how a theory can be translated into a working program without itself displaying impressive levels of precision and detail; programs can lack a principled theoretical basis for developmentally significant aspects of their design; and there is often doubt about the degree to which a program's behaviour really parallels that of human subjects.

An important direction for progress lies with developmental psychologists providing data that offer tighter constraints on computational models. What kind of data should that be? It is noteworthy that there have been remarkably few attempts to devise computational models of data from conventional independent–dependent variable experimental studies – taken alone, such data are unlikely to offer the rich detail necessary for constraining the design of computational models and evaluating their success as cognitive models. Virtually all of the modelling directed at developmental data is covered by work on production systems (as reviewed by Thornton) or by the cognitive modelling aspect of the ITS framework (as introduced by Sleeman). With few exceptions, these have relied on collecting their own data rather than using ready-available but unsuitable experimental results. Sleeman's chapter illustrates a type of data-collection and analysis that plays an important role in cognitive science. Other chapters draw attention to related techniques, such as the microanalytic study of behaviour patterns and individual case-studies, that are increasingly being used to good effect in developmental studies of cognition.

Additionally, the coming chapters consider how developmental psychology and cognitive science can come together to refine their concepts and questions for future research in this area. The necessity for two-way interchange is well illustrated in Draper's chapter. On the one hand, machine-learning work offers precise models for developmentalists to explore. On the other hand, it may be founded on overly simple ideas about what learning is; in this respect, it suffers from inattention to the facts and theories of human development. The engineering-oriented approach of AI practitioners designing a learning system contrasts in important ways with general principles of change that emerge from Lawler's (1985, 1986) case-studies of cognitive development. However, Draper suggests that machine-learning is reaching the point where it can move beyond task performance and mimicry (simulation) to address a basic question of equal relevance to developmental psychology: 'what is learning for?'

Many other fundamental questions are raised in the following chapters, such as: How can we most usefully talk about learning and development? Are there distinct developmental processes? Is it worthwhile striving for precise models of cognitive development in limited domains, or are more general models of the subject's motives, expectations and knowledge essential? To answer such questions, none of these chapters proposes that we should, to use Sharkey's (1986) words, 'throw away the protective armour of our own disciplines and rush naked to become born-again cognitive scientists'. They show clearly, however, that developmental psychology and cognitive science already share important areas of mutual concern. It will be a wasted opportunity for both enterprises if they pursue their inquiries independently. The most urgent need is to bring together computational and developmental approaches to provide the foundation for a genuinely developmental cognitive science.

## REFERENCES

Boden, M. A. (1982). Is equilibration important? – A view from artificial intelligence, *British Journal of Psychology*, **73**, 165–173.

Boden, M. A. (1983). The educational implications of artificial intelligence. In W. Maxwell (ed.) *Thinking: An Interdisciplinary Report*, Franklin Institute Press, Philadelphia, Pa.

Brown, J. S., and Van Lehn, K. (1980). Repair theory: a generative theory of bugs in procedural skills, *Cognitive Science*, **4**, 379–426.

Johnson-Laird, P. N. (1983). *Mental Models*, Cambridge University Press, Cambridge.

Lawler, R. W. (1985). *Computer Experience and Cognitive Development: A Child's Learning in a Computer Culture*, Ellis Horwood, Chichester.

Lawler, R. W. (1986). Natural learning: people, computers and everyday number knowledge. In R. W. Lawler, B. Du Boulay, M. Hughes and H. Macleod (eds) *Cognition and Computers: Studies in Learning*, Ellis Horwood, Chichester.

McVicker Hunt, J. (1961). *Intelligence and Experience*, Ronald Press, New York.

Mandler, J. (1983). Representation. In *Cognitive Development* (Volume eds, J. Flavell and E. Markman), Vol. 4 of *Handbook of Child Psychology* (ed. P. H. Mussen), 4th edn, Wiley, New York.

Neisser, U. (1976). *Cognition and Reality*, Freeman, San Francisco.

Newell, A. (1980). Physical symbol systems, *Cognitive Science*, **4**, 135–183.

Newell, A., and Simon, H. A. (1976). Computer science as empirical inquiry, *Communications of the Association for Computing Machinery*, **19**, 113–126. Reprinted in *Mind Design* (ed. J. Haugeland), MIT Press, Cambridge, Mass.

Pylyshyn, Z. W. (1984). *Computation and Cognition: Toward a Foundation for Cognitive Science*, MIT Press, Cambridge, Mass.

Sage, M., and Smith, D. J. (1983). *Microcomputers in Education: A Framework for Research*, Social Science Research Council, London.

Sharkey, N. (1986). *Advances in Cognitive Science*, Vol. 1, Ellis Horwood, Chichester.

Sloman, A. (1982). Computational epistemology, *Cahiers de la Fondation Archives Jean Piaget*, Geneva, June, No. 2–3.

Computers, Cognition and Development
Edited by J. Rutkowska and C. Crook
© 1987 John Wiley & Sons Ltd

CHAPTER 9

# Computational Models and Developmental Psychology

JULIE C. RUTKOWSKA

## SUMMARY

Understanding and evaluating computational theories and programmed models: two theories of the same developmental data.
What the programs do: sufficiency analysis.
How and why the programs work: success as process models; relationships between theory, program and programming language.
Microanalytic behavioural data and the equivalence of computational models and psychological processes.

## INTRODUCTION

Occasionally, after seeing what a program can do, someone will ask for a specification of the theory behind it. Often the correct response is that the program *is* the theory (Winston, 1977, p.258).

As for theory-testing, our claim is that the existence of a program which is successful in some limited domain does not provide a test of explanatory adequacy (or of procedural adequacy, for those who prefer that term), and this is true whether there exist many competing theories or no theory at all (Dresher and Hornstein, 1977, p.148).

It has been frequently suggested that psychological theories of development would benefit from the adoption of a more computational approach. The most influential way of developing computational theories focuses on constructing models in the form of computer programs, the method that has been the mainstay of artificial intelligence (AI) research. Within cognitive science, an extreme (but by no means unusual) viewpoint among AI and other researchers has been that the experiments and observations of disciplines such as psychology have provided us with more than enough facts, now urgently in need of a scientific (computational) explanation (Boden, 1981, ch.3). In the main, developmental psychology has not concurred with this perspective, and computational methods have not been widely adopted. Two main problems face developmental psychologists who wish to take up this challenge. One is that, within cognitive science, the status of computer programs in theory development is controversial, as the above quotations illustrate. The other is that the implied relationship is uni-directional. It includes no explicit guidelines as to the contribution developmental methods might make towards establishing an *interdisciplinary* framework for research.

My conviction is that computational and developmental methods can complement each other in essential ways, and the aim of this chapter is to explore the reciprocal interplay between them. In the next section, I briefly sketch the main features of computational models and their 'empirical' status. Accounts of such models can be fairly obscure, and the following sections are devoted to detailed analysis of examples to illustrate what developmental psychologists may have to gain. At a general level, I outline the main features that should be looked for and expected in a useful account. More specifically, the issues that are raised offer a range of criteria against which the relative success of models can be judged and illustrate debates concerning the role of programs. In the section that considers the contribution of developmental data, I follow the view that computational models offered as cognitive models must be compatible with developmental concerns (Norman, 1980; Pylyshyn, 1978, 1979) but dispute the view that enough 'facts' are already available. I believe that we are still in need of many facts of the right kind and will suggest that microanalytic developmental studies that are informed by the computational metaphor offer a route to better theory in developmental psychology and more suitable data for constructing and validating computational models.

## PROGRAMS AS TOOLS FOR THEORY DEVELOPMENT

The main features of an explanation in traditional experimental psychology and in approaches that make use of computer programs in their theorizing are schematized in Figure 9.1. Both types of approach share the aim of constructing theories that explain *how* intelligent functions are possible. It is in their methods and criteria for what constitutes a satisfactory explanation that they differ. The psychologist relies on behavioural data from experiments and observations to operationalize explanatory psychological constructs. From the computational and cognitive science perspective, this shows too exclusive a preoccupation with predicting behaviour and cannot do justice

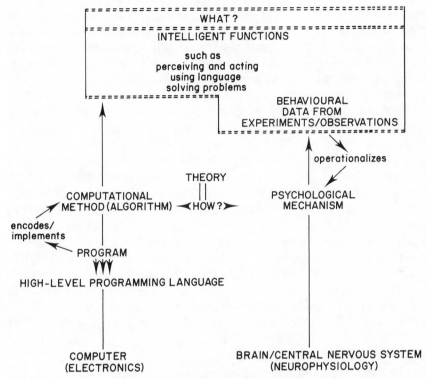

FIGURE 9.1 Theory and explanation in approaches making use of computational concepts and models (left) and in traditional psychology (right)

to the complexity of underlying psychological mechanisms. The proposed solution is to develop new ways of conceptualizing mechanisms and an alternative to behavioural operationalization.

Computationally oriented theorists will begin their explanation by drawing on ideas from AI and computer science concerning the nature, organization and use of knowledge in order to specify a detailed *computational method* through which the performance(s) in which they are interested could be generated. This articulated theory may then be tested by encoding or *implementing* the method in a *computer program* in some suitable *programming language*. To achieve this, the theorist will have to make explicit: *data* and its representation (symbol-structures specifying the basic or primitive elements of information and the relations between them); *procedures* (the 'instructions' that control internal processes for adding, deleting or changing database items and overt behavioural processes); and *control* (the manner and sequence in which procedures are to be activated).

In contrast with traditional psychology, this provides a *working model* of processes involved. It is important to emphasize that this is a model of a computational theory by virtue of its origins in AI/cognitive science ideas and concepts, not simply because it is encoded in a computer program. A computer could be used to explore theories that are not themselves computational. Theories in chemistry or meteorology, for instance, or behaviourist psychological theories without any cognitive constructs could be and are tested through appropriately designed computer programs. In such cases, however, we would have a computer simulation but not a computational theory.

This programming step is considered to be the computational equivalent of the psychology experiment. Newell and Simon (1976) maintain that a program only has to be inspected over a few runs to see if it does or does not behave in the manner hoped for. There is no need to build 100 copies of a program to gain statistical evidence concerning its performance. More recently, however, the assumption that a program need not be re-built and re-run has been questioned. Ritchie and Hanna (1984) point out that published accounts of repetitions are extremely rare. It is unclear if this is because large AI systems are only rarely successfully re-implemented; successful repetitions are not considered to be interesting; or failure is seen as evidence of incompetence rather than evidence of a possible gap between the original theory and its program. This, they believe, may be inhibiting continuity and the establishment of scientific standards.

The results of computational experiments include evidence concerning the *output* or external behaviour of the system, and the theorist whose aim is cognitive modelling will require that this is compatible with what is known of human behaviour in the domain concerned. Additionally, evidence is provided of the system's *internal dynamics*. Neither of these can be foreseen easily – if at all – when many interacting processes are involved. Thus, constructing a program and observing its functioning offer a powerful way of testing whether or not the theory really predicts what it claims. Johnson-Laird (1983) argues that psychologists should not even consider a theory as a possibility unless (at least) those parts of it that give rise to predictions can be expressed in terms of *effective procedures* (ones that we know could be executed by a simple machine).

What issues and criteria should developmental psychologists bear in mind in assessing accounts of computational theories and programmed models? The theory–program relation of this computational approach poses no lesser problems than the theory–experiment relation in psychology. What aspects of such (often complex) 'experiments' need to be presented for evaluation (Ritchie and Hanna, 1984)? Because a theory could be expressed in a computer program, does this mean that it should be, or might some other presentation such as axiomatic statements prove equally useful (Johnson-

Laird, 1983)? How might a model's psychological validity or equivalence be established (Pylyshyn, 1979, 1984)?

Such questions make it necessary to pay careful attention to the relationship between the various components of computational explanations, which have been outlined above. I will approach this through comparison of two theories that feature working programs and purport to explain data from the same developmental studies. A single detailed computational model might be provisionally accepted as being better than none at all, but when at least two exist, issues of evaluation and validation are cast into sharp relief. Additionally, one piece of work is due to an AI researcher while the other uses a computer program to test a theory previously constructed by developmental psychologists. This enables the potential benefits of both computational ideas and programming experiments, and their relationship, to be considered.

## EVALUATING TWO THEORIES OF INFANT OBJECT UNDERSTANDING

**The data and the problem**

Prazdny (1980) and Luger, Bower and Wishart (1983) offer computational explanations of infants' *object understanding*. The behavioural observations concerned are records of head and eye movements in situations including one or more of the following: brief occlusion of an object; change in the trajectory an object has been following; and substitution of an object by another differing in features such as shape and colour. In a series of experimental studies, Bower and his co-workers demonstrate two types of performance in infants of about 8–12 weeks ('Level 1') and 20–24 weeks ('Level 2'). (Key studies are reported in Bower, Broughton and Moore (1971) and Bower and Patterson (1973); related studies and reviews in Bower (1971, 1974/82).) These can be illustrated by behaviour in three situations, all of which are included both by Prazdny and by Luger, Bower and Wishart. Table 9.1 briefly summarizes the studies and typical infant behaviour. Luger, Bower and Wishart offer a model of Levels 1 and 2, Prazdny of Level 1 only, and the behaviour of these computer models will be discussed later.

The following broad pattern has to be explained: The visual anticipation behaviour of extremely young infants suggests that they 'know' that objects continue to exist while out of sight, contrary to the traditional view of Piagetian theory (e.g. Study A in Table 9.1). However, closer inspection reveals that Level 1 infants' understanding of objects is far from adult. In some situations they do not appear to discriminate between what are, from an adult perspective, quite different objects (e.g. studies A and C). In others they appear to look in several places for an object, as if they 'believe' it can

TABLE 9.1 Three studies illustrating the developmental data addressed by Prazdny (1980) ('P') and Luger, Bower and Wishart (1983) ('LB&W'), shown with behaviour recorded for Level 1 ('L1') and Level 2 ('L2') human infants and behaviour produced by the two computer programs for these levels

| STUDY A | AN OBJECT MOVES, THEN DISAPPEARS FROM VIEW BEHIND A SCREEN; A DIFFERENT OBJECT EMERGES. |
|---|---|
| L1 | Visually track the moving object and turn to look at the opposite side of the screen as if 'anticipating' the reappearance of the unseen object. They continue to do this even if a different object appears there. |
| P L1 | Continues to track during disappearance and when object emerges. |
| LB&W L1 | Sees one object and continues to track it during and after its disappearance. |
| L2 | Do not continue following the different object that emerges but look back to the screen. |
| LB&W L2 | Sees two objects, original and new. (No information on whether it looks back.) |

| STUDY B | AN OBJECT MOVING IN A LINE OR A CIRCLE STOPS IN FULL VIEW. |
|---|---|
| L1 | Fixate it for up to half a second, then continue tracking along the empty movement path. |
| P L1 | Follows then stops. Fixation oscillates between the stationary object and empty movement path. |
| LB&W L1 | Continues on empty movement path when object stops; looks back to stationary object; then looks back to empty movement path again. |
| L2 | Pause briefly; continue tracking; then return to fixate the stopped object. |
| LB&W L2 | Continues on empty movement path; looks back to stopped object; keeps fixating it. |

| STUDY C | A MOVING OBJECT IS REPLACED BY A DIFFERENT ONE IN MID-PATH. |
|---|---|
| L1 | Continue tracking. |
| P L1 | Follows the object and continues to do so when it changes. |
| LB&W L1 | Identifies and follows the object; ignores the substitution; continues to see and follow what, for it, is a single object. |
| L2 | Appear 'confused' and look 'back and forth between places of different objects' (Bower, Broughton and Moore, 1971, p. 28). |
| LB&W L2 | Notes the substitution; calls this a new object; looks back to place of previous object; then continues to follow the new one. |

be in more than one place at a time (e.g. studies A and B). And even the Level 2 infant, who succeeds in these situations, will fail on the standard Piagetian manual search tasks. This example is similar to many developmental psychology problem areas. There is greater ability than was previously believed, but it is too simplistic to conclude that subjects can simply do things earlier. A re-conceptualization is needed of the mechanisms underlying early competence, how and why these change, and what it is that is developing.

## Operationality and appropriate language

To begin assessing the efforts of the two theories with respect to such questions, it is helpful to consider Newell's (1970) reflections on relationships that might exist between cognitive psychology and AI. Toward the 'weaker' end of his hierarchy we can expect potential gains in clarity and precision. The computational approach can serve as a form of 'mental hygiene' because it forces *operationality* of fuzzy or mentalistic theoretical constructs. The language of programs and data structures provides an *appropriate language* for phrasing theories of behaviour.

Neither of these suggestions necessarily involves the construction of a working computer program. Although the label 'computational theory' has been most commonly and influentially used in the context of writing and running computer programs, it is also applicable to theorizing based on computational concepts and assumptions. Such ideas may offer new 'tools for thought' (Waddington, 1977) to increase understanding in an area and suggest new questions for investigation, even though the account of the 'human program' may be too incomplete for a computer model to be feasible.

At this level of analysis, it is possible to ask to what extent the theories proposed by Prazdny (1980) and Luger, Bower and Wishart (1983) benefit from precise and useful computational concepts. Both theories begin by assuming that the infant's perceptual processes provide accurate information about the world (contrary to the traditional Piagetian view). The characteristics of Level 1 and Level 2 behaviour, including the apparent 'errors' of Level 1 infants, stem from how that information is extracted, organized and used to guide visual behaviour.

Prazdny's theory draws extensively on AI ideas concerning *problem-solving* and *vision*. A problem is conceptualized as a discrepancy between an actual state of the world and some desired state, and problem-solving as the selection and activation of procedures to reduce that discrepancy. The infant's problem is to keep track of a particular object, across changes such as movement and disappearance, through program procedures controlling internal processes and behavioural processes such as fixation and following.

A key issue uncovered by AI problem-solving work concerns *database consistency*. To be successful, the subject must have an accurate representation of the world at any particular time. New information cannot simply be added cumulatively to a system since new assertions may contradict or alter the import of those already present. Nor can old information simply be deleted whenever new information arrives or it will be impossible to construct descriptions of events that occur over time. Processes are needed to decide which assertions should be added, removed or changed at any point, and a computational model must state what they are. Underlying Level 1 infants' performance are such processes for maintaining internal consistency in the database 'view of the world' and consistency between that view and the actual state of the external world. Say the world alters in an unpredicted way; decisions must be made concerning how to alter the database. This may involve collecting perceptual information while still keeping track of new external 'developments' – a computationally complex situation.

Prazdny makes use of recent AI ideas on vision to clarify the contribution of perception to the infant's database model of the world. The key assumption is that vision involves several levels of processing and is divided into independent 'modules', each offering a different representation of the input. A modular process is one that operates on the type of data appropriate to it, when that data is available, without taking into account what will occur at later levels. It is designed to compute or make explicit a particular type of information, which can then be used in further processing or to guide particular behaviour.

These ideas are used to construct a theory of infant mechanisms involving three levels of computation, as sketched in Figure 9.2. The two *perceptual* levels include separate channels for computing information about object features and movement. (Obviously, the program that tests this theory will not be able to 'see' in the conventional sense; its processes will operate on a sequence of 'snapshots', each consisting of symbolic descriptions or assertions that are fed into the computer to convey input information on position, size, colour and rough shape of objects.) The first, *motion detection* level produces an instantaneous characterization of the situation from consecutive pairs of snapshots. Its processes can compute that the object is moving/stationary, appeared/disappeared, or partially occluded, and add assertions to this effect to the database. The new information this provides can be used by processes of *trajectory computation*, which produce a description spanning a larger time interval. This makes explicit information such as trajectory, trajectory change (e.g. stopping), and occlusion. This organization makes it possible to pass control of the system's processes to various parts of the system depending on the circumstances. For example, distinct ways of describing movement can support procedures controlling different types of visual behaviour: the motion description offers adequate information for visual pursuit movements; when there has been enough time to compute a trajectory description, the necessary information for extrapolation or predictive movements will be available.

The third, *conceptual* level of the system has access to information from all autonomous lower levels and can intervene in difficulties with building and maintaining a detailed and accurate integrated 'object description' on

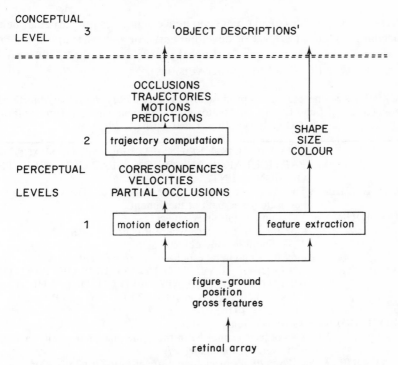

FIGURE 9.2 Three levels of processing of the infant perceptual system, showing the main computational components and the information each makes available. (Modified from Prazdny, 1980)

the basis of the information they provide. It asserts one object to be 'interesting' and commands lower levels to keep it in sight. This conceptual level accepts any identity judgements the lower levels make; if a conflict arises, the processes of this highest level can compare rival object descriptions and try to resolve inconsistencies in the database. Prazdny proposes an infant strategy for resolving inconsistency through perceptual investigation if information from the perceptual levels conflicts with the system's 'object description'; This involves taking time to build a new 'object description', then comparing it with the old one by 'looking' to the place where each predicts an object to discover which one is correct.

The general features of the alternative theory are not taken from computational work but originate in *identity theory*, which Bower, and subsequently Wishart, began to formulate to explain their impressive array of experimental findings. It aims to bring together the infant's understanding of objects and of spatial relations, arguing that infant performance is governed by a series of *conceptual rules* that interpret perceptual information and generate behaviour. Each rule embodies different criteria for attributing identity to successive appearances of an object and hence generates the particular behaviour characteristic of a level of development. For Levels 1 and 2, the rules shown in Table 9.2 are proposed (Luger, Bower and Wishart, 1983, pp.24–25; see Bower, 1974/1982 for earlier versions).

TABLE 9.2 Two conceptual rules proposed by identity theory to explain object understanding in Level 1 and Level 2 infants, together with their corollaries and behaviour. (After Luger, Bower and Wishart, 1983)

| | |
|---|---|
| RULE I | AN OBJECT IS A BOUNDED VOLUME OF SPACE IN A PARTICULAR PLACE OR ON A PARTICULAR PATH OF MOVEMENT. |
| COROLLARIES | Two objects cannot be in the same place. Two objects cannot be on the same path of movement. |
| BEHAVIOUR | 1. To find a stationary object, look for it in the place where it is usually seen. 2. To find a moving object, look for it along its usual path of movement. |
| RULE II | AN OBJECT IS A BOUNDED VOLUME OF SPACE OF A CERTAIN SIZE, SHAPE, AND COLOUR WHICH CAN MOVE FROM PLACE TO PLACE ALONG TRAJECTORIES. |
| COROLLARIES | As Rule 1, plus: Two objects cannot be in the same place nor on the same path of movement *simultaneously*. |
| BEHAVIOUR | 1. To find an object, search for it in its usual place or, if it has moved, along its path of movement. 2. To find an object that has disappeared mysteriously, remove the object which has replaced it. 3. To find an object that has disappeared mysteriously, remove the object which is now in the place where it was last seen. |

The essential distinction is that Rule I does not employ object features as a criterion of identity. Basically, no feature change should affect its operation. Thus, if an object changes its place or path of movement it should, in fact, be interpreted as two objects. But if a stationary or moving object is changed for one with different features, this should be interpreted as *transformation* of a single object rather than as a replacement. The use of features in the identity criterion of Rule II means such violations will be interpreted as *replacement* of the object concerned. (Behaviours 2 and 3 associated with Rule II are mostly relevant to later developing behaviour on manual search tasks in which an object is covered by a cup or a cloth – the 'mysterious' disappearance.)

How, then, do these two theories fare in terms of the 'operationality' and 'appropriate language' dimensions introduced above? Prazdny was not impressed by the original form of identity theory (which does not differ in any substantive way from the present version outlined here). He suggests it fails to use appropriate concepts, so cannot illuminate mental phenomena. Identity theory and Piagetian explanations suffer from the same problem: 'They lack precision, are not detailed enough, and cannot be formulated as a process model without (probably extensive) modifications. The notion of mechanism they employ is of a very abstract nature, if it exists at all' (Prazdny, 1980, p.129). Static lists of rules cannot address questions of mental process as they do not tell us what occurs when there is dynamic interaction between such rules.

Certainly, Prazdny has made use of computational ideas to spell out, in considerably more detail than is usual in developmental psychology, a process model of what he believes infants 'know' or 'believe' about objects and the way this controls their behaviour. It is important, however, to be clear on the way(s) in which this can be considered beneficial. Both theories offer more or less complex ways of saying that younger infants do not use 'features' to understand and unify the various appearances of an object. Considering the apparently simple nature of the performance data, demanding detail/ complexity may seem like overkill. For instance, there are no clear guidelines as to whether the most detailed and interactive theory is more satisfactory or simply less parsimonious.

A key point is that Prazdny's theory is more than a re-description of the phenomena it is trying to explain. A common criticism of psychological explanations, from the computational perspective, is that constructs offered as explanations actually pose questions (Boden, 1981), or are of essentially the same character as what they purport to explain (Sloman, 1978). This criticism does seem applicable to identity theory. Conceptual Rules I and II are so high-level that they could be considered re-descriptions of the general behaviour patterns of Level 1 and Level 2 infants, or what Pylyshyn (1984) terms 'generalizations stated over properties of the represented domain'. Level 1 infants, for example, look for objects in places or on paths of movement and are said to represent objects in terms of places or paths of movement.

Additionally, Prazdny's theory is phrased in terms of known (compu- tational) mechanisms. This increases our confidence that it is not merely a re-description: there is independent evidence for such mechanisms, apart from the existence of the infant abilities that they are being used to explain.

Such reservations apart, Luger, Bower and Wishart have succeeded in taking identity theory further by implementing it in a running computer program. They argue that Rules I and II of identity theory can be operational- ized as *grammars* or *re-write rules* that translate perceptual inputs to the system into sets of behavioural responses. The input to the two grammars is 'perceptual' information including position, size, colour, and shape. (Similar to Prazdny's system, the program will operate on a sequence of 'snapshots' consisting of static symbolic descriptions representing this information and the time at which it is present.) The rules of each grammar check these descriptions in various ways to produce a new symbol structure that makes explicit the number of objects present and their characteristics in terms of the particular grammar. The system's task is to 'find' objects and to maintain contact with the object it initially identifies as 'interesting'.

Grammar 1 (Rule I) tests 'snapshots' to determine if there is a permanent object at a location through the following checks:

(a) Look for an object structure within a fixed radius of the location.
(b) Check whether previous snapshots would indicate that a permanent object should be at this location.
(c) Test the object structure for 'interest' (the structure is tested from two slightly different views to check if it has mass/volume).
(d) Check whether the object structure is intact (whether it or any of its boundaries are occluded).
(e) Based on this object structure look to an appropriate position for the next object structure.

Grammar 2 (Rule II) includes an extra rule. This checks perceptual values such as size and colour between the snapshots.

Identity theory becomes more detailed and less obviously circular in its predictions in this computational form, but has it moved beyond re-description? Does this translation offer a more satisfactory explanation in terms of the functional properties of the system underlying the observed regularities in infant behaviour? To say that one theory is better or more plausible than the other in this respect, two broad issues must be considered: How do they map onto behaviour? And how successful are they as process models? These questions can be addressed by looking at the relevant programs to see *what* they do and *how and why* they do it.

### What the programs do: sufficiency analysis

Running a program has become established as a key way of demonstrating the *sufficiency* of computational theories. If there is no known way of producing a particular performance and we devise a system that does not use any capacities obviously beyond those of a human subject, then we have evidence of at least one mechanism that is sufficient for the task (Newell, 1970). Psychologists may suggest that their predictive experimental techniques do essentially the same thing, but the computationally-oriented theorist would dispute this. For example, Johnson-Laird (1983) uses Piaget's explanations of developmental data as a key illustration of how impossible it is to be sure that empirical claims follow from many psychological theories, noting that the gap between theory and data 'runs through all of his work like a geological fault' (p.25) (cf. Boden, 1978). This suggests one aspect of a reply to the question: 'Can we be sure that computers do things the way humans do?' The psychological processes proposed by traditional theories may not actually 'do' anything at all in the absence of a sympathetic audience adding many unspecified missing assumptions (Sloman, 1978, p.54).

The relative performance of the two program models in terms of the sufficiency criterion can be checked by considering the 'behaviour' each generates in the three example studies. The main features of this behaviour are shown beneath the performance of human infants in Table 9.1.

Is the behaviour of the programs close enough to that of infants? The answer to this is determined by how concerned we are with the details of behaviour. If we adopt a 'pass/fail' criterion of whether the programs exhibit a successful or errorful 'search' outcome – as a standard psychology experiment well might – then *both* models match up for *all* studies. If we move beyond this to take account of the *micro-structure* of behaviour, we find differences between the programs and discrepancies between programs and infants in study B.

Luger, Bower and Wishart's program does not pause when infants pause, even though the original empirical study placed great stress on this as evidence that the infant's following is not simply overshooting or an inability to stop head movement. Apart from this, the Level 1 behaviour of both programs in study B appears very similar: whereas infants simply go on to follow the now empty movement path, the programs show rather more 'looking back and forth' between the empty movement path and location of the now stationary object. Prazdny and Luger, Bower and Wishart respond to this differently.

Prazdny considers the difference between his program and infants to be evidence of its inadequacy in some not fully understood respect; it cannot say why infants want to hold on to the 'old' description. He points out that his program's behaviour could be brought into line with that of infants very easily by adding a single procedure telling it to attend to the moving object whenever object descriptions for stationary and moving objects exist. However, this would be unreasonably *ad hoc* unless it arose from some principled reconceptualization of the system's operation.

Luger, Bower and Wishart do not mention the discrepancy and express no reservations concerning their program's sufficiency. Do such fine behavioural details and this degree of discrepancy matter? I believe they must if developmental and programming methods are to be brought together in the construction of more than superficial theories, and will return to the reasons for this in the next section. Admittedly, the Luger, Bower and Wishart program prints out how many objects it 'perceives', but it is inappropriate to argue that the program's internal beliefs are more important to the experiment than its overt behaviour. It is, after all, the power of such beliefs (operational-ized in computational terms) to explain performance that is at issue.

It is intuitively appealing to try comparing the fidelity of the two models to the data in terms of their overall number of matches with it. This proves very difficult to do. Three example studies have been discussed, but both models are tested more extensively. Prazdny's model is tested in a more comprehensive set of studies, while Luger, Bower and Wishart's model covers two levels of subject performance. Each attempts to model some data that the other does not, and there is some data that neither of them attempts to replicate. Since conventions for comparing and assessing computational models are not yet well established, it seems important for the future use of these methods that competing models should be tested with a comparable range of similar situations so that their relative sufficiency can be established.

Recently, Priest and Young (1986) have attempted to begin developing *quantitative* criteria for evaluating 'micro-theory sysems'. (A 'micro-theory' consists of the set of core procedures and their variants that generate a segment of data in some domain, and a 'micro-theory system' is the set of such theories used to explain the whole body of data.) Traditional statistical approaches cannot be used. The theory is built after the data have been collected. And the behaviour generated is rarely a point on a one-dimensional scale; often it is a complex data structure such as an algebraic equation or a chess move with a negligible probability that it could have been obtained by chance. They note also that even an exact fit of model to data is neither surprising nor impressive. The theorist is free to select for their theory just those data points that actually occur in the data, and theories constructed in this way can be considered 'trivial'. For example, if Prazdny had added the special-purpose procedure discussed above to ensure that his program model generated the particular piece of behaviour involved, this aspect of his theory would have been trivial.

The main criteria Priest and Young believe an evaluation measure should satisfy involve a theory's accuracy and inaccuracy in fitting the data, parsi-mony and triviality, as discussed above. Essentially, their approach hopes to replace the question 'are these results obtained by chance?' with the question 'are these results obtained trivially?' As it stands, the approach is applicable to models where each behaviour is linked with a specific procedure as the number of micro-theories is easily counted (e.g. the production-system models discussed in Chapters 10 and 11 of this volume). With models in which procedure interactions are called on to generate behaviour, such as Prazdny's model, the use of this approach is less clear-cut. However, further developments along such lines will be particularly welcome if they lead to greater uniformity in the way program models are constructed and presented for evaluation.

## How and why the programs work: is the theory in the program?

Sufficiency analysis demonstrates that the mechanisms of a program model can produce the performance under investigation, but it cannot simply be concluded from this that the theory it models is also adequate for this task. Computational theories are like others in being underdetermined by the evidence for them. Questions must be raised concerning how the program achieved what it did to ensure that this was due to the theory encoded in it. There can be a complex interplay between theory, program and programming language. Program models do not simply eliminate the problem conventional psychological theories face in establishing their predictive and explanatory power, but they do offer a unique way of attacking it because the program and details of its operation are available for inspection.

When a program is offered as a working model of psychological processes, its creator should be expected to provide a discussion of which parts of the model are relevant and which are not. Winston (1977), in the work from which this chapter's opening quotation is taken, argues that often the program *is* the theory; provided it is written in a high-level, expressive language it can give a crisp account of processes, offering a tool similar to mathematics in the older sciences. But the word 'crisp' is crucial here; real-life programs invariably contain 'patches', 'hacks' or 'kludges', components that are included to make the program run but which are not derived from the theory being tested.

Minimally, an account of a program experiment needs to be explicit about which aspects of the program are *implementation details*. Implementation refers generally to the process of translating a computational theory into a program. Counter-intuitively, the implementation details or features are not the essentials of this process but aspects of the mapping that are made for the sake of convenience and to which no theoretical significance is attached.

Both Prazdny and Luger, Bower and Wishart are clear in discussing the elements of their respective implementations that are not pertinent to their conceptualization of infant object understanding. For example, Prazdny notes that the way his system represents occlusion does not employ texture or optic flow information, which is probably used in human vision. Luger, Bower and Wishart's program applies rules serially, in the order described previously, but this is not suggested as an aspect of infant mechanisms. They emphasize that they consider the infant rules operate in concert in some way.

Separating theoretically important from insignificant aspects of a program's operation is often hard to do, particularly in the case of large-scale systems. For example, Ritchie and Hanna (1984) highlight this problem through their analysis of Lenat's seminal work in machine learning. Lenat (e.g. 1979) develops a theory of mathematical discovery as a systematic form of inference, based on a particular type of knowledge structure and a particular arrangement of rules. His AM program (the 'automatic mathematician') begins with pre-numerical knowledge and 'discovers' the concepts of elementary mathematics. The program is large and impressive looking. The program's behaviour is impressive. But Ritchie and Hanna find many significant gaps between the official overview of the theory and the implemented program. In trying to explain how the program *really* works, the term they have most recourse to is 'obscure'. It seems, however, that important aspects of the discovery process are performed by *ad hoc* program procedures *not* specified in the theory.

The point at issue here is neither that Lenat has described his 'experiment' in any worse fashion than is usual, nor that he has intentionally concealed how his program works. It is that computational theories and their program models are often of such complexity that this 'slippage' between levels of explanation may, in practice, be extremely difficult to avoid. In many cases, too little program information is supplied to make thorough re-analysis possible, and it is most unlikely that a developmental psychologist would, in any case, have either the background or the desire to pursue a similar exercise. What can be stressed, however, is that evaluations should pay close attention to the match between theory and program. In particular, accounts of how a program works – what happens when it runs – can be checked to see if they offer convincing process models and conform to the theory. While far from perfect, this check may reduce the likelihood of an inadequate theory being camouflaged by an impressive program. It can be addressed to the two programs under consideration by returning to the example studies mentioned previously and looking further at *how* the programs produced the behaviour that was outlined in evaluating their sufficiency.

### The two programs as process models

Prazdny's account is reasonably successful in showing how his program's operation provides evidence for the roles of the processing components he has emphasized and the interactions between them. Studies A and B can serve as examples. In *Study A*, we are offered a process account of how an object's disappearance and 'anticipation' of its reappearance are understood. Comparison of 'snapshots' by the first-level motion component results in object movement being detected by the system and, when the object that is consequently followed moves behind a screen, partial occlusion and disappearance are computed. This makes available information relevant to the computations of the second-level trajectory component. It interprets the combination of disappearance and partial-occlusion information as meaning that the object has not 'gone out of existence' but is currently occluded by the object that previously partially occluded it; the database is altered accordingly. Further, it activates 'fixation' in the region of the opposite side of this occluding object: the system's 'expectation' of reappearance.

If the appearance of an object in that region is detected by the first-level motion computation, this confirms the first part of the expectation. An attempt is then made to update the system's 'object description' (pertaining to the occluded object) with this new movement information. This procedure *implicitly* embodies the system's 'belief' that the 'same' object that disappeared should reappear. The updating is successful when parameters of the new movement, such as velocity, match those of the previous description, as they do in this study because the trajectory computations on which this continuity of identity is based have no access to feature information.

Updating is unsuccessful if, for instance, the velocity of the object that appears in the predicted location is too great or it emerges sooner than information from the predictive trajectory component suggests. This situation brings in the conceptual level processes to try to resolve the conflict between perceptual information from the trajectory component and the old 'object description'. The system enters a *latency mode*, 'fixating' the object while a new object description is constructed. This offers an explanation of *Study B* behaviour: when the trajectory changes, an 'object description' for a moving object will conflict with perceptual information concerning a stationary object. Infants' pausing when they see a moving object stop corresponds to the latency mode. The outcome of the update attempt at the conceptual level is that two 'object descriptions' eventually exist for the one object in the database, the older one specifying a moving object, the newer one a stationary object. 'Looking' back and forth between the locations specified in the two descriptions to resolve this conflict gives us the oscillatory behaviour that did not quite match human subjects.

Overall, Prazdny's model appears internally consistent and closely matches his theory's stress on different levels of computation. As a process model, although there are certain lacunae in the account of how feature information is transmitted, it offers a possible mechanism to explain object understanding in the situations studied. Both the infant's understanding of events and search 'errors' emerge from the interaction of more basic components of the system. At a molar level, the theory stresses 'objects' and 'events', but its decisions about correspondence or identity are embodied in considerable procedural knowledge of motion and change in motion. As such, it could be considered a possible mechanism for the type of high-level rules that are the concern of identity theory. The process model shows no obvious gaps leading to the question: why does the program do that? One might wish to dispute assumptions of the model – a task beyond the scope of this chapter – but the detail that makes for ease of criticism is, itself, an advantage all too rare in much theorizing.

The case of Luger, Bower and Wishart's model is quite different. It proves extremely difficult to separate out the theoretically essential details of why the computational model works as it does from the account of the program and the features of the particular AI language in which it is implemented. Some effort is needed to familiarize oneself with characteristics of programming languages, but this does permit an informed assessment of work that might otherwise appear complex because of the technical nature of the formalisms it uses. I shall not go into detail here because this would place too much stress on features of PROLOG, the programming language in which Luger, Bower and Wishart's 'grammars' or 're-write rules' are expressed. I shall, however, outline in general form the main problems.

In principle, there is no reason why a clearly formulated program could not be written in any AI programming language. But it is important not to lose sight of the fact that a programming language is an extremely powerful tool. It provides more than a static notation; it is also a 'virtual machine' with its own principles of operation. A highly declarative formalism such as PROLOG can be especially seductive. It allows fairly trivial theories that are little more than common-sense descriptions to be stated, and a PROLOG program will draw the 'conclusions' that they predict.

Luger, Bower and Wishart emphasize that their grammars for object understanding, which were outlined earlier, 'follow fairly closely' the two conceptual rules of identity theory. But this match does not offer support for their theory. A criticism of the original identity theory was that its rules were too static to offer a process account of mechanisms. The fact that the PROLOG program runs and returns infant-like 'behaviour' does not mean this criticism was misplaced. A computational method or algorithm for performing a task is expected to make clear the computational steps that will occur and their sequence or the circumstances in which processes will be activated. In the case of this particular theory, its main individual 'rules' are expressed in PROLOG, but how they operate on the changing database of 'snapshot' information and interact with one another to generate behaviour is quite obscure. So far as one is able to tell, these active processing aspects of the program's operation rely as much or more on general PROLOG processes as on processes that have been formulated in the theory and then encoded in the PROLOG program.

For example, in *Study A* Grammar 1 anticipates and sees the emergence of a single object from behind a screen. But how is understanding of the object's disappearance being modelled? One of the rules in the PROLOG program checks 'snapshots' for occlusion, and the description of the computational model says the program can detect boundary violations like partial occlusion. It is unclear, however, what information and processes are involved in computing this, or how occlusion information interacts with prediction of future object positions. How, for instance, is the next 'appropriate position' looked to affected by whether the object is visible, partially or totally occluded? Without such details, the theory appears *superficial*: its explicit component processes are too molar because further necessary and important processing must be contained within them.

It has already been noted that Luger, Bower and Wishart consider the particular order in which rules are applied to be an implementation detail. They suggest that specifying interdependence and/or parallelism would be premature since 'concrete hypotheses about the nature of such parallelism are beyond the ken of current cognitive theory' (1983, p. 27). Such hypotheses, however, are exactly what a great deal of computational work in AI is trying to clarify. The notions of modularity and processing control included in Prazdny's model draw directly on such work. There is no reason why a PROLOG program could not incorporate explicit hypotheses concerning the order of computational processes.

A consequence of the absence of process information is that the way the program generates behaviour is made to look alarmingly like sleight of hand. When a moving object stops in *Study B*, the program based on Grammar 1 does not stop, unlike infants or Prazdny's program: it *continues*; finds no object; *looks back* to the now stationary object and describes it as a new object; then *returns* to the movement path to look for the 'old' object it initially found interesting. Looking back to the stopped object offers a closer fit to infant behaviour, but why it occurs is not spelt out. It could be generated by the kind of *ad hoc* (trivial) program modification that Prazdny was explicitly avoiding. Nor can we tell why the program returns to the old path despite previously having found no object there. Luger, Bower and Wishart's model needs to clarify how representations of past, present and future situations interact to explain each component of behaviour, as Prazdny's account does.

In summary, Luger, Bower and Wishart's deeper conception of the mechanisms that underlie the general rules of identity theory remain implicit in their program, which adds little to their verbally-stated theory. To what extent this is due to incompleteness of the account of the program's design is difficult to know; there are, at least, important gaps in presentation. The aim of further work in this vein should be to make the theoretically relevant ideas explicit. A further aim for both of the models should be *replication*. It is difficult to establish all of the reasons why a program 'works', and attempts to construct further programs using the design principles they have suggested should offer very valuable clarifications.

## EQUIVALENCE BETWEEN COMPUTATIONAL MODELS AND PSYCHOLOGICAL PROCESSES

Asking to what extent a computational model accurately reflects the theory it is testing leads to the final yet central question: is the theory a valid theory of human psychological processes? Here, I will consider this problem in the context of two closely related issues. The first is concerned with the type of *behavioural data* that developmental psychologists need to collect. Were the 'facts' that the two theories discussed above attempted to explain suited to the construction and validation of precise computational models? The second brings in *developmental change* as both problem and method. What general strategy should developmental and computational theorists adopt in trying to explain it? And is there anything special that developmental methods can offer those who are trying to model human abilities?

### Establishing useful facts: microanalytic representational studies

Pylyshyn (1984) distinguishes between 'weak' and 'strong' equivalence of processes. There is weak equivalence if two systems show the same input–output relationship, producing similar behaviour. Establishing strong equivalence, however, entails showing that this is achieved through the same computational method or process. To demonstrate strong equivalence between a computational model and psychological processes, it would be necessary to reveal all of the basic cognitive or representational states that underlie regularities in behaviour. Pylyshyn (1979, 1984) proposes several empirical constraints that psychologically valid computational models might be expected to obey. These suggest ways in which empirical data can help to tease out the basic components and processes of a system.

An important comparison that can be made between computational and human systems is the *relative difficulty* they have with a range of problems in the area of ability under investigation. Finding the same rank-ordering for both systems would imply a similar process organization underlying the behavioural regularities. Both the likelihood of making an *error* and the relative *time taken* for the tasks could play a part in establishing rankings of relative difficulty or complexity. Relative time measures are straightforward enough; Prazdny's model, for instance, may be moving in the right direction by trying to incorporate assumptions about the relative time taken for the various computations (of motion, trajectory and object descriptions). Error data require further attention in this context because a great deal of the data with which developmentalists are concerned consists of wall-to-wall 'errors' when viewed from the perspective of mature performance on the tasks involved. Thus, the likelihood of an error will prove less pertinent to analysis than will the nature or form of that error.

This concern meshes with a further important dimension of comparison: *intermediate state information*. An assumption of the computational perspective, amply reinforced by psychological observations, is that subjects' task or problem performance involves various stages of computation. A goal or problem-solution is rarely achieved in a single step. Techniques that go beyond capturing performance on a single dimension – whether that is pass/ fail, proportion of trials correct, or time taken – to reveal *intervening states* that subjects pass through can provide the basis for a powerful comparison with computational models.

Data suited to such purposes are unlikely to be the outcome of psychological studies that are restricted to dependent–independent variable experimental designs and use predetermined criterion measures for assessing their subjects' performance. Returning, for example, to the observations of infants that featured above, Bower's descriptions of their behaviour are more detailed than in many experimental studies and move beyond simplistic pass/ fail criteria. Nevertheless, the research conforms to the conventional logic:

If subjects do/do not possess process(es) 'A'
then they will/will not produce behaviour 'B' in situation 'C'.

Even when the criterion behaviour 'B' appears to be a fairly complex pattern of behaviour, as it is in the infant visual tracking studies, it generally derives from the experimenter's rational analysis of the demand characteristics of the task. As such, it may implicitly embody a premature theory of what subjects are doing and offer a very selective account of their actual performance.

Because behaviour is not of interest in its own right, criterion measures will rarely offer the precision required for analysis of error patterns or intermediate states. In the tracking studies, for instance, 'anticipation' of the reappearance of an object that disappears is assumed to demonstrate that subjects 'know' the object continued to exist out of their sight. However, the way in which 'anticipation' is operationalized in the experimental setting involves a very molar behavioural measure, allowing quite different behaviour patterns to qualify as achievement of the same criterion (Bower, Broughton and Moore, 1971). When it comes to comparing such behaviour with that of a computational model, as was attempted in the discussion of sufficiency analysis, a genuine problem emerges. There is no way of telling whether an imperfect fit results from deficiencies of the computational model or from incomplete, selective reporting of relevant aspects of subjects' behaviour.

It would be wrong, however, to conclude that empirical psychological studies cannot contribute further to theory development – the view of 'aggressive AI intellectual imperialism' (see Boden, 1981, ch. 3). A more profitable vein of data is available. It is striking that theorists who are intent on computational modelling and believe that behavioural observations (as opposed to their own intuitions) should provide their core material have, by and large, felt it necessary to go out and collect their own data. The most highly developed technique has become the analysis of subjects' *protocols* as they think aloud while tackling problems (Newell and Simon, 1972; Ericsson and Simon, 1984). Non-verbal behaviour, such as eye and hand movements, have also been relied upon (e.g. Young, 1976). Even the 'clinical' method of Piagetian studies rarely captures the level of detailed description that is aimed at, as a quick comparison of Piaget's (1976) summary of the Tower of Hanoi task with Anzai and Simon's (1979) work will show.

Within developmental psychology, what I will call *microanalytic* studies of representational development have most in common with the protocol techniques of the cognitive scientist, and are beginning to offer discernible methodological guidelines. Their broad aim is to move away from criterion measures that embody the experimenter's view of a task to a subject-oriented methodology, and they assume that analysis of the micro-structure of behaviour offers a powerful tool. In order to show what microanalytic studies might contribute, I will briefly outline their main features and how they compare with other methods. Illustrations will be taken from work on infant performance in a visual tracking situation (Rutkowska, 1983), and from studies of children's problem-solving (Karmiloff-Smith, 1979, 1984; Karmiloff-Smith and Inhelder, 1974).

Microanalytic studies of behaviour distinguish between outcome and process, and an intimate relationship is assumed between what subjects can be said to have achieved and how they achieved it. Thus, a primary goal is to describe the range of *behaviour patterns* shown by subjects. Taken in isolation, any element of behaviour is open to multiple interpretations, but ambiguity can be reduced if that element is located as one component of a range of patterns. On the visual tracking paradigm, for instance, the sequence of head and eye movements and fixation positions can be recorded throughout each trial involving an object's disappearance, not simply whether subjects are or are not looking at where the object will reappear before it comes back into view (Rutkowska, 1983). On a block-balancing task, there is the order in which blocks are selected and the type of movement involved in attempting to balance them on a fulcrum (Karmiloff-Smith and Inhelder, 1974). Obviously, not just *any* behavioural detail matters, but a useful level of description can be achieved by looking for patterns that occur across subjects and that permit us to classify the behaviour of individuals without recourse to an enormous 'other' category.

Several points of general interest emerge from describing subjects' performance in this way. One is that there are far more behaviour patterns than the criterion measures of dependent–independent variable design studies may suggest. For instance, at least ten patterns were necessary to describe infant performance on a basic tracking task. These patterns subsumed the criterion measures that had been used by various researchers, but also made clear that a tremendous amount of information relevant to how subjects perform is lost if data collection is restricted to the presence or absence of a pre-specified criterion behaviour or to a single quantitative measure such as the time taken. Of greatest importance is the fact that subjects of different levels achieve the same outcome through quite distinct behaviour patterns. The 'anticipation' of a 3-month-old infant takes the form of continued tracking during the object's disappearance; a 9-month-old will stop tracking as the object disappears, then turn to the exit region prior to the reappearance. Subjects initially balance blocks by moving them back and forth until they are stable; later they will begin by immediately placing the geometric centre on the fulcrum. What would be considered to be 'doing the same task' from an experimenter's 'outcome-perspective' may involve quite distinct forms of understanding on the part of the subject.

Do these more detailed descriptions of behavioural processes provide *intermediate-state* information, or are they simply tuning in to shallow surface phenomena of no relevance to explaining the subject's knowledge and understanding? Something akin to the latter view is implicit in a great deal of developmental theory. Luger, Bower and Wishart (1983), for instance, do not share Prazdyn's (1980) dissatisfaction with the 'macroscopic' level at which infant visual tracking behaviour has been described. They assume that different behaviours can provide evidence of the same conceptual rule; either visual or manual search offers access to the subject's object concept. While sympathizing strongly with their intention to emphasize the complexity and significance of infant mental processes, the plausible intuition that what subjects 'know' can be expressed through quite different behaviours may be misleading except at a superficial level of description.

Boden (1983) has noted that computational ideas have been an important motivating force behind microanalytic studies of the interplay between action-sequences and changing cognitive representations. Within this context, Karmiloff-Smith (1979, 1984) refers to her behavioural analysis as a study of the child's *procedures*. The term 'procedure' is more than a useful shorthand for how subjects set about doing tasks; it is a theoretical construct expressing commitment to the view that behavioural processes offer us access to the human subject's program for dealing with the world. To describe looking, object manipulation, language use, and so on, as procedures implies that these behavioural processes are governed by internal program procedures and are therefore part of the subject's knowledge.

In this vein, the development of understanding in a domain may be viewed as the acquisition and organization of a wide range of procedures for interacting with the world, not as the formation of a narrow range of static concepts. Several areas of research now support the conclusion that subjects do not develop a unitary representation of what a pre-computational perspective would consider to be a single piece of knowledge. In the area of language, for example, work on children's knowledge of word meanings reveals quite distinct procedures for comprehension and production of the 'same' lexical item (Clark, 1983). Lawler's (1981) case-study of mathematical understanding shows how his daughter employed quite different procedures to add the same two numbers if the sum was presented verbally, on paper, or in financial terms (as when the number of cents concerned corresponded to the price of two packs of her favourite chewing gum). Influenced by computational concepts concerning knowledge and understanding, Lawler (1985) develops in detail the notion that mental development is founded on disparate, active structures that he calls 'microviews'.

Microanalytic studies that are informed by computational ideas assume that even apparently simple performances involve an ongoing *transaction* between environmental information and the subject's understanding (an assumption that was shared by Prazdny's computational view of infants). Thus, emphasis is placed on exploring tasks and contexts that *externalize* aspects of the subjects' processing through their behaviour. This may appear to be unduly restrictive, but that is not the case. On closer inspection, there are few experimental contexts that cannot be approached in this way. Analysis of middle-years conservation tasks, for instance, normally pays most attention to whether subjects give the conserving or non-conserving answer, but they offer the opportunity to study verbal justifications (e.g. Neilson, Dockrell and McKechnie, 1983), eye movements (e.g. O'Bryan and Boersma, 1971), and so forth. Recordings of the probability with which infants make manual search errors can be enriched through attention to the behaviour sequences involved (Willatts, 1984).

A microanalytic approach can differ from both traditional dependent–independent variable experimental designs and individual case-studies. The form of hypothesis testing characteristic of the experimental method may be prematurely and inappropriately constrained unless a microanalytic analysis has preceded it. The collection and analysis of data through case-studies, on the other hand, may be under-constrained, resulting in anecdotally fascinating transcripts of very limited theoretical significance. Microanalytic studies based on individual and group observations offer a balance between these two approaches, providing rich data that are also amenable to a range of statistical techniques of analysis. They have a good deal of commonality with ethological techniques of naturalistic observation, but are indebted to a computational framework as opposed to the evolutionary perspective of ethological study. While similar data-collection techniques have been adapted for the study of social development, they hold a great deal of unexploited potential for the analysis of cognitive issues.

## Developmental constraints on computational models

A more general though important empirical constraint on a computational model of some ability is that it should be possible to see how the system could have developed (Pylyshyn, 1978, 1979, 1984). Developmental psychologists, however, know that the nature of development is controversial. Thus, a close link is established between questions concerning how developmental insights can be used and how they might be gained.

Despite their differences, Prazdny (1980) and Luger, Bower and Wishart (1983) share fundamental assumptions about how to set about explaining development. First, we should model each of the levels of ability encountered. Then, it ought to be possible to work out what processes are needed to change the structures of one level into the those of the next. Bower (1982) expresses the hope that AI research may provide a precise specification of the rules determining such changes. This seems straightforward, but it may be overoptimistic. Neither of the computational models discussed in this paper suggests a clear route to conceptualizing the mechanisms of development.

An alternative strategy, and the one I will emphasize here, is that levels or stages of ability cannot be understood independently of each other. Looking at how a system is transformed in development offers valuable insights as to what is being transformed as well as how. A point of particular concern is that the levels that are isolated in describing a developmental sequence in some domain of understanding may not all have the same status. This is not to say that some are less significant than others, but that they may have different roles or functions in the developmental process. The prevailing view is that the behaviour characteristic of a given level of performance reflects *qualitatively* distinct representations, strategies or hypotheses for tackling the *task* concerned. But some regularities may demonstrate errors due to no interpretation of the task or situation being available to subjects (cf. Cromer, 1980). More significantly, certain levels may be revealing characteristic *transitional* patterns of investigation or exploration in the subject's construction of their understanding.

The microanalytic studies that were discussed above offer evidence of such 'exploratory' levels in the changing performance of human subjects. In infant tracking, for instance, a striking finding is that the behaviour of continuing following while an object is moving out of sight, then looking back to where it disappeared, is found regularly even if the same object emerges and its speed remains constant. It does not appear to be a search for the original object following a replacement, but is one of a group of behaviour patterns that involve heightened attention to the disappearance point and intervene between the occurrence of the two forms of 'anticipation' mentioned above. In the context of the other levels of performance, these behaviours are plausibly interpreted as explorations of the situation. The infant could be said to be learning about 'disappearance' rather than exhibiting errorful search.

In a language acquisition study, Karmiloff-Smith (1979) noted children initially used the French word 'même' appropriately in its two contexts ('same kind' and 'same one'), but these two uses appeared to be quite distinct from the perspective of the children's representation – two procedures were involved, not a single procedure applicable in two contexts. At a second, transitional level of development, the term 'même de' was introduced, which does not appear in grammatical adult usage. Its function appeared to be the marking of a distinction between the two uses. The single form was eventually resumed, but revealing an integrated use in the two contexts.

What is important about such levels of functioning is that the child's understanding has become a concern in its own right. The child is trying to understand his or her tools for understanding, not to increase the degree of success on the task as the experimenter might conceptualize it, even though the end-result is coming to 'do the task' in a mature way. Karmiloff-Smith argues that there is evidence for three recurrent phases in the development of children's representations of many domains. In the initial phase, the child may achieve a successful outcome but his or her knowledge of the situation is implicit in as yet unrelated procedures. In the intervening phase, there may appear to be a regression in task performance from the experimenter's perspective. This, however, is due to processes that mark an advance in the child's representation because they make explicit aspects of the situation and the child's behaviour that were previously implicit. She suggests that the motivation underlying these restructurings is greater control over both the environment and their own processing. Such findings and the further questions they raise offer a potentially strong link with current developments in computational work.

The field of machine learning is devoted to building computational models of change that improve a system's performance. Scott and Vogt (1983) have emphasized that, in order for this endeavour to succeed, it must concern itself not only with *task-oriented learning* but also with *knowledge-oriented learning*. They define knowledge-oriented learning as 'the construction of an organized representation of experience' (p. 432) and argue that it is not motivated by the attempt to improve performance on any particular task. Their own system involves ideas such as increasing its certainty about the possibility and consequences of applying particular behaviours in its environment. As with other systems in this vein, these ideas are based primarily on the intuitions and logical analysis of the designer. Lenat incorporated no less than 59 heuristics to assess 'interestingness' in the discovery processes of the AM system which was mentioned previously.

Scott and Vogt suggest that children's play is a naturally occurring form of knowledge-oriented learning worthy of inspection by the cognitive scientist. But this is too restrictive; the empirical studies discussed above offer a valuable source of insights concerning the interplay between task-oriented and knowledge-oriented learning in human interactions with the environment. Empirical studies that bring together programming experiments and behavioural observations of this type offer a potentially powerful route to conceptualizing change and producing psychologically valid models.

## CONCLUSIONS

The aim of this chapter has been to explore the proposal that theory development, computational modelling and developmental techniques of data collection can inform each other and proceed as joint endeavours. There can be no short cut to constructing effective theories, and to appreciate the complementary power of computational and developmental experiments we must be aware of both their strengths and limitations.

The discussion of computational theory and computer programs illustrated how evaluative questions can be addressed to program models that are difficult or even impossible to pose for conventional theories. It can be concluded that computational concepts and methods offer a potentially valuable complement to those more familiar in developmental psychology. Emphasis was on the importance of being clear as to the relationship between theory and program. The examples that were compared suggest that better theories may be constructed by making use of computational concepts appropriate to explaining the nature and organization of knowledge, independently of whether they are complete enough to be implemented in a programmed model. Conversely, the fact that a theory can be translated into a working program need not mean that it meets acceptable criteria of precision or detail. Questions need to be asked beyond whether it produces the pertinent behaviour, but this method makes such questions possible.

It was suggested that behaviourial data from developmental studies can play a role in the construction and evaluation of computational theories and models. Microanalytic techniques may provide a route to understanding the process of performance and change, and they offer data more suitable for the evaluation of computational models.

At present, it may well be that the computational approach can serve developmental psychology best through concepts that clarify and guide our thinking about knowledge and its development. We may be some way from theories complete enough to be implemented in useful programmed models. Where possible, however, attempts should be made to bring the methods sketched in this chapter together, and a first step in that direction is increasing our awareness of their respective potential.

## ACKNOWLEDGEMENTS

Thanks to Tom Khabaza for helpful discussions concerning this chapter, and to Steve Draper and Stephanie Thornton for their comments on an earlier draft.

## REFERENCES

Anzai, Y., and Simon, H. A. (1979). The theory of learning by doing, *Psychological Review*, **86**, 124–140.

Boden, M. A. (1978). Artificial intelligence and Piagetian theory, *Synthese*, **38**, 389–414.

Boden, M. A. (1981). *Minds and Mechanisms: Philosophical Psychology and Computational Models*, Harvester Press, Brighton.

Boden, M. A. (1983). The educational implications of artificial intelligence. In W. Maxwell (ed.), *Thinking: An Interdisciplinary Report*, Franklin Institute Press, Philadelphia, Pa.

Bower, T. G. R. (1971). The object in the world of the infant, *Scientific American*, **225**, 30–38.

Bower, T. G. R. (1974/82). *Development in Infancy*, Freeman, San Francisco.

Bower, T. G. R., Broughton, J., and Moore, M. K. (1971). Development of the object concept as manifested in changes in the visual tracking behaviour of infants between 7 and 20 weeks of age, *Journal of Experimental Child Psychology*, **11**, 182–193.

Bower, T. G. R., and Patterson, J. G. (1973). The separation of place, movement and object in the world of the infant, *Journal of Experimental Child Psychology*, **15**, 161–168.

Clark, E. (1983). Meanings and concepts. In *Cognitive Development* (Volume eds J. Flavell and E. Markman), Vol. 3 of *Carmichael's Manual of Child Psychology* (ed. P. H. Mussen), 4th edn, Wiley, New York.

Cromer, R. F. (1980). Empirical evidence in support of non-empiricist theories of mind, *Behavioral and Brain Sciences*, **3**, 16–18.

Dresher, E., and Hornstein, N. (1976). On some supposed contributions of artificial intelligence to the scientific study of language, *Cognition*, **4**, 321–398.

Ericsson, K. A., and Simon, H. A. (1984). *Protocol Analysis: Verbal Reports as Data*, MIT Press, Cambridge, Mass.

Johnson-Laird, P. N. (1983). *Mental Models*, C.U.P., Cambridge.

Karmiloff-Smith, A. (1979). Micro- and macrodevelopmental changes in language acquisition and other representational systems, *Cognitive Science*, **3**, 91–118.

Karmiloff-Smith, A. (1984). Children's problem solving. In M. E. Lamb, A. L. Brown and B. Rogoff (eds), *Advances in Developmental Psychology*, Vol. 3, Erlbaum, Hillsdale, N. J.

Karmiloff-Smith, A., and Inhelder, B. (1974). If you want to get ahead, get a theory, *Cognition*, **3**, 195–212.

Lawler, R. (1981). The progressive construction of mind, *Cognitive Science*, **5**, 1–30.

Lawler, R. (1985). *Computer Experience and Cognitive Development: One Child's Learning in a Computer Culture*, Ellis Horwood, Chichester.

Lenat, D. (1979). On automated scientific theory formation: a case study using the AM program. In J. E. Hayes, D. Michie and O. I. Mikulich (eds), *Machine Intelligence*, Vol. 9, Ellis Horwood, Chichester.

Luger, G., Bower, T. G. R., and Wishart, J. (1983). A model of the development of the early infant object concept, *Perception*, **12**, 21–34.

Neilson, J., Dockrell, J., and McKechnie, J. (1983) Justifying conservation, *Cognition*, **15**, 277–291.

Newell, A. (1970). Remarks on the relationship between artificial intelligence and cognitive psychology. In R. Banerji and M. D. Mesarovic (eds), *Theoretical Approaches to Non-Numerical Problem-Solving*, Springer Verlag, Berlin.

Newell, A., and Simon, H. A. (1972). *Human Problem Solving*, Prentice-Hall, Englewood Cliffs, N. J.

Newell, A., and Simon, H. A. (1976). Computer science as empirical inquiry: symbols and search, *Communications of the Association for Computing Machinery*, **19**, 113–126.

Norman, D. (1980). Twelve issues for cognitive science, *Cognitive Science*, **4**, 1–33.

O'Bryan, K. G., and Boersma, F. J. (1971) Eye movements, perceptual activity and conservation development, *Journal of Experimental Child Psychology*, **12**, 157–169.

Piaget, J. (1976). *The Grasp of Consciousness*, Routledge and Kegan Paul, London.

Prazdny, K. S. (1980). A computational study of a period of infant object concept development, *Perception*, **9**, 125–150.

Priest, A., and Young, R. M. (1986). Methods for evaluating micro-theory systems, Paper presented at ICAI Research Workshop, Windermere, Cumbria.

Pylyshyn, Z. W. (1978). Computational models and empirical constraints, *Behavioral and Brain Sciences*, **1**, 93–99.

Pylyshyn, Z. W. (1979). Complexity and the study of artificial and human intelligence. In M. Ringle (ed.), *Philosophical Perspectives in Artificial Intelligence*, Humanities Press, Atlantic Highlands, N. J.

Pylyshyn, Z. W. (1984). *Computation and Cognition: Toward a Foundation for Cognitive Science*, MIT Press, Cambridge, Mass.

Ritchie, G., and Hanna, M. (1984). AM: a case study in AI methodology, *Artificial Intelligence*, **23**, 249–268.

Rutkowska, J. C. (1983). Patterns of behaviour on the visual tracking paradigm in the first year of life, Paper presented at the Annual Conference of the British Psychological Society Developmental Section, Oxford.

Scott, P. D., and Vogt, R. C. (1983). Knowledge oriented learning, *Proceedings of the 8th International Joint Conference on Artificial Intelligence*, Vol. 1, pp. 432–435, Karlsruhe.

Sloman, A. (1978). *The Computer Revolution in Philosophy*, Harvester Press, Brighton.

Waddington, C. H. (1977). *Tools for Thought*, Paladin, London.

Willatts, P. (1984). Stages in the development of intentional search by young infants, *Developmental Psychology*, **20**, 389–396.

Winston, P. H. (1977). *Artificial Intelligence*, Addison-Wesley, Reading, Mass.

Young, R. M. (1976). *Seriation by Children: an Artificial Intelligence Analysis of a Piagetian Task*, Birkhauser Verlag, Basel.

Computers, Cognition and Development
Edited by J. Rutkowska and C. Crook.
© 1987 John Wiley & Sons Ltd

CHAPTER 10

# Adaptive Production Systems as Models of Human Development

STEPHANIE THORNTON

## SUMMARY

This chapter reviews adaptive production systems as models of childhood cognitive development, and argues that these have various limitations, being often atheoretical, *ad hoc* and psychologically naive. The chapter also argues the need for a more effective means of integrating psychological and programming insights in a genuinely interdisciplinary way.

## BACKGROUND AND INTRODUCTION

The problem of accounting for the nature of changes in cognition, and for the nature of the processes which bring about these changes, is a research area which historically has produced controversy rather than progress.

Developmental psychologists are not agreed as to what changes in cognition as the child grows. On the one hand, there is the view that cognitive development involves the radical reconstruction of intellectual structures, so that the child's mind is profoundly different in its organization from that of the adult (Piaget, 1970). On the other, there is the view that development cannot involve such changes, because the creation of entirely new cognitive structures is not possible (Fodor, 1976); or the view that cognitive growth is not a matter of change in intellectual structures, but a change in the ways in which knowledge is brought into use, or in the extent to which knowledge can be voluntarily manipulated outside its habitual framework (Donaldson, 1978); or even the view that developmental change is simply a change in

217

the amount of knowledge the child has so far acquired (Gagne, 1968). Correspondingly, mechanisms responsible for yielding cognitive growth are conceived in very different terms by different theorists. Some believe the fundamental mechanisms to be located primarily in the child's head, to operate by reviewing and revising the child's cognitive structures (Piaget, 1970, 1972; Karmiloff-Smith, 1979, 1984). Others locate developmental processes outside the child, in the social or cultural pressures with which the child interacts (Vygotsky, 1962), for example in the conceptual tools or training provided by formal education (Donaldson, 1978; Cole and Scribner, 1974). Within either perspective, there are variations in the exact form of hypothesized developmental mechanisms.

Discourse between these different perspectives is problematic. Areas of consensus are beginning to form – for example, certain aspects of the Piagetian tradition have been modified in the light of work from other perspectives (Piaget, 1972; Inhelder, Sinclair and Bovet, 1974). But there remain many issues which are profoundly controversial. Psychology has traditionally relied on experimental data to resolve such conflicts, but the controversies involved here are not readily amenable to solution by that route. The problem is that the controversies which face us now centre not so much on the overt behaviour produced by the child at any particular age or in any particular situation, or on the forms of change in overt behaviours, but on the interpretation to be put upon that behaviour, from the point of view of diagnosing what underlying process produced it. Any specific behaviour or change in behaviour can be produced in a multiplicity of ways. Critical experimental tests of alternative views would make sense only in the context where these alternative views were expressed in process models of sufficient detail to allow the discovery of different predictions from each model, on some testable measure. In other words, the problem currently faced by developmental psychology is the need to elaborate theoretical ideas in clearer, more detailed and concrete terms, in order to come to grips with the issues.

It has been widely argued that developmental psychology is ill-equipped to handle this problem, that as a discipline psychology lacks a suitable medium in which to discuss any kind of cognitive process, and that the discipline is profoundly atheoretical (for example, Boden, 1977; Sloman, 1978). In this context, work in AI has been advanced as a saving solution, as offering the theoretical input which is seen as lacking in developmental psychology. It has been argued that computer programs provide a medium in which cognitive processes can be expressed and explored, and in which the coherence and viability of specific mechanisms can be examined. Concepts from the 'computational metaphor' have been promoted as providing the best available conceptual framework which allows a concrete theoretical exploration of developmental change in processing or of self-modificatory processes. The way forward for developmental psychology would then involve working towards the construction of computational models of the mechanisms involved in cognitive developmental change, testing the theories through demonstrating the extent to which a program built on those principles could reproduce the phenomena observed in children.

Developmental issues have not yet received all that much attention in AI. There is a growing literature on machine learning (e.g. Lenat, 1974; Mitchell *et al.*, 1981.; Quinlan, 1983; Sussman, 1975; Waterman, 1970; Winston, 1975), which has explored various aspects of the mechanisms involved in transforming one level of processing into another. Some of this work has produced interesting ideas, but from the point of view of developmental psychology, machine learning work remains fairly esoteric. Such work is not concerned to address the problem of human development. It has not yet produced programs which come anywhere near simulating the kinds of developmental change of interest to developmental psychologists. Work in most other areas of AI has indirect implications for models of human development, but again, such work is presently hard to map onto the problems of developmental psychology. There is, however, a body of AI work which directly attempts to illuminate the theoretical problems of developmental psychology: this work draws on a particular type of programming technique, known as a production system, to simulate both the changes in cognitive skills between younger and older children, and the mechanisms which generate these developmental changes.

The remainder of this chapter presents a review and evaluation of the AI developmental work based specifically on production systems. Other types of AI approach are considered elsewhere in this book (see Chapter 12). The aim here is not to provide a comparative evaluation of the production system approach *vis-à-vis* other types of AI methodology, but rather to look at those production systems which specifically lay claim to address issues in developmental psychology, and to explore the nature of their contribution.

## PRODUCTION SYSTEM MODELS OF DEVELOPMENT

The term 'production system' refers to a particular way of structuring a computer program. In essence, a production system has three elements. The first is a set of condition → action rules, called *productions*. As the names suggest, the left-hand side of each rule stipulates the condition under which the rule applies, and the right-hand side stipulates the action which is determined by that condition. For example,

If I am hungry → cook a meal

The second element of the system is a *database*, consisting of information associated with the task, including the goals and subgoals currently active, such as whether or not you are hungry. The third element is a *control process*, which determines which rules will be compared to the database first, and which will have priority when the conditions for several are met at the same time.

Below is a simple example of a production system. This system deals with the problem of putting a pan of water on to boil. The production system has three rules, which are compared in turned to the database, wherein is recorded the current status of the task.

P1:  if the pan contains cold water → turn on the heat under the pan
P2:  if the pan is empty → fill the pan with water
P3:  if there is no pan on the cooker → fetch a pan

This extremely simple production system generates behaviour without the need for any goals. Here, the productions are triggered simply by beliefs about the situation. More sophisticated production systems would have both belief components and goal components in the left-hand 'condition' side, and the right-hand 'action' side would include setting up new goals, or forming new beliefs, as well as performing external actions.

With such a simple production system as the one described above, control problems hardly exist. But even small increases in the complexity of the task will mean that some kind of control process becomes necessary. For example, suppose that the water is being boiled to cook a carrot. The production system would have to be extended to include instructions for fetching and preparing the carrot, for example:

P4:  if there is no carrot → fetch a carrot
P5:  if the carrot is dirty → scrape the carrot clean
P6:  if the carrot is clean → put it in the pan

Now there is a control problem for the system. What should it do first? At any one time, the database (state of affairs) may include elements meeting the conditions of two rules. For example, the carrot is dirty and there is no water in the pan. Control processes would determine which rule should be activated first. This problem seems a relatively easy one to solve, as the conflicting rules can be treated as part of two independent tasks. But control problems can be very complex. For example, even in the simple system described here, the two tasks must actually be integrated: if the carrot is put in the pan before the water, then, as these rules stand, you won't get cooked carrot: production rule P2 will never fire, because the pan will not be empty, so the heat will never be turned on because there will never be any water in the pan (the condition for production rule P1 to fire).

Production systems were originally developed by Newell and Simon (cf. Newell and Simon, 1972) as a particularly useful way of simulating the processes underlying adult problem-solving in tasks like cryptarithmetic, and 'move' problems such as the 'missionaries and cannibals' problem. The way in which a production system is structured means that, up to a point, new rules can be added without revision or alteration of the existing rules. This type of flexibility is particularly valuable for models of developing systems. It means, for example, that a production system can model gradual learning, through the gradual acquisition of new rules. The use of condition → action rules facilitates the process of modelling the relation between behaviour and situation: where the database changes, the behaviour of the system changes. Condition → action rules are also particularly comprehensible to psychologists, perhaps because their format recalls the familiar S–R bonds.

Computer programs can, of course, be structured in other ways. A production system methodology is only one of a number of different types of approach to structuring a computer program. But the production system approach is very general. Any computational process whatsoever can be modelled in a production system, even though a production system does not always provide the optimal structure for programming a particular function.

The basic production system technique has been developed, mainly by students of Newell and Simon at Carnegie-Mellon University, to model the different problem-solving skills shown by children of different ages. For example, production systems have been implemented successfully to model some aspects of children's behaviour at various ages in class inclusion tasks (Klahr and Wallace, 1972), length and weight seriation (Baylor and Gascon, 1974), length seriation (Young, 1976), quantification tasks (Klahr, 1973), conservation tasks (Klahr and Wallace, 1973), language acquisition (Langley, 1981), balance scale tasks (Klahr and Siegler, 1978), and arithmetic tasks (Young and O'Shea, 1981). These Piagetian tasks are at the centre of much current work in developmental psychology, and production system analyses are therefore potentially of great value in illuminating the issues surrounding them

The basic idea behind all such programs is that children of different ages use different sets of rules in approaching a given problem. For example, Richard Young's work on 4- to 6-year old children's approach to length seriation has shown how the differing performances of the children, from fairly extensive incompetence to accurate skill, can be conceptualized in terms of the particular seriation rules a child does or does not possess. Young divides the seriation task into three components, which he describes as follows (Young, 1976, p.194):

Selection:     the block he chooses to work with next.

Evaluation:    his decision whether or not to accept a block as an addition to the line.

Placement:      whereabouts in the line he puts a new block; of which a major
                aspect is *correction*: what he does with a block once he realizes
                that it's wrong.

Young argues that children of differing levels of skill have different rules
for each of these components of the task. For example, he describes the
following alternative possibilities for 'selection' rules, each of which would
obviously produce a different type of behaviour, corresponding to a different
level of skill in seriation (Young, 1976, p.195):

1 Get nearest: select by proximity
2 Get suitable: choose any block of the right size
3 Get-in-mind: select any block that was recently tried or considered
4 Get biggest first: start with the biggest block
5 Get near last: pick a suitable block from near where the last one came from
6 Get from subpool: take one from the collection of blocks which have been tried
                and put aside.

Conceptualizing children's skills in terms of production system models has
a number of advantages. For example, as Young points out, his production
system approach provides a more extensive account of children's seriation
skills than was given by the Piagetian tradition. It constitutes an explicit
account of the processes which yield the child's performance at each stage,
as opposed to the more implicit model of processes provided by Piaget. The
production system account is also more detailed, and covers aspects of skill
which are not included in traditional accounts: where Piaget talks only of
the logical structure of skill, the production system model provides a working
model of the child's knowledge in use. Young's production system approach
attributes a greater flexibility and adaptability to the child's skill than is
allowed for by traditional models such as Piaget's. His production system
model of seriation allows the subject to tackle the task in a variety of ways,
allowing him flexibility in the way in which he uses the rules available
to him. Piagetian accounts of seriation, in contrast, assume a much more
determinate approach on the child's part, an approach constrained by the
logical form of seriation. The more flexible model is intuitively a better match
to reality. In addition, the production system approach offers a new approach
to various issues such as the continuity or discontinuity of developmental
change: Young argues, for example, that his models suggest that the
phenomena traditionally conceptualized as reflecting major reorganizations
in the child's mind – Piagetian 'stages' – may be explicable in terms of
'cumulative progress along a developmental trajectory through the space of
seriation structures' (Young, 1976, p.209). In effect, the poor performance
of the young child, and his gradual improvement, may reflect not radical
change in the basic cognitive structures invoked for the task, as Piaget argued,

but the initial absence of good rules for seriating, and the gradual addition of more and better ones.

Thus work based around building production system models of cognitive change in childhood offers developmental psychology a powerful conceptual tool, which can, in effect, allow the detailed exploration of the processes going on in the child's head in ways which traditional psychological approaches cannot. It can reveal aspects of processing previously inaccessible to analysis. As such, it offers a powerful tool through which many of the theoretical problems of developmental psychology, such as the controversies as to what it is that changes with cognitive growth, could receive fresh illumination.

Early production system work on children's cognition was confined to modelling the different rule sets implied by different levels of skill in performance. More recently, production systems have been implemented which also include developmental mechanisms, i.e. mechanisms which act to transform one level of skill into another, by revising and improving old rules, or by adding new ones (Anderson, 1983; Anzai and Simon, 1979) Langley, 1981; Young and O'Shea, 1981). Developmental mechanisms are conceptualized in such adaptive production systems as a set of 'meta-rules' – i.e. rules which act upon problem-solving rule systems to revise old rules and create new ones. In other words, these programs propose that developmental mechanisms can be thought of as a special kind of production system, which acts on and reforms other problem-solving rule systems, by reviewing a trace of how the existing production system worked in addressing a particular problem, and applying certain tests to detect where developmental transformations can be made. The specific developmental mechanisms for effecting these transformations may be unique to a particular production system model. Each individual programmer solves the problems of creating his or her program as best they can, in an *ad hoc* way. There is no general theory as to the ways in which particular functions should be handled in creating programs to model childhood cognitive development. At some levels, this does not really matter. The fine details of a computer program have small claim to be accurate representations of human processing. It is the general properties of the processing which are pertinent to a psychological theory. At this more global level, there is a well-established 'case law' which provides the common ground between one program and another, and which yields some characteristics general to most self-modifying programs. One common type of 'meta-rule' is a procedure whereby a collection of separate procedures which act systematically and successfully in combination with one another are reorganized or 'chunked' into a single procedure. For example, in cooking a carrot, putting the carrot in the pan (production P6) and putting the water in the pan (P2) act systematically and successfully together; they could profitably be 'chunked' into a single production, which in effect explicitly captures what was only implicit in the previous rule-set, namely that water must be cooked with the carrot:

P7: if the carrot is clean → put it in an empty pan and fill the pan with water.

This kind of 'chunking', or 'composition', as Anderson (1983) calls it, in effect has the character of allowing the child to 'internalize' a regularity already occurring, unacknowledged, in his problem-solving, by creating a new rule which explicitly represents the regularity. This rule is then added to the system, and can contribute to the discovery of other regularities, and the creation of fresh rules.

Another very common type of developmental mechanism involves rules which act to prune problem-solving rule-sets so as to eliminate unnecessary or redundant productions or productions which lead to diversions in solving the problem. Such a mechanism works by looking at the trace of a particular episode of problem-solving, and locating any instances where a production fired which was irrelevant to solving the problem, or which involved a step which was unnecessary *vis-à-vis* the goal. Having located the redundancy and the conditions in which it arises, the rule set can then be restructured appropriately. For example, consider a production system for cooking carrots as above. If this production system includes P7, P2 and P6, then P2 and P6 are redundant, since they perform actions already covered by P7. This redundancy can be detected, and the rule-set restructured accordingly. Another kind of redundancy might be eliminating a rule which put the clean carrot down on a plate before putting it into the pan. Adaptive production systems also normally include procedures which 'tune' successful rules, by discriminating more finely the applicability of the rule, or generalizing successful rules. Such a mechanism acts by looking at the effects of rules in relation to task goals. For example, in the system for cooking carrots given above, the applicability of P1 might be generalized so that the heat will be turned on if the water in the pan is initially tepid rather than cold.

Through such devices adaptive production system models have yielded more specific models of developmental mechanisms than have previously been produced by developmental psychology. Mechanisms for selectively eliminating, adding, combining and tuning rule-sets have been shown to be potent in transforming the performance of a system in ways that are suggestive of developmental phenomena. The process of 'chunking' together separate procedures into one has the effect of allowing the system to use knowledge in more integrated ways, and of allowing things to be done in a single step which were previously done in a number of separate moves. Such streamlining or automatizing of the system has been argued to be an important factor in the difference between novice and experienced processors (cf. Boden, note 1), and provides an interesting model for some developmental change. Similarly, the implementation of actual programs in which developmental change is triggered within rule-sets which are successfully handling a problem, as well as being failure driven, has provided substantial support for psychological claims for a re-examination of the Piagetian dictates as to the relation between development, success and failure (Karmiloff-Smith, 1984).

## A CRITICAL EVALUATION OF PRODUCTION SYSTEMS AS MODELS OF DEVELOPMENT

It is clear that the production system approach provides a powerful tool for developmental psychology. In common with other computational techniques, the production system techniques have great potential for modelling complex cognitive processes in ways that offer theoretical accounts of the nature of developmental change which far outstrip traditional approaches open to developmental psychologists in terms of concrete detail. However, from the point of view of developmental psychology, there remain certain difficulties in accepting that the specific production system programs written to date constitute a useful basis for a theoretical account of cognitive development. These reservations centre around the validity of the programs as theories of childhood cognitive development.

This question of validity seems at first to be open to fairly straightforward empirical exploration. One can ask whether or not a program successfully mimics the performances produced by children of differing ages. The answer is 'yes'. Proponents of such programs as developmental theories make much of the fact that their programs often produce traces which show a close parallel to the protocols produced by real children, and that their self-modifying systems show the same patterns of change in performance as does a developing child. The degree of matching achieved between some aspects of the program's performance and that of the child does indeed provide a plausible basis for the claim that the computer programs accurately model the child's cognitive processing. But in fact, the conclusions which can legitimately be drawn from such a degree of match are weaker than one might suppose. The programs are written to mimic the child's behaviour; so it is neither surprising nor impressive that they produce traces which parallel the child's growth. Such simulation is the criterion for completion of the program. Certainly, if a program could not mimic the child, then one would have grounds for concluding that it was an inadequate or innaccurate model of the child's processing. But it does not follow that accurate mimicry of a child's behaviour necessarily implies that the program is an adequate model: Louis (XVI)'s clockwork men were accurate mimics of some human behaviours, but no one would take that to mean that clockwork mechanisms parallel human processing in yielding those behaviours. The more general point is that any piece of behaviour could be generated by a plethora of different mechanisms. Similarity of output is no guarantee of similarity of processing. If one wants some kind of empirical test of the parallel between program and human processing, then the only legitimate type of test would be if a program were to predict some new measurable effect which experimental psychologists could go out and look for. Successful prediction of this kind would provide a much stronger (though still conditional) support for the claims of the production system models. This point is, in fact, well accepted by people working on production systems. But as yet, there is very little empirical work attempting to fulfil this function. Gaps of this sort are a general weakness of the interaction between AI and psychology.

It is worth adding that the degree of accuracy achieved by current programs in simulating children's performances should not be overestimated. Existing programs based on production systems can cope only with the circumscribed tasks for which they were written, and can only handle input of a limited range within those tasks. They do not simulate the child's capacity to deal effectively with distractions, or with social interactions, while doing the task. And in one respect, there is already strong evidence that adaptive production systems are not adequate models of childhood cognitive development. There are serious discrepancies between the developmental characteristics of the child and the programs in that whereas self-modifying programs (to the limited extent that they develop at all) develop very rapidly, children take time, sometimes years, to achieve the progress apparently gained by the machine in seconds. This discrepancy cannot be dismissed under the general rubric: 'Well, machines do everything faster than people.' The speed discrepancies are orders of magnitude different between program and child, and are associated with other mismatches – children falter, showing a complex fragility in their new achievements which is not matched by the programs. These areas of mismatch almost certainly indicate areas of poor fit between child and program, at the level of underlying processing.

It has been argued that, even if the psychological validity of particular programs is a matter of controversy, such models still have a powerful claim to be taken up by developmental psychology, since they are more complete than alternative accounts. If a program successfully simulates children's behaviour, then, it is argued, it has been empirically demonstrated that the processes embodied in that program are adequate or sufficient to yield the behaviours involved. This conclusion would be far from trivial. Psychological theories of developmental processes are notorious for their sketchy nature. Piaget's theory has been endlessly criticized for its inadequacy in failing to embody any model of performance factors, or to state mechanisms clearly; the same criticism can be made of his critics, such as Donaldson, whose model of children's processing includes only a vague account of the processes which underlthe any particular performance. No psychological theory to date can make any claim to represent a full account of the processing sufficient to yield the performances under consideration (and this is perhaps the key factor in our failure to resolve many of the controversies currently facing developmental psychology). Indeed, only when a theory is expressed in terms of a computer program could a claim to provide such a stringent level of theoretical adequacy be tested. On this basis, one might put forward a strong argument that the production system models written to date should have pride of place in our theoretical thinking, even where there are mismatches between the performances of children and programs, on the grounds that it is better to have a coherent theory, even if it is wrong, than to have no theory at all. But here again, the strong claims for the programs are open to criticism. The arcane descriptions of such programs to which the reader normally has access are difficult for a psychologist to fathom in detail. But close inspection often reveals that the program does not do quite what its author says it does, or that it does things in a different way from the way its author claims. Computer programs operate not only through principled processes, but also through 'cheats', such as *ad hoc* and highly local rules, which allow them to get over difficulties in running for which no principled solution is known. Through such devices, lacunae are allowed to exist in current production system models of childhood cognition which vitiate their claims to embody processes *sufficient* to account for the phenomena of cognitive developmental change.

An example of particular significance to developmental psychology is the fact that the programs are often completely devoid of actual models of the circumstances which trigger developmental change. Some programs even have a separate unit which embodies the developmental mechanism. When this unit is 'switched off', no development occurs. When it is 'switched on', such development as the program simulates is rapid and complete. In effect, in such programs, developmental processes are triggered by nothing more sophisticated than a lever-pulling exercise by the programmer. Other programs have developmental elements more tightly integrated into the basic program. But again, these programs do not constitute full accounts of how these functions might work. For example, one of the commonest developmental operators is the process of collating or 'chunking' into a single unit procedures which are often and successfully used in combination, as has been described above. But programs incorporating this function have no principled mechanism for determining how such combinations are to be detected. They operate on the basis that if some sequence of instructions is used more than once in various tasks, then the sequence is worth recording as a sequence. But not all co-occurring procedures should be chunked into a single unit. Beliefs about causality, etc., as well as contiguity, determine which procedures should be coordinated into a single unit. For example, the actions of changing gear and driving round a corner often occur in contiguity. The utility of representing these actions as a unit depends not on their contiguity, but on the significance of the relationship between the actions. The two should be flexibly coordinated in terms of the effect of changing gear on safe cornering, and not on the basis of contiguity *per se*. Currently available production system programs modelling childhood development are weak in terms of their representations of such causal relationships. They emphasize contiguity at the expense of causality, and rely on *ad hoc* rather than principled criteria for resolving when such a move is appropriate.

This means, in effect, that programs expressed as production system models have, as yet, made little contribution to our understanding of how and when knowledge changes. Indeed, even the general form of the heuristics which such programs propose as developmental mechanisms provides little illumination for developmental psychology. The concrete substance of these heuristics is, in effect, nothing more than a 'reification' of the start–end state transformations which they are alleged to produce. Thus when a developmental change shows a surface characteristic of procedures having become more economic in form, the tendency in current programs is to postulate the existence of heuristic meta-procedure for detecting and eliminating redundancy. This is an extremely simple model of the way developmental mechanisms might work. Other lacunae exist in these programs: for example, control processes are tailored to specific contexts. There is no principled work on control processes for developmental mechanisms, i.e. no actual model of such things. Thus even programs which successfully transform one level of skill into another do not presently constitute adequate theories of how this could be done, leaving aside the problem of how such theories stand as models of how children actually do it.

In sum, the programs written to date using production system techniques have generated some interesting ideas about developmental mechanisms, but have not shown that they embody processes equivalent to those occurring in the child, nor that their mechanisms are sufficient to account for the phenomena of developmental growth. But to say this is not necessarily to attack the basic idea of using computational concepts to clarify developmental issues, nor the specific claim that production system techniques constitute the most convenient tool within such a framework. There is a distinction between the medium in which a theory is expressed, and the substantive content of that theory. The potential for representing and exploring cognitive processes is far greater with computational concepts of any kind than without, even if this promise has not yet been realized.

## A MORE FRUITFUL LIAISON BETWEEN AI AND DEVELOPMENTAL PSYCHOLOGY?

Adaptive production systems may well have a lot to offer developmental psychology. But will this potential be achieved? It will be argued here that this depends to a large extent on our ability to construct a genuinely interdisciplinary interaction between AI and developmental psychology. At present, there is only a trivial liaison between work in the two disciplines. Can this be expanded to create a genuine cognitive science of development?

Currently, much of the work based on production system techniques does not concern itself with the issues which direct developmental psychologists: while developmental psychology is caught up in controversy as to the extent to which cognitive development represents change in underlying skill as opposed to change only in the processes involved in deploying existing skill across novel situations, people working on production system models tend to act as though development can be treated straightforwardly as a matter of developing skills. Their programs are presently written on the assumption that the young child performs poorly because he or she lacks the skills embodied in certain rules possessed only by older children. These specific programs cannot successfully simulate the recent discoveries that the young child's performance is strongly affected (Donaldson, 1978) by the detailed *social* context of the situation in which the test is made, as well as by features of the context more directly relevant to the skills under consideration. Alternative possibilities, such as production system models incorporating processes of the kind discussed by Donaldson, are in principle perfectly feasible. But such models have so far simply been ignored, with no discussion, justification or rationale for such a position, at a time when developmental psychology is taking these matters to be more and more problematic. There are to date no programs which attempt to incorporate developmental processes relying on social or cultural factors to induce and guide growth, despite the general consensus that such effects must contribute to human development. An obvious area for the development of interdisciplinary cooperation would be in the introduction of psychological ideas on such topics into the framework of production system modelling. From such a collaboration, psychologists would be provided with the means to express and explore their theoretical models in a coherent and rigorous medium, and programmers would gain perspective as to the phenomena to be explored. The rephrasing of psychologists' questions in the more explicit form demanded by programming might well lead us all into a more fruitful search for principled solutions as to the nature of developmental mechanisms.

A first target for a truly interdisciplinary cognitive science of development must surely involve a reappraisal of the basic constraints and assumptions which circumscribe our research efforts. The notion usually advanced under this heading is that developmental psychologists must alter their ways, by rethinking their basic approach to theorizing about cognitive processes so as to develop conceptual frameworks commensurate with (if not actually based on) the kinds of concrete processing concepts which characterize computer models, as the best means of producing theories capable of explaining cognitive development. They must also evolve empirical techniques capable of yielding data which genuinely bear on conceptual issues phrased in this way. But the other side of the coin is that programmers must become genuinely responsive to input from psychology, and must evaluate the constraints and limitations which their working assumptions may place on developmental models, against the input from psychology.

For example, adaptive production systems (and indeed, all AI programs) are written for microworlds. That is, the program operates in a universe bounded by the task in hand. There is no hidden agenda in the test situation so far as the program is concerned, and only a trivial history of other, analogous but different tasks in different situations to draw on in constructing its solution to the problem before it. Problem-solving in a microworld is disembodied, lacking any context of motives and expectations beyond those integral to the task in hand. Although it has been argued that much cognitive processing must be modularly organized (Fodor, 1983), no psychologist has ever suggested that processing operates in modules as circumscribed as this. Indeed, it is easy to demonstrate that children's performance in a given task is a product of factors going well beyond the bounds of the usual program microworld. Human reasoning is embedded in the framework of our general knowledge and expectations, both in the sense that our knowledge is tied to familiar, concrete contexts (Donaldson, 1978; Gelman, 1978; Johnson-Laird and Wason, 1977) and in that social norms and expectations irrelevant to the task in hand may determine the child's interpretation of what is going on, and hence the success or failure of his efforts (McGarrigle and Donaldson, 1974; Donaldson, 1978). The strong suggestion is that the universe in which developmental models operate should be expanded to include a more general model of the child's motives, expectations and knowledge of the world. This conclusion has implications for both sides of the AI – developmental psychology collaboration, in that just as AI programs presently assume a circumscribed microworld, so psychological models emphasize some but not all of these factors (compare Piaget and Donaldson, for example). Solving the problems of developing models which integrate these factors into a more viable whole is obviously an exercise better suited to an interdisciplinary approach than to the efforts of either psychology or AI alone.

Another area ripe for interdisciplinary research concerns assumptions common to both AI and psychology as to the nature of the structural relationship between developmental and other processes. Work in both disciplines commonly makes the strong assumption that developmental mechanisms are independent of ongoing problem-solving processes (cf. Klahr's, 1982, review). Models of development are seen as two-phase models, in which there are processes which develop, and processes which act on them to actually produce the development (Klahr, 1982; Thornton, note 2). Thus in present-generation adaptive production systems, developmental change is produced by a set of very general heuristic meta-processes, which stand separate from ordinary processing, and which operate in domain-neutral ways across all facets of cognitive skill, i.e. applied across all tasks and at a ll age levels, as has been described above. Similar assumptions underly psychological concepts, such as Karmiloff-Smith's notion of the switching in of 'meta-procedural' processes. In fact, the whole notion of a separate 'meta-level' of productions to generate developmental change may prove to have fallen into the old fallacy of assuming that because a change is produced, there must be a 'something' to produce the change. The analogy in biological terms would be to say that because evolutionary change occurs, there must be an organ, or physiological mechanism within the organism, which acts explicitly to supervise evolution. The fallacy in that context is obvious. Evolutionary effects derive not from evolutionary organs, but from selection pressures in the interaction between organism and environment. Similarly, the generality and the motive force of developmental processes in cognition can be conceptualized in ways other than separate, specifically 'developmental' functions (Thornton, note 2). The point here is that this issue is an open question, and one which needs to be explicitly explored by a cognitive science of development. The assumption that developmental mechanisms stand separate from the rest of cognitive processes constrains us to theorize about such processes in certain ways, and to ignore other possibilities. There is little psychological research which bears explicitly on this question. There is some empirical work which does not support it: for example, Thornton's (1985) analysis of the goals and operations which actually trigger and effect change in children's problem-solving in the 'Twenty Questions' task suggests that these are so closely allied to the goals and operations which constitute the actual problem-solving that it becomes meaningless to make a distinction between problem-solving and developmental processes. The validity of such a distinction is not an issue which will easily be resolved through a purely theoretical policy of seeing how far one can get under the 'two-phase' assumption, since our models of development are far from testable against a realistic criterion of being adequate to generate the observed phenomena, and are likely to remain so for a long time. Again, here is an area in which AI can help psychologists to phrase the question, and psychologists can provide analyses of what people actually do in ways that will illuminate the problem.

## CONCLUSIONS

On the one hand, the conceptual power of AI approaches offers to developmental psychology the tools for making progress with problems which have always eluded us. The potential of the production system approach, which is presently the main AI approach applied directly to psychological issues, is formidable. On the other hand, present work in that vein suffers from grave defects, which seriously limit its relevance to developmental issues. Present-generation programs fail to deliver the 'goods', because of their psychological naivety, their *ad hoc* approach, their unexamined assumptions, and their programming 'cheats'.

The obvious solution to the problem for developmental psychology (and perhaps for AI too) lies in a more sophisticated interaction between AI and psychology, wherein methodologies are developed for carrying the strengths of each discipline into a truly interdisciplinary collaboration. The problems of present-generation production systems are not inevitable aspects of the production system approach. AI techniques can be used to carry and develop theories of virtually limitless range. Production systems can perform anything programmable (though they may not always represent the optimal programming structure). But the approach cannot be expected to solve all the problems of developmental psychology without drawing on the subject matter of psychology. If developmental psychology is to profit from the computer revolution, we need to be more concerned with developing frameworks within which psychological work can be incisively informative to computer models, as well as driven by the computational metaphor.

## REFERENCES

Anderson, J. R. (1983). *The Architecture of Cognition*, Harvard University Press, Cambridge, Mass.
Anzai, Y., and Simon, H. (1979). The theory of learning by doing, *Psychological Review*, **86**, 124–40.
Baylor, G. W., and Gascon, J. (1974). An information processing theory of aspects of the development of weight seriation in children, *Cognitive Psychology*, **6**, 1–40.
Boden, M. (1977). *Artificial Intelligence and Natural Man*, Basic Books, New York.
Cole, M., and Scribner, S. (1974). *Culture and Thought*, J. Wiley and Sons, New York.
Donaldson, M. (1978). *Children's Minds*, Fontana, London.
Fodor, J. (1976). *The Language of Thought*, Harvester Press, Brighton.
Fodor, J. (1983). *The Modularity of Mind*, MIT Press, Cambridge, Mass.
Gagne, R. M. (1968). Contributions of learning to human development, *Psychological Review*, **75**, 177–191.
Gelman, R. (1978). Cognitive development. *Annual Review of Psychology*, **29**, 297–332.
Inhelder, B. Sinclair, H., and Bovet, M. (1974). *Learning and the Development of Cognition*, Harvard University Press, Cambridge, Mass.
Johnson-Laird, P. N., and Wason, P. C. (1977). *Thinking*, Cambridge University Press, Cambridge.
Karmiloff-Smith, A. (1979). Micro and macro developmental changes in language acquisition and other representational systems, *Cognitive Science*, **3**, 81–118.
Karmiloff-Smith, A. (1984). Children's problem-solving. In M. E. Lamb, A. L. Brown and B. Rogoff (eds), *Advances in Developmental Psychology*, Vol. 3, Erlbaum, Hillsdale, N.J.

Klahr, D. (1973). A production system for counting, substituting and adding. In W. G. Chase (ed.), *Visual Information Processing*, Academic Press, New York.

Klahr, D. (1982). Nonmonotone assessment of monotone development: an information processing analysis. In S. Strauss and R. Stavey (eds), *U-shaped Behavioural Growth*, Academic Press, New York.

Klahr, D., and Siegler, R. S. (1978). The representation of children's knowledge. In H. W. Reese, and L. P. Lipsitt (eds), *Advances in Child Development*, Vol. 12, Academic Press, New York.

Klahr, D., and Wallace, J. G. (1972). Class inclusion processes. In S. Farnham-Diggory (ed.), *Information Processing in Children*, Academic Press, New York.

Klahr, D., and Wallace, J. G. (1973). The role of quantification operators in the development of conservation of quantity, *Cognitive Psychology*, **4**, 301–327.

Langley, P. (1981). *Language acquisition through error recovery*. CIP working paper 432, Carnegie-Mellon University.

Lenat, D. B. (1974). The role of heuristics in learning by discovery: three case studies. In R. S. Michalski, J. G. Carbonell, and T. M. Mitchell (eds), *Machine Learning: An Artificial Intelligence Approach*, Tioga Publishing Company, Palo Alto, Calif.

McGarrigle, J., and Donaldson, M. (1981). Conservation accidents, *Cognition*, **3**, 341–350.

Mitchell, T. M., Utgoff, P. E., Nudel, B., and Banerji, R. (1972). Learning problem-solving heuristics through practice. In *IJCAI 81*, International Joint Conference on Artificial Intelligence,

Newell, A., and Simon, H. (1972). *Human Problem-solving*, Prentice-Hall, Engle-wood Cliffs, N.J.

Piaget, J. (1970a). *Genetic Epistemology*, Columbia, NY.

Piaget, J. (1970b). Piaget's theory. In: P. Mussen (ed.), *Carmichael's Manual of Child Psychology*, Wiley, New York.

Piaget, J. (1972). Intellectual evolution from adolescence to adulthood. *Human Development*, **15**, 1–12.

Quinlan, J. (1983). Learning efficient classification procedures and their application to chess games. In R. S. Michalski, J. G. Carbonell, and T. M. Mitchell (eds), *Machine Learning: An AI Approach*, Tioga, Palo Alto, Calif.

Sloman, A. (1978. *The Computer Revolution in Philosophy: Philosophy, Science and Models of Mind*, Harvester Press, Brighton.

Sussman, G. (1975). *A Computer Model of Skill Acquisition*, American Elsevier, New York.

Thornton, S. (1985). Processes of change in children's problem-solving. End of grant report for ESRC project grant C00230087. British Library.

Vygotsky, L. S. (1962). *Thought and Language*, MIT Press, Cambridge, Mass.

Waterman, D. A. (1970). Generalization learning techniques for automating the learning of heuristics, *AI Journal*, **1**, 121–170.

Young, R. (1976). *Seriation by Children: an Artificial Intelligence Analysis of a Piagetian Task*, Birkhauser Verlag, Basel.

Young R., and O'Shea, T. (1981). Errors in children's subtraction, *Cognitive Science*, **5**, 153–177.

*Notes*

Note 1: Boden, M. (forthcoming)

Note 2: Thornton, S. Mechanisms of change in children's problem-solving. (in preparation)

Computers, Cognition and Development
Edited by J. Rutkowska and C. Crook
© 1987 John Wiley & Sons Ltd

CHAPTER 11

# Cognitive Science, AI and Developmental Psychology. Are There Links? Could There Be Links?

DEREK SLEEMAN

SUMMARY

Protocol analysis of students' difficulties learning algebra is discussed and used to illustrate individual variation in performance and change. 'Repair theory' and 'mis-generalization' are compared as explanations of why errors occur. Student/user modelling techniques for AI intelligent tutoring systems are introduced and a process model of the algebra data outlined.

## ARTIFICIAL INTELLIGENCE, PSYCHOLOGY AND DEVELOPMENTAL PSYCHOLOGY

Over the last two decades a strong symbiosis has developed between AI (artificial intelligence) and psychology. Human–computer interaction studies have taken seriously the information-processing limitations of humans suggested by psychology (Card, Moran and Newall, 1983). Further, there has been *discussion* in the community of a radically different approach to designing new artefacts, say a program to play a novel game: namely, study in detail humans solving the task, analyse these protocols, and use these analyses as a basis for the design. These illustrate how psychology has influenced AI. The influence of AI on psychology has been even more pervasive. In the 1960s and 1970s AI formulated a range of high-level data-structures – often termed representational schema – including predicate calculus, production systems, semantic networks, frames and LISP data-

235

structures. Many of these schema have subsequently been 'adopted' by psychologists who have used these structures to summarize their observational data. Others have suggested that these schema are in fact accurate, or reasonably accurate, models of human representational schema. For instance, the Carnegie-Mellon School of Information Processing have frequently advocated the use of production systems to represent human knowledge (e.g. Newell, 1973; Anderson, 1983). Similarly, many workers have used semantic networks to represent a particular subject's domain knowledge; Collins and Quillian (1972) being probably the first. On the other hand, Johnson-Laird (1983) has argued that semantic networks are really inadequate to express the extensional knowledge which a person has.* In passing, I would like to point out what I believe are some important and pertinent negative results from AI. The early natural language systems, which used predicate calculus as their representational schema, did not carry out human–like dialogues. This suggests to me that humans do not have their knowledge represented in this form. The search for more powerful representational schema continues as an important research area within AI.

For some (strange) reason the sub-field of developmental psychology – maybe wisely – seems to have been largely uninfluenced by AI and cognitive science to date. The machine-learning sub-field of AI might be expected to have the greatest resonance with developmental psychology; see Carbonell, Michalski and Mitchell (1983) for an introduction to this field. (Chapter 12 of this volume discusses this topic in more detail.) Given the widespread adoption of representational schema from AI into psychology, we might have expected to see developmentalists using the several learning algorithms as models of child development and producing criticisms (analogous to those offered by Johnson-Laird) of their shortfall. Similarly, the experimental work done by developmentalists has not (greatly) influenced the design of existing learning algorithms. It is clear that there are some fascinating questions to be addressed in both these sub-fields, and it would appear that greater communication between the two activities could be very beneficial.

There are two additional areas from AI and cognitive science which I believe are pertinent to developmental psychology (these areas will be dealt with in separate sections below). They are:

1. Cognitive science's probing of difficulties which students have in learning – largely in the area of high-school subjects. The detailed analysis of protocols which characterizes this work is of particular relevance to developmental psychology in revealing great individual variation in performance

---

*In fact, I believe Johnson-Laird's criticism should have been broader and included all of AI's current representational schema.

and change. (Additionally, I will put forward a mechanism/theory to explain a part of the data discussed.)

2. Student/user modelling techniques – which enable significant differences between users to be represented in intelligent systems. The prime purpose of discussing this issue is to make psychologists who are concerned with modelling human knowledge aware of an additional range of (AI) techniques and representational schema. (For completeness, I will show how some of the data introduced in the high-school case study can be modelled using one of the techniques introduced in the discussion of modelling.)

Before treating these topics in some detail, it seems appropriate to add that taken together these techniques have given cognitive psychologists/scientists another important tool for model building. The standard approach of cognitive – including developmental – psychology has been to use statistical techniques. Such techniques essentially provide models which stress the *common* elements of how the target population solves tasks; frequently, this 'summary' is not in a form which makes it clear how the inferred model(s) would perform on a *particular* task. On the other hand, Piaget's very rich interviews were largely anecdotal, and again were not transformed into models for individuals on specific tasks.

Given the combination of rich/deep interviews and more powerful representational schema, cognitive scientists are now (sometimes) able to produce models to explain the problem-solving of a range of individuals on a specific task. These models then give additional possibilities (as noted above and discussed further in the following section) for theorizing on the cause of the individual differences noted. A model/theory which can explain both the commonalities *and* the individual differences of subjects' performance would have greater predictive power than the theories of 'common activities' produced by traditional statistical methods, and thus in a Kuhnian sense would be a more powerful theory.*

## REVIEW OF COGNITIVE SCIENCE AND INSTRUCTION

In the last decade workers in cognitive science have done detailed analyses of the performance of novices and experts in a variety of areas including chess (Chase and Simon, 1973), high-school mathematics (Davis, 1984; Sleeman, 1985a), physics (McCloskey, 1983), programming (Ehrlich and Soloway, 1984; Sleeman *et al.*, in press; see also Chapter 8 of this volume); and even the language-arts areas (Langer, in press). The following important issues have been raised by these studies:

---

*Some developmentalists – principally Klahr and his co-workers – have used process-orientated models to describe how children solve specific tasks; see Klahr (1978).

1. Experts and novices frequently appear to have different knowledge and, more significantly, different organization of knowledge.
2. A topic is very difficult to learn if its concepts conflict with the student's real-world knowledge. For example, in physics 'work' and 'force' are defined very precisely – and these definitions 'clash' with the real-world definitions to which students tend to regress.
3. Students sometimes display the ability to use complex *procedures* but demonstrate a naive *conceptual* knowledge of a domain. For example, McCloskey (1983) has reported a study in which college engineering students were able to get a high percentage of motion tasks correct using Newton's equations, but gave incorrect solutions when asked to sketch the trajectory of an object dropped from an aeroplane.
4. Individual students' knowledge and its organization seem to vary considerably.

To a less or greater degree, all the above points stress the greater variability in the knowledge (both factual and procedural) of students in these domains. A number of us believe that this variability is such that it cannot be explained by a single mechanism, and that what is being learnt by a student at any one point is greatly influenced by the knowledge which the student has prior to the current learning episode. Our inescapable conclusion from all this substantial body of experimental evidence is that the students in these studies were following individualistic learning paths. This conclusion challenges a central assumption long held by developmentalists – of the consistency of the steps through which all children progress; see Piaget (1954) and Flavell (1985) for classical and neo-classical arguments supporting this position.

Arguments have also been presented for a *universal* model of child language acquisition (e.g. Brown, 1973). Recent language work, however, has drawn closer to the cognitive science perspective by focusing on acquisition differences between *languages* (Slobin, 1986); *sub-cultures* (Romaine, 1984); and, albeit to a lesser extent, *individuals* (Wells, 1986).

As this appears to be an important point, I give below a somewhat more detailed look at one 'novice' study, and the tentative psychological interpretation given to the data. Once one has collected extensive 'bug catalogues' – examples of student mistakes or errors – it is very natural to speculate about the *cause* of the variability. Also I believe this will nicely illustrate the alternative approach to model and 'theory' building in psychology discussed in the introduction to this chapter. Because of familiarity with the data, I have chosen to illustrate the point with one of my own studies of high-school algebra students. (This data was originally collected to enable an intelligent tutoring system to be built which would diagnose student errors by observing them solve a series of related tasks. The construction of student-user models for such systems is discussed further in a later section.)

## A case study of high-school algebra students*

Once one has identified misunderstandings which one believes arise fairly consistently in a subject domain then a series of additional investigations are possible. These include:

1. Hypothesizing the nature of the processes used by students to solve tasks given the incorrect/buggy/mal-rules.
2. Adding this knowledge to an intelligent diagnostic and tutoring system, like LMS (the Leeds Modelling System), so that in future it would be able to spot an additional set of errors. And related to this, building a remedial subsystem which exploits the inferred student model (this will involve analysis of teacher–student remedial dialogues in the particular subject domain).
3. Undertaking studies aimed at improving the initial instruction in the domain so as to avoid (some of) the observed difficulties.

In this chapter I discuss the first of these issues in the context of extensive studies undertaken with 14- to 15-year-old algebra students. The Leeds Modelling System, LMS, was implemented and a database of examples, correct and incorrect or *mal*-rules had been established which was sufficient to diagnose the majority of difficulties encountered by 15-year-old students (Sleeman, 1982a). The same database was then used with twenty-four 14-year-old students and the outcome was very different. A high percentage of the student errors were *not* diagnosed by LMS. (The majority of errors made by 15-year-olds were *manipulative*, whereas the 14-year-olds made principally *parsing* errors. Both these terms will be defined subsequently; for the moment, we can say that the 14-year-olds appeared to have major misunderstandings of algebraic notation, whereas the 15-year-olds appeared, by and large, to 'understand' algebraic notation but made errors of omission, i.e., omitted to carry out systematically *all* the substeps of a procedure, like moving an integer from one side of an equation to the other.)

The investigator analysed these protocols in some detail and then carried out individual interviews to determine the nature of the students' difficulties (Sleeman, 1985a). The pertinent observations from this latter experiment are:

1. Students appear to regress under cognitive load. That is, they are often able to use a particular rule correctly in the context of simple tasks, but make errors with this same rule when the tasks are more complex. (This analysis *assumes* that domain rules are independent and one rule does not subsume another.) See Sleeman (1985a) for examples.

*This section is taken from an earlier article published by this author in the 1984 proceedings of the Cognitive Science Society's annual conference, entitled 'Misgeneralization: an explanation of observed mal-rules'; and to a lesser extent from Sleeman (1984).

2. There appears to be a number of clearly identifiable *types* of error.
3. Students use a number of alternative 'methods' to solve tasks of the same type.

### Observed types of student errors

From the protocols and the interviews I concluded that in this domain errors could be classified as: manipulative, parsing, execution/clerical and random. The first two topics will be dealt with in some detail in the rest of this section; see Sleeman (1984) for details of the others.

### *Manipulative errors*

I define a *manipulative* mal-rule to be a variant on a correct rule which has one substage either omitted or replaced by an inappropriate or incorrect operation (cf. Young and O'Shea, 1981). For example, MNTORHS is a mal-rule which captures the movement of a number to the other side of an equation, where the student omits to *change* the sign of the number. (MNTORHS is short for *mal-number-to-rhs* rule.) MXTOLHS is the mal-rule which corresponds to the analogous X-to-lhs rule. (Most of the errors noted with 15-year-old students were manipulative.) Note that this general schema would also generate many mal-rules, which we have not yet observed; in the next subsection we give an explanation of why some of the possible mal-rules are not observed.

(a) *Analysis of some manipulative mal-rules: A schema for generating manipulative mal-rules*

In a recent experiment we noted three (additional) mal-rules which can be explained by this mechanism. Two of them will be analysed in some detail.

(i) *A variant on SOLVE.* The variant on SOLVE transformed:

$$4 * X = 6 \text{ to } X=6$$

whereas SOLVE would change the same expression to
$X = 6/4$, i.e., SOLVE is activated by the pattern

$$M * X = N$$

and returns

$$X = N/M$$

where $M$ and $N$ are both integers. In the case of this mal-rule it is suggested that the student realizes she/he has a task in which the SOLVE rule should be activated and omits or (forgets) to apply one of the operations, namely dividing by $M$. SOLVE has three principal actions: noting down $N$, the divide symbol and $M$, and so this mal-rule could be said to be omitting one of the principal steps. Furthermore, it appears that students have an idea about the acceptable *form* of answers and so given the above task we have *not* seen $X = 6/$ or $X = /4$.

(ii) *A variant on SIMPLIFY*. Examples of the two mal-rules noted here, which have occurred reasonably frequently are:

$$X = 6/4 => X = 3/4$$
$$X = 6/4 => X = 6/2$$

(The SIMPLIFY rule transforms the same expression to $X = 3/2$).

Again we argue that the above observations can be explained if we assume that this rule has several principal steps including: calculate the common factor, divide 'top' by common factor, divide bottom by common factor, write down the components; and that each of these mal-rules corresponds to one step being omitted.

## (b) *'Grain size' and manipulative mal-rules*

There is a sense in which detailed analyses of manipulative mal-rules allow one to infer the *substeps* processed by students, and this in turn allows one to predict the set of mal-rules that will be encountered in a domain (bearing in mind the idea of acceptable form outlined above). Further, one might argue that the representation of the tasks should be at this 'lower' level; the justification for the representation chosen and illustrated above is that this appears to be more consistent with the verbal and written protocols collected for students solving these tasks. The schema discussed above for generating manipulative mal-rules by omitting, or modifying, one substep is thus consistent with Young and O'Shea's (1981) modelling of subtraction.

## *Incorrect representation of the task or parse errors*

I assert that many of the students whom we interviewed carried out steps of the computations in ways which would not fall within the definition given earlier for manipulative mal-rules. Below, I give typical protocols for two students working the task $6*X = 3*X + 12$:

| I: | | II: | |
|---|---|---|---|
| $6*X = 3*X + 12$ | | $6*X = 3*X + 12$ | |
| $9*X/12$ | | $X + X = 12 + 3 - 6$ | |
| $X = 12/9$ | | $2*X = 9$ | |
| $X = 4/3$ | | $X = 9/2$ | |

When I pressed the 'first' student for an explanation of how the original equation was transformed into the second, i.e., $9*X = 12$, the student talked about moving the $3*X$ term across to the left-hand side. Thus the interviewer concluded that this was an instance of a student using a variant of the correct rule, namely a manipulative mal-rule. The 'second' student, when pressed, simply asserted that the change from the original equation to the second line 'was all done in one step'. Hence the interviewer concluded it was a very different *type* of mal-rule involved and *not* a simple variant on the correct rule. Thus the interviews provided *essential* additional information as, of course, the second student's protocol could have been explained by the use of MXTOLHS and the mal-rule:

$$M * X => M + X$$

which some people might wish to argue constitutes a *manipulative* mal-rule: replacing the * operator by the + operator. (In the above example, where $M$ stands for an integer, $6*X => 6 + X$ and $3*X => 3 + X$.) Even if we did not have the additional experimental evidence, this investigator would maintain that such a transformation belays a profound misunderstanding of algebraic notation and so *should* be considered as a *parsing* mal-rule. See Sleeman (1984) for additional discussion of this issue.

### Explaining why student errors occur

The discussion of manipulative and parsing errors illustrated how different types of student error may occur on a single task. Cognitive modelling attempts to analyse students' understanding also reveal that individual students may use alternative methods. With the same type of task, the student may display different bugs both during the same test period and between different tests: the observed phenomenon of *bug migration*. Why should this occur? Brown and Van Lehn's (1980) *repair theory* gives a neat explanation for this in the domain of multi-column arithmetic; namely, that the student will use a related family of mal-rules, and possibly the *correct* rule, during a single session with one type of task.

BUGGY (Brown and Burton, 1978) analysed the responses which students gave to multi-column subtraction tasks. The system reported a diagnosis for each student in terms of correct procedures, or procedures which had some of their substeps replaced by incorrect variants, which they called 'bugs'.

Young and O'Shea (1981) point out that, although BUGGY produces models that behave functionally as the students do, these models are not very convincing as psychological models. Many of the bugs appear to be very similar (many are connected with borrowing from zero) yet this relationship is not made clear. More particularly, Young and O'Shea show that some of the BUGGY data can be analysed more simply in terms of certain competences being *omitted* from the 'ideal' model.

Repair theory (Brown and Van Lehn, 1980) is a further attempt to provide a psychological explanation for the same data. Here Brown and Van Lehn take a correct procedure for performing subtraction and apply a deletion operator to the procedure. This perturbed procedure is then used to solve tasks. When it encounters an impasse, such as a situation where it is about to violate a precondition (e.g. attempting to take a number from 0), a repair is applied to the perturbed procedure, and it attempts to continue solving the task. This process also uses critics to throw out some repairs which are considered impossible at a given impasse. In its initial form, some impossible bugs – bugs *not* found in the protocols of student subjects – were generated and only 21 out of an observed set of 89 bugs were generated by repair theory. These considerations show its limitations as a complete theory of behaviour in this domain, but they also illustrate the complexity and scale of the task facing the researcher who wishes to construct a detailed model of mechanisms underlying successful and unsuccessful performance.

More recently, Van Lehn (1983) has suggested a variant of repair theory, which does not delete steps from procedures – as it is argued that the blocking, or inhibition, of the deletion operator was unprincipled. This version overcomes the difficulty that certain core procedures *cannot* be generated easily by rule deletion. Instead, Van Lehn has suggested a series of core procedures, which correspond to the various stages of instruction (cf. Sleeman and Smith, 1981). From this perspective an impasse impasse occurs when the student encounters a sub-task which he has not yet learnt, or has forgotten.

Both variants of repair theory explain what Brown and his co-workers have called bug migration. Moreover, Van Lehn (1981) has analysed protocols in which it was possible to generate *all* the observed bugs in a migration class by applying different repairs to a common (partially learnt) core procedure. So Van Lehn suggests *consistent* bugs can be explained by supposing the student stores the 'patch' and merely uses it with the next task. The argument for inconsistency (so-called 'bug migration') is that the patch is *not* retained and that one of the repair-set is selected randomly.

There seems to be an alternative explanation which should also be considered: 'mis-generalization'. Although a task-set may have been designed to highlight one particular feature, the student may spot completely different feature(s) and these may dominate his or her solution.* Repair theory

*Earlier Sleeman and Brown (1982) have argued '. . . Perhaps more immediately, it suggests that a Coach must pay attention to the sequence of worked examples, and encountered task states, from which the student is apt to abstract (invent) functional invariances. This suggests that no matter how carefully an instructional designer plans a sequence of examples, he can never know all the intermediate steps and abstracted structures that a student will generate while solving an exercise. Indeed, the student may well produce illegal steps in his solution and from these invent illegal (algebraic) 'principles'. Implementing a system with this level of sophistication still presents a major challenge to the ITS/Cognitive Science community . . .'

accounts for some bugs by hypothesizing that the student had not encountered the appropriate teaching necessary to perform the task. Suppose we make the converse assumption, that the appropriate teaching had been carried out, and further suppose that *some* students (I am *not* claiming that there is a *single* mechanism) do not gain competence in this domain by being *told* the rules but rather by *inferring* rules for themselves by noting the transformations which are applied to tasks by the teacher and in texts.* It seems reasonable that the student's inference procedure should be guided by his or her previous knowledge of the domain, in this case the number system, and that the student will normally infer several rules which are consistent with the example, and not just the 'correct' rule. Indeed, due to some missing knowledge the 'correct' rule may not be inferred. (And so the fact that the student *never* uses the 'correct' method along with several 'buggy' methods is *not* evidence that he or she has not encountered the material before.) We shall refer to this process as 'knowledge-directed inference of multiple rules', or *mis-generalization* for short.

Suppose the student saw the following stages in an algebraic simplication:

$$3*X = 6 \quad => X = 6/3$$

Then s/he might infer

$X$ = RHS number/LHS number *OR* $X$ = LARGER number/SMALLER number.

We will surmise how a student would use such a rule-set. We will suppose that the abler students actively experiment with different 'methods', and use their own earlier examples, examples worked by the teacher and in the text to provide discriminatory feedback. From our experiment with 14-year-old students we have direct evidence that some students are aware of having a range of applicable rules and of being unsure of when to select a particular method (Sleeman, 1985a). That study did not provide any insights into the rule-selection processes used by these students. We could suggest the common default, i.e., that the process is random. However, studies in cognitive modelling have already discredited this explanation many times, so we will postulate that the process is deterministic but currently 'undetermined'. It is further suggested that tasks which show a rule is inadequate will weaken belief in the rule, but once a (mal-)rule is created it may not be completely eliminated – particularly if the 'counterexamples' are not presented to the student for some period. Thus given this viewpoint, the phenomenon of bug-migration occurs because the (less able) students have inferred a whole range of rules and select a rule using a 'black-box' process. Given a further task, they again choose a method and hence select the same or an alternative

---

*Independently, Van Lehn has come to a similar conclusion; the Sierra system described in his thesis relies heavily on inference (Van Lehn, 1983).

algorithm, influenced partly by the relative strengths of the rules. That is, if the relative weights are comparable, it is more likely that the students will select a different method for each task. If one weight 'dominates' then it is likely that the corresponding method will be selected frequently. Further, if only one (mal-)rule is generated by the induction process then this approach predicts that the students will consistently use that rule.

We suggest that many of the bugs encountered in the subtraction domain can be accounted for by this (inference) mechanism. For instance, the 'smaller-from-larger' bug, where the smaller number is subtracted from the larger *independent* of whether the larger number is on top or the bottom row, seems one such example (Brown and Burton, 1978; Young and O'Shea, 1981). Brown and Van Lehn (1980) report that because borrowing was introduced, with one group of students, using only tasks with two columns, these students inferred that whenever borrowing was involved they should borrow from the leftmost column, their 'always-borrow-left' bug. So it appears important to ensure that the example set includes some examples to counter previously experienced mal-rules. Indeed it seems as if task-sets can be damaging if they are too preprocessed and contain too little 'intellectual roughage'; Michener (1978) puts a similar argument. Additionally, Ginsburg (1977) quotes several instances of young children inferring the name 'three-ty' for 30, given the names for '3', '4' and '40', and '5' and '50'. So given the wealth of experimental evidence this alternative explanation should be given serious consideration.

Further, I have two philosophical reservations about repair theory. Firstly, that by some mechanism not articulated all students acquire a *common* set of impasses, and moreover they consistently observe these. Secondly, repair theory, which sets out to explain *major* individual differences at the task level, itself proposes a specific mechanism *common* to all students. On the other hand, mis-generalization predicts that the individual's initial knowledge profoundly influences the knowledge which is subsequently inferred, and captures the sense in which learners are active theory builders trying to find patterns, making sense out of observations, forming hypotheses, and testing them out.

### Summary of the algebra case study

Firstly, there are two hypotheses which explain bug-migration: the one given by repair theory and the one put forward here, namely mis-generalization. Of course it is possible that each may be applicable in different situations. Secondly, several 'algorithms' have been presented for creating student models. I believe these are suggestive about the processes used when a student solves (these) tasks. Repair theory suggests that it can be explained by making 'repairs' to incomplete core-procedures, whereas Young and

O'Shea suggest that it is adequate to take a correct procedure and merely delete components. The data for the algebra manipulative mal-rules can be adequately explained by either. However, Young and O'Shea's approach seems inadequate to explain the parsing mal-rules. Indeed, we have to extend revised repair theory before the results reported here can be accommodated. This chapter claims that there are two very different types of mal-rules at large with algebra students – namely manipulative and parsing mal-rules – and that this second category of algebra errors, and much of the data collected in other areas, appear to be best explained by a further mechanism, namely mis-generalization. However, once *inferred* I believe rules are additionally *applied* incorrectly, and that the mechanism(s) described by Young and O'Shea, repair theory and my previous discussion of manipulative mal-rules are appropriate for this stage.

## MODELLING THE ALGEBRA DATA

I noted earlier that psychology has adopted many of the representational schema developed by AI for representing human knowledge. Although I agree with Johnson-Laird's criticism of current AI schema, I would argue that they have much greater expressive power than, for example, the mathematical formalisms Piaget used to describe thought structures. There would be virtue in a 'reinterpretation' – a 're-representation' – of Piaget.

One criticism of this work is that the AI representational schema have been used merely as convenient formalisms to summarize the information and that the 'models' of the subjects' domain knowledge have not been used predictively. (Prediction being, of course, the hallmark of a true scientific model.) On the other hand, another body of researchers, largely from within the intelligent tutoring systems community, have developed techniques for inferring models by observing students' problem solving. These models have been used predictively and are often implemented within one of the representational schema discussed earlier – but at a somewhat higher level of abstraction.

In the next subsection, I give a review of techniques currently available for student/user modelling.

### Student/user modelling techniques*

In a recent paper Rich (1983) gives three 'dimensions' for classifying user models:

(a) a model of a single stereotype-user *versus* a collection of models of individual users;

*This is based on a section of Sleeman (1985b).

(b) models specified by the user or systems designer *versus* models inferred by the system based on the user's behaviour.

(c) models of long-term user characteristics *versus* models of the current task.

Rich's review illustrates that useful systems have been implemented which require the user to essentially provide his or her own 'model'. For example, Rich cites several electronic mail and LISP systems, where the user can set parameters which determine aspects of the system's performance. However, she concedes this is not a serious option for naive users. This review will consider *only* systems which infer models for each individual user and do this as a result of interaction with users. The third dimension is considered an important one and is discussed in some detail below. Additionally I believe there is an important fourth 'dimension', namely:

(d) the nature and form of the information contained in the user model and the inference engine needed to interpret that information.*

Sleeman (1985b) reviews the five types of user models used to date: Scalar, Ad-hoc, Profile, Overlay and Process. Below, I discuss in some detail *process models* of the type used to model the algebra students' performance; finally, I shall discuss more generally the problem of modelling.

Self (1974) was the first person to suggest explicitly that a student-user model should be executable, so that models could be used predictively, and in some sense capture the *processes* by which the user solves the task. The BUGGY project (Brown and Burton, 1978) was the first significant instantiation of the idea of a process model. Further, the concept of a process model was extended significantly to include incorrect or buggy sub-procedures so that the BUGGY system was able to replicate the performance of students with (consistent) errors. Sleeman (1982a) used a similar technique to capture previously encountered errors made by algebra students.†

In common with BUGGY (Brown and Burton, 1978), LMS uses a *generative* mechanism to create hypotheses/models from a set of primitive components. Without a generative facility, the ability of a system to model complex errorful behaviour is severely limited. However, the use of such a mechanism also causes difficulties, since such an algorithm can readily lead to a combinatorial explosion. For example, if there are $N$ primitive rules in a domain where the order is significant, then there are $N$ factorial, $N!$, models to be considered. BUGGY uses a collection of primitive bugs from which to

---

*Sleeman and Brown (1983) review several different forms (data-structures) which have been used to represent user-models, namely: overlay, differential and perturbation. For a review with a somewhat different perspective see Clancey (1982b).

†Subsequently Sleeman (1982b) has implemented an extension by which more knowledge is brought to bear on protocols which cannot be analysed in terms of the existing set of rules and mal-rules. This sub-system thus *adds* to the collection of mal-rules at run-time.

generate models; LMS uses correct domain rules and corresponding mal-rules (incorrect) rules, which have been observed in the analysis of earlier protocols. On the other hand, whereas BUGGY uses heuristics to limit the size of its model space, a major feature of the LMS work has been the formulation of the search to focus each task-set on particular rule(s). As has been demonstrated (Sleeman and Smith, 1981, and more particularly, by Sleeman, 1983) this technique drastically reduces the number of models that must be considered at each stage.*

LMS is data-driven, i.e. for each new domain the user has to provide a database of rules, mal-rules and tasks which are sufficient to discriminate between the models generated. We briefly review the production system (PS) representation which has been used for student models and explain the main features of the PS interpreter used to execute these models.

The algebra case study discussed previously gave examples of some typical rules and mal-rules used by students, such as SOLVE and MSOLVE. Table 11.1(a) gives a set of eleven production rules, used with LMS, which are *sufficient* to solve linear algebraic equations of one variable. The *rule name* is shown with the *condition* in which the rule will be activated and the *action* taken when this occurs. Table 11.1(b) gives a set of mal-rules for this domain which have been observed in protocols analysed earlier and Table 11.1(c) shows pairs of correct and 'buggy' models executing typical tasks. (These are typical of the models which LMS infers.) A task-set is a set of 5–7 tasks which *highlights* the use of one or more domain-rules; Table 11.2 gives a typical task for each of this domain's task-sets and the rules which each set focuses on. The layout of the tasks in Tables 11.1 and 11.2 is *exactly* that used by LMS; this format has also been used in all subsequent sessions with the students.

In this work, a model is an *ordered* list of rules. Order is significant, as the interpreter used executes the action of the *first* rule in the model whose conditions are satisfied by the state (i.e. the task or the partially solved task). In this way we are able to capture *precedence* which is important in this subject domain. The match–execute cycle continues until no further rules fire. In fact, LMS infers a model for each task which the student works and produces *summary* model(s) for each task set. If the student's behaviour is random or conforms to a previously unencountered mal-rule, then LMS returns a null model; for more details see Sleeman (1982a). LMS continues presenting task-sets to a student until its example bank is exhausted or the student opts to 'retire'.

What should a comprehensive user model contain? People have very diverse sources of knowledge. For example, they know how to *do* things, i.e. they have process information, they have a great deal of factual infor-

---

*Initially, we made the assumption that the domain was hierarchical and so we have referred to the stages as *levels*; and thus modelling proceeds by first considering level 1, then 2, etc.

TABLE 11.1 (a) Rules for the Algebra domain (slightly stylized)

| Rule name | Condition | Action |
|---|---|---|
| FIN2 | $(X = M/N)$ | $((M\ N))$ or $((M))$ |
| SOLVE | $(M * X = N)$ | $(X = N/M)$ or (INFINITY) |
| SIMPLIFY | $(X = M/N)$ | $(X = M'/N')$ |
| ADDSUB | (lhs $M$ +! − $N$ rhs) | (lhs [evaluated] rhs) |
| MULT | (lhs $M * N$ rhs) | (lhs [evaluated] rhs) |
| XADDSUB | (lhs $M*X$ +!− $N*X$ rhs) | (lhs $(M$ +!− $N)$ * $X$ rhs) |
| NTORHS | (lhs +!− $M$ = rhs) | (lhs = rhs −!+ $M$ |
| REARRANGE | (lhs +!−$M$+!−$N*X$ rhs) | (lhs+!−$N*X$+!−$M$ rhs) |
| XTOLHS | (lhs = +!− $M*X$ rhs) | (lhs −!+ $M*X$ = rhs) |
| BRA1 | (lhs < $N$ > rhs) | (lhs $N$ rhs) |
| BRA2 | (lhs $M*<N*X$ +!−$P>$ rhs) | (lhs $M*N*X$ +!− $M*P$ rhs) |

Where: $M$, $N$ and $P$ are integers
lhs and rhs are general patterns (which may be null)
+!− means either + or − may occur,
< and > represent standard 'algebraic brackets'.

(b) Some mal-rules for the domain

| Rule name | Condition | Action |
|---|---|---|
| MSOLVE | $(M*X = N)$ | $(X = M/N)$ or (INFINITY) |
| MNTORHS | (lhs +!− $M$ = rhs) | (lhs = rhs +!− $M$) |
| M2NTORHS | (lhs1 +!− $M$ lhs2 = rhs) | (lhs1 +!− lhs2 = rhs −!+ $M$) |
| M3NTORHS | (lhs1 +!− $M$ lhs2 = rhs) | (lhs1 +!− lhs2 = rhs +!− $M$) |
| MXTOLHS | (lhs = +!− $M*X$ rhs) | (lhs +!− $M*X$ = rhs) |
| M1BRA2 | (lhs $M$ *<$N*X$ +!− $P>$ rhs) | (lhs $M*N*X$ +!− $P$ rhs) |
| M2BRA2 | (lhs $M*<N*X$ +!− $P>$ rhs) | (lhs $M*N*X$ +!− $M$ +!− $P$ rhs) |

Using the same conventions as above.

(c) Pairs of correct and 'buggy' models executing typical tasks

(i) Shows (MULT ADDSUB SOLVE FIN2) and (ADDSUB MULT SOLVE FIN2) solving
$$3 * X = 5 + 3 * 4.$$
[The first line gives the initial state and all subsequent lines give the rule which fires and the resulting state.]

| | $3 * X = 5 + 3 * 4$ | | $3 * X = 5 + 3 * 4$ |
|---|---|---|---|
| MULT | $3 * X = 5 + 12$ | ADDSUB | $3 * X = 8 * 4$ |
| ADDSUB | $3 * X = 17$ | MULT | $3 * X = 32$ |
| SOLVE | $X = 17/3$ | SOLVE | $X = 32/3$ |
| FIN2 | (17 3) | FIN2 | (32 3) |

(ii) Shows (NTORHS ADDSUB SOLVE FIN2) and (MNTORHS ADDSUB SOLVE FIN2) solving $4 * X + 6 = 19$.

| | $4 * X + 6 = 19$ | | $4 * X + 6 = 19$ |
|---|---|---|---|
| NTORHS | $4 * X = 19 − 6$ | MNTORHS | $4 * X = 19 + 6$ |
| ADDSUB | $4 * X = 13$ | ADDSUB | $4 * X = 25$ |
| SOLVE | $X = 13/4$ | SOLVE | $X = 25/4$ |
| FIN2 | (13 4) | FIN2 | (25 4) |

250     COMPUTERS, COGNITION AND DEVELOPMENT

TABLE 11.2 Typical task for each task-set and which rule(s) are being focused on

| Task-set | Rules focused on | Typical task |
|---|---|---|
| 2 | SOLVE | $5 * X = 7$ |
| 3 | ADDSUB | $3 * X = 5 + 3$ |
| 4 | MULT | $5 * X = 2 * 2$ |
| 5 | XADDSUB | $2 * X + 3 * X = 10$ |
| 6 | NTORHS | $2 * X + 4 = 16$ |
| 7 | REARRANGE | $4 + 2 * X = 16$ |
| 8 | XTOLHS | $4 * X = 2 * X + 3$ |
| 9 | BRA1 | $2 * X = 5 * <3 + 1>$ |
| 10 | BRA2 | $6 * X = 2 * <2 * X + 3>$ |
| 11 | ADDSUB/MULT | $2 * X = 2 + 4 * 6$ |
| 12 | ADDSUB/XADDSUB | $2 + 3 * X + 4 * X = 16$ |
| 13 | ADDSUB/BRA2 | $15 * X = 2 + 4 * <2 * X + 3>$ |
| 14 | MULT/XADDSUB | $2 * 4 * X + 2 * X = 12$ |
| 15 | MULT/BRA2 | $14 * X = 2 * 3 * <2 * X + 3>$ |

mation, and strategies and heuristics to indicate when pieces of knowledge are applicable. Why then have we been able to model users *at all* with the simplistic knowledge-sparse models used to date? The answer has to be that workers have chosen to work at very well-defined sub-areas – and like all good scientists have made strong simplifying assumptions until forced to relax them. For example, in the BUGGY project Brown and Burton (1978) assumed initially that students both understood the notion of number and had stable bugs. So far they have only needed to relax the second assumption. Initially when modelling algebra students, Sleeman (1982a) assumed that if a student worked tasks correctly using a rule, this rule would be used correctly in all subsequent tasks and that the student's arithmetic was sound. (The first assumption was removed by a subsequent version of LMS; Sleeman, 1983. And the assumption about the arithmetic has been challenged by data collected recently; Sleeman, 1984.) In the NEOMYCIN project, Clancey (1982a) continues to assume that medical students do not have any factual error and they do not use incorrect strategies.

Some of the protocols collected in the field of, for example, naive physics reveal that students not only bring to bear knowledge of the real world, but are also unable to manipulate algebraic equations and arithmetic expressions. Tutors well understand that students' difficulties occur because of the lack of understanding of more 'basic' concepts, in the same or related subjects, and that diagnostic teaching involves probing until one has identified the source(s) of the students' difficulties. This is exactly what a 'real' modelling system needs to do. Modelling is a very open-ended task because people have a great deal of diverse knowledge which they structure in many different and often idiosyncratic ways. To date, the field has chosen, wisely, small-scale tasks. I would like now to consider a scenario which makes the potential size of the task clearer. A very open-ended task is implementing a user modelling system to cope with a wide range of users, as at an information bureau. Lenat, Borning, McDonald, Taylor and Weyer (1983) discuss a user modelling system for an online encyclopaedia. In this latter case, one needs to identify the seriousness of the reader (browser, general interest, specific task to be achieved) the background knowledge of the reader (type of profession, student), and some idea of his preferred learning style (textual explanations, examples, graphical presentations), and so on.

It seems clear that these more open-ended modelling tasks will require a much richer knowledge base, a series of representational schema to capture the user's knowledge, and an extensive range of inference techniques. Future modelling systems should use their models *predictively* and report to the investigator situations where the models persistently fail to predict subsequent user behaviour. Alternatively, future systems might use *additional* knowledge to resolve the conflict.

Although workers in both dialogue analysis (see Grosz, 1979), and belief systems, e.g. PARRY (Colby, Weber and Hilf, 1971), discuss how their systems should be sensitive to their users, none of these systems has a separate user modelling subsystem. Making this component explicit would in my view be a significant step forward.

## CONCLUSIONS

Studies carried out by cognitive scientists of high-school and university students strongly suggest that these students demonstrate that there are substantial differences among students in all subject areas investigated. In this chapter I have illustrated how protocol analysis and interviews can be combined to arrive at detailed models of the mechanisms underlying students' understanding of algebra. These cognitive models can play an important role in the design of intelligent tutoring systems, and their inclusion in such systems enables them to be used predictively.

AI has provided a range of basic representational schema, and more recently through the efforts of researchers in student/user modelling a further set of techniques for modelling individuals' problem solving. Some of these techniques might be useful for building simulations of child development at several stages. Additionally, the sub-field of machine learning has devised several algorithms which are capable of, say, inferring 'new' knowledge given a set of examples.

Future challenges for developmental psychology include:

(a) using AI's representational schema (including the modelling techniques introduced here) to build additional models of child performance;
(b) critiquing the learning algorithms so far produced by AI;

(c) giving the machine learning workers clear guidance about the constraints of human processing at each stage of development from infancy to young adulthood; and maybe most critically of all,

(d) interacting with AI workers to evolve a common language for describing the topic of mutual concern, namely, learning.

## ACKNOWLEDGEMENTS

Mr M. McDermot and students of Abbey Grange School, Leeds, provided fascinating sets of protocols. Pat Langley, Kurt Van Lehn, Jaime Carbonell, Stellan Ohlsson, Peter Jackson, Alan Bundy and William Bricken have helped with numerous discussions about this work. Rosemary Martinak gave valuable feedback on an earlier draft.

## REFERENCES

Anderson, J. R. (1983). *The Architecture of Cognition*, Harvard Univ. Press, Cambridge, Mass.

Brown, J. S., and Burton, R. R. (1978). Diagnostic models for procedural bugs in basic mathematical skills, *Cognitive Science*, **2**, 155–192.

Brown, J. S., and Van Lehn, K. (1980). Repair theory: a generative theory of bugs in procedural skills, *Cognitive Science*, **4**, 379–426.

Brown, R. (1973). Development of the first language in the human species', *American Psychologist*, **28**, 97–106.

Carbonell, J. G., Michalski, R. S., and Mitchell, T. M. (1983). An overview of machine learning. In R. S. Michalski, J. G. Carbonell and T. M. Mitchell (eds), *Machine Learning*, pp. 3–24, Tioga Press, Palo Alto, Calif.

Card, S. K., Moran, T. P., and Newell, A. (1983). *The Psychology of Human–Computer Interaction*, Erlbaum, Hillsdale, N. J.

Chase, W. G., and Simon, H. A. (1973). Perception in chess, *Cognitive Psychology*, **4**, 55–81.

Clancey, W. J. (1982a). Tutoring rules for guiding a case method dialogue. In D. Sleeman and J. S. Brown (eds), *Intelligent Tutoring systems*, pp. 201–225, Academic Press, London.

Clancey, W. J. (1982b). ICAI systems design. In A. Barr and E. A. Feigenbaum (eds), *The Handbook of Artificial Intelligence*, pp. 229–235, Wm. Kaufmann, Los Altos, Calif.

Colby, K., Weber, S., and Hilf, F. (1971). Artificial paranoia, *Artificial Intelligence*, **2**, 1–25.

Collins, A. M., and Quillian, M. R. (1972). How to make a language user. In E. Tulving and W. Donaldson (eds), *Organisation and Memory*, Academic Press, New York.

Davis, R. (1984). *Learning Mathematics: a Cognitive Approach*, Croom Helm, London.

Ehrlich, J., and Soloway, E. (1984). An empirical investigation of tacit plan knowledge in programming. In J. Thomas and M. L. Schneider (eds), *Human Factors in Computer Systems*, Ablex, New York.

Flavell, J. H. (1985). *Cognitive Development* (2nd edn), Prentice-Hall, Englewood Cliffs, N. J.

Ginsburg, H. P. (1977). *Children's Arithmetic: the Learning Process*, Van Nostrand, New York.

Grosz, B. J. (1979). Utterance and objective: issues in natural language communication, *Proceedings of 6th International Joint Conference on Artificial Intelligence*, 1067–1076.

Johnson-Laird, P. N. (1983). *Mental Models*, Harvard University Press, Cambridge, Mass.

Klahr, D. (1978). Goal formation, planning and learning by pre-school problem solvers or: 'My Socks are in the Dryer'. In R. S. Siegler (ed.), *Children's Thinking: What develops?*, pp. 181–212, Erlbaum, Hillsdale, N. J.

Langer, J. A. (in press). Reading, writing and understanding: an analysis of the construction of meaning, *Written Communication*.

Lenat, D. B., Borning, A., McDonald, D., Taylor, C., and Weyer, S. (1983). KNOESPHERE: Building expert systems with encyclopedic knowledge, *Proceedings of International Joint Conference on Artificial Intelligence*, **8**, 229–235.

McCloskey, M. (1983). Naive theories of motion. In D. Gentner and A. L. Stevens (eds), *Mental Models*, pp. 299–324, Erlbaum, Hillsdale, N. J.

Michener, E. R. (1978). Understanding understanding mathematics, *Cognitive Science*, **2**, 361–383.

Newell, A. (1973). Production systems: models of control structures. In W. G. Chase (ed.), *Visual Information Processing*, Academic Press, New York.

Piaget, J. (1954). *The Construction of Reality in the Child*, Basic Books, New York.

Rich, E. A. (1983). Users are individuals: individualizing user models, *International Journal of Man-machine Studies*, **18**, 199–214.

Romaine, S. (1984). *The Language of Children and Adolescents*, Blackwell, Oxford.

Self, J. A. (1974). Student models in computer-aided instruction, *International Journal of Man-Machine Studies*, **6**, 261–276.

Sleeman, D. H. (1982a). Assessing competence in basic algebra. In D. Sleeman and J. S. Brown (eds), *Intelligent Tutoring Systems*, pp. 185–199, Academic Press, London.

Sleeman, D. H. (1982b). Inferring (mal) rules from pupil's protocols, *Proceedings of the 1982 European Artificial Intelligence Conference*, pp. 160–164. (Republished in *Proceedings of the International Machine Learning Workshop*, Illinois, June 1983.)

Sleeman, D. H. (1983). A rule directed modelling system. In R. Michalski, J. Carbonell, and T. M. Mitchell (eds), *Machine Learning*, pp. 483–510, Tioga, Palo Alto, Calif.

Sleeman, D. H. (1984). An attempt to understand students' understanding of algebra, *Cognitive Science*, **8**, 387–412.

Sleeman, D. H. (1985a). Basic algebra revisited: a study with 14-year-olds, *International Journal of Man-Machine Studies*, 127–149. (Also published as Stanford University memo HPP 83–9.)

Sleeman, D. (1985b). UMFE: A user modelling front-end subsystem, *International Journal of Man-Machine Studies*, **23**, 71–88.

Sleeman, D. H., and Brown, J. S. (1982). Intelligent tutoring systems: an overview. In D. Sleeman and J. S. Brown (eds), *Intelligent Tutoring Systems*, pp. 1–11, Academic Press, London.

Sleeman, D. H., and Smith, M. J. (1981). Modelling pupil's problem solving. *Artificial Intelligence*, **16**, 171–187

Sleeman, D., Putnam, R., Baxter, J., and Kuspa, L. (in press). Pascal and high-school students: a study of misconceptions, *Journal of Educational Computing Research*.

Slobin, D. I. (1986). *The Crosslinguistic Study of Language Acquisition* (2 vols), Erlbaum, Hillsdale, N.J.

Van Lehn, K. (1981). Bugs are not enough: empirical studies of bugs, impasses and repairs in procedural skills, Xerox PARC, *Cognitive and Instructional Sciences Technical Report*, CIS-11.

Van Lehn, K. (1983). Felicity conditions for human skill acquisition: validating an AI-based theory, XEROX PARC, *Cognitive and Instructional Technical Report*, CIS-21.

Wells, G. (1986). Variation in child language. In P. Fletcher and M. Garman (eds), *Language Acquisition* (2nd edn), pp. 109–140, Cambridge University Press, Cambridge.

Young, R., and O'Shea, T. (1981). Errors in children's subtraction, *Cognitive Science*, **5**, 153–177.

Computers, Cognition and Development
Edited by J. Rutkowska and C. Crook.
© 1987 John Wiley & Sons Ltd

CHAPTER 12

# Machine Learning and Cognitive Development

Stephen W. Draper

## SUMMARY

Reviewing machine learning, and its relevance to cognitive development. The functionalist framework. A range of abstract learning functions: rote learning, deductive learning, inductive summarization, and inductive generalization (inter- and intra-dimensional). Limitations of existing work: dependence on built-in description languages. Connectionist work. What is learning for? Bricolage: going beyond functionalism to study true development?

## INTRODUCTION: AI AND FUNCTIONALISM

There is now a sizeable body of literature from the field of artificial intelligence (AI) on programs that exhibit learning. This topic has recently shown accelerated growth and is generally referred to as 'machine learning'. The programs often strike one as clever by machine standards, but can they help us to understand human learning or even larger issues of development? In this chapter I shall review work in machine learning and discuss its potential for contributing to an understanding of cognitive development. We must first look at the attitudes AI brings to bear, then at how these have shaped work on machine learning so far, and finally at whether and how such work can be linked to issues in human cognitive development.

One view of work in AI stems from the perspective of extended functionalism. One form of functionalism is the doctrine that what the subject of study does is the primary concern, how it does it is at most secondary: it is summed up by the phrase 'implementation details don't matter'. Applied to,

255

for example, the heart, functionalism identifies it as an organ for pumping blood. This approach allows prediction of the consequences of heart failure, and the design of mechanical replacements for the heart which are nothing like the original heart. On the other hand, repairing rather than replacing the heart (as in coronary bypass surgery) does require an understanding of the implementation. Applied to mental life, functionalism entails the idea that the mind can be studied independently of the brain. When combined with the idea that the mind is an information processor, a doctrine that we might call 'extended functionalism' emerges. It holds that the mind's function is computation – the computation of functions in the mathematical sense of input–output mappings; and that what matters are the functions computed, and not primarily how they are computed. (See Johnson-Laird, 1983, pp.8 ff., for a concise exposition and further references.)

On this view, the main problem in understanding the mind is to identify the functions it computes. Since human behaviour is adaptable and flexible, the problem is particularly hard because any observed behaviour might be the response of a very general function to the particular circumstances. Functionalism is a pervasive perspective and is consonant not only with AI, but with engineering and in particular computer science which are concerned with constructing mechanisms for human purposes, and also with biological sciences such as physiology and evolution theory which seek to understand organs in relation to their functions. However, in the final section of this chapter we shall question its applicability to developmental issues. Nevertheless, most existing work in AI is best understood in the context of functionalism.

One kind of contribution to this programme is empirical work aimed at identifying the functions. Another kind is to consider various proposals for functions and establish whether or not they could possibly be computed by any mechanism – if not, then they cannot be computed by a human mind. One reason that this is a significant problem is that not all the plausible English descriptions that have been proposed turn out to specify a definite function (i.e. make definite predictions by specifying what output will be generated for a given input); but in addition Turing showed that even mathematically well-defined functions are not always computable. (That is, even when there is a perfectly precise definition which allows us to verify whether any given input–output pair belongs to the function, there may be no possible mechanism that can calculate the output given the input for all cases.) If, however, a function is established as computable, then exploring the possible ways of computing the function can generate hypotheses (to be investigated empirically) about how humans compute it, and identify the cost, limitations, accuracy, etc., of each of these, which might be linked to observation of reaction times, error rates, etc.

Much AI work consists of this kind of exploration of function implementation, first to establish the computability of a proposed function (and hence its status as a solid proposal, not just a piece of rhetoric in English), and then to explore some of the implementation issues. Since the most obvious way of demonstrating that a function is computable is to invent an implementation and show that it works by running it, a novel piece of work in AI typically bears on both aims simultaneously.

From this functionalist perspective, AI work always hangs on a hypothesis or guess about a function computed by the mind. If the guess is wrong, the work is not invalid, but irrelevant to psychological aims. In this, AI is rather like applied mathematics: mathematics is valid independent of application, but applied mathematics aims to explore just those mathematical ideas that do indeed have an application. Lines of work in AI may be organized around developing a technique (e.g. a family of functions with economical implementations) independently of its applications, or around a search over alternative techniques for a single problem, thus stressing validity or relevance respectively. In the end, however, both AI and applied mathematics are suspended between theory and application: the validity of a piece of work depends on its theoretical soundness; its relevance on its applicability. Of course psychology is not the only kind of application for AI – there can be commercial or other practical interest in methods of computing some of the functions AI explores. Some of the work on learning has already found non-psychological application.

Since AI studies both functions and their implementation, it can fail to model the human mind (i.e. to be psychologically relevant) in two separate ways: it may have studied the wrong function, or the wrong implementation. (Not only AI has this problem: some of the favourite measures of experimental psychology – e.g. reaction time – relate only to implementation issues, and can lead to studies that are open to charges of irrelevance because they assume on very slight grounds that the function they presuppose, by discussing its implementations, is psychologically real.) Finally we should note that even when AI work has no direct psychological relevance, it often contributes in the long run to our understanding by showing us a set of possibilities: such sets of possible alternatives constitute the context needed to appreciate the solution (in this case, a psychological function) actually observed.

AI work, then, starts with a guess about a function. Where do the guesses come from? What kind of function should be considered? Answers to these are central to proposing ideas about the nature of learning and its relationship to cognitive development. This chapter is organized around the different ways of defining learning that AI workers have adopted. We shall have to recognize that often the guesses come from overly simple ideas about what learning is. This is where much AI work on learning visibly suffers from insufficient attention to the facts and theories of human development. I shall argue, however, that AI has the potential for raising and pursuing interesting issues in development.

## LEARNING DEFINED BY TASKS

The most obvious way to apply a functionalist approach is to define a learning function in terms of an external task. An early example of this was Samuel's program that learned to play the game of checkers (draughts), or rather to play it better (Samuel, 1963).

### Samuel's checkers program

Like most game-playing programs, it chose a move by performing lookahead: considering each move in turn, and for each possible move considering each reply its opponent might make and assuming the best would be chosen, and so on. Because the number of alternatives quickly 'explodes' into more than can be considered in any reasonable time, the lookahead is limited to a few moves. The positions envisaged at this point (e.g. after looking three moves ahead) must then be evaluated statically, on the basis of features such as number of pieces, control of the centre squares, and so on. The program learned in two kinds of way. Firstly, after choosing a move, it remembered the board position and the score calculated for (the best move from) that position. In future games if this position was reached after lookahead, the remembered score could be used instead of the statically calculated one; this effectively increased the depth of the lookahead for that position. Since only a limited number of such positions could be stored (a few thousand), this memory was managed so as to retain only the most frequently considered positions. The second kind of learning concerned the features contributing to the scoring used in static evaluation. Scores were a linear combination of separate features (such as number of pieces, control of the centre squares, etc.) from a more or less arbitrary collection. The weight given to each feature was continually adjusted depending on how well it seemed to be doing at predicting statically the value of a position in the light of subsequent play (see Samuel, 1963, for details), and features that seemed to contribute nothing reliable were dropped and others introduced for a trial period.

### Criticism of Samuel's program and strategy

Samuel's program is a straightforward attempt to write a program specially designed to learn one thing – checkers – and its success is judged by its playing ability (it approached the level of a minor master). As a piece of AI the next thing we want to know is what its success depended on, i.e. what has been demonstrated about the techniques used and the claims made for them. As Good (1968) pointed out, Samuel's program can be criticized here because it is unclear from his report that the weights given to the scoring features had settled down to a stable value, and this lack of stability allows us to doubt that they were playing any useful role in the program's playing successes. Nevertheless, clearly more, and more careful, work could clear this up. (These criticisms in fact have a form similar to that of critiques of experimental designs – the design of a program, like that of an experiment, contains many features and the question arises of which features are in fact responsible for the main effects. A single implementation can establish computability, but by itself is unlikely to satisfy our consequent curiosity about why it works.)

Samuel's program is, however, only interesting if the techniques it used turn out to be more widely applicable than to learning checkers. This possibility motivated the work, and will certainly govern whether there will be long-term interest in it. The strategy is: pick a specific learning problem, develop any methods that seem to work on that problem, then look for other problems that can also be solved using those methods. Good (1968) argued that Samuel's method would not work for other games, and chess in particular: he attributed the program's success largely to the stored positions, which allowed it in effect to know all the useful openings by heart, and recognize all the usual end-game positions, but said that this would not work for games like chess with a substantially larger number of possible positions.

If this analysis is correct, then the program fails to command sustained interest because its techniques fail to apply widely. How might we change the research strategy to improve the chance of success? Close attention to a fixed problem task might seem to be the pitfall (although this is a potential pitfall in psychology too, e.g. conservation is assumed to be a particularly significant task). An alternative is to study a different kind of definition of a learning task, one that is not specified in terms of a problem domain but in terms of what changes are to be made on the basis of what kind of input. This approach has been widely adopted, as I shall now discuss, for instance in studies of 'concept learning' by machine.

## ABSTRACT LEARNING FUNCTIONS

This section is concerned with learning functions abstracted from both the problem domains they have been applied to and the details of their implementation. As well as describing a number of programs, it introduces a classification scheme, and discusses a common weakness. Later sections step back to consider machine learning work as a whole, and its relationship to development.

AI learning work is often categorized by learning type, e.g. learning by exploration, failure-driven learning, and many others – see for instance the categories used by Charniak and McDermott (1985, ch.11), or by Michalski in his survey chapter (Michalski, 1986). However some of these categories are more illuminating than others, and here I want to focus on a three-way distinction based on the logical status of the knowledge learned:

(a) Rote learning, which consists of storing and being able to recall items imparted by an external source, e.g. memorizing facts about converting kilograms to pounds.

(b) Deductive learning, which consists of storing items originally generated by the program itself from built-in knowledge, e.g. remembering what the square of 13 is, rather than working it out each time.

(c) Inductive learning, which consists of inferring a general rule from a set of examples, or a concept from a set of instances.

**Rote learning and deduction**

Rote learning may seem uninteresting (it is what a tape recorder does, after all), and will not be discussed much further here, but it should be noted that in general it can involve significant issues: for instance, how memory is organized, why it should be that most people in fact have trouble in learning quantities of arbitrary items, the problems of translating a 'fact' told to us in English (say) into an internal representation for storage, and more generally of 'operationalizing' a communicated fact into a form that affects action directly, e.g. converting a spoken warning 'do not touch the wire' into modifications to motor movements in future actions (see Mitchell, 1983, p.1147). Programs such as 'Teiresias' (Davis, 1982; Charniak and McDermott, 1985, give a brief account), that learn by being told, can be seen as an exploration of rote learning, with attention being focused on the problem of the communication channel between teacher and learner, and how teachers can make contact with the concepts of the learner.

Deductive learning, that is the learning of items generated by the program itself and whose validity thus depends on its inbuilt knowledge, is widespread and important, although called by a variety of names in the literature (often, confusingly, 'rote learning'). The board positions stored by Samuel's program are an example of deductive learning: nothing outside the program told it how good those positions were, it simply stores its own conclusions to improve speed and accuracy in future. This idea was generalized under the name of 'memo functions' (see Marsh, 1969). The same phenomenon is behind Rosenbloom and Newell's (1986) program which models the power law of human performance: the essential idea (developed in detail and matched to a large body of empirical data) is that people's speed of performance improves with practice because they store the results of mental operations involved in generating the plan for a sequence of actions, so that it goes faster on each trial as more and more can be retrieved as a chunk instead of being recalculated.

In fact deductive learning goes far beyond the speeding up of performance. In principle, once you have learned Euclid's five simple axioms, you can deduce all the theorems of his geometry. In practice, only exceptional individuals find even one interesting theorem, so mostly we also learn the theorems together with the proofs, i.e. the path of reasoning connecting it to the axioms. The fundamental reason for this is that the space of valid chains of deduction from those axioms is huge, but only a tiny fraction of the points thus reached are interesting. Because of this, learning those points by heart does not just save time, but in practice is all that allows us to find them at all. Thus deductive learning can be more than a performance issue, and instead concern questions of discovery and mathematical creativity. Lenat's program 'AM' addressed this. The program searches for interesting mathematical concepts in number theory, starting from a few axioms and some heuristics about what counts as interesting. It continually creates new definitions of concepts, and then explores their properties to see if they turn out to be interesting ones. See Charniak and McDermott (1985) for a short description, and for more details Lenat (1983a, 1983b).

Deductive learning, then, concerns drawing out and perhaps reorganizing knowledge that is already latent in the learner. This may consist of remembering things worked out in the course of performing a task (e.g. Samuel's program); of working out consequences of new facts learned (this is where rote learning can merge into deductive learning over the issue of operationalization); or of 'goal-directed learning', e.g. in the program LEX2 (Mitchell, 1983; and also see below), where the learner works out rules just in order to remember them for future use. When such rules are wholly derivable from prior knowledge, the learning is deductive. When, however, they are summaries or generalizations from experience, it is inductive. This brings us to the remaining category, inductive learning, which has by and large formed the centre of interest in AI work on learning, and is discussed at length in the following subsections.

## Data compression (inductive summarization)

The next type of learning may be called data compression but is also the first kind of induction because it summarizes examples as a general rule. It is the problem of how, given a set of known examples which you wish to store in order to improve future performance, you can economize on memory space by summarizing many separate examples in a rule. For instance, in a checkers-playing program which remembers board positions and their values, if all positions of three kings against one will result in a win for the side with three kings, it would be more economical to replace the storage of all the many distinct such positions by a rule. The success of such a technique can be measured by the amount of storage saved (the ratio of data compression). In the pure form stated, it replaces only derivable examples and its content therefore has the status of deductive knowledge; but it is also inductive in the sense of summarizing examples by a generalization (i.e. a rule). It is like using induction to infer 'all swans are white' on the basis of inspecting a number of swans – but in the case where you inspect *all* existing swans: as long as the rule describes only finite sets, however large, it need never involve incorrect generalizations, and so has the validity of deductive learning.

Quinlan (1983) describes such a program for storing some classes of chess end-games. It summarizes millions of board positions in a rule consisting of a few dozen nodes (the rule says whether each possible position is won or lost). The rule is generated ('learned') automatically by a program. Quinlan makes it clear that his program is crucially dependent on the description language provided for classifying board positions: although it selects from the range of descriptive terms provided those that are most useful, the time it takes to construct the rule depends on how many terms it has to consider, so providing all possible terms is not feasible. Quinlan reports that months of work go into devising plausible terms, i.e. abstract features of chess positions likely to be diagnostic of imminent checkmate.

## Inductive generalization

The seminal AI work on inductive learning is often considered to be Winston's program (Winston, 1975), which learned concepts from training sequences of line drawings. Here the emphasis is not so much on summarization (data compression) as on generalization from a few specific instances. For instance, to learn the concept of an arch, it would be presented with a series of drawings depicting either examples of arches or 'near-misses', i.e. examples that only just fail to count as arches. It would be told what concept the drawing related to, and whether it was an example or a near-miss. The program interpreted the drawing, converting it into an internal description in terms of blocks, their type and shape (e.g. brick, wedge) and the relationships of the blocks to each other (e.g. touching, on top of). It constructed a definition of the concept by comparing examples to determine which properties were necessary, e.g. that the cross-section of the pillars does not matter, but that there must be a gap between them, the cross-piece must rest on both pillars, etc. Basically, new examples might cause it to broaden (generalize) its definition to cover new features, while near-misses might cause it to narrow (specialize) the definition to exclude a feature of the near-miss. Such learning of concepts is inductive, because its outcome is an abstract description based on a set of particular examples, but going beyond them so that it will apply to 'similar' ones it has not yet seen.

In recent years there has been a lot of work following this lead in various ways: see the edited collections by Michalski, Carbonell and Mitchell (1983, 1986), the review chapters heading those volumes, and the review by Bundy, Silver and Plummer (1985). Different domains have been used, and different ways of presenting or finding the training examples. A noteworthy example is Mitchell's program LEX which learns about mathematical integration techniques (Mitchell, 1978, 1982, 1983; Mitchel et al., 1983). In calculus there is no general method for integration; instead, for those problems which turn out to have solutions at all, you must discover which of a large set of possible methods ('operators') to apply and in which order. With experience you become much faster at estimating which method is likely to work at each step. LEX begins with a set of methods, and at first solves problems by exhaustive search, i.e. trying all sequences of methods until success is achieved. It then analyses the sequence that succeeded (the ideal solution path), and remembers in a rule each successful method and the pattern of the problem that it applied to. If it remembered only the exact example, this would be deductive learning of past successes; it is inductive because it sets out to discover the class of similar problems which that method will also succeed on. This inductive generalization of problem patterns is carried on by a form of the 'empiricist algorithm' comparable to Winston's: new examples of success for that method broaden its trigger pattern; examples of failure narrow it. The latter come from analysing all the method applications that turned out to lead off the ideal solution path. LEX achieves an increase of about 100 times in problem-solving speed as it discovers the range of conditions for trying each method.

LEX differs from Winston's program in domain (integration problems rather than objects constructed from blocks), in the fact that it extracts its own training examples from the problem-solving task that forms the motivation for the learning rather than relying on a teacher, and because it is not told which example applies to which concept (rule) but calculates that itself.

Although the various inductive programs differ in many ways, it is becoming clear that a number of them use much the same underlying method, which following Charniak and McDermott I have called the 'empiricist algorithm', consisting of a combination of generalization and specialization (or discrimination) to zero in on the correct concept. Bundy et al. (1985) compare and contrast a number of such programs (concentrating on variants they call 'focusing' and 'candidate elimination'). In this area, then, enough work has been done to abstract a common technique from several different application domains, and to begin to discern the limitations that remain even when weaknesses in one author's work have been addressed by another. The common bottleneck that is becoming perceptible is discussed in the next subsection.

## The description language

Induction goes beyond the available evidence to form a generalization whose validity is hoped for, but not proven. The success of AI programs at this turns out to depend on the description language used, and its implicit match to the domain. The description language is usually built into the programs before they begin learning, and determines how the examples are described: learning consists of the manipulation of expressions in this language.

A description can be thought of as composed of terms that denote values on independent description dimensions. For instance, in describing structures like arches, we could consider the colour of a pillar to be one description dimension, and its cross-section another. The basic values on one dimension are mutually exclusive and exhaustive, e.g. if a pillar is round it cannot also be square. In addition a dimension may have an associated 'generalization hierarchy': that is, its basic values may be organized into larger and larger groups, e.g. the cross-section dimension might have a 'rounded' concept comprising circular and oval cross-sections, and a 'polygonal' concept comprising square, triangular, etc.

Empiricist algorithms embody two kinds of induction – intra- and inter-dimensional (within a description dimension, and between dimensions) – and both may lead to false conclusions if the language turns out not to fit the task exactly.

Intra-dimensional induction occurs when two examples have been seen with different values on that dimension: the current definition of the concept is generalized to use the description in the generalization hierarchy that covers both. For instance, if square and triangular pillars were seen, then the concept definition would contain 'polygonal pillars'. If the example values are widely spaced enough or no descriptions of intermediate scope are present, then the description becomes fully generalized on that dimension, e.g. if a blue pillar and a red one are seen, the concept definition would allow any colour. This is both plausible and unreliable. On the one had, it should be possible to infer that colour does not matter to the concept of 'arch' without showing an example with every possible colour – two or three should be enough. On the other hand, if the description 'polygonal' were not supplied, the algorithm could never notice if only square and triangular pillars were being used and not round ones: after seeing square and triangular examples it would generalize to 'any shape' if 'polygonal' is not present in its generalization hierarchy.

Besides such intra-dimensional induction and its problems, empiricist algorithms rely on the assumption that descriptive dimensions are independent to perform a second kind of induction. For instance, they would tacitly assume that the range of colours seen are independent of the range of pillar cross-sections. Again this is plausible but unreliable, and leads to a failure to learn concepts in which properties described on separate dimensions turn out to have a mutual dependence. Failure to make this assumption would mean multiplying the number of examples to demonstrate a concept, e.g. the examples showing that colour does not matter to the arch concept would have to be duplicated for each of the allowed types of pillar cross-section. On the other hand, if the description language is not perfectly tailored to the problem, by having strictly independent dimensions, then the assumption can cause trouble. For instance, an empiricist algorithm could not notice that pillars were always either blue and round, or red and square. (If this seems an unnatural 'concept', consider learning what a mallard is: either male and green-headed, or female and mottled brown.) These problems too can be made to vanish by tailoring the description language, but techniques like the empiricist algorithm cannot do such tailoring for themselves, though a few steps have been taken (e.g. the 'tree-hacking' method described by Bundy *et al.*, 1985).

All the programs discussed are seriously limited by their dependence on the prior provision of a description language matched to the task. Any concept can be represented and learned given the right descriptive terms, but inability to find these automatically means that current 'empiricist' techniques have solved only half the problem. Similarly, Quinlan's program can only select the best combination of the descriptive terms given it, and its success at data compression depends on how good these are for the task in hand. Future work then should centre on the generation of missing descriptive terms.

## Motivations for learning

Three overlapping motivations for learning can be constructed from the three kinds of learning discussed above: speed-up of performance by remembering cases (deductive learning), data compression (inductive summarization), and extrapolating known examples to similar but not yet explored cases (inductive generalization). Each is associated with programs that have concentrated on them, and each implies a criterion for how well learning succeeds in being useful; but in fact all three criteria apply to all learning programs, and should be applied and optimized together, although no one has yet done this. We shall consider each in turn in more detail.

The first motivation, associated with deductive learning, has as its ultimate motive and criterion for success a speed-up in overall performance. As a more immediate measure, it suggests optimizing the proportion of items needed that are stored in memory as opposed to requiring recalculation. If time and space were infinite resources, then a learner would maximize performance speed by generating and storing in advance all items it would ever need, so in practice this criterion implies a tacit trade-off of performance speed against learning time and memory space. (Rosenbloom and Newell's work tacitly assumes infinite memory size, and their results can be used to show the trade-off of performance improvement against learning time.) The relationship of the ultimate and the immediate criteria – performance speed and optimizing the proportion of needed items stored – depends on several additional factors such as whether past experience turns out to be a good predictor of the items needed in future, and the amount of time saved each time an item is found ready-made in memory.

The second motivation, data compression, clearly embodies a criterion for learning techniques: economy of storage. In fact two things should ideally be minimized: the ratio of the space needed to store the rule learned to the space saved by the cases it replaces, and the time taken to apply the rule when it is used. It is no good using concise descriptive terms in the rule that turn out to take so long to apply that they spoil the time-saving which motivated the use of stored examples in the first place. (In the case of Quinlan's program, applying the rule means using it to decide whether a given new board position is won or lost.) Quinlan gives measurements demonstrating his program's success on both counts, though he has no argument to show it performs optimally.

The third motivation for learning (extrapolating the use of known examples) is latent in generalization from examples. It is similar to saving time by remembering cases, but here the idea is not just to store examples for re-use if the same situation recurs, but to extend their use to novel cases by some kind of analogy or generalization. In this way a relatively few, isolated experiences might come to cover a large part of the space of possibilities. In the task performance phase, such a program assimilates a new problem to the most similar known case, and in the learning phase it accommodates (modifies) its case-descriptions in the light of the success or failure of the assimilations tried. Because it does not have access to the complete set of possible examples, it can be wrong (unlike Quinlan's program), but it has a clear measure of success.

Mitchell's LEX is in this situation: it remembers examples of successful operator use and hopes to improve its future performance even on cases it has not met before by generalizing. Mitchell gives figures for LEX's improvement in problem-solving speed as it learns, but it would perhaps be better to show explicitly the trade-off between speed gained in future problem-solving against time and effort spent in learning in order to show the trade-offs in this approach to capitalizing on past experience by extrapolating it. That would demonstrate not just that LEX does learn, but why it was advantageous for it to do so.

The ultimate motive for extrapolation is to save performance time (or optimize the sum of performance and learning times), but the immediate criterion it suggests is to maximize the number of items potentially covered by each stored experience, rule, or 'concept'. Obviously such a criterion of maximizing generalization or extrapolation implies an interaction with accuracy (wild generalizations are unhelpful if untrue), but complete accuracy is not required as long as the program can recover, as LEX does by detecting that the generalization was false in the new instance and falling back on search and recalculation.

Deductive learning (e.g. Samuel, and Rosenbloom and Newell) is motivated by a desire to improve the speed of performance with practice. Two generalizations of this appear, both involving induction: compressing the amount of storage involved by replacing many separate items by a rule that summarizes them (data compression or induction as simplification and summarization), and extending the usefulness of stored items by treating new problems as 'similar' to old ones (induction as generalization). In summary, then, we see that we can gain performance speed at the cost of some learning time and memory space; that we can save memory at the cost of learning time (to do data compression); and we can extend the use of memory in saving performance time if we trade some accuracy for increased generality in each stored item. These ideas suggest how AI work might go beyond vague simulations of 'learning', and begin to define some functional advantages of a learning component with quantitative measures of success, and thus offer the possibility of an explanation of *why* programs should, and humans do, learn. They also suggest that induction can be motivated by a desire for simplification and/or generalization, and so the accuracy and reliability (i.e. the truth) of its conclusions are not the only criteria.

## CONNECTIONIST WORK

A rather different kind of work on machine learning has begun to be prominent, motivated primarily by a class of mechanism and not by the kind of functional advantages of learning discussed so far, and their associated explanatory potential. It is characterized by the use of models consisting of large numbers of simple units (broadly analogous to neurons) which compute in parallel, and is known as connectionism since much of the models' content is in the specification and strength of the connections between the units. (See Rumelhart and McClelland, 1986, for a large collection of this work.) It is broadly inspired by considering the nature of the brain and asking what kind of computational behaviour might be exhibited by that kind of mechanism. In stressing mechanism and attending to function only secondarily, it is in a quite different tradition from other AI (and machine learning) work, which attends to function and regards mechanism as 'implementation detail': however, it has begun to come up with results that are unquestionably interesting, while not fitting into mainstream work. Connectionism seems primarily oriented around exploring computational techniques or algorithms that seem natural for these networks, and then discovering their properties and possible applications, which include interesting kinds of learning. In some cases they show close modelling of human data but there is often no suggestion of why they work (beyond a description of the network), or why humans should show such mental behaviour. It is almost as if human memory properties were arbitrary side-effects of an arbitrary mechanism.

One such piece of work is that by McClelland and Rumelhart (1985) and consists of a model of human memory that attacks the distinction between a memory for specific instances and for prototypes, i.e. between deductive or rote memory and inductive memory, by providing one uniform mechanism which exhibits both kinds of behaviour depending on the set of inputs given it. The program will not remember an example with precision on one exposure, but can retain exact memories for specific cases if trained on them repeatedly. On the other hand, if exposed to a series of variations it will retain the theme or prototype more exactly than any of the actual examples shown it. It can do both of these at once without confounding independent examples: it does not have to be told which kind of learning to do nor what the input is an example of. Thus it displays inductive learning of prototypes (as well as memorizing specific examples) without the need for an internal or external teacher to direct learning, and pre-segregate examples into training sets.

McClelland and Rumelhart (1981) describe another model whose ostensible purpose is to perceive words from printed letters, but which exhibits as a side-effect a kind of induction of morphological regularities from the words it knows, such that its response is different (in exactly the way that people's responses are) to non-words that are like real words (e.g. 'mave') and non-words that are not (e.g. 'xpqj'). This is an example of an algorithm with more than one function, i.e. it has side-effects (induction) at the functional level that are at least as interesting as the original function (word recognition).

Another significant piece of work (Hinton, 1986) suggests an interpretation of what connectionist networks do: they use their internal layers to compute a new description language adjusted to the learning task on hand, then the input descriptions are translated into this new internal language, and then concepts are learned and remembered in it. His model is given a set of facts about family trees to learn for later recall, in the form of triples naming facts like 'Andrew is the father of Jennifer'. The data has many hidden regularities which the program is not told, such as that there are really two disjoint family trees, one English and one Italian, that individuals have a unique and constant gender, and that gender constrains which relationships an individual can take part in (e.g. father versus mother). The program adjusts its units in a way that can be interpreted as analysing these hidden descriptive dimensions, so that one unit comes to represent nationality, another generation (i.e. height in the tree), and so on. This may point the way to escaping from built-in description languages, since the program appears to analyse more basic atomic descriptive dimensions behind a pattern of data, e.g. it discovers that it should divide the names on the basis of a dimension that we can see corresponds to nationality.

To understand the relationship of connectionist work to other work on machine learning we need to develop the idea of functionalism a little more fully, which the next section does.

## FUNCTIONALISM AND MACHINE LEARNING

Having discussed some existing work on machine learning, some issues raised by it, some weaknesses, and likely developments in the near future, we can now step back to consider how the pieces of work relate to each other and to the programme of extended functionalism sketched in the introduction. To provide a framework I shall expand the latter a little by making explicit a distinction between levels in a computational model, each of which may be associated with a separate set of issues and problems.

### Three levels in modelling

Simple functionalism is concerned with one kind of abstraction in which we concentrate on one property of a mechanism (its function) and ignore others (its implementation). Thus we might see the heart as a pump, and separate this from how it does its pumping. Extended functionalism, which views the functions of mind as computational ones, involves an additional kind of abstraction, because computation itself is not a physical operation like pumping but an abstract or symbolic one. This abstraction, although perhaps philosophically mysterious, has in fact been familiar to us in its manifestations from childhood, because it is present in even the simplest applications of mathematics, including arithmetic. Any such application involves several levels, although we do not usually need to notice this.

For instance, suppose you want to calculate whether you can afford to buy a new car. First you study the problem in the world and decide on exact definitions for terms such as 'afford'. Then you do some calculations about your finances, which amounts to a function of the various quantities such as your income and the number you chose as representing what you can afford. Once the mapping has been established between the real-world statement of the problem (the first level) and a function using addition and subtraction (the second level), the function can be computed without thinking of its meaning: it is just a piece of arithmetic and might have been about miles travelled or some other problem entirely, because the functions of arithmetic are independent of their application. This level of abstract function is a second level: motivated by the real-world problem, but definable separately from it. The third level is that of algorithms: methods for computing the function (e.g. column addition), and again could be studied separately.

These three levels are also involved in developing AI theories, but here none of them are familiar and ready for use: so research in AI may have to do original work on all three levels at once. It is as if in order to decide whether you can afford a car (level 1 – the specific problem in the world), you also had to join a debate on whether addition could be applied to negative numbers and decimals as well as to natural numbers (i.e. on the definition of the functions to be used – level 2), and also invent, improve, or find alternatives to, column addition (level 3 – algorithmic methods). Because of this, early work on any AI topic is at best exploratory and ambiguous. However, as more work is done on the same topic, comparisons between programs allow increasing clarification of the separation of levels, and of the definitions and results belonging to each.

What is sought, ideally, is a way of specifying functions independently both of the practical demands of the task (level 1), and of what people do (level 3), just as addition is defined independently of both the financial problems it can be applied to, and of how people (or calculators) do it. It is this independence that allows us on the one hand to say a calculator is doing addition correctly, and on the other to claim explanatory force in saying that we make financial decisions using arithmetic (this would be empty if 'arithmetic' meant only 'financial calculations'). This is the aim behind proposing functional criteria like data compression. The functionalist approach advocates moving away from using either specific tasks (level 1) or mimicry (simulation) of human performance (level 3) as primary criteria, and searching for independently defined ones that can suggest answers to the question 'what is learning for?', which is discussed in the section after next. As just argued, this is only to be expected after enough work has been done to support comparative analysis – a state into which the field of machine learning is currently emerging. The next section groups machine learning work by its potential for such comparisons.

### The three levels as foci for learning work

All real programs must make specific choices on each level, but as discussed in the introduction, a line of work may focus on one level. Thus one might study a fixed task and all the various ways (employing various functions) of carrying it out, or study a fixed function (e.g. deductive learning) and on the one hand the various tasks it can help to achieve, and on the other various implementations (algorithms) for computing the function. A given learning program, then, cannot be usefully classified in any one way (e.g. by task) since it represents at least three partly independent choices. (They are only partly independent because a given function, for example, may be relevant to more than one task but not to all possible tasks.) With these provisos in mind, we may group work on machine learning as belonging to lines of work focused on one of the three levels, although in principle a given program could be important to more than one line. We shall take the levels in reverse order.

The connectionist work can be thought of as mainly focused on the third level of implementations or algorithms: connectionists study such algorithms, finding what they can do, and most interestingly discovering that one algorithm can often simultaneously compute effects that we might previously have supposed were unrelated functions, e.g. recall and prototypical completion, or perception and induction. This approach is unusual in AI: since there are many functions that might help a given domain task, and many implementations for each defined function, it has seemed better to work top-down from the problem to an implementation. However, the effects demonstrated by this approach seem likely to revise our ideas about the relationship between learning and what are usually conceived of as quite separate faculties such as perception, similarity judgements, and the use of prototypes to do inference.

Much of the work on machine learning is best seen as focusing on the second level of functions. We must first recognize that there are several independent functions that may be used together to make up a particular learning program, but which should be analysed separately. Samuel's program, for instance, learned both by remembering board positions and by adjusting coefficients. LEX, besides a module for solving problems given some state of knowledge, had three others: one that did inductive learning given positive and negative examples of rule (concept) use, one to extract such examples from a problem-solving episode, and another to generate new problems, i.e. 'experiments' to cause more learning.

Thus besides the range of deductive and inductive learning described earlier, there is another range of functional variation with respect to the occasion for learning. For instance, Samuel's program learns only the board positions encountered in play, and so even though the content of the items learned is internally generated, which items are learned depends on the particular games the program is trained on. Thus external events determine the occasions of learning, and so indirectly what gets learned. In contrast, Lenat's program is entirely internally driven: it decides what to explore itself. Mitchell's program LEX can be run either way (on human-generated problems or on problems it generates itself), and one can imagine a program intermediate between the two, that after being set a problem externally decided what training problems to set itself, just as serious chess players may set themselves problems in the hope of improving their performance against future opponents. This kind of variation is concerned in contrasting learning by being taught versus learning by exploration or eduction versus self-teaching, but affects what data are presented to a learning algorithm rather than what lesson that algorithm extracts and how.

Again, as LEX illustrates, there is a third independent functional issue of how data for learning are extracted from an event such as a problem-solving episode and directed to the appropriate concepts for assimilation. (This is called the credit-assignment problem by Charniak and McDermott, 1985, p.634.)

Comparisons of AI programs have allowed these to be provisionally identified as functions independent of each other and of the task domain they are applied to. It has not yet advanced far enough to give a complete specification of these in usefully abstract terms. The suggestions above concerning measures of data-compression, etc., are steps in this direction for the first of these function types (the inductive/deductive one) only.

Work focused on the first level – the problem domain – has been surprisingly lacking. It would consist of exploring a number of ways of doing the task, only some of them using learning. This would show whether and under what conditions learning is a useful function. It is extraordinary that this question is seldom raised, either in AI or the other behavioural sciences, although it is central to a functionalist approach. One place it has been raised is in the context of ethology (Gould, 1982), where it takes the form of asking under what conditions it is advantageous to an organism to learn something instead of inheriting it as an innate behaviour.

### What is learning for?

The basic question is 'what is learning for?', i.e. what functions does it perform, when will it be advantageous, and can learning be classified in this way? This seems a good basic question for AI, and one that could open the way to a contribution to the study of development. Since little work seems to have been done on this line, we can only illustrate the kinds of answer that might be considered in (future) work of this kind.

One partial answer is that an organism must learn what it cannot be genetically programmed with, e.g. the appearance of its own parents, or its own home. Since these details are different for each individual they must be learned. Computers exhibit a form of this when they test at 'boot' time (i.e. when they start up and inspect their environment) to see what peripherals are connected to them in this incarnation, and adjust their operating systems accordingly. (Some current UNIX systems do this, for instance.) A variation on this would be self-tuning of various parameters: for instance, as we grow up the distance between our eyes and their height above the ground change, so these parameters of visual perception need to be acquired (and slowly but continually adjusted). Work on (human) adaptation to inverting prisms suggests that this kind of learning extends also to some parameters that might from a design viewpoint have been made innate.

Another idea of this kind is that it is wasteful to learn information that you can pick up whenever it is needed. Indeed, despite our vague belief that people will become familiar with things they regularly encounter, there is evidence that people are very poor at remembering things like the detailed appearance of the building they work in, or even the kind of handle on their office door. Thus it seems that we do not, and for efficiency should not, learn just because we are exposed, but should learn only those things that both might be helpful in future and would be some trouble to find out when needed.

Yet other ideas about what learning is for are those given earlier: saving memory space by data compression, and performance time by memorizing derivable results.

These ideas may be wrong, or may only apply to relatively small areas of learning, but they are of the right kind: they offer theories of the usefulness of learning, an issue missing from most AI work, yet a natural component of a functionalist approach. They are important because to date most work on machine learning, like much psychological work on memory, attempts to describe or mimic human mental functions without examining the reasons for them, and hence without any hope of explanatory content.

## BEYOND FUNCTIONALISM

We have now reviewed a functionalist approach to learning and showed how AI work on machine learning fits into that and is beginning to fill out that framework, though with surprising neglect of the top level, which should ask why learning might be useful in the design of the task-performing behaviour. The functionalist approach, however, assumes that the task is given, and studies how mechanisms to perform it might be designed and optimized. This view of learning seems generally to lead to proposals of a fixed general mechanism which uses learning to tailor itself to a particular environment whose details were not known when the mechanism was designed. This is true of Samuel's program (learning board positions it encounters, which improves its performance provided future opponents play comparable games to past ones), of Chomsky's ideas of a universal grammar and language acquisition devices (a child just has to learn how a particular language fits into the universal pattern), and of gull chicks imprinting on their own particular parents.

Such programmed learning, in which what to learn, and when and how to extract it from experience are built into special learning machinery, is doubtless important in animals, and perhaps in humans. (Gould, 1982, ch. 16, describes how bees learn characteristics of food sources in a way that is both strikingly mechanical, and yet equally strikingly adaptive.) Work on machine learning usually also seems to have this character, both in its dependence on what is already built in (e.g. the description language) and in the functionalist outlook which relates learning as a means to a task as a predestined end.

But, as Thornton discusses in the introduction to Chapter 10, this is not the only view of cognitive growth. Surely this programmed, purpose-driven learning cannot apply to cognitive development in general: surely the hall-mark of human minds is that they can learn anything, and that they are self-transforming (rather than merely adapting by a little self-tuning). What if, in contrast to 'what is learning for?', we accept as a hypothesis or premise that humans do have a general learning mechanism that allows entirely novel behaviours to emerge without a special learning mechanism for this being previously built in? I shall now try to show that AI could also contribute to this side of the debate. While most existing work on machine learning essentially belongs to the 'learning' side, and contributes to modelling cognitive change as accumulation within a fixed framework, it is in principle possible to explore a computational perspective on the contrasting view which emphasizes development as restructuring. However, to do so undermines a simple functionalist approach in two ways.

Firstly, it may be that the constraint of having to learn (develop) an ability is severe enough that the final ability attained is not optimal: learning may not merely affect *how* a function is implemented by also *what* function appears. Ordinary programming, and its application to computational cognitive modelling, normally proceeds by identifying a function to be computed and then finding an implementation of that function. In cognitive development, as in evolution and ontogenesis (physical development of an individual organism's body from the original single cell), a major constraint is that construction is not organized for the end alone and independently of other considerations, but is affected firstly by the previous state of the individual and secondly by the need for the intermediate forms to be at least partially functional.

Secondly, we may not be able to find any criterion of optimality for judging the final abilities observed; indeed we may not be able to tell what the learning was supposed to achieve. For instance, just because I can count backwards from one hundred does not show that I ever tried to learn to do so or benefit from being able to do it: it may be an irrelevant side-effect of something else. (This is comparable to a problem in evolution theory with understanding features of organisms as adaptations: you cannot be sure which are the features.) Lawler, who was trained in AI but performed a developmental observation study, uses the metaphor of 'bricolage' to offer some ideas on this.

## The metaphor of bricolage

Bricolage is a concept of Levi-Strauss adopted by Lawler (1985) as a central idea about development. Levi-Strauss introduces it in *The Savage Mind* (1962/1966, pp.16ff.) as part of his attempt to characterize the difference between intellectual activities in 'primitive' cultures and in Western science. *Bricoler* literally means to swerve from one's direct course. The metaphor contrasts the engineer and the *bricoleur*, who is the sort of handyman whose work reflects what he has to hand as much as the task itself: his work is 'deflected' from a pure solution.

The contrast with a *bricoleur* is not absolute, since engineers too cannot do exactly as they choose but also are subject to some constraints, such as the laws of physics, how much they know, and perhaps economic limits. Nevertheless there is a clear dimension of control, as an example may make clear. Consider someone coming home from work and deciding what to have for dinner. The 'engineer' would decide what the best dinner would be on general grounds, and then set out to buy and prepare what was necessary; the *bricoleur* would look in the fridge and devise a meal based on what was available. From a theoretical point of view, the significance is that one could probably predict an engineer's behaviour on general grounds, but to understand a *bricoleur* well enough to predict behaviour we would have to know many personal details such as what he ate yesterday and whether some was left over – in other words his behaviour would depend on his history as well as his goals and general competence.

## Implications for an AI approach to development

The heart of the implied problem is that AI people naturally tend to think in terms of knowing what function you want to implement, and writing a program that does that as well as possible; whereas a skill ('program') in a child evolves rather than is designed, and may owe as much to its origins and idiosyncratic path of development as it does to the function it is 'meant' to implement. This means that development constitutes a distinctive challenge to AI, because the applicability of its dominant trend of thought is always in question.

While humans learn skills over a period, and probably never stop learning and adapting, most software is written to perform a fixed function and is not meant to change once installed. Furthermore, the mode of transmission of skills is not by one machine teaching another but by direct copying of the internal structure – what would be called telepathy if done by humans. That is, once a program has been constructed on one machine, copies are transferred and installed in other machines, usually without any modification at all. Furthermore, it is the identity, not the changes that are stressed: if a program in a high-level language is transferred, it will be recompiled on the new machine, i.e. translated into the machine code of the new machine. But this is thought of as the 'same' program, and the compilation is not thought of as learning or assimilation (even though it might be interesting to do so – see below). Thus neither teaching, learning nor development have any recognized place in contemporary software. To a programmer, 'development' means 'program development' and is what the programmer does during the creation and testing of a program; it is not an activity performed by the machine itself. (Thus in this case the theoretical use of computer modelling is being retarded rather than helped by the analogy with existing computational technology.)

AI might nevertheless do some interesting work, even though it means moving away from the functionalism that is grounded in the engineering approach of normal computer science, and abandoning any informal help from simple analogies between human cognitive development and existing computer technology. AI could begin by exploring evolving programs. Some first steps are already in existence (although not usually described in these terms). Again I shall just illustrate the possibilities of an approach that has not yet taken off.

How can a new function or skill emerge from old ones? In particular, can it emerge gradually, or only in one large step? Production rule models such as Young's (1976) model of seriation (discussed in some detail in Chapter 10 of this volume) show how new functions can emerge as the result of incremental learning of small 'units' (production rules). Similarly, Lawler's observations also show how a 'skill' such as addition can be seen as an emergent phenomenon based on the accumulation of many small skills. Furthermore, the set of rules at each stage is viable, i.e. it allows the child to perform the task in at least some cases. It thus exhibits intermediate viability, a condition associated with the notion of bricolage: if solutions may be arrived at by incremental modification of solutions to an earlier task, then not only will the solution depend on the starting point as well as the desired target ability (the feature of bricolage discussed above), but it may also be affected by the need to be of at least some use at each intermediate stage. Thus although current software does not develop in this way (but usually collapses completely if some unit is not present), Young has shown that such development can be modelled computationally.

This kind of learning, in which the scope rather than the speed of the function improves, is in contrast to Mitchell's program. LEX can always solve all integration problems (in principle) given enough time: its learning radically improves its speed, but it develops new skill only in the sense of bringing new problems within its time limits. Simple functionalism, especially in computation, regards speed and accuracy as performance measures determined by the implementation and secondary to a fixed function specification, and this has tended to carry over into machine learning. Mitchell measured LEX's speed increases with learning, while regarding its ability to do integration as predetermined. However, it would take only a small change in outlook to measure the increase in problem range or difficulty made possible by learning (for instance, without learning perhaps LEX can only afford to tackle problems that can be solved with a single transformation, while with experience it can solve harder ones without giving up). As children develop they can appear to become worse at some tasks as they develop internal representations of greater generality. The apparent paradox is generated by the use of fixed-task criteria, and would disappear with criteria of task range. While experimentalists might try to develop such criteria, AI workers could start thinking about the design of learning mechanisms that are not aimed at learning (speeding up) a fixed task but at broadening the range of their function. One of the attractions of Young's production rule model of seriation is that it does indeed model increase in the *range* of seriation tasks successfully performed. Thus we could view Young's work as a hint on how to broaden the functionalist perspective, instead of merely as an attempt to model human data closely (level 3 in the terms of our discussion of the levels of modelling in the previous section), without explaining why humans should exhibit such imperfect implementations of the (presupposed) function of seriation.

Another phenomenon of development is present in embryo in the Hacker program (Sussman, 1975) which learns to write blocks-world programs, and which really models an interdependent cluster of skills. Although this was not addressed in Sussman's study, it could provide a testbed for demonstrating the effects, separately and together, of several kinds of learning concerned in one skill. One kind of learning is remembering solutions to old problems, which might be though of as prompted by problems set it or as taught directly (as mathematicians are trained by learning other people's proofs). Another is its ability to assimilate new problems to the nearest remembered problem as LEX does, which is affected by the way it learns to change (generalize) the description of a learned solution. Another is its skill in debugging the retrieved solution to work on the new problem ('accommodation'), which changes when it modifies its bug detection or analysis routines (e.g. the 'critics'). Studying the *interaction* of kinds of learning on a task which they all affect, and perhaps eventually understanding how this might be coordinated and controlled, is as much a pure developmental issue as a functionalist one.

## CONCLUSION

This chapter used an account of the functionalist approach to cognitive science to review work on machine learning, show how the pieces of work relate to each other, and show what kind of work and results can be foreseen as a direct progression. This functionalist perspective can be expected to culminate in answering the question of what learning is for when viewed as an available technique to support fixed functions such as perception. However, the more basic phenomena of development – at least as usually perceived and described – do not fit into this approach. Nevertheless, AI might contribute to this developmental (as opposed to learning) perspective too by starting an essentially new line of research, which, instead of assuming that task performance is the given around which behaviour (and learning) is structured, focused on phenomena of behavioural change. The first pieces of such work would probably be little more than mimickings of such apparent phenomena, until enough work had been done to discern some structure and constraints behind the simulations. It is possible that connectionist work will prove to be a pioneer in this, because of its focus on algorithms first and their applications second, and the way that it builds learning into almost all its projects from the start.

## ACKNOWLEDGEMENTS

The writing of this chapter was supported by SERC fellowship B/ITF/94. The intellectual debts I am aware of – and there are probably others – are owed to Alan Bundy for the analogy between AI and applied mathematics; to Chris Thornton for discussions on machine learning; and to Andrew Law, Claire O'Malley, and Josie Taylor for discussions on what AI should have to say about development, even if it doesn't yet.

## REFERENCES

Bundy, A., Silver, B., and Plummer, D. (1985). An analytical comparison of some rule-learning programs, *Artificial Intelligence*, **27**, 137–181.

Charniak, E., and McDermott, D. (1985). *Introduction to Artificial Intelligence*, Addison-Wesley, Reading, Mass.

Davis, R. (1982). Teiresias: applications of meta-level knowledge. In R. Davis and D. B. Lenat (eds), *Knowledge-based Systems in AI*, McGraw-Hill, New York, pp.227–490.

Good, I. J. (1968). A five-year plan for automatic chess. In E. Dale and D. Michie (eds), *Machine Intelligence 2*, Oliver & Boyd, London, pp.89–118.

Gould, J. L. (1982). *Ethology: the Mechanisms and Evolution of Behaviour*, Norton, New York.

Hinton, G. E. (1986). Learning distributed representations of concepts, *Proceedings of the Cognitive Science Society Conference*, Amherst.

Johnson-Laird, P. N. (1983). *Mental Models*, Harvard University Press, Cambridge, Mass.

Lawler, R. W. (1985). *Computer Experience and Cognitive Development*, Ellis Horwood, Chichester, pp.250–255, and ch.1.

Lenat, D. B. (1983a). Theory formation by heuristic search, *Artificial Intelligence*, **21**, 31–59.

Lenat, D. B. (1983b). The role of heuristics in learning by discovery: three case studies. In Michalski et al. (1983), pp.243–306.

Levi-Strauss, C. (1962/1966). *The Savage Mind*, Weidenfeld & Nicolson, London, pp.16ff.

McClelland, J. L., and Rumelhart, D. E. (1981). An interactive activation model of context effects in letter perception, *Psychological Review*, **88**, 375–407; **89**, 60–94.

McClelland, J. L., and Rumelhart, D. E. (1985). Distributed memory and the representation of general and specific information, *Journal of Experimental Psychology*, **114**, 159–197.

Marsh, D. (1969). Memo functions, the graph traverser, and a simple control situation. In B. Meltzer and D. Michie (eds), *Machine Intelligence 5*, Edinburgh University Press, Edinburgh, pp.281–300.

Michalski, R. S. (1986). Understanding the nature of learning: issues and research directions. In Michalski et al. (1986), pp.3–25.

Michalski, R. S., Carbonell, J. G., and Mitchell, T. M. (eds) (1983). *Machine Learning*, Tioga, Palo Alto, Calif.

Michalski, R. S., Carbonell, J. G., and Mitchell, T. M. (eds) (1986). *Machine Learning*, Vol. 2, Morgan Kaufman, Los Altos, Calif.

Mitchell, T. M. (1978). Version spaces, Ph.D. dissertation, Dept. of computer science, Stanford University. Report STAN–CS–78–711.

Mitchell, T. M. (1982). Generalization as search, *Artificial Intelligence*, **18**, 203–266.

Mitchell, T. M. (1983). Learning and problem solving, *Proc. IJCAI–83*, Karlsruhe, pp.139–1151.

Mitchell, T. M., Utgoff, P. E., and Banerji, R. (1983). Learning by experimentation: acquiring and refining problem-solving heuristics. In Michalski et al. (1983), pp.163–190.

Quinlan, J. R. (1983). Learning efficient classification procedures and their application to chess end games. In Michalski et al. (1983), pp.463–482.

Rosenbloom, P. S., and Newell, A. (1986). The chunking of goal hierarchies: a generalized model of practice. In Michalski et al. (1986), pp.247–288.

Rumelhart, D. E., and McClelland, J. L. (eds) (1986). *Parallel Distributed Processing: Explorations in the Microstructure of Cognition*, Bradford Books,

Samuel, A. L. (1963). Some studies in machine learning using the game of checkers. In E. A. Feigenbaum and J. Feldman (eds), *Computers and Thought*, McGraw-Hill, New York, pp.71–105.

Sussman, G. J. (1975). *A Computational Model of Skill Acquisition*, Elsevier, New York.

Van Someren, M. W. (1986). Knowledge based learning: reducing the description space for rule learning, *Proc. ECAI–86*, pp.1–7.

Winston, P. H. (1975). Learning structural descriptions from examples. In P. H. Winston (ed.), *The Psychology of Computer Vision*, McGraw-Hill, New York, pp.157–209.

Young, R. M. (1976). *Seriation by Children: an Artificial Intelligence Analysis of a Piagetian Task*, Birkhauser Verlag, Basel.

Computers, Cognition and Development
Edited by J. Rutkowska and C. Crook
© 1987 John Wiley & Sons Ltd

CHAPTER 13

# The Need for Developmental Theories in Cognitive Science: Children and Computing Systems

MICHAEL SCAIFE

## SUMMARY

Children and computers; cognitive development; novice programmers; cognitive science; sensorimotor learning; computational approach to psychology; virtual machines; Soviet psychology; interiorization; learning to use computer input devices; interfaces.

## PREAMBLE

How should we prepare our children for the 'computer age'? If psychologists have any role to play in this process, have they made any progress to date? The answer is as predictable as it is disappointing: reading the contemporary psychological literature makes it clear that next to nothing is understood about how the child goes from the stage of dealing with computer systems as novel, complex toys to treating them more as the 'information prosthesis' (Papert and Weir, 1978) wherein their ultimate importance lies. The psychologist's lack of success in this area has more than academic importance since it serves to reinforce the inclination of computer systems designers to pay little or no attention to them when designing their products. The case for taking psychological research into consideration has not yet been made self-evident and to believe otherwise is delusion. Therefore in this chapter I feel it necessary to indicate some of the reasons why psychological investigation *is* a vital ingredient in information technology development and to point to the methodological basis required for such an enterprise.

The main concern of this chapter is, however, with the question of what form a theory of human–computer interaction (HCI) should take and whether we need a theory that is somehow qualitatively different from existing accounts of learning. In addressing this issue I shall argue that we currently lack a suitable, comprehensive developmental theory in which to locate the interactions between the child and computers. For progress to be made it will be necessary to evolve an approach based on theoretical presuppositions that are novel to contemporary information-processing psychology.

## FIRST STEPS IN DEFINING THE HUMAN–COMPUTER INTERACTION

### The cognitive status of the computer

As a starting point here we should first construct a crude taxonomy of the ways in which HCI has been glossed in the literature. Such a scheme serves merely to establish a set of pointers to the different kinds of claim that could be made in this area and no more.

### (a) *The computer as display device, super-calculator or word-processor*

This is the lowest level of conceptual sophistication where there is no particular reason to consider the user in special terms. Here the psychologist's input tends to be focused upon such things as the psychophysical specifications of optimum screen display parameters or menu layouts (e.g. Card *et al.*, 1983). Such research may not therefore suggest the need for any novel theoretical principles and falls squarely within established work in motor skills and ergonomics.

### (b) *The computer as remedial assistant*

Here the emphasis is on the use of the system to solve practical problems such as helping to shape handwriting or other skills (e.g. Lally and Macleod, 1983). The speed and accuracy (within task limits) of the computer come to the fore and in this sense the system is no different in principle from other aids to acquisition such as the learning machines of the 1950s. However, the feedback nature of the situation does pose greater complexities in understanding than case (a) especially when considering the nature of the control systems, which are not located solely in the machine or the user but are more properly regarded as incorporating the two.

## (c) The computer as teacher

This is much more interesting than the preceding cases in the sense that it involves the use of computers with flexible strategies for dealing with a variety of levels of learning standards in the same situation. Such work would be typified by the acquisition of concepts within some defined content area such as set theory (e.g. Lally, 1980). Interesting consequences for cognitive development may follow from the adoption of particular teaching programs but there is no necessary commitment to the notion that computing devices are more than a useful substitute for traditional tutorial methods.

## (d) The computer as cognitive catalyst

There are a variety of claims in the literature that can be incorporated under this heading. Among the more modest are attempts to demonstrate that mathematical skills are fostered in virtue of experience with a variety of programming languages (e.g. training in APL elevates test scores; Elliot, 1978). According to more radical views, however, one is justified in talking of cognitive revolutions brought about by the 'mere' activity of being exposed to the formal apparatus of programming *per se*. Although claims of such advances to tend to be more or less monopolized by proponents of the LOGO programming language, it is not obviously the case that the general claim is in fact dependent on the specific content of this particular vehicle. There is not space here to review the evidence for and against these various claims. However, it can safely be stated that there is certainly not yet a substantial body of evidence to support any strong claims that programming computers *per se* will produce cognitive enhancements that are general in their applicability (cf. Pea and Kurland, 1984).

## Should we worry about not having a theory for HCI?

One implication of the failure to demonstrate the uniquely mind-enhancing properties of computing devices might be that we should consider the computer environment simply as a contemporary equivalent of the teaching machines of old. After all, we should not forget that many of the same hopes/grand claims that are being made for computers today were being made two or three decades ago for learning machines. In this sense one might regard a psychologist, conservative of view and method, as justified in refusing to become exercised about the likely impact of 'new technology' on development. Are there any reasons to believe that this is misguided? I think that there are. Firstly, there is the certainty that computing devices will become ubiquitous in a way that teaching machines did not. While this does not argue for a special theory of HCI it means that at the very least there is an urgent need to fine tune our general theories of learning to this particular situation. Secondly, and much more importantly, computers will soon attain a sophisticated level of interactive competence (albeit perhaps in restricted domains) which means that children will have access to systems that will pose problems of communication of a complexity that teaching machines never approached. The term 'communication' is not used here in an idle way: there does not seem, a priori, any reason to assume that the complexity of the representations of intentionality and meaning in the interactions between the child and the computing system should ultimately be orders of magnitude less than between, say, peers. If one takes this line of argument seriously then the task, for psychologists, becomes one of understanding the interaction between child and computer in terms of a distributed intelligent system.

## THEORETICAL DIRECTIONS

If we grant that HCI is a suitable case for the psychologist's treatment and that contemporary information-processing psychology has failed to provide the necessary direction, we must look elsewhere for inspiration. Two candidates appear to have some promise, albeit for different reasons. The first of these is the (purportedly) new discipline of cognitive science with its emphasis on the integration of concepts from psychology, philosophy, artificial intelligence and linguistics. The promise here is of advance towards a general theory of intelligence which might allow us to derive some part of the framework we need for describing HCI. The second approach is from French-language and Soviet literature, much of which has been ignored by English-speaking psychologists but which, it will be seen, allows us to consider learning at a level that has been neglected in English-language theory.

### What can cognitive science contribute?

Cognitive science is not an easy organism to classify. However, for present purposes we might regard it as encompassing those aspects of the behavioural sciences that are committed to the study of the mind considered as a computational system. The inspiration for this enterprise is from within the area of computer science and, more particularly, artificial intelligence. The productivity of this approach can scarcely be doubted when one looks at the burgeoning literature in the field of cognitive simulation (see Boden, 1985). The most obvious virtue of the computational approach is that it requires the user to be explicit about details of processes, particularly where the model is to be implemented as a program. Computational accounts are consequently good, for example, at representing the flow of information at different levels of control. In many instances the model that is adopted employs directly concepts taken from the theory of computer science as analogies for the understanding of behavioural processes. For example, Arbib (1976) likens the level of neural operations to that of a machine-code program whereas organization at the level of sequences of goal-directed actions can be compared to planning strategies in a high-level programming language.

The computational approach has been applied to many problems in behavioural science. The reason why it has such a powerful generality derives from the assumption that understanding the logic of computational processes does not require consideration of the details of the hardware on which the computation occurs. In principle any computing machine can support any program. To be more precise, a physical machine can support a variety of 'virtual machines': so that the same computer can be a LISP machine or a POP11 machine, or whatever. It is argued that there are few constraints between operations of the different sorts of machine. This belief (which may be problematic even for computers) will cause difficulties if extrapolated uncritically to biological organisms as the methodological basis for a computational approach to cognition (Scaife, 1985). Here the assumptions held about the virtual computing machine become mirrored in the idea that the important properties of cognition are independent of the facts of biological organization, just as any computing machine can support any program. Thus to describe the essential nature of mental processes we need pay no attention to neurophysiological or neuropsychological data.

There are serious difficulties with such a formulation. A computational account of mental processes should not ignore potential constraints operating between levels of functioning. One of the main arguments advanced here is that too much of the work on theoretical cognitive modelling has become so to speak 'disembodied' with no explicit relationship between 'pure' knowledge structures and activities in the physical-social world. Thus English-language psychology has been greatly concerned with how abstract, logical cognition works (e.g. Johnson-Laird, 1983). Such work is of great interest but it has become such a dominant approach that very term 'mental model' has come to denote a virtual space of action, a tendency which may have been reinforced by the modelling techniques used in artificial intelligence (e.g. the blocks world pioneered by Winograd, 1972). Yet one of the most robust demonstrations of developmental psychology is that of the fundamental role of sensorimotor (bodily) processes in the ontogenesis of cognition (Piaget, 1936; Wallon, 1959; Werner and Kaplan, 1963). Further, as Mounoud and Hauert (1981), Pailhous (1978) and others have observed, there is good reason to believe that sensorimotor processes are important in this respect throughout the developmental period. Cognition, in the framework of cognitive science, then needs to become somehow re-embodied in subjects acting in a real world.

**New directions: the need for another type of psychological theory**

One major criticism then of much contemporary cognitive science is its studied ignorance of the real constitution of (biological) subjects. A possible counter would be to constrain our description of mental processes (which of course might themselves be couched in some high-level descriptive language) by what we know of the functional principles of nervous system activity. This follows from the acceptance as a major research objective of the task of identifying the origins, that is to say the development, of intelligence. The best accounts that are currently offered within psychology (the Piagetian and Soviet models), different as they are, both stress the need to specify the relationship between biology and psychology. In both cases the descriptive language of psychological process is abstracted across biological structure, e.g. the Piagetian reflex or Luria's functional system, but this abstraction rests upon an analysis of the nature of the biological system that supports development. Thus we may point to the neural-psychological activity relationships that Luria (e.g. Luria, 1966) attempted to describe. He demonstrated that the result of neurological investigation does not have to take the form of mapping localization of functions in the brain but can underpin a theory of cognitive processes based on functional descriptions at various levels: motor control zones at one level, functional systems at another, and so on.

Soviet psychology has a double importance for present purposes in stressing the interactive and fundamentally social nature of cognitive change. Most importantly, as with Piagetian theory, it is based on the assumption of the operation of constant developmental processes or tendencies. The point here (and it cannot be overemphasized) is not the theoretical adequacy or otherwise of the particular concept of equilibration or the laws of the dialectic, but rather that ideas of this kind are fundamental for descriptions of intelligent systems. This point has not been widely appreciated in the artificial intelligence literature where synchronic modelling is the norm and indeed, in cognitive science approaches to mind generally, developmental concepts do not figure prominently. It should be immediately remarked, however, that this is nothing new to English-language psychology where much of the literature purporting to be 'developmental' is really synchronic adult-experimental work with age added on as a parameter or variable. In most of this work there is very little recognition of the fact that the inherently developmental nature of cognition has to be taken as its fundamental characteristic.

A second important aspect of Soviet psychology for our consideration of the possible impact of information technology lies in its insistence that development proceeds as much by the recalibration of psychological functions against each other as by the maturation of particular neural structures. Part of this development involves processes that are initially inter-psychic, shared between individuals such as infant and adult, and become intra-psychic as internalized actions. From this interactional perspective, if one were to consider the computer as a possible partner in such a process then perhaps significant developmental change may be effected in a similar fashion.

## PUTTING THE BODY BACK

In one respect it is not surprising that cognitive science has such a disembodied view of cognition for, as Kelso (1982) has pointed out, psychologists themselves (within English-language psychology, that is) too often regard motor development as uninteresting or trivial in theories of behavioural change. Skill acquisition research has not provoked a great deal of interest from psychologists with a more 'cognitive' orientation, so that few accounts of development articulate the importance of reciprocal interactions between motor and cognitive development. All too often they are regarded as separate domains, although there have been notable exceptions in that literature which emphasizes learning within the context of the overall goal of the movements (e.g. Bruner, 1970; Elliott and Connolly, 1974).

By contrast, theorists within French-language psychology have made much more of the analysis of processes at the level of sensorimotor functioning to bridge the motor–cognition 'divide' (e.g. Wallon, 1959; Paillard, 1971; Pailhous and Bullinger, 1978; Mounoud and Hauert, 1981). Sensorimotor development is seen as neither a trivial problem nor merely a stage in the development of representational intelligence. By comparison, within English-language psychology the analysis of sensorimotor processes is usually either limited to infancy, characterizing a stage of development left behind with the emergence of representational intelligence, or to adult perceptual-adaptation research as when considering eye–hand coordination.

The usefulness of the French-language psychology approach in this area derives from a conjunction of ideas. Of these one of the most important is the extension of the concept of interiorization (Galperin, 1966) to describe the mechanisms of sensorimotor-based learning. In a key paper Pailhous and Bullinger (1978) question the usual (tacit) assumption that exploratory activity with hand or eye is a direct and unambiguous index of the cognitive processes that direct search. There are many factors which affect the observable form of activity. One important consideration is the fact that the properties of the sensorimotor apparatus itself must themselves be interiorized before exploration with this apparatus can be efficient. Thus Pailhous and Bullinger comment that the eye or hand is an *instrument*, in the sense of a tool, which 'only permits cognitive apprehension of the world to the extent that certain of its properties have been interiorised'. It is important to realize that this perspective does not apply solely to the young child learning to use its sensorimotor apparatus for the first time but also to learning in a wide variety of situations. As they point out, one can easily envisage tasks, e.g. in industrial situations, where this will occur.

This approach to the analysis of sensorimotor learning has at least two important consequences:

(a) It allows us to conceive of learning in terms of two poles of activity. On the one hand we have the situation where the subject is engaged in a process of exploration of objects in the world. In this case the pattern of motor activity is guided by the spatial arrangement of the field. Here the interiorization of properties of the sensorimotor systems may be an inadvertent, although important, consequence of exploration. At the other pole we have the situation where the subject's task is the acquisition of a new skill which involves the reorganization of previously elaborated actions. A good example of this may be taken from Pailhous's (1978) study of the acquisition of a suppleness exercise in trainee and expert ballet dancers. The action involves the rhythmic movement of the spinal column in a series of regular waves. To produce a smooth motion requires that the separate blocks of muscles that control movement for different sections of the vertebral column be recoordinated at a functional level. In such cases learning is directed exclusively towards the properties of the body itself. The complexities of learning involved here are highlighted by consideration of the acquisition of complex skills like dancing or sports activity. Within French-language psychology there is a much stronger tradition of looking at these activities, something which is often disregarded within English-language psychology as being too applied or the domain of ergonomic theorists (cf. Maigre and Destrooper 1975; Le Camus, 1984). These studies are of great value in the search for a *general model* of sensorimotor-based learning that can assist us when looking at interactions with any novel device.

(b) A second consequence of the French-language psychology analysis is a methodological one: we need an ontogenetic dimension to allow investigation of the process of interiorization to be studied at different cognitive levels. Each developmental period will allow different degrees of interiorization for any given task. This perspective is essential for any detailed analysis of the relationship between the cognitive and the sensorimotor components of learning. An excellent example of the investigation of such processes is afforded by Pailhous and Bullinger (1978) who administered a task to young children and adults that required them to copy a model village from information supplied via a subject-operated video camera. The subjects thus had to interiorize the properties of the prosthetic camera device (e.g. that the camera image moved right when the camera moved left, etc.) before they could make progress with the task. Marked developmental differences were found, the most important of which for present purposes was that the younger (4–5 year old) subjects could not correlate the 'cause' of moving the camera with the obtained perceptual effects of the changing field of view. The problem of dissociation meant that they thus could not proceed with the interiorization of the camera's properties and hence use it for systematic exploration of the spatial properties of the model.

This general line of theorizing has direct implications for the study of children interacting with computers. The computer environment must be regarded from the child's point of view as a new system with properties that the child has to learn. No matter how self-evident to adults the properties may appear to be, some learning must occur. The nature of the interaction with the physical machine is not to be dismissed as trivial. The child has to master the user interface before it can make adequate use of the software which characterizes the machine at higher levels. In order to provide an adequate account of such learning we need to move towards a general developmental theory of the interactions between children and computers that takes account of both the sensorimotor and the cognitive aspects of the interaction. In line with the criticisms made previously about 'disembodied cognition' it comes as no surprise to find that very little consideration has been given to how difficult or otherwise computer input devices actually are for children. They are simply assumed to be transparent. Where data do exist on user performance with devices of various sorts, they have been almost entirely confined to studies in adults of the accuracy of pointing to text elements in screen-editing tasks (e.g. Goodwin, 1975; Card et al., 1978; Embley and Nagy, 1981). Some studies have been done in the context of graphics input but developmental considerations have not been noticeable and the emphasis has been on criteria for functional efficiency (e.g. Ritchie and Turner, 1975).

How seriously should we take such considerations? To represent the child's problems as being purely cognitive is clearly not an accurate assessment. In addition, considerations to do with real-world object-directed activity are directly relevant to the attempt to produce an adequate model of the novice child programmer. The nature of the initial interaction with the physical machine is important in determining the subsequent acquisition of programming skills. The link here is in the role of sensorimotor representations in the formulation of the more abstract 'cognitive' procedural skills utilized in skilled programming. For young children it is likely that the same kinds of sensorimotor processes that mediate 'everyday' action are also responsible for giving meaning to initial interactions with computers. The mental model that the child forms of the computer will be based on such understanding.

This assumption is consistent with work relating the acquisition of programming skills to knowledge of action. A good example of this is work with

LOGO. The basic philosophy as set out by Papert emphasizes the developmental importance of 'body knowledge' in reasoning by analogy about the physical world and new spatial concepts (e.g. Papert, 1980, p.11). This knowledge is taken to underpin programming skills. Sometimes dramatic examples of this process have been described. Weir and Emmanuel (1976) report on the way in which a 7-year-old autistic boy, previously uncommunicative and uncooperative, made rapid progress with a button-box driven screen 'turtle', interpreting the LOGO command structure by direct reference to his own bodily axes (up–down–back–forward).

For both children and adults, it has also been noted repeatedly that the more concrete that concepts and procedures are made in teaching novice programmers (e.g. using button boxes, joysticks, coloured cards and slot machines, etc.), the easier is the transition to using abstract programming terms. For young children the problem in interacting with computers is not 'merely' in learning to program; it is in learning to become familiar with, and to control, a series of related machines. These include the physical machine (keyboard/button box, screen, etc.) and the virtual machines of the software that the child has available. As du Boulay et al. (1981) point out, it is critical that the novice be given details of the machine at the right level. They suggest the use of a 'notional machine' (or 'conceptual computer') for instruction. This would have 'a small number of parts that interact in ways that can easily be understood, possibly by analogy to other mechanisms with which the novice is more familiar' (O'Shea and Self, 1983, p.184). Clearly, especially for the young child, a model which explicitly employs analogy with a known space of actions is going to be desirable, not to say essential.

The question remains, however, as to whether we can actually apply these theoretical speculations to the problem of understanding the learning processes of the user of information technology. Can we take a specific learning situation and give a psychological account of the ways in which knowledge is acquired during the course of interaction and subsequently restructured? This is not going to be an easy task and we should not expect such a complex problem to be completely tractable in the first instance. Therefore, as a starting point, we shall constrain the problem space to the specific issue of how novices, especially children, come to operate the plethora of currently available input devices, e.g. mouse or touchscreen or window interfaces.

An example of such research comes from work on children and adults interacting with computerized display devices being done at Sussex University by the author, Peter Coles and Freda Gardner as part of the ESRC Cognitive Science Initiative.* This particular project looks at the ways in which 3- to 10-year-old children learn to use common computer input devices (mouse,

*The support of an Economic Science Research Council grant (no. CO8250010) to M. Scaife is gratefully acknowedged.

touchscreen, joystick, trackball, etc.). The devices present the user with a learning situation that involves the interiorization of novel properties. The primary empirical task is to see how different features might affect performance in a range of graphics tasks. Given that these devices are manufactured without (apparently) any substantial empirical research being done on their suitability for the tasks for which they might be employed, then any data that are gathered on fundamental ergonomic performance will themselves be valuable. However, consistent with the position taken in this paper, the main aim is to advance a theoretical framework that attempts to provide a fuller psychological account of the interaction process. In order to do this we shall conceptualize the interaction in terms that employ concepts from both psychology and computer science. We shall use as a basic concept that of the 'interface'. The idea of an interface here is taken to be something which connects two systems, functioning to facilitate the flow of information and transforming this flow into a form that is usable by the recipient.* In this respect one can regard the devices that any learner uses to interact with the computer as interfaces with properties that will be the object of learning: he must interiorize the properties of the material interface which connects him to the (computer) world. This process of interiorization is one that involves the discovery of the properties of the current interface and their reconstruction in the cognitive domain. The research programme will provide the empirical data necessary to make the features of this process explicit.

## CONCLUSIONS

The main thrust of this paper has been to argue:

(i)  that understanding the child's interactions with computers involves more than considering the child as a programmer;
(ii)  That psychologists have not been successful in understanding that a novel type of theoretical account is required to explain the child's mastery (or otherwise) of the computer system.

In the paper I have argued that we have to be aware of the contribution of sensorimotor processes to the acquisition of knowledge. It is important here to re-emphasize that the scope of the term 'sensorimotor' is wider than that commonly understood by Piagetian students (although not so obviously by Piaget himself). In the same vein it is also germane to point out that previous attempts to use developmental theory explicitly in talking about novices' interactions with computer systems have often seemed either to be rudimentary or to employ conceptual notions which are inadequate as they stand for the task in hand, e.g. Papert's use of Piagetian theory in *Mindstorms*.

*I am grateful to Aaron Sloman for a clarification of this point. The gloss is my own, however.

The problems that confront the psychologist in the area of information technology systems in general and computing devices in particular are formidable. There are so many 'variables' in the situation that classical experimental methods are simply inappropriate. If we consider the problems from the broad perspective of cognitive science we see that it does not provide an adequate base for empirical work nor is it adequately developmental in its orientation. In these important respects the science largely spawned by information technology is inadequate for explaining information technology itself. Further, as this paper demonstrates, it is not crystal clear precisely what route to follow instead. The alternative that I have argued for in this paper is by no means totally satisfactory. I have suggested that some amalgam of Soviet and Francophone psychology will prove to be a profitable starting point for our investigations. Yet both of these sources are themselves beset by difficulties in their theorizing, e.g. in discussing precise mechanisms of social appropriation. For all these reasons we should be much more concerned with developing novel formulations than continuing to force new problems into the procrustean bed of old theoretical ideas.

## REFERENCES

Arbib, M. A. (1976). Program synthesis and sensorimotor coordination. *Brain Theory Neurology*, **2**, 31–33.

Boden, M. (1985). Is computational psychology constructivist?, *Archives de Psychologie*, **53**, 103–112.

Bruner, J. S. (1970). The growth and structure of skill. In K. Connolly (ed.), *Mechanisms of Motor Skill Development*, Academic Press, London.

Card, S. K., English W. K., and Burr, B. J. (1978). Evaluation of mouse, rate-controlled joystick, step keys and text keys for text selection on a CRT, *Ergonomics*, **21**, 601–613.

Card, S. K., Moran, T. P., and Newell, A. (1983). *The Psychology of Human-Computer Interaction*, Lawrence Erlbaum Associates, Hillsdale, N.J.

Du Boulay, J. B. H., O'Shea, T., and Monk, J. (1981). The black box inside the glass box, *Int. J. Man-machine Studies*, **14**, 237–249.

Elliott, J. M., and Connolly, K. J. (1974). Hierarchical structure and skill development. In K. Connolly and J. Bruner (eds), *The Growth of Competence*, Academic Press, New York, pp.135–168.

Elliott, P. C. (1978). Computer 'glass boxes' as advance organisers in mathematics instruction, *Int. Journal Math. Educ. Sci. Technol.*, **9**, 79–87.

Embley, D. W., and Nagy, G. (1981). Behavioural aspects of text editors, *Computing Surveys*, **13**, (1) 42–70.

Galperin. E. (1966). Essai sur la formation par etapes des actions et des concepts. In *Recherches psychologiques en URSS*, Editions du Progres, Moscow.

Goodwin, N. C. (1975). Cursor positioning on an electronic dispay using light pen, lightgun or keyboard for three basic tasks, *Human Factors*, **17**(3), 289–295.

Johnson-Laird, P. N. (1983). *Mental Models*, Cambridge University Press, Cambridge.

Kelso, J. S. (1982). The process approach to understanding human motor behaviour.

In J. S. Kelso (ed.), *Human Motor Behaviour*, John Wiley & Sons, Chichester, pp.1–20.

Lally, M. R. (1980). Computer-assisted development of number conservation in mentally-retarded schoolchildren, *Australian Journal Developmental Disabilities*, 6, 131–136.

Lally, M. R., and Macleod, I. (1983). The promise of micro-computers in developing basic skills. In J. Megary, D. Wallace, S. Nisbett and E. Hoyle (eds), *Computers and Education*, Kogan Page, New York.

Le Camus, J. (1984). *Pratiques Psychomotrices*, Soledi, Liège.

Luria, A. (1966). *The Higher Cortical Functions in Man*, Basic Books, New York.

Maigre, A., and Destrooper, J. (1975). *L'education Psychomotrice*, Presses Universitaires de France, Paris.

Mounoud, P., and Hauert, C. A. (1981). Development of sensorimotor organisation in young children. In G. Forman (ed.), *Action and Thought: from sensorimotor schemes to symbolic operations*, Academic Press, New York.

O'Shea, T., and Self, J. (1983). *Learning and Teaching with Computers*, Harvester Press, Brighton.

Pailhous, J. (1978). Conditions cognitives de l'acquisition d'habilites sensori-motrices. Working paper, Laboratoire de Psychologie de l'Apprentissage, CNRS, Marseille.

Pailhous, J., and Bullinger, A. (1978). The role of interiorisation of material properties of information-acquiring devices in exploratory activities, *Communication and Cognition*, 11, 209–234.

Paillard, J. (1971). Les determinants moteur de l'organisation de l'espace, *Cahiers de Psychologie*, 14, 261–316.

Papert, S. (1980). *Mindstorms*, MIT Press, Cambridge, Mass.

Papert, S., and Weir, S. (1978). Information prosthetics for the handicapped, *MIT Artificial Intelligence Memo 496*.

Pea, R., and Kurland, M. (1984). On the cognitive effects of learning computer programming, *New Ideas in Psychology*, 2, 137–168.

Piaget, J. (1936). *La Naissance de l'intelligence Chez l'enfant*, Delachaux & Niestle, Neuchatel.

Ritchie, G. J., and Turner, J. A., (1975). Input devices for interactive graphics, *Int. J. Man-Machine Studies*, 7(5), 639–660.

Scaife, M. (1985). Psychology and the possibility of a developmental cognitive science, *Artificial Intelligence and Simulation of Behaviour Quarterly*, 52, 20–22.

Wallon, H. (1959). Importance du mouvement dans le developpement psychologique de l'enfant, *Enfance*, 3–4, 235–239.

Weir, S., and Emanuel, R. (1976). Using Logo to catalyse communication in an autistic child. *Research Report 15*, Dept. of AI, Edinburgh Univ.

Werner, H., and Kaplan, B. (1963). *Symbol Formation*, Wiley, New York.

Winograd, T. (1972). *Understanding Natural Language*, Academic Press, New York.

# Author Index

# Subject Index

306

integration, 224
organization, 70, 177 f
pre-existing, 129
procedural, 122, 155
representation, xii, 109, 168
static, 122
syntonic, 74
variability, 238
Knowledge-directed inference, 244
Knowledge-oriented learning, 212

Language acquisition, 180, 211 f, 238
Language acquisition device, 273
Language development, 70
Learner–computer interaction, 182
Learning
  accretion, 71
  autonomous, 36 f
  collaborative, 36 f (*see also*
    Collaborative learning)
  deductive, 255, 260 f, 265 f, 270
  discovery, 38, 100, 104
  exploration and discovery, 100
  exploration, 259
  failure-driven, 225, 259
  general mechanisms, 274
  goal-directed, 261
  gradual, 221
  independent, 36 f
  individualistic, 238
  inductive, 260 f, 271
  knowledge-oriented, 212
  mastery, 137
  motivation, 265 f, 269 f
  motivations for, 212, 265 f, 269 f
  programmed, 273
  purpose-driven, 274
  rote, 260 f
  self-directed, 38, 49
  self-discovery, 116, 123, 124, 129
  structuring, 71
  task-oriented, 212
  transfer, 94, 112, 125
  trial and error, 101
  tuning, 71
Learning algorithms, 236, 251
Learning difficulties, 73
Learning disability, 73 f
Learning environment, 72, 78, 100, 104
Learning machines, 273, 282
Learning theory, 80 f, 88

Leeds Modelling System (IMS), 239
Lego sets, 155
LEX, 261, 263, 266 f, 271, 272, 276 f
Linear programs, 99, 100, 101
Linguistic creativity, 77
Linguistic development, 136
Linguistics, 178, 180
LISP, 89, 90, 109, 153, 247, 285
  and LOGO, 89
  data structures, 89, 236
  symbol manipulation, 89
Logic, 164, 207
  classical, 164
  diagrammatic representations, 165
  formal, 164
  human, 155
  natural, 164
  predicate, 155, 164
Logic programming, 89, 90, 91
Logic programming languages, 90, 155
Logical expressions, 165, 167
  misinterpretations, 165
Logical reasoning, 95
LOGO, xii, 17, 31, 37 f, 40, 42, 49, 74,
    81, 88 f, 90, 91, 92, 93, 105, 109
  and LISP, 89
  collaborative learning, 40, 42
  social interaction, 92

Machine code, 285
Machine independence, 163
Machine learning, 181 f, 184, 201, 212,
    219, 236, 251, 252, 255 f, 267 f
Mal-rules, 239, 240 f, 245 f, 248
Manipulative errors, 239, 240
Matches, 156 f
Matching, 225
Mathematical discovery, 201
Meaning, 167
Meccano sets, 107, 119, 155
Mechanisms, 154, 178
Memory
  deductive, 268
  dynamic, 71 f
  economy, 261
  inductive, 268
  rote, 268
  schemata, 72
Mental model, 11 f, 24 f, 31 f, 70 f, 72,
    81, 285, 289
Meta-processes, 231